More Praise for
Design for All Learners

"*Design for All Learners* is a must-read for professionals who are serious about creating inclusive spaces and learning experiences. This book provides practical, actionable insights that will benefit anyone committed to making education accessible for everyone. If you're ready to break down barriers and design with accessibility in mind, this book will show you how."
—**Keely Cat-Wells**, CEO, Making Space; Disability Rights Advocate

"Accessibility isn't just about compliance. It's about the potential and dignity of a world created for all learners, and how that world is better for everyone. Full of heartfelt stories and practical insights, this book should be on every learning designer's bookshelf."
—**Julie Dirksen**, Author, *Design for How People Learn*

"Accessibility is a laudable goal stymied by a complicated set of issues and a dearth of clear advice. This engaging and well-structured book, authored by a stellar cast and assembled into a coherent presentation by a committed editor, is the handbook we all need to make sense of, and progress, on this valuable area of endeavor."
—**Clark Quinn, PhD**, Executive Director, Quinnovation

"I love that this book not only gave me practical strategies I can use right away to create more inclusive learning experiences, but it also helped me truly understand why accessibility is so important. It's got real examples, tools, and templates that make championing accessibility and improving learning experiences more achievable."
—**Melissa Milloway**, Learning Experience Design Leader

"If you're serious about reaching every learner, *Design for All Learners* is a must-read. It's a game-changer for anyone designing learning experiences and it provides actionable steps to make learning effective for all."
—**Nick Floro**, Learning Architect and Co-Founder, Sealworks Interactive Studios

"*Design for All Learners* is an essential toolkit for anyone who wants to go beyond mere accessibility compliance to create truly inclusive learning experiences. It is packed with practical tools and expert insights that bridge the gap between theory and transformative results."
—**Mike Taylor,** Learning Consultant, Nationwide; Author; Professor; and International Speaker

"Rarely am I as captivated by a nonfiction book as I was with *Design for All Learners*. This is a breakthrough book for learning designers who want to create equitable learning experiences for everyone, and its rich stories from unique voices will open your mind and challenge your assumptions. We've needed a book like this for a very long time."
—**Connie Malamed,** Publisher, The eLearning Coach Website and Podcast

"A must-read for anyone involved in creating learning experiences, this book champions Design for All principles and offers practical guidance on making learning accessible and inclusive for everyone. Readers will learn how to create inclusive experiences in any setting, from adapting group work for neurodivergent learners to ensuring in-person presentations are accessible and designing virtual events with accessibility in mind."
—**Hadiya Nuriddin,** Chief Learning Strategist, Duets Learning

"Sarah Mercier has gathered thoughtful stories, examples, and processes from a wide range of experts to offer thoughtful approaches to developing inclusive learning experiences. By addressing common myths about accessibility, this book aims to shift our own personal perspectives to be more inclusive and make better design choices so everyone can learn."
—**Tracy Parish,** Learning Consultant, Parish Creative Solutions

"Inclusive design may seem complicated and scary to many designers. *Design for All Learners* collects a wide breadth of knowledge, resources, and experiences, without being overwhelming. Each chapter can be read in one sitting and ends with something you can do right away. The diversity of authors is a real plus, which allows many kinds of challenges to be highlighted and backed up with personal stories and case studies."
—**Dave Gray,** The School of the Possible

Sarah Mercier, Editor

Design for All Learners

Create Accessible and Inclusive Learning Experiences

atd PRESS
Alexandria, VA

© 2025 ASTD DBA the Association for Talent Development (ATD)
All rights reserved. Printed in the United States of America.

28 27 26 25   1 2 3 4 5

No part of this publication may be reproduced, distributed, or transmitted in any form or by any means, including photocopying, recording, information storage and retrieval systems, or other electronic or mechanical methods, without the prior written permission of the publisher, except in the case of brief quotations embodied in critical reviews and certain other noncommercial uses permitted by copyright law. For permission requests, please go to copyright.com, or contact Copyright Clearance Center (CCC), 222 Rosewood Drive, Danvers, MA 01923 (telephone: 978.750.8400; fax: 978.646.8600).

ATD Press is an internationally renowned source of insightful and practical information on talent development, training, and professional development.

ATD Press
1640 King Street
Alexandria, VA 22314 USA

Ordering information: Books published by ATD Press can be purchased by visiting ATD's website at td.org/books or by calling 800.628.2783 or 703.683.8100.

Library of Congress Control Number: 2024945223

ISBN-10: 1-95715-789-5
ISBN-13: 978-1-957157-89-4
e-ISBN: 978-1-95715-790-0

ATD Press Editorial Staff
Director: Sarah Halgas
Manager: Melissa Jones
Content Manager, Learning Technologies: Alexandria Clapp
Developmental Editor: Jack Harlow
Production Editor: Katy Wiley Stewts
Text Designer: Shirley E.M. Raybuck
Cover Designer: Faceout Studio, Elisha Zepeda

Printed by BR Printers, San Jose, CA

*Christian, Ian, and Nathaniel—I'm so proud of you.
You give me hope for the future.*

Contents

List of Tools ix

Design for All Accessibility and Inclusion Statement xi

Preface xiii

Introduction: A Journey to Design for All 1

Part 1. Exploring an Inclusive Mindset

1. Accessibility Benefits Everyone 17
   by Leah Holroyd
2. Misconceptions and Myths: "No One Is ___ in My Organization" 21
   by Leah Holroyd
3. Thinking Outside Your Ability 25
   by Brian Dusablon
4. Lessons in Persona Design 37
   by Kristin Torrence
5. Design and Develop With People in Mind 53
   by Yvonne Urra-Bazain
6. Intersectional Inclusion: Understanding How Dimensions of
   Social Identity Play Into Accessibility to Help Everyone THRIVE 65
   by Jess Jackson
7. Personal Discoveries: Accessible Does Not Always Mean Accessible for All 83
   by Jean Marrapodi
8. Understanding Neurodivergent Learners 89
   by Judy Katz
9. The Importance of Testing With Real Users 93
   by Diane Elkins
10. Beyond Accessibility Checklists: Integrating an Inclusive Design Mindset 97
    by Leah Holroyd
11. Jobs That Require a Certain Ability 101
    by Diane Elkins
12. A Proactive Approach to Inclusion: Universal Design for Learning 105
    by Sarah Mercier

Part 2. Designing Inclusive Digital Content

13. Perspectives: Thinking Through Lenses 113
    by Brian Dusablon

14. Busting Myths About Accessible Digital Content 127
    by Diane Elkins
15. Keyboard Navigation, Headings, and Focus Order 133
    by Michelle Jackson
16. Designing Visual Hierarchy With Headings 141
    by Judy Katz
17. What Frozen Shoulder Taught Me About Accessible Layout 145
    by Diane Elkins
18. Screen Reader Overload: Considering Changes of
    Context When Demonstrating Assistive Technology 149
    by Yvonne Urra-Bazain
19. My Personal Experience With Color Contrast 159
    by Leah Holroyd
20. Navigating Color Blindness in Digital Content Creation 165
    by Michelle Jackson
21. What Air Hockey Taught Me About Color Contrast and Alt Text 171
    by Diane Elkins
22. Why Include Alt Text in Digital Learning? 175
    by Michelle Jackson
23. Typeface, Text, and Captions: A Creative Journey in
    Making Digital Content Accessible 191
    by Alan Natachu
24. Closed Captions: When Sound Matters 219
    by Sarah Mercier
25. The Case for Transcription 223
    by Yvonne Urra-Bazain
26. Audio Description Versions 233
    by Diane Elkins
27. Embracing Simplicity: Making a Complex Table Accessible 239
    by Yvonne Urra-Bazain
28. Accessible Documents—Why Bother? 249
    by Diane Elkins
29. Complex Topic, Plain Language: Harnessing Plain
    Language Guidelines to Support Complex Learning 251
    by Yvonne Urra-Bazain
30. Accessibility Lessons for Augmented Reality (AR) 263
    by Betty Dannewitz
31. Virtual Reality: A Request for On-the-Knees Angled Training 267
    by Kristin Torrence

Part 3. Creating an Inclusive Physical Classroom

32. New to Mastery: How Applying UDL
    Crafted the Path to CNC Machining Careers 285
    by Cara North

33. Inclusive Design Considerations for Physical Learning Environments.............................297
    by Suzanne Ehrlich and Michelle Bartlett
34. Unlocking Focus: The Vital Role of Fidget Toys
    in Enhancing Concentration for Neurodivergent Learners..309
    by Judy Katz
35. Beyond the Rules: A Lesson in Accessibility and Empathy 313
    by Jean Marrapodi
36. Tailoring Group Work for Neurodivergent Learners...315
    by Judy Katz
37. Describe Your Visuals in Instructor-Led Programs 317
    by Diane Elkins
38. Improving Accessibility With Presentation Captioning...319
    by JD Dillon
39. Driving Dreams: Overcoming Dyslexia With
    Adaptive Learning and Technology 331
    by Jean Marrapodi
40. Don't Forget Interpreting Needs! 335
    by Mary Henry Lightfoot
41. Working With Sign Language Interpreters...339
    by Diane Elkins
42. Creating Sensory-Smart Spaces: Strategies for
    Crafting Neurodivergent-Friendly Training Environments 343
    by Judy Katz
43. Addressing Speech Access Needs in the Physical Classroom 345
    by Susi Miller and Sarah Mercier
44. Beyond Barriers: Creating Inclusive Learning
    Pathways for Nonliterate Liberian Elders in Providence...347
    by Jean Marrapodi
45. Left in the Margins: Discover an Unexpected Accessibility Barrier....................................353
    by Sarah Mercier

Part 4. Creating an Inclusive Virtual Classroom

46. Inclusive Design Considerations for a Welcoming Virtual Learning Space....................357
    by Michelle Bartlett and Suzanne Ehrlich
47. Revolutionizing Remote Learning:
    A Guide to Crafting Inclusive Virtual Classrooms..365
    by Karen Hyder
48. Redefining Engagement: Designing Accessible and Inclusive
    Activities in Virtual Classrooms..379
    by Kassy LaBorie
49. Strategies to Overcome Auditory Processing Challenges 389
    by Judy Katz
50. Optimizing Virtual Training Accessibility: Addressing Speech Access Needs 391
    by Susi Miller

Part 5. A Primer on Accessibility Standards

51. Interpreting Accessibility Standards 397
    by Haley Shust
52. Practically Applying WCAG Standards to Learning Content 409
    by Susi Miller
53. Testing WCAG Standards 425
    by Susi Miller

Part 6. Adopting an Inclusive Mindset in Your Organization

54. The Invisible Why 435
    by Daron Moore
55. Breaking the "Serving One" Mentality 445
    by Belo Miguel Cipriani
56. Accessibility Advocacy in Corporate Environments 449
    by Haley Shust
57. Hiring an Accessibility Consultant 473
    by Belo Miguel Cipriani
58. Incorporating Accessibility in Development: Guidance for Quality Assurance 479
    by David Lindenberg
59. Keeping Neurodivergent Learners in the Flow With Quality Content 485
    by Judy Katz
60. Accessibility Is Better When You're in It Together 487
    by Sarah Mercier

Part 7. Taking Action

61. When Efforts to Be Inclusive Don't Go as Planned 491
    by Todd Cummings
62. Progress Over Perfection 497
    by Meryl K. Evans

Acknowledgments 515

Take Action Toolbox 517

Additional Resources 553

Book Club Questions 557

Endnotes 559

About the Contributors 571

Index 579

About the Editor 587

About ATD 589

Tools

Tool 1-1. Persona Pitfalls and How to Avoid Them 519

Tool 1-2. Testing With Real Users 521

Tool 2-1. Lenses of Accessibility Questions 524

Tool 3-1. Reflection Prompts for In-Person Learning Spaces 528

Tool 3-2. Tips for Working With Sign Language Interpreters 529

Tool 3-3. Sensory Accommodations Checklist 530

Tool 3-4. Ways to Include Learners With Speech Access Needs 531

Tool 4-1. Reflection Prompts for Inclusive Virtual Learning Spaces 533

Tool 4-2. Virtual Classroom Shopping List for Platform Accessibility Features 534

Tool 4-3. Virtual Event Marketing Materials Checklist 535

Tool 4-4. Example Presession Attendee Survey to Determine Needs 537

Tool 4-5. Facilitator and Producer Setup Checklists 539

Tool 4-6. Recipe for Successful Virtual Training Activities 542

Tool 6-1. Accessibility Specialist Business Case Example Outline 545

Tool 6-2. Accessibility Audit Report Example 548

Tool 6-3. Inaccessibility Log Example 550

Tool 6-4. Quality Control Checklist Example 551

Design for All Accessibility and Inclusion Statement

The authors in this book are professionals who were asked to share their expertise in one or more topic areas for which they have deep experience.

Some authors have self-identified as Blind, visually impaired, Deaf, Hard of Hearing, mobility-challenged, and neurodivergent. Others have self-identified as being part of one or more of the following communities: BIPOC (Black, Indigenous, and people of color) and LGBTQIA+ (lesbian, gay, bisexual, transgender, queer, intersex, asexual, plus other identities). **Each author who self-identified used the terminology and capitalization that they preferred.**

The authors in this book strive to use the terminology known to be of acceptable use at the time of writing. Visual examples include alternative text for digital versions of the book and image descriptions where appropriate.

A third-party sensitivity reviewer, Isabelle Felix at Writing Diversely, provided feedback that was incorporated into this book prior to publication.

The EPUB adheres to WCAG 2.0 AA guidelines, and the PDF has been validated using Adobe Acrobat Accessibility Checker and PAC 3 (PDF Accessibility Checker 3).

We are committed to accessibility and inclusion and welcome your feedback. Contact Sarah Mercier at contact@buildcapable.com or use the contact form at DesignForAllBook.com with any questions or comments you have.

Preface

Sarah Mercier
CEO, Build Capable

Several years ago, I listened to an episode of the *99% Invisible* podcast called "Invisible Women."[1] It explored lessons from the book *Invisible Women: Data Bias in a World Designed for Men* by Caroline Criado Perez.[2] The episode shared one particularly interesting example about the design of crash test dummies, which are human-shaped dummies used to test the human response during a vehicle crash. These dummies are based on the male body, which just so happens to exclude half the world's population. And, when female versions of test dummies are included, they are usually slight adaptations of the male version and placed in the passenger's seat.

The result is that women are 73 percent more likely to be injured or die in a car crash.[3]

I share this story to say this: If you want to be a good designer of anything—products, built environments, or learning experiences—you must account for the broad spectrum of people who make up your target audience, not just a watered-down perception of "normal" that doesn't actually exist. At its core, that's what the concept of "Design for All" is about—getting better at designing for people. To do that, you must better understand people, especially people who aren't like you.

From a very young age, my mom taught me to value diversity. Let me share another story with you, one that she shared with me when I was little.

In 1969, my mom and her friend were traveling cross-country (from Tennessee to California) when they stopped in Oklahoma to buy some souvenirs. They were wearing their hair in braids, bell bottom jeans, and crop tops. The shop owner refused to serve them because they were hippies. My mom said that experience was one of the worst feelings she'd ever had, but she went on to tell me that as a young child, she had visited Selma, Alabama, and was confused by the "No Blacks" signs she saw everywhere. She thought it was horrible that people would be treated that way. She also told me about the times when her best friend and his husband got death threats because they were gay. After describing these experiences, she said, "Even though I had that one experience of someone discriminating against me, it's nothing compared to what a lot of people experience every day. You always need to remember that."

As a child, I couldn't understand why people would do these things. It didn't make any sense to me. It still doesn't.

It's also worth mentioning that my mother was diagnosed with multiple sclerosis (MS) when I was 12 years old. Throughout my adult life, I have had countless experiences of helping her navigate access to airports, restaurants, event venues, shops, beaches, parks, and many other public places. The effort required to do something as simple as having dinner or going to a show has ranged from being easy to completely impossible, depending on things like access to accessibility information, the availability of ramps, the distance from the parking lot, the space to maneuver her rollator, or access to a wheelchair.

The worst thing is when someone tells you that their venue is accessible, but when you arrive, you realize it's not. It's like showing up to a high-rise office building for an appointment on the 30th floor, but there are no elevators. Would you be upset if you were expected to climb 30 flights of stairs whether you have a disability or not? This analogy is small in comparison to the absurdity of many of the barriers unnecessarily put in front of those with disabilities.

But, this book is not about trying to tackle all the world's injustices. It's about what *you* can do. You've chosen this book to find ways to help remove barriers and create inclusive learning experiences, and for that, I am grateful.

In research for this book, I've had the opportunity to hear stories that brought me to tears. But, I wasn't crying because I felt sorry for the people who shared their experiences with me. They have been innovating around poor design of the world around them, often throughout their lives. I was emotional because I felt embarrassed by my own assumptions and actions. Their stories gave me hope because they helped me change, and now I can share what I've learned with you.

However, it's important to note that I knew writing this book on my own would undermine the premise. I knew that I could write about the topics from my own research, experience, and professional practice, but that's not enough. I didn't want to speak for anyone. Instead, I wanted to move over and make space for others to speak for themselves. Design for All came to life when its principles were applied in the approach to this book. You'll learn from experts with a wide range of lived experiences, both professional and personal.

I told everyone that I'd never write a book until it was something that I cared about enough to spend the time it would take to do it right. This is that book.

Introduction
A Journey to Design for All

Sarah Mercier
CEO, Build Capable

My journey to inclusive design is full of good intentions and plenty of mistakes. Allow me to take you back in time to 2004. Not only was this the year that Mark Zuckerberg launched Facebook from his dorm room and Google introduced Gmail, but it was also the year I began my first "official" role in the learning and development field. As a senior technical trainer for a major credit card processing company, I was primarily responsible for onboarding new hires and providing ongoing training for call center representatives.

I spent most of my time in the classroom demonstrating tasks in our systems. In addition to classroom training, I worked across a variety of departments to identify weekly training topics and created e-learning content using an authoring tool in the learning platform. This training material was delivered directly to learners' email inboxes. Thanks to a co-worker, I even discovered a shiny new tool called RoboDemo (which would become Adobe Captivate) that allowed me to record system simulations so learners could practice tasks without any risk to real customer accounts.

Although I believe that I was a great trainer, there was something I didn't do. I didn't make the e-learning accessible. As opposed to being highly interactive and participant centered in the classroom, my e-learning programs were content centric. I have no idea whether there were people who completely missed out on their weekly training because I didn't know anything about digital accessibility or inclusion. I never even considered it.

Just a few years later, in early 2008, I traveled to Milton Keynes in England as a training consultant to support the launch of a new call center. For the first time, I began to realize just how different the English language is based on where you live. Something as simple as telling classroom participants where the bathroom is (WC, or water closet) or where they can throw away their trash (or rubbish—in the bin) changed the way I thought about teaching. There were participants in my classroom from other countries with different ways of thinking. Even the concept of credit (which was ubiquitous in the United States) was foreign to most folks there at the time. The individuals in my classes frequently laughed at my American analogies and examples during training.

I quickly began to work with other local trainers to improve my teaching approach, and it was certainly a learning experience. Within a few short months, I customized (localized) my classroom training. It's fair to say that, although I was just becoming aware of ways to be more inclusive, I still was not thinking enough about accessibility needs or barriers at this point in my journey.

In the latter part of 2008, I started a new job as a call center training supervisor for a national company in the automotive industry. Something about this job was quite different than what I had experienced in my journey to date—I was training blind and partially sighted call center representatives. I started to learn how to make accommodations so the training was more accessible. For example, at the request of one representative with low vision, I increased the font size on my job aids and other training documentation to 90-point, resulting in upwards of 100 pages of printed materials. I also created e-learning content that could be read aloud by JAWS, a popular screen reader application. Yet, there were still many limitations with our authoring tools, learning management system, and, unfortunately, my lack of knowledge. I often needed to engage a supervisor or co-worker to help their colleagues read through the content, complete activities, and take online tests. This process was extremely time consuming and, frankly, not a great experience for anyone.

At this point in my journey, I began to realize just how much of an impact inaccessible training can have on individuals with disabilities. The processes they had to go through to participate in even the most basic training was unnecessarily daunting, but I had no idea how to solve the problem. It was frustrating, but I did my best to learn and change what I could.

Fast forward to 2012. At this point, I specialized almost exclusively in designing and developing online content, including content delivered on mobile devices. I launched a company and worked with organizations across a variety of industries. I was creating fun games, mobile applications, e-learning—the whole package. I built solid knowledge of user interface (UI) and user experience (UX) principles to the point where I was also consulting large-scale companies and their teams on making better design decisions.

To be completely transparent, even though I had some experience training individuals with disabilities, I still didn't have great digital accessibility skills outside alt text for images and captions for videos. It's not accurate to say that I didn't care, but rather anything beyond that wasn't part of my design mindset yet. I didn't have enough context for the various ways I could avoid excluding people and reduce barriers to their ability to learn. To make matters worse, it was not something that companies prioritized. Some even refused to invest resources to create accessible content because "no one with a disability works here."

In 2016, more than 12 years into my formal training career, I attended Brian Dusablon's accessibility keynote, "Design for All: Accessible Learning Experiences," at a training conference. He shared stories that I had never considered. One was his experience trying to navigate a computer using a keyboard because he had a broken wrist and couldn't use his mouse. Another was a time when he designed an online course with low color contrast and received feedback about it from a colleague. He provided tools and processes to address many accessibility pitfalls that I had never really considered.

Finally, I was beginning to identify ways to improve my design process right from the start.

It was also during his presentation that I realized accessibility went beyond permanent disabilities. What about a temporary or undisclosed disability? How about those of us who wear glasses or hearing aids? Or are colorblind? Or speak a different native language? Brian said, "We are all on a spectrum." That stuck with me.

Consider this example. Figure I-1 shows three children at a baseball game standing behind a wooden fence. This image originated at The Inclusion Solution blog from The Winters Group, a Black women–owned and led diversity, equity, inclusion, and justice consulting firm. It's now widely adapted, shared, and discussed.

Figure I-1. Equality. *Source: Image adapted from The Interaction Institute for Social Change interactioninstitute.org, original concept by Craig Froehle.*

Notice that the children have all been given the same size box to see the game over the fence. This is an example of equality—each child has the same accommodation. Unfortunately, despite having a box, the middle child can barely see over the fence, and the child in the wheelchair is unable to use the box or see the game.

As an alternative, what if each child is given exactly the accommodation needed to comfortably see over the fence? Now, there is a ramp for the child using a wheelchair, the middle child gets two boxes, and the tallest child doesn't need a box—each one gets just what they need to see the game over the fence (Figure I-2). This is an example of equity. Each child receives the accommodation needed to experience the game.

Figure I-2. Equity. *Source: Image adapted from The Interaction Institute for Social Change, original concept by Craig Froehle.*

Or, what if it was a chain link fence that the kids could see through? Now, none of them require accommodation to see the game because the barrier is removed (Figure I-3).

Figure I-3. The barrier is removed. *Source: Image adapted from The Interaction Institute for Social Change, original concept by Craig Froehle.*

Mind. Blown. These images completely changed my perspective. Could I identify the barriers? Could I start designing better fences?

In 2018, I joined a team that was passionate about accessibility and inclusion. We wrote about it, spoke about it, shared resources, and even created a free text-based SMS course to help others learn about it. We formally implemented processes to ensure we were designing with an inclusive mindset from the start, and that we caught anything in quality control that may have been missed. No matter how many projects I worked on, I constantly discovered ways we could improve. Ways to do better.

This also meant taking a close look at our organization. At my first strategic retreat with the company, we began discussing a rebrand to change our name, Learning Ninjas. Although it certainly wasn't the only reason for the change, we had learned that using "ninjas" to describe ourselves may be considered offensive, and that was not how we wanted to show up in the world. As an organization that prioritized being inclusive, we were excited to ditch the old name and begin the process of rebranding as Build Capable.

By 2019, I was working on a large mobile learning application with a few other organizations. This multiyear project consisted of continuous design and development iterations as we revised and added content in the app. In that year's phase of the project, I pushed for a full accessibility and inclusion audit. We spent hours adding missing alt text to images, testing screen reader functionality, verifying that videos contained closed captions, and ensuring images represented a more diverse population. How was this missed in the first place? It wasn't intentional. It was a lack of awareness. Once I brought it up with the project team, everyone moved forward with a thoughtful, intentional process for future design cycles.

Then, it was late 2020. Or, was it 2021? It all runs together. I was attending a virtual online event during a global pandemic. The speakers had recorded videos of their presentations, and I was excited to do something other than bake bread or scroll social media. I logged in to the event in my home office alongside my son, who was busy working. Where are my wireless headphones? Dead. Probably from the kids watching TikTok videos. I opened the first presentation intending to watch with my computer muted so I wouldn't disturb my son. I searched for the "cc" button, but there were no closed captions. When I provided feedback to the event host, they responded, "We didn't turn that feature on because we didn't think anyone would need it." I actually felt a little guilty. Did I need it? I suppose the answer is yes because I never came back to those presentations.

2022 was the year that I put my experience to the test. I began working with a client that provides braille training and other learning opportunities to individuals with vision loss or blindness. Similar to my experience back in 2008, they were struggling with the accessibility of their e-learning content due to the technical challenges and limitations of their authoring tool, which also happens to be the most popular tool in our industry. Even after scaling back their courses to an extremely simplified format, screen reader behavior and device functionality (from desktop to mobile devices) was inconsistent during testing.

I reached out to the authoring tool vendor and found someone on their development team who was more than willing to work on this with us, which was very encouraging! While they were logging tickets to establish bug fixes, I worked on a short-term solution. I wrote some custom code and shared the fix with the authoring tool vendor as well as the client's learning platform vendor. With this, we were able to address most of the issues. In addition to end-user testing, my team validated the fix by using screen readers, including Apple's accessibility feature, VoiceOver. Even with that, a few bugs remained that required workarounds. The vendors assured us, "It's on our road map.

* * *

Now, I am sharing these parts of my journey with you. How exciting! And you picked up this book to find answers. Despite the tools you have to work with, your corporate culture, and the fact that you're probably overwhelmed with demands vying for your time, you want to find ways to Design for All. That's badass.

So, how do you begin your own journey to accessible, inclusive design? Let's start with a level set on some important terminology.

Accessibility, Universal Design, UDL, Inclusion, DEI, and More!

I don't know about you, but I find that terms like *accessibility*, *universal design*, *inclusion*, and *DEI* are often tossed around and used interchangeably. However, each one carries a unique, important perspective.

Accessibility

According to the US Department of Education, "Accessibility means a person with a disability is afforded the opportunity to acquire the same information, engage in the same interactions, and enjoy the same services as a person without a disability in an equally effective and equally integrated manner, with substantially equivalent ease of use."[4] Many of the examples in this book are accessibility focused, like my example of making accommodations for call center representatives who were blind or had low vision.

Let's apply an accessibility perspective to the fence illustration I mentioned earlier. What about a child who is blind? How will they experience the baseball game? The accommodation they would need has nothing to do with the fence.

Accessibility needs are an increasingly popular topic for designers for many reasons—from legal considerations to personal experiences. It can be challenging if you're not familiar with the wide range of individual needs of people with disabilities. Add in the frequent objections like "There's no one in my company who is [*enter disability here*]," and you pile on the lack of buy-in from necessary decision makers in your organization.

Universal Design

Universal design is the practice of designing something in a way that maximizes usability for as many people as possible. There are seven principles of universal design:

1. **Equitable use.** The design is useful and marketable to people with diverse abilities.
2. **Flexibility in use.** The design accommodates preferences and abilities.
3. **Simple and intuitive use.** The design is easy to understand how to use.
4. **Perceptible information.** The design can be perceived by a person's senses, regardless of environment or sensory abilities.
5. **Tolerance for error.** The design minimizes hazards and adverse consequences of accidental or unintended actions.
6. **Low physical effort.** The operation is efficient and comfortable.
7. **Appropriate size and space for approach and use.** The design allows the space for mobility and is appropriate for reach and use, regardless of the person's body size, posture, or mobility.

Universal design can be applied to built environments, the digital world, and yes—even learning experiences.

Universal Design for Learning

According to CAST (formerly known as the Center for Applied Special Technology), *universal design for learning* (*UDL*) "is a framework to guide the design of learning environments that are accessible and challenging for all. UDL aims to change the design of the environment, reducing barriers so that all learners can engage in rigorous, meaningful learning."[5] Although this framework is intended to serve as a systematic approach to applying universal design in a learning context, it may not address the specific needs of learners with disabilities in the way that an accessibility focus does. It may not fully support individual circumstances, even if the goal is to consider these individuals more broadly. That said, UDL can be a useful framework to begin ideating ways to create more accessible and inclusive learning experiences.

Diversity, Equity, and Inclusion

Diversity, equity, and inclusion (*DEI*) is "a conceptual framework that promotes the fair treatment and full participation of all people, especially in the workplace, including populations who have historically been underrepresented or subject to discrimination because of their background, identity, [or] disability."[6] *Inclusion*—both as a component of DEI and its own practice within the workplace—is "the act or practice of including and accommodating people who have historically been excluded (because of their race, gender, sexuality, or ability)."[7]

While DEI is a commonly used acronym, many have criticized and revised it, suggesting alternatives like DEIB (diversity, equity, inclusion, and belonging), IDEA (inclusion, diversity, equity, and access), and even JEDI (justice, equity, diversity, and inclusion). I believe that the meaning behind each of these these letters is incredibly important, and the problem is less about choosing an acronym and more about inadequate implementation.

Some organizations have established DEI departments and leadership to work toward this goal. Although this is a critical step, it doesn't always extend to the learning and development (L&D) function in ways that have a systematic influence. There are still deep skills gaps, mindset changes, and political pressures that must be addressed to make real progress. Workplace policies, processes, environments, and cultures, among other things, often fall short when it comes to diversity, equity, and inclusion. Many companies fail to create a safe space where all people feel confident they're in a place where they belong. Also, consider the popular phrase, "Nothing about us without us." Initiatives that exclude the people they are meant to represent lack credibility and likely won't succeed.

Design for All

This book intends to help you Design for All—exploring design where these perspectives intersect and overlap. When learning about accessibility, you'll find ways to ensure that individuals with disabilities (whether permanent, temporary, or even situational) can fully participate in the training you offer. When you focus on UDL, you'll find ways to offer training with options that accommodate the most people with the least barriers. By gaining knowledge about inclusion, you'll also consider things like education, language, computer literacy, economic conditions, internet connectivity, microaggressions, lack of representation, and more. ("Microaggressions are the everyday slights, insults, putdowns, invalidations, and offensive behaviors that people experience in daily interactions with generally well-intentioned individuals who may be unaware that they have engaged in demeaning ways."[8]) Focusing on DEI can help with operationalizing inclusion efforts across an organization. Design for All explores what happens when you foster a mindset that takes all these perspectives into account. It's not a model or a framework, and it's not new.

The Design for All concept has been around since at least the late 1990s, bringing together user-centered design, accessibility, and universal design.[9] You'll find applications of Design for All everywhere—in architecture, products, and services. I even found a Design for All initiative to foster inclusion across Europe (EIDD—Design for All Europe). In this book, we will explore what Design for All can do for the L&D field.

I began this introduction with my journey to inclusive design, and I chose the word *inclusive* on purpose. I believe that possessing an inclusive mindset is the key to Design for All. It will drive you to remember that *learners* are *people* who have unique experiences, perspectives, backgrounds, and abilities. This book will help you make better design decisions so everyone can learn.

Is This Book for You?

Before I can answer that, I have to ask: Do you truly care about helping people learn? Take that a step further: Do you care about helping *everyone* learn? Is your goal to be a compliant designer or a great designer? Do you want to lead a team that creates "check the box" courses or training that is effective?

What is your current role? Are you a "team of one" responsible for everything from instructor-led training to e-learning, perhaps even managing your company's learning platform? Are you a training manager responsible for implementing processes and practices in your organization while leading a team? Maybe your job responsibilities include a mashup of classroom training, in a face-to-face or virtual environment, and sharing subject matter expertise. Regardless, you are likely juggling competing priorities and trying to figure out how something so important can be part of your work in a meaningful way.

I have great news. This book was designed especially for you.

What you take from this book won't change much based on your job title, whether you are a team of one, or if you work in a large organization with many resources—but what you do with the information might. And, if your goal is to become a better teacher, designer, and leader, I can promise that you will leave here with a packed toolkit.

This is where it gets good. Anyone who is creating training content; facilitating in-person or virtual training, meetings, or events; building or supporting systems and software (I'm talking to you, IT departments and system vendors); or feeding content into and out of these areas (like communications, marketing, sales, and IT staff) will benefit from the wide range of information shared in this book.

As the most hopeful version of myself that I can be, I will take this a big step further. Anyone who picks up this book, no matter what they do for work, will learn something they can use to help make the world a better place for all of us.

How Is This Book Organized?

Each part of this book has been thoughtfully structured around what you need to know about Design for All and what you can do with that information. Some strategies are at the organizational implementation level, some are at the design and development level, and others are focused on how to shift your individual mindset. Many are led with stories that inspired practitioners and experts to change the way they think about designing for people.

- **Part 1, Exploring an Inclusive Mindset,** contains practical ways to develop your own personal goals for inclusive design. It also addresses common myths about accessibility and ways to shift your perspective.
- **Part 2, Designing Inclusive Digital Content,** is perfect for designing and developing any type of digital content, such as PowerPoint presentations, PDFs, e-learning content, videos, and other digital materials and experiences. You'll find that this part has the most information, which is great because nearly all of us create some form of digital content! The chapters include real stories, examples, processes, tools, and tips to support you.
- **Part 3, Creating an Inclusive Physical Classroom,** covers important considerations for classroom facilitators and presenters. This is where you'll find excellent examples for inclusive design practice in today's classroom or in-person presentation settings.
- **Part 4, Creating an Inclusive Virtual Classroom,** is an important topic, especially in recent years due to the overwhelming increased use of digital meeting platforms. Expect to learn about how you can shift to a more inclusive practice with lessons learned from virtual event facilitators and producers.
- **Part 5, A Primer on Accessibility Standards,** is all about translating the standards and legal aspects of accessibility. Expect

to learn more about a wide range of accessibility standards, such as the Web Content Accessibility Guidelines (WCAG), the Americans with Disability Act (ADA), European Accessibility Act, and many others.
- **Part 6, Adopting an Inclusive Mindset in Your Organization,** focuses on areas such as quality assurance, quality control, whether you should hire or outsource accessibility resources, governance and audits, and how to have important conversations with decision makers.
- **Part 7, Taking Action,** is a lesson in what might happen when you start to design for all, and how to strive for progress over perfection when things get tough.
- **Take Action Toolbox** is where you'll find a quick reference to the gold mine of resources, guides, templates, and examples shared throughout the book!

I am so glad that you've decided to embark on your own journey to Design for All. Are you ready to begin?

Part 1.
Exploring an Inclusive Mindset

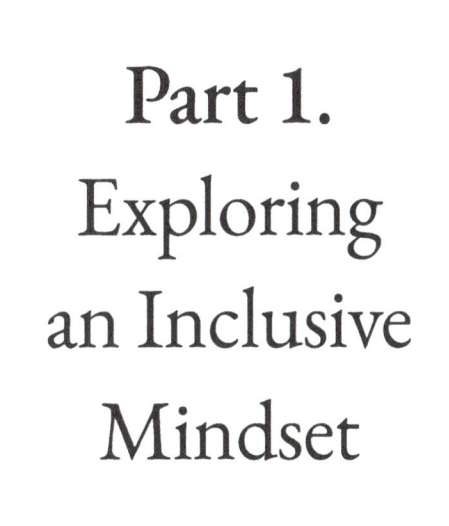

1.
Accessibility Benefits Everyone

Leah Holroyd (she/her)
Learning Designer and Director, White Bicycle

> "Accessible design is just good design." —Becky Brynolf, Royal National Institute for the Blind (UK)

Prioritizing accessibility is a brilliant thing for so many reasons. When I talk to organizations about accessibility, I speak about the moral arguments for inclusion, the legal requirements, and the business case. On the last, the World Health Organization has estimated that one in six people have a disability.[10] Additionally, research has shown that 69 percent of people will simply leave a website if they encounter accessibility issues.[11] Therefore, you're missing out on a sizable portion of prospective customers or participants if you're not thinking about accessibility. However, to my mind, the moral argument alone—that everyone has a right to be included—is sufficient.

The great thing about accessibility is that accessible design practices benefit everyone, whether they have a disability or not. All of us might be affected by permanent, temporary, or situational barriers at some point in our lives. Consider an example in the learning design context: Providing captions and a transcript for any video or audio content means that it can be accessed by a deaf person (a permanent barrier), a person with an ear infection (a temporary barrier), someone who's working in a noisy open office or at a kitchen table with their kids (a situational barrier), or someone who is learning in a second language.

I once attended a conference where a woman recounted her own experience of falling ill while studying for an online qualification. She explained that her medication sometimes affected her hearing, so she would turn on the video captions on the days when this was an issue for her. Her accessibility requirements varied from one day to the next, depending on the severity of the medication's side effects.

We can probably all think of a time when we've experienced some sort of barrier that was (or could have been) alleviated by more inclusive design choices. A few years ago, I was hit by a taxi while crossing the road outside a hotel where I was staying. Luckily, I came away with just one broken toe and a lot of bruises, but I spent a few days using crutches to help me get around. I had to go into London to attend meetings during this time, and I remember finding it very challenging to navigate the Tube (the London Underground system). I had brought a small suitcase with me, not realizing that it would be impossible to carry a suitcase while holding a crutch in each hand. Some Tube stations have step-free access, but many don't, and I was close to tears as I tried to get up and down the stairs with my luggage. Obviously, this experience doesn't mean I know what it's like to have a disability that affects my movement. But this temporary injury did give me insight into how inaccessible some Tube stations are. As in the video captioning example, providing elevators and ramps at all stations would benefit many people, including wheelchair users, people with lots of luggage, people with children in pushchairs (or strollers)—the list goes on!

When I talk to people about digital accessibility, I like to emphasize that there is a lot of overlap between the accessibility measures that can help different groups of users. For example, while in a video call with a new client, I described some accessibility issues I'd encountered on their website and in their social media posts. I pointed out several instances in which they had used a heavily stylized font in all caps and explained that it was very hard to read for someone like me with central vision loss. The woman I was speaking to could see my point straightaway and told me that she had dyslexia and also found text in all caps harder to parse. This was the perfect illustration of how a particular approach—using a plain font and avoiding all caps—could benefit both people with visual access needs and people with cognitive access needs.

What You Can Do Right Away

Think about any permanent, temporary, or situational barriers to accessibility you've faced in your day-to-day life and how your experiences in the physical or virtual world might have been impaired by them. As you embark on your journey to more accessible and inclusive learning design in this book and beyond, maintain this mindset: Accessibility benefits everyone.

2.
Misconceptions and Myths

"No One Is _____ in My Organization"

Leah Holroyd (she/her)
Learning Designer and Director, White Bicycle

Let's start with a question: What do the following things have in common?
- A multimillion-dollar peanut butter brand
- A fashion line for the British retail chain Warehouse
- The *New York Times* bestselling cookbook *Recipes From My Home Kitchen: Asian and American Comfort Food*

Answer: They were all created by people who are blind or have other visual disabilities.

Serial entrepreneur Pic Picot started out making sugar-free nut butter in his garage in New Zealand. He now has a factory and a team of people working for him, and his products are sold in 12 countries. He also has macular degeneration.

Kimberley Burrows is an interdisciplinary artist who has created paintings for the Wellcome Collection, UK Scouts, and the Holocaust Memorial Day Trust, as well as designed clothes for Warehouse. She became blind due to a retinal detachment while at university.

Christine Hà won the third series of *MasterChef* in the US and went on to open restaurants in Texas, host an accessibility-focused cooking show on Canadian TV, and serve as a culinary envoy for the American Embassy. She has neuromyelitis optica.

I collect these stories. I arm myself with them. Sadly, in my work as a learning designer, I still occasionally encounter people who switch off when I mention accessibility. Sometimes they just gloss over what I'm saying and move on to the next point on their agenda; other times they are more explicit: "Oh, well, this course is aimed at [*insert profession here*] so that isn't an issue for us."

So, I counter by telling them about Dr. Tim Cordes (an American physician who was diagnosed with Leber hereditary optic neuropathy as a child), Jessikah Inaba (the UK's first blind black female barrister), or Chris Downey (an architect who teaches universal design at the University of California, Berkeley, and who lost his vision following surgery on a brain tumor).

I also counter by pointing out that I'm an award-winning entrepreneur and education professional with Best disease (also known as vitelliform macular dystrophy), which affects my central vision.

Unfortunately, some people make assumptions about what people with sight loss—or indeed any kind of disability—are capable of. Whether conscious or otherwise, they sort jobs into categories that they think only certain types of people can do. This smacks of the medical model of disability, which means viewing disability as a problem or a deficiency on the part of the individual, rather than in terms of the barriers created by society.

I've experienced this myself. At a large educational technology conference in London, I approached the exhibition stand of a company whose software I use to create e-learning courses. I introduced myself to the company rep and explained that I have a condition that affects my central vision. I told her that I experienced issues when using the software because some user interface (UI) elements were inaccessible. For example, the program's checkboxes or radio buttons were a very pale grey on a white background, meaning that the color contrast was very low. The rep listened and nodded sympathetically but offered no reassurances. She told me that the company's road map for accessibility was focused on the learner experience (meaning the end users of the e-learning courses). They had no plans to improve the experience for customers like me until they'd met all the Web Content Accessibility Guidelines (WCAG) for the learner-facing output. I couldn't help feeling that there was an underlying assumption here: Someone with a visual impairment probably wouldn't be working as a learning designer.

The key message here is to not make assumptions about what anyone can or can't do. It's also worth thinking about the numbers. Around one in six people has a disability or long-term condition, so statistically speaking, unless you work in a tiny organization, some of your colleagues will likely be people with disabilities.[12] And thanks to advances in technology, it's becoming increasingly possible for people to remain in their job roles even after experiencing a disability or impairment simply by adjusting their setups—whether that means using assistive technology like screen readers or using built-in functionality.

I'm in the early stages of my macular degeneration, so I use my computer's accessibility settings to make the cursor and icons larger. I also typically view documents and online materials zoomed in at 125 percent, and, when possible, I adjust color contrast to make things clearer and avoid the eye strain that often occurs if I stare at black text on a white background for long periods. This is the norm for me, and I often forget that I've adjusted my settings to support me in this way. On the odd occasion that I have to look at someone else's computer—perhaps to check the work of a freelancer who's supporting me on a project—I struggle to read text and I often lose the mouse pointer! Ultimately, I'm perfectly capable of continuing my work as a learning designer while my eyesight deteriorates. In fact, I think that my lived experience of sight loss has given me a better appreciation of the importance of accessibility, which has made me better at my job.

What You Can Do Right Away

What assumptions do you make about participants in the learning experiences you design? What misconceptions or myths have you internalized that you might need to overcome to design more accessible and inclusive training? When you are open to becoming more self-aware about your own design practices, you reduce the risk of excluding people from development opportunities.

3.
Thinking Outside Your Ability

Brian Dusablon (he/him)
Consultant and Inclusive Design Advocate

I want to share what I know about perspective—how mine has shifted and how important other perspectives and experiences are to your design process. Design for All is an approach, a mindset, a process, and a mission. It's about equal access to learning.

Learning presents some of the greatest opportunities we have as humans. Learning enables us to change our minds. Learning allows us to change our careers. Learning grants us the ability to change our lives and the lives of those around us. I imagine you picked up this book because you wanted to learn something.

Everyone Deserves the Opportunity to Learn!

I was ignorant. When I started creating e-learning content, I didn't know anything about accessibility or inclusion. For more than a decade, I created e-learning courses and websites without considering accessibility. I didn't pay attention until someone in my organization told me they couldn't read the text in an information security compliance course our training department had created.

We had designed a dark, vault-themed course that received positive feedback from our pilot group. We had spent a considerable amount of time working through content reviews and making sure we had the right images and appropriate alt text. Our interactions were solid.

Unfortunately, we had not considered color contrast. The use of grays and blacks in our design made it nearly impossible for one employee to read the content. Upon learning about his experience, we apologized and immediately pulled the course from the learning management system (LMS). We adjusted the design and sent it to him for a review. This incident initiated my journey toward understanding accessibility and inclusive design.

I know I am not unique in this experience. I now know about contrast checking tools and online tests for color blindness and low vision that I can use on my designs. I have also learned that the best testing is conducted by working with a diverse pilot audience and asking specific questions about accessibility from the beginning, not the end.

Designing for Real Life

As my journey into accessibility progressed, I discovered it extends beyond accommodating specific disabilities to encompass the entire spectrum of human diversity. The more I experienced the world—the more people I met with different backgrounds, lived experiences, and abilities—the more my perspective broadened.

At the 2016 Penn State Web Conference, which was focused on online accessibility, I met Eric Meyer. His keynote was centered around a remarkable personal experience and greatly influenced me.

Imagine urgently rushing to the hospital to be at the bedside of a loved one in critical condition. In this moment, your sole focus is to reach them. You know which hospital they are going to, so you go to its website to try to find out where they will be taken. You are in a state of panic. You are emotional. You are distraught. You are crying and your hands are shaking. Desperately, you search for essential information—a contact number, a directory of hospital wings, anything to guide you to your loved one. But, as you dig through the pages, you can't find what you need.

The designers of this website failed to create an accessible experience because they did not consider the needs of their primary audience: people in crisis. In this experience, Meyer described a different kind of temporary disability than we might normally consider: emotional distress.

In *Design for Real Life*, Meyer and Sara Wachter-Boettcher share real, lived experiences in which designers let them down.[13] They also share what we can do about it to be better. They advocate for designing with compassion, provide techniques for identifying and considering stress cases, and guide readers to consider more people, more of the time.

Some may argue that this approach is extreme and not relevant to learning. But in dismissing certain scenarios as edge cases and choosing not to address them, we demonstrate negligence. We have the ability and responsibility to push these boundaries and extend our care and consideration.

We can explore the entire spectrum of human interaction with our content. If people at either end of the spectrum have an equitable experience, everyone in between is more likely to have a positive experience too. By questioning, listening, and including diverse perspectives, we amplify voices that are often marginalized.

In the end, we create more accessible and inclusive content, improving quality and usability for everyone.

Applying Compassion to Learning Experience Design

Imagine the possibility of pilot or driver training that's accessible to those who are blind or have low vision. At first, the concept of a blind pilot may seem outlandish. Yet, haven't you ever pursued learning something simply out of interest or curiosity, regardless of its relevance to your job?

Consider recent advancements in technology. Self-driving cars and driver assistance tools are increasing in number. Why limit an individual's understanding of vehicle functionality or operation because we think they will never drive? This knowledge could empower them to leverage technology for easier and more accessible transportation. Why prevent them from learning? Similarly, why dismiss the idea of accessible pilot training?

You may find the idea of accessible pilot training to be absurd. The notion initially seemed odd to me. But let's consider Stefan's story. Despite a severe vision disability, he harbors a deep curiosity about flying, something inspired by stories from his father, a pilot. He wants to learn, even if he may never pilot a plane. Should we deny Stefan the opportunity to learn about flight because the training is designed for the fully sighted?

Imagine Stefan learns of a new medical procedure that could potentially restore his vision. If he wanted to begin studying flying now in preparation, he would not have access. He has limited options because designers made choices and assumed that a blind person would never fly a plane. In that case, Stefan must wait until after his procedure to begin learning, delaying his passion even further.

This scenario underscores the impact of inclusive design. Why prevent Stefan, or anyone, from learning based on assumptions? What authority do we have to restrict access to knowledge? Embracing a Design for All philosophy ensures anyone with a desire to learn has the opportunity to do so.

Overcoming Bias

It can be easy to spot biases in others but quite challenging to recognize our own. In training and organization development, this becomes particularly evident. Too often, people say, "We don't have anyone like that in our organization." Yet, can we predict everyone who may join the organization in the future? Of course not. Leave this excuse behind.

Education and empathy are key in recognizing our biases. By valuing and seeking out diverse experiences, we confront our biases directly, leading to greater understanding and compassion.

Adopting a Design for All mindset ensures our content remains accessible to all learners, both now and in the future. This approach requires thoughtful design work, resulting in more inclusive and enriching learning experiences for everyone. Although this may require some initial design work, the outcomes—more inclusive and enriching learning experiences—far outweigh the effort.

We All Benefit From Accessible Design

Let's explore a few stories that illustrate the importance of accessibility in various situations. These narratives highlight diverse challenges people face, emphasizing that accessible design is not just a specialized need but a universal benefit.

Encountering Temporary Disabilities

Have you ever broken a bone or sprained an ankle and required some kind of temporary or permanent accommodation? I broke my hand playing rugby in college and had to wear a compression cast on my dominant hand. It was long before I knew anything about accessible software. Reflecting on this experience now, I am grateful for the keyboard accessibility in the online patent research tool I used in my part-time job because that cast made traditional mouse-based navigation challenging.

Think about the prevalence of drag-and-drop interactions in e-learning courses. Could I have effectively navigated one without a mouse? I'm not sure. Although it's possible to design these interactions to be accessible, they rarely work well for people *with* a mouse, much less for people using touch screens or other forms of interaction. We must choose the interactions and templates we design wisely, ensuring they are universally accessible.

Living With Undisclosed Disabilities

My friend Mary's journey through college further emphasizes the importance of accessibility. She has a moderate learning disability and didn't want to make a big deal about it to her professors by asking for accessible resources. Her experience with accessible e-books marked a turning point in her academic career. Once she realized her device could read class books aloud, she saw significant improvements in her grades. She now works with children with learning disabilities! If she did not have this accessibility feature, it might have taken years longer for her to graduate and robbed us of a great teacher.

Mary's reluctance to disclose her disability caused me to pause and reflect on the content I produced. I thought of my audience and wondered who hadn't spoken up. Her story reminds us to consider those who might not voice their challenges.

Challenging Incorrect Assumptions

Have you ever made assumptions about your audience? Imagine that a team created a new-hire training program for a national car dealership. They worked hard to make sure the courses were accessible for employees who used the JAWS screen reader.

But there was a problem. One employee, who was legally blind, didn't use JAWS. Instead, she magnified the text on her screen and used other tools built into her computer and web browser to read and interact with the material. The team did not consider someone using the content this way, and thus, she had a tough time with the courses. When we take a more inclusive approach, we can account for all without making assumptions.

> "We need to change the way we talk about accessibility. Most people are taught that 'web accessibility means that people with disabilities can use the Web'—the official definition from the W3C [The World Wide Web Consortium]. This is wrong. Web accessibility means that people can use the web. Not 'people with disabilities.' Not 'blind people and deaf people.' Not 'people who have cognitive disabilities' or 'men who are color blind' or 'people with motor disabilities.' People. People who are using the web. People who are using what you're building. We need to stop invoking the internal stereotypes we have about who is disabled." —Anne Gibson[14]

Often, our efforts to make things accessible focus on two groups: those considered "normal" and those with limited mobility, total blindness, or profound deafness. We end up offering specific accommodations, such as text versions of courses, targeting these disabilities. But this approach leaves out a large portion of the population with varying abilities.

The Americans with Disabilities Act (ADA) talks a lot about providing accommodations, suggesting there's such a thing as a "normal" or "average" person.[15] However, no one is average. What does *average* even mean? Over time, most of us will face some kind of limitation, whether temporary or permanent.

Think about it. Are you wearing glasses right now? If you aren't, you may be one day. It's common for our vision to deteriorate as we get older. We might not hear as well or move as easily. Accessibility, then, isn't just about helping others. It's about making things easier for all of us. Whether due to injury, accident, or age, our abilities fluctuate. Yet, we still tend to design for an imaginary average user.

Charting a New Path

Adopting inclusive, universal design principles is a way forward. These principles encourage us to create content that's accessible to anyone, regardless of their abilities. It involves simplifying content, establishing clear standards, and paying attention to people's needs.

We can aim to design for a wide range of abilities, rather than an imaginary "average" user. When we make content accessible and inclusive from the start, we create opportunities for more people to learn and benefit.

> "I'm not broken. I'm not bent. I'm not incapable. I might not work the same way everyone else does, but that doesn't mean I'm unable to accomplish those things others can accomplish."
> —Sarah Chorn[16]

Design for All is more than just a goal—it's a commitment to constantly learn from and listen to a wide range of people. This approach helps set the bar for making learning accessible to everyone. It ensures we think about different abilities and perspectives right from the start. My mission is to keep questioning what I think I know and to keep getting better. This way, I can help create learning experiences that empower everyone. When we design with everyone in mind, it makes things better for all of us.

So, what's next after learning from these different perspectives? Consider how empathy, compassion, and thoughtfulness can shape your design approach in new ways.

Empathy Maps

> "The more we build websites and digital products that touch every aspect of our lives, the more critical it becomes for us to start designing for imperfect, distressed, and vulnerable

> situations—designing interfaces that don't attempt to make everything seamless, but instead embrace and accommodate the rough edges of the human experience." —Eric Meyer[17]

One of my favorite tools in my Design for All practice is the empathy map (Figure 3-1). It helps me see things from other people's perspectives. I use it to think about what different users might be thinking, seeing, saying, doing, and hearing, which helps me understand their needs better.

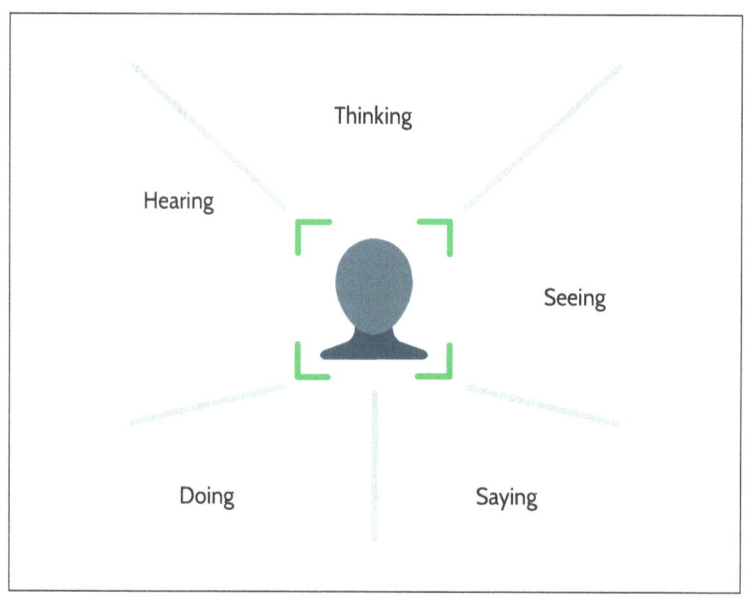

Figure 3-1. An empathy map template in Whimsical, an online design tool, showing a structured layout used to articulate user behaviors and attitudes. At the center, there's a simplified icon representing a person's head surrounded by sections labeled with the sensory experiences of that person. Starting from the top right and moving clockwise, the quadrants are labeled "Thinking," "Seeing," "Saying," "Doing," and "Hearing."

Empathy is the ability to understand and share another person's feelings. Creating an empathy map is a focused exercise in which you create a comprehensive profile using data from an analysis of your audience. Include a name, job title, and location, making the persona more tangible and relatable.

The next step involves dissecting various dimensions of the persona's experience. Use individual sticky notes (either in a digital format or on a physical board) for each observation and add them to the map. The resulting visualization can help you consider the multitude of factors influencing your design decisions.

Empathy mapping is the single most successful activity I do to raise awareness about the different types of users I'm designing for and the unique experiences they bring to the learning environment. Facilitating separate empathy mapping sessions with decision makers, practitioners, and learners is particularly advantageous. This process uncovers gaps in understanding that can inform design and communication strategies and even help shift organizational culture.

But empathy mapping is only an initial step in the user experience research process. It reveals areas to conduct further investigation. The complexity of human experiences demands that we go further—moving from understanding (empathy) to actively addressing and supporting individuals' needs (compassion).

> "Individuals are a faceless and voiceless mass. Alice and Bob, on the other hand, are people. An advocate's third task is to make the impersonal personal by articulating the interests of a group and helping decision makers to see them as people rather than numbers." —Lyle Mullican[18]

The Power We Wield as Designers

Accessibility is not an add-on or a feature. It's a requirement. If our content is not accessible, then our design has flaws, and our work remains unfinished. If we don't solve these problems at the design phase and push the vendors who develop the tools and systems we use, we limit the positive impact we want to have. This results in some people not being able to learn because they can't access the content. Let's commit to amplify unheard voices, actively listen to feedback, and drive progress.

In our work, we often have to decide whether to focus on what the client wants or to think bigger and consider everyone who will use our content. Meeting client expectations is important, but we all benefit if we listen and learn from a diverse range of voices. This way, we can craft experiences that are easy for everyone to use and learn from.

Accessibility is about all of us, our spectrum of abilities and disabilities, and how we interact with the world. We want people to learn. We can empower them to transform their minds, careers, relationships, and beyond through learning. We won't be perfect, but we can continue to improve. So, design for all, with intention, grace, and curiosity.

From This Day Forward—A Commitment to Design for All

I will leave you with this final, compelling story. At the 2016 Penn State Web Conference, I attended a presentation by Target. They showcased an interactive, universally accessible Star Wars–themed orientation for new hires. Their creative approach was impressive, but what truly struck me was their commitment to designing equitable experiences for all users.

After the presentation, I talked with the team about their plans to make their entire course catalog accessible. With hundreds, if not thousands, of courses, you can imagine how large an undertaking that would be. Their response was direct and inspiring: From that day forward, everything they designed would be fully accessible. They pledged to uphold accessibility best practices in all new materials and improve existing content over time.

We can all adopt this forward-thinking commitment. By committing to a Design for All mindset, we positively influence our organizations and empower our learners. Viewing accessibility as an opportunity, not a burden, unites us in our efforts to create more inclusive learning experiences, contributing to a more equitable future for all.

What You Can Do Right Away

How often have you made empathy a core component of your design? The next time you're preparing to create a new learning experience, use an empathy map (like the one in Figure 3-1) to establish a better understanding of your learners' needs.

4.
Lessons in Persona Design

Kristin Torrence (she/her)
Immersive Learning Engineer

At my first instructional design job fresh out of graduate school, I was working at an educational technology company that translated psychology research into educational products and services to help students and educators increase their motivation and achievement. We received a grant from the US Department of Education Institute of Education Sciences to create a role-playing game aimed at teaching scientific inquiry skills and learning strategies and fostering growth mindsets in students.

I didn't know about the concept of personas during this time, and evidently, neither did my team. The design team primarily comprised psychologists, so in alignment with their learning science research practices, we used a design-based research approach paired with a standard software development process to create the educational science game. We took a content-focused approach to conceive the initial learning design. Only in retrospect has it become obvious that a learner-centered approach would have been ideal for this type of immersive learning solution.

Our experience with designing for K–12 students had taught us that a content-focused approach was the best way to go. We had previously designed a blended learning product that taught neuroscience concepts and aimed to cultivate growth mindsets in students. It proved to be a successful flagship product.

While that product reached saturation among educators who began championing a growth mindset, gaining traction with a broader audience was a more challenging endeavor. Because the lessons were not aligned with the widely adopted Common Core State Standards, school decision makers had trouble justifying and finding room in the budget for supplementary programming. As we embarked on creating a science game, we committed to aligning the curriculum to the Next Generation Science Standards (NGSS) to make it more marketable and applicable to audiences across the country.

The science game was aimed at teaching middle school students in grades six through eight. We involved our target learners in the design process from the very beginning. We recruited a K–8 school in New York City to host a weekly focus group of about 15 students, which allowed us to collect students' thoughts, ideas, and feedback to inform our initial designs. We used participatory design techniques to get a clear understanding of the direction of the game from the ideation phase to the paper, low-, and high-tech prototyping phases.

We then released an alpha prototype and ran a larger pilot study in which we recruited schools from California, New York, and Washington, DC. The pilot study yielded mixed results when it came to efficacy, interest, and engagement. Looking back, these findings aren't surprising to me. We had heavily relied on our focus group as a generalized sample of our target learners, but that assumption was inaccurate.

Our focus group students represented a very specific demographic. They attended a lower-performing inner-city public school; in addition, these students had opted into an after-school science enrichment program. So, they were a very specific subset of learners among an already specific group of learners. The game's alpha prototype needed major improvements to attract and motivate the breadth of our target audience.

Our leadership made a strategic decision to shift gears and adapt the science game for students in grades three to five. The company needed a product that fit the late elementary age group so our product catalog spanned all grades. Without any input from grades three to five, we made adaptations to the game—for reading level, iconography, and activity types—geared toward that age group in hopes that it would work.

When the beta prototype for a full level of the game was complete, we conducted user testing with the target age group, but the game didn't meet the students' needs. Our initial assumptions, which were based on middle school students, did not hold true for the younger group. The game was too text heavy, it wasn't engaging enough, and the activities were not age appropriate. Internally, we struggled with simplifying scientific concepts without losing the core principles being taught. Our findings revealed that the game was not catering to students' interests, and it was not aligning well to the concepts they were learning in their science curriculum at that time. Unfortunately, this product was never able to see the light of day. What had begun as a learning experience with tremendous potential ended in total disappointment.

We completely failed to understand our new target learners at a deeper level—their interests, reading levels, prior knowledge, motivations, and context. Instead, we made assumptions. However, this major setback proved to be a great learning experience for me and my team. Through our failure, we realized the importance of understanding our target demographic well before embarking on the design process.

It was only later, when I learned about the concept of personas, that I realized that tool could have made the ultimate difference for this project. Now, I firmly believe that without creating personas, understanding our learners' needs, or testing our assumptions, we are bound to miss the mark. Similarly, using personas in your design approach can help you create inclusive learning experiences that consider accessibility barriers.

Personas, Their Purpose, and Their Components

Personas originated in the user-centered design and human-computer interaction fields as a way to bring a people-centered focus to software development by creating detailed descriptions of fictitious users. As the principles of user-centered design influenced the instructional design field, the evolution and use of learner personas became more prevalent.

Learner personas are hypothetical archetypes that represent a subgroup of target learners who engage with a learning solution (Figure 4-1). The purpose of personas is to create reliable and realistic representations of different user groups in terms of their demographics, behavior, and goals. Your aim is to have an array of learner personas that showcase the major variations across members of the targeted learner population. These personas enable a design team to focus on a memorable cast of characters, representing the needs of the larger user group.

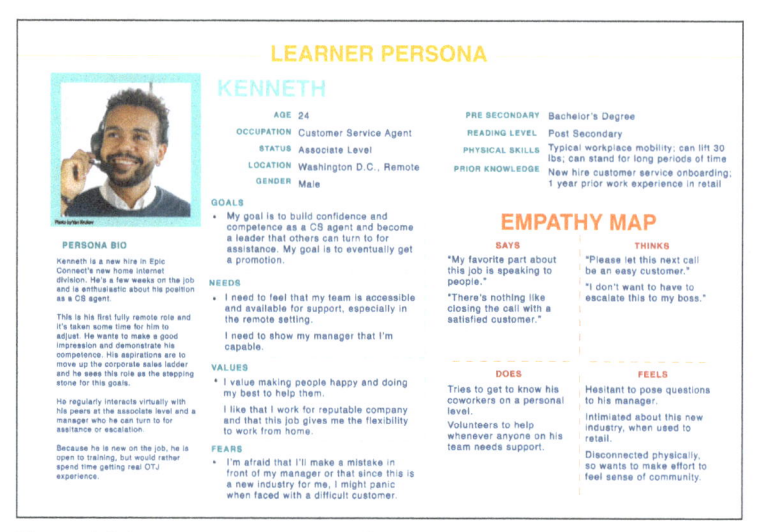

Figure 4-1. Learner persona example.

As depicted in Figure 4-1, learner persona components can vary depending on need, but some of the most common are:

- **Demographics.** Age, gender, ethnicity, occupation, location, education, reading level, and physical abilities
- **Bio.** A description of their characteristics, including what a typical day is like for them, team working dynamics and dispositions, and their likeliness to respond to training
- **Prior knowledge.** What they already know about the subject or skills they possess in that area
- **Goals.** What drives them to succeed, what they aspire to learn, and what their personal or professional goals are in the short and long term
- **Needs.** What they need to feel engaged, confident, and motivated to complete and act on the training program, and the support they need to be successful in the training program and in their job

- **Values.** What they value most about their job, their core values or life philosophy, and what and whom they value
- **Fears.** What keeps them up at night or otherwise affects their behavior or mindset
- **Challenges.** Pain points and problems they face, cognitive or physical barriers, and obstacles such as time, access to technology, and language proficiency

The learner persona detailed in Figure 4-1 is for an individual named Kenneth. On the left side, there is a photograph of a smiling man with short curly hair wearing a headset. He appears to be in a remote work setting.

Kenneth's bio says he's a new hire in Epic Connect's new home internet division. He's a few weeks on the job and is enthusiastic about his position as a customer service (CS) agent. This is his first fully remote role, and it's taken some time for him to adjust. He wants to make a good impression and demonstrate his competence.

His aspiration is to move up the corporate sales ladder, and he sees this role as the stepping stone for that goal. He regularly interacts virtually with his peers at the associate level and a manager who he can turn to for assistance or escalation.

Because he is new on the job, he is open to training but would rather spend time getting real on-the-job (OTJ) experience.

Other details are as follows:

- **Age.** 24
- **Occupation.** Customer service agent
- **Status:** Associate level
- **Location.** Washington, DC; remote
- **Gender.** Male
- **Presecondary.** Bachelor's degree
- **Reading level.** Postsecondary
- **Physical skills.** Typical workplace mobility; can lift 30 pounds; can stand for long periods of time
- **Prior knowledge.** New-hire customer service onboarding; one year prior work experience in retail

- **Goals.** "My goal is to build confidence and competence as a CS agent and become a leader that others can turn to for assistance. My goal is to eventually get a promotion."
- **Needs.** "I need to feel that my team is accessible and available for support, especially in the remote setting. I need to show my manager that I'm capable."
- **Values.** "I value making people happy and doing my best to help them. I like that I work for a reputable company and that this job gives me the flexibility to work from home."
- **Fears.** "I'm afraid that I'll make a mistake in front of my manager or that since this is a new industry for me, I might panic when faced with a difficult customer."

One additional component that can be created separately, but I tend to include within my learner personas is an empathy map. Empathy maps help provide insight into a learner's mind by identifying things they may say, think, do, and feel. They usually capture:

- What the learner says out loud about reactions to their current circumstances at work
- What the learner thinks, such as why training does or doesn't make sense for them or their organization
- What the learner does in their spare time, who they interact with, and their interests
- What the learner feels, including feelings they may express to themselves, their tolerance level for change, and their perceived risk or sacrifice of changing the way they do things

Empathy maps can help you understand a learner's cognitive and emotional state during their learning journey and provide a deeper understanding of their needs and challenges.

Kenneth's persona includes an empathy map in Figure 4-1, which shows that he:

- **Says:**
  - "My favorite part about this job is speaking to people."
  - "There's nothing like closing the call with a satisfied customer."

- **Thinks:**
  - "Please let this next call be an easy customer."
  - "I don't want to have to escalate this to my boss."
- **Does:**
  - Tries to get to know his co-workers on a personal level
  - Volunteers to help whenever anyone on his team needs support
- **Feels:**
  - Hesitant to pose questions to his manager
  - Intimidated about this new industry because he's used to retail
  - Disconnected physically, so he wants to make effort to feel a sense of community

This detailed persona helps instructional designers and developers understand Kenneth's characteristics, goals, and needs to tailor training and support effectively.

By constructing a set of comprehensive learner personas and consistently referencing them during design, you can more readily evaluate the degree of resonance of the designs with the target audience and make more informed decisions to adapt content to meet the audience's needs more broadly. Using learner personas during the instructional design process facilitates greater understanding and empathy for target learners, their perspectives, and their needs, enabling you to effectively customize learning design to the target audience.

Strategies for Creating Personas

Designing effective learning solutions requires a deep understanding of learners and their needs. Creating learner personas can be quite overwhelming at first, because of the sheer amount of inputs to consider and time they can take to develop, but the more practice you have with creating personas, the faster you'll be. Over time, you will become more attuned to identifying trends and patterns across your data sources. The persona creation process can be broken down into three stages: gathering data, identifying patterns and drafting personas, and iterating and validating personas.

Gathering Data

The first step in creating learner personas is to gather data about the target learners. The easiest way to collect this data is to speak to them. Consider conducting interviews or focus groups with a diverse, representative group.

Interviews involve speaking directly to target learners and asking probing questions that get to the root of the persona elements I described in the previous section. Because interviews are typically conducted on a one-on-one basis, they can be time consuming and resource intensive both in terms of data collection and analysis.

A less resource-intensive option is a focus group because it allows you to collect a variety of viewpoints from target learners at once. Focus groups typically comprise six to eight participants who offer their perspectives, insights, and shared experiences. This option allows you to detect common pain points or nuances through collaborative and interactive discussions. Interviews and focus groups require recruitment efforts and oftentimes incentives for participants, which can quickly increase the cost.

A more cost-effective method for gathering data from learners is to administer surveys. Surveys enable you to collect data from a large sample of target learners and typically require less analysis effort compared to interview and focus group transcripts. Surveys are helpful for collecting both qualitative and quantitative data from learners. Online survey tools enable quick and efficient creation and distribution, which means learning designers can administer surveys to a sizeable sample of target learners and, if designed well, amass a wealth of valuable learner data.

You may also have access to system data that is worth leveraging for creating personas. Learning management systems (LMSs), learning experience platforms (LXPs), human resources information systems (HRISs), and other platforms are a gold mine for learner information. Find out what data you have permission to access, what is useful for gleaning insights about your target learners, and what aligns with the learner persona components.

Identifying Patterns and Drafting Personas

After collecting data about your learners through interviews, focus groups, surveys, or system data, review it to analyze trends and find recurring themes. These patterns provide the foundation for the construction of learner personas. Identify the target population subgroups and use the data from your investigation to formulate representative archetypes for each group. The goal is for your learning solution to resonate with the learners in your target population, so you'll need to ensure that the scope of learners is captured across the collection of personas you create.

Here are some guiding questions to help you complete each section of the learner persona. Some have been adapted from Rance Greene's book, *Instructional Story Design*.[19]

- **Age.** What is the typical age range of the learner?
- **Occupation.** What industry or company do they work for?
- **Status.** How long have they been in this field of work?
- **Location.** Where does the learner live? Are they remote or in office?
- **Gender.** What are the demographics of the company?
- **Presecondary.** What is their education or background? What are the learner's cognitive abilities?
- **Reading level.** What is their reading level?
- **Physical skills.** Does the learner have important physical characteristics or skills?
- **Prior knowledge.** What prior knowledge is the learner already equipped with?
- **Persona bio:**
  - What is a typical day like for the learner?
  - What challenges them at work or in life?
  - Has anything happened professionally to make them feel vulnerable?
  - Who or what has influence over them and who do they have influence over?
  - How likely are they to respond to training in light of their circumstances?
  - How will this stretch them?

- Are they willing to commit time and effort to taking and acting on the training?
- How will they personally benefit from the training?
- What's in it for them?
- **Goals:**
    - What does the learner want to achieve personally and professionally?
    - What motivates the learner?
- **Needs:**
    - What things do they need to feel engaged, confident, and motivated to complete the training?
    - What will motivate them to act on the training?
    - What does the learner want to help them reach their goals?
    - What supports does the learner think they need to be successful in the training? In their job?
- **Values:**
    - What do they value most about their job?
    - What are their core values, morals, or life philosophy?
    - What or whom do they value?
- **Fears:**
    - What keeps them up at night?
    - What fears or other mental or practical barriers prevent them from taking action?
    - Can these fears be remedied? How?

Here are some guiding questions to help you complete each section of an empathy map:

- **Says:**
    - What types of things does the learner say (out loud)?
    - What are their current circumstances at work? How are they reacting to them?
- **Thinks:**
    - What types of things does the learner think to themselves?
    - Why might they believe the training doesn't make sense for them or their organization?

- **Does:**
  - What does the learner do in their spare time?
  - Who do they interact with?
  - What types of music, games, movies, humor, sports, and so forth do they like?
- **Feels:**
  - What is their tolerance level for change?
  - What is the perceived risk or sacrifice of changing the way they do things?

This template is structured to help instructional designers and developers understand their learners better by answering specific guiding questions, creating a detailed persona bio, and mapping out the learner's thoughts, actions, and feelings.

Iterating and Validating Personas

After drafting your learner personas, validate them with your target audience, and, if possible, people adjacent to your target audience. Share the collection of personas with your target learners and ask them, "Do any of these personas resonate with you?" "Do these personas resemble real people you work with?" If the answer to either of these questions is no, you'll need to identify what does not seem authentic and iterate on the persona collection accordingly. Continue the iteration process until the target learners and stakeholders can validate that the personas indeed capture the breadth and depth of the target learner population. Remember, personas are artifacts that are continually referenced and used for various facets of design (including ideation, critiquing, idea refinement, and validation of design decisions), so it's imperative that these personas are true representations of target learners.

Persona Pitfalls and How to Avoid Them

Returning to my experience with personas, let's fast forward to when I had six years of instructional design experience under my belt and was designing virtual reality (VR) learning solutions for adult learners. While in the discovery phase of creating an HVAC training program for a trade school, I created two very detailed learner personas and empathy maps to represent the target audience. I had studied videos of prior students' reflections, analyzed demographic information from the trade school's reports, interviewed subject matter experts (SMEs) about their student populations, and had the SMEs and stakeholders validate the personas. One SME shared that a persona reminded him exactly of a student of his. We studied these personas and used them as the basis of our design. We thought we had done a great job, and to an extent, we did.

However, we were unaware that this product was not only meant to serve the trade school we were designing for, but also intended to be sold to companies who would use it for continuing education and practice for their seasoned HVAC technicians. Suddenly, we realized that we'd completely left out a whole subset of our target audience and did not consider them in our design. We failed to account for the broader audience that the solution would sell to, and we found this out the hard way.

Some of the design decisions we made to support novice learners' acquisition of procedural skills were unfit for veteran technicians. During the discovery phase, SMEs highlighted that cross-threading of hose connectors was a common error made by technicians in training. With this in mind, we wanted to promote and reinforce turning hose connectors slightly to the left prior to securing them tightly by turning them to the right. We made this a prerequisite for every hose connection step within the series of modules so this behavior would become automatic. This design was well received by HVAC instructors and students. However, the joystick cross-thread prevention movement hindered the experience for seasoned technicians so much that they were turned off by it. This product had trouble selling when released to the market and unfortunately was only able to serve a portion of the target demographic effectively.

It is possible to miss the mark on accurate and representative learner personas, even if you do go through the entire process of creating and validating personas with target audiences and stakeholders. Even with the best intentions, designers are susceptible to mistakes during the learner persona creation process. Here are four common learner persona pitfalls and how to avoid them.

Pitfall 1. Too General—Personas Represent the Average Learner

One of the most common pitfalls occurs when the collection of personas depicts the "average" learner, not the diverse spectrum of learners within the target audience. While analyzing the data gathered about learners, it's easy to overlook the outliers and put too much emphasis on average characteristics and behaviors. This can result in overlooking the unique characteristics of different groups. To avoid this pitfall, check for nuanced trends among learners and lean into specifics about their underlying traits and tendencies to ensure that the collection of learner personas represents your entire target audience. Your learning solution should resonate with the breadth of learners in your target audience, so it's imperative that the learner personas you design meet the needs of and account for the diverse perspectives and dispositions of your learners.

Avoid this pitfall by:
- Basing your learner persona descriptions on data you've collected from learners and peripheral personnel
- Highlighting specific characteristics gathered from nuanced trends in the data rather than generalized traits
- Ensuring your learner personas are clear and detailed enough to represent distinct individuals

Pitfall 2. Too Narrow—Personas Don't Represent the Range of Learners

Another common pitfall is not creating enough personas to represent a wide range of target learners. This can lead to a design that completely excludes a segment of target learners by failing to adequately address their needs, as evidenced by the HVAC learning solution dilemma. This pitfall can be avoided with a thorough analysis of the diverse learner groups that make up the target audience. This could range from two or three to as many as 10 groups—the goal is to represent diverse perspectives. Ensure you create multiple personas tailored to different aspects of your learners, such as prior knowledge, skill level, roles, perspectives, and contexts. It's critical to clearly understand the scope of different learners early on and create a collection of personas that accurately capture the wide array of learners who will be exposed to the learning solution. The goal here is to use personas during design so learners believe the training applies to them—and they can't feel that way unless they're represented in the collection.

Avoid this pitfall by:
- Identifying the meaningful subgroups within your target learner population (such as categories based on role, experience level, and context)
- Creating learner personas to represent each subgroup

Pitfall 3. Stereotypical—Personas Include Biases, Social Judgments, or Invalid Assumptions

Avoid including stereotypes or social judgments in learner personas. Reflect on your collection of learner personas and identify if you've included any gender stereotypes that are not supported by the data from your investigation, such as typecasting more senior-level personas as men who are driven by competition, or women personas as more emotionally driven and inclined toward artistic subjects. Analyze your learner persona collection for probable cultural or age-related stereotypes, such as expecting individuals from East Asian cultures to excel in STEM subjects, or assuming that older individuals are uninterested in or challenged by technology. Evaluate your personas for socioeconomic stereotypes, such as assuming individuals of lower socioeconomic status will have lower aspirations, poorer habits, and decreased critical thinking skills compared with those of a higher socioeconomic background. Avoid assuming that a person with a disability will not do certain jobs or will only have an accessibility testing role. Allowing these stereotypes to go unchecked in learner personas does a disservice to your learners and can perpetuate misinformation.

We need to ensure that we are creating genuinely representative personas. It's important to be vigilant in avoiding such biases and base learner persona development on data gathered from your target audience rather than relying on assumptions. To avoid these issues, involve a broad range of individuals in the persona creation process and collaborate with diverse teams when analyzing data and constructing personas. The more folks you involve in the validation process, the more perspectives you can draw upon to ensure that the personas accurately reflect the actual characteristics and behaviors of learners. You may also choose to consult with a sensitivity reader during the persona review phase to identify and eliminate any instances of unintentional stereotyping.

Avoid this pitfall by:
- Conducting a thorough persona review and correcting any biased assumptions or stereotypes, including those based on race, gender, culture, age, disability, socioeconomic status, and education level
- Validating learner persona attributes with real learners to ensure accuracy and cultural sensitivity
- Hiring a sensitivity reader to help identify instances of stereotyping, if possible

Pitfall 4. Fixed—Personas Not Updated to Evolve Over Time

A misconception about personas is that they are concrete and final once they are created. However, as you engage in user testing and learn more about the target learner audience during the learning experience design process, you should update your personas to account for any new information. Failing to iterate on personas can result in learning experiences that are disconnected from the learners' needs. To address this pitfall, you can establish a dynamic process of routinely reviewing and updating personas based on new data and insights to ensure that the design decisions you're making as you undergo the instructional design process are relevant and aligned with learners' evolving needs.

Avoid this pitfall by:
- Planning for regular reviews to update your collection of learner personas based on new information gathered from learners or the learning solution's needs
- Continuing to validate the collection of learner personas with learners and peripheral personnel to ensure the range of learner

personas is still relevant and create additional learner personas if the need arises

It's important to know how to mitigate these pitfalls so you are better equipped to create learner personas that genuinely represent the diversity of your target learners and provide a solid foundation for designing effective and inclusive learning experiences geared toward meeting learners' unique needs.

What You Can Do Right Away

Before designing your next learning experience, create at least two learner personas. Then, design the learning experience for those personas. Ask yourself questions like, "What would Persona 1 think about this scenario?" "How will Persona 2 complete this activity?"

5.
Design and Develop With People in Mind

Yvonne Urra-Bazain (she/her)
E-Learning Developer at Briljent

We live in the most advanced and globally networked time in documented history. This gains truth with every second that positions itself as the new now. As a resident of this timeline, you may encounter people who represent diverse identities, generations, physical locations, abilities, disabilities, cultures, belief systems, and specializations.

The onus is on us to be responsible, respectful, and ethical global citizens. While this may have been true in varying degrees before, the diverse needs and opportunities now fall to us. They are as numbered as the people who share the world.

In the 10 years that I was a classroom teacher, my students' needs were something I could anticipate. I got to know the same group of people, in proximity, over a year of direct interaction. Now, I build digital learning experiences in brief contractual bursts. I may never meet people who use what I help create. I may never read their names on a roster. The divide between what I create and whom I create it for is often bridged by my best intentions and assumptions.

As an e-learning developer for state departments, I must ensure the digital accessibility of content. I am learning to deliver products that account for a diversity of situations and preferences, including:

- **Mode of operation.** This means the hardware method someone uses to engage with content, whether through a mouse pointer, dragging actions, keyboard navigation, or other assistive technologies that allow them to access an interface or information.

- **Preferred user agents.** These comprise any software that presents digital content, including web browsers, plug-ins, media players, and assistive technology programs, such as screen readers or browser extensions.
- **Bandwidth limitations.** Some users may be traveling, using a metered connection, living in rural areas with limited internet connectivity, or accessing the internet through outdated hardware.

Every time I talk to someone about their access needs, I gain insight into their user experience. It is a humbling and critical practice to receive feedback that your solution did not work.

Accessibility for all people is a high standard. I cling to Meryl Evans's reminder to focus on "progress over perfection." As a practitioner, increasing accessibility is my persistent goal. I've taken on helping others develop empathy for user access needs as a personal undertaking. My role is to provide experiences that simulate the usability and accessibility of digital environments to newer practitioners. This depends on presenting various sources and perspectives about accessible and inaccessible experiences.

Sources of Digital Accessibility Recommendations

According to SeeWriteHear, web accessibility is "the practice of making information, activities, and/or environments sensible, meaningful, and usable for as many people as possible."[20] Accessibility is often measured by a pass or fail metric that asks: Can all people access the information with equity?

Guidelines about user accessibility are informed by three classifications of sources: primary, secondary, and tertiary.

A *primary source* provides a first-hand report on a unique experience or documentation of original information. Examples include:

- **User testing.** Testing digital products with users who represent a range of abilities and disabilities provides a primary testimonial of their user experience.
- **Surveys and interviews.** One of the most direct ways to determine how a user can or will interact with a product is by observing and interviewing the people using it.

A *secondary source* offers an analysis or restatement of primary source information. It may describe, interpret, or synthesize the original information. Examples include:

- **User personas.** Creating user access personas based on primary source information of similar groups serves as a second-hand source of user accessibility information. A persona is a fictitious character based on the characteristics of people who share a similar experience.
- **Simulations.** Tools that simulate user experiences may be based on commonalities among user data or feedback, so they can represent a larger collection of people with similar needs.

A *tertiary source* indexes, organizes, compiles, and digests primary and secondary sources to generalize ideas. As a result, they are typically not credited to a particular author. Examples include:

- **Guidelines and standards.** The World Wide Web Consortium (W3C) publishes and maintains the Web Content Accessibility Guidelines (WCAG) as the international standard for web accessibility.
- **Recommendations.** Other groups offer checklists and additional distillations of recommended best practices.

Ideally, a timeline for accessible development should be guided by tertiary recommendations, informed by secondary user personas and simulations, and validated by primary user testing, surveys, and interviews. However, not every product timeline or work order contract may account for these planning, prototyping, and testing cycles. The minimum current practice may include accessibility testing using tertiary checklists and tools that simulate diverse user experiences.

WCAG recommendations are a necessary aggregate of primary and secondary source information. The guidelines represent the widest range of situations and variabilities of the three source classifications. While all sources are valuable, introducing new practitioners to tertiary sources of accessibility information alone poses a challenge I refer to as the hidden object conundrum.

The Hidden Object Conundrum

In a hidden object puzzle, the player must locate a list of items within a dense or chaotic scene. In other variations, the player must pinpoint one unique item hidden among repeating objects or characters. While it is meant to be a visual brain teaser, the task of finding objects can be difficult because the player may have a different concept of what a listed object is or how it might be represented in the static image. If the player is uncertain what a listed item looks like, how can they recognize it?

Figure 5-1 depicts an illustrated scene with a desk near a window. On the desk are various items unusual to the setting, including a suitcase, a sheet of paper, and a feather quill. Try locating these three items, but consider how this list could be problematic:

- Pepper
- Chips
- The Capricorn symbol

Figure 5-1. Close up of hidden object puzzle scene. A desk is near a window. There are various items unusual to the setting on the desk. *Source: Image generated using Adobe Firefly 2.0 from the prompt "Assortment of items on a desk, including a suitcase, a sheet of paper, a feather quill, a box of potato chips, a chili pepper, a pepper mill, and poker chips."*

In addition to the visual complexity inherent in this puzzle, terms can be ambiguous and represent disparate items depending on context.

In English, *pepper* is a term that refers to a canister of ground or whole peppercorns or any variety of fresh capsicum pepper fruits.

Regional and international differences in language also affect how a player expects *chips* to display in the puzzle. Chips in American English are thin, crunchy snacks, but the same term in Australian or British English means pommes frites, crisps, or what Americans call french fries. In addition, chips could reference gaming pieces, such as the poker chips also displayed in the image.

Lastly, the Capricorn symbol may be an esoteric visual for people to find, partially due to needing specialized knowledge and schema for varying representations.

Similarly, when clients ask for an accessible e-learning program, consultants, designers, and developers may rely on tertiary checklists to pinpoint which elements of a deliverable need to be addressed to meet accessibility requirements. However, for new practitioners, anticipating different ways success criteria could present for various users and understanding what specialized terms mean can increase the difficulty of making e-learning content accessible.

Take for example, the WCAG 2.1 Success Criterion (SC) 1.3.1:[21]

Principle 1 Perceivable

Guideline 1.3 Adaptable: Create content that can be presented in different ways (for example simpler layout) without losing information or structure.

Success Criterion 1.3.1 Info and Relationships (Level A): Information, structure, and relationships conveyed through presentation can be programmatically determined or are available in text.

A new practitioner may need clarification to make reasonable modifications for accessibility based on this text. Indeed, W3C provides further explanation for the key terms *structure*, *relationships*, *presentation*, and *programmatically determined*, as well as the intent, benefits, examples, related resources, sufficient techniques, advisory techniques, and failures pertinent to this success criterion. However, the full text that documents this, "Understanding SC 1.3.1: Info and Relationships (Level A)," may require hours of study to completely read and mentally digest.

This represents the complexity of one of the 50 or more success criterions required for minimum WCAG Level A and AA conformance.

When our early experiences designing for accessibility are relegated to lists, it is no wonder it feels like we're searching for a hidden object we don't understand. We risk creating best practices based upon reasonable best guesses. It can feel like getting a list of calculus algorithms after mastering addition. Furthermore, a reliance on tertiary checklists as the sole source for best practice may cloud the key to accessibility: designing for as many people as possible.

User Access Personas and Simulations

While primary source information is as person centered as possible, it may be both unreasonable and too narrow for new practitioners. First, it is rare to have access to user testing and feedback from an assistive technology (AT) user for every deliverable. Second, if you can have at least one user test some of your deliverables, the usability information you could learn from observing or surveying them may only inform you about their specific access needs. And third, you ideally want to plan learning experiences with accessibility in mind from the beginning. User testing is typically reserved for when a deliverable or product has already gone through at least a prototyping phase.

Instead, I suggest that new practitioners supplement their accessibility approaches with secondary source information, such as user access personas and simulations. For this reason, I facilitate a monthly virtual meeting that blends an empathy lab with personal usability analyses. It is my hope that by discussing our diversity of user experiences and simulating various user needs, we can build stronger intuitions and lay the foundation for testing practices that maintain user experience at the core.

The W3C publications are leaning toward more usable, people-centered guidelines, as well. The W3C Working Group Note, "Making Content Usable for People With Cognitive and Learning Disabilities," is written in more understandable language and includes a section on use cases and personas that gives context to user experiences, including the problems users may encounter and a description of what works well for that user.[22] In addition, the section is written in the various personas' voices, as if they were quotations from a user testing interview.

The WCAG 3.0 Working Draft proposes that the updated standard guidelines should be written in plain language and focused more on user needs instead of technology. While version three of the guidelines may be years from publication, other examples of user personas and simulations could aid our accessibility discussions now. The United States General Services Administration's Technology Transformation Services digital services agency 18F provides insight into how to build useful, research-based personas and a framework for groups to practice the skill.[23] And in 2017, the United Kingdom's Central Digital and Data Office published personas as user profiles that practitioners can use today as they build their skills.[24]

Design for People

I am working toward consistently designing and developing with people in mind, so I strive to ensure my discussions about accessibility prioritize people. While guidelines, checklists, and other recommendations are necessary, they are often process or tool focused. This further disconnects me from the unknown users for whom I create materials and products.

Considering this challenge, I've made it a habit to imagine how something I am designing would be used by people I know or have met. As an RVer, I've had the privilege of meeting incredible people, including a chief software engineer with one hand, a musician with hearing loss, and an early-retired EMT with reduced vision in one eye due to amblyopia. In the following sections, I'll share some stories about the people I consider when I develop e-learning experiences.

V: A History of Febrile Seizures

V is a young woman who experienced prolonged febrile seizures between the ages of two and four years old. The seizures could last 30 minutes and were focalized around her mouth. The risk factors were severe enough for V to take medication regularly to prevent seizure events and to be monitored by a neurologist.

Although her physician has said V shows no indication of long-term effects or signs of epilepsy, she must take seizure warnings seriously. She avoids flashing or strobing lights whenever possible.

While she has a tolerance for motion, V does have sensitivity to light in motion and brightness. Digital experiences that provide a mix of still-frame presentation with video or animation are important to her. Eliminating media that poses a seizure risk further protects her health.

B: Blindness and Foreign Language Barriers

B was my childhood neighbor. When I was a teenager, I woke up early in the morning to wait with him for his school bus. He attended a school for the deaf and blind that was an hour's drive away.

B spoke Tagalog. I learned some Tagalog words, but had difficulty communicating with him beyond saying hello, goodbye, and other simple phrases. At the time, B used a cane and needed assistance for mobility.

Finding braille in his native language was difficult. He relied on his family for conversation, company, and entertainment. When cell phones and other technology became mainstream, B's opportunities similarly grew, although AT language support in Tagalog lagged compared with other languages.

When I consider language differences and test for auditory and tactile modes of operation, I think of B.

D: Profound Hearing Loss

I recently listened to D speak as a presenter at an accessibility conference. He shared what it was like to meet one of his role models as a child, but to not be able to hear him, or understand why classmates around him were smiling. During the virtual conference, the closed captions were not working correctly. When the session's host tried to speak with D to communicate, he expressed some confusion. Although D uses hearing aids, the message he was receiving was not coming through clearly.

For D, visual modes of communication are vital. Sound-based alerts must also be presented visually to properly signal him. I think about D when I deliver a speech-based presentation. I consider if live captioning is an option, if there is a backup for live captioning, and what other ways I can represent what I am saying with visuals and other expressions.

E: Dementia

E was my mother. For five years, I provided caregiving to her in our home. Over time, her cognitive abilities began to change. We used visual boards for needs prompting. We used songs to remind us of daily tasks, mealtimes, and hygiene routines. As her ability to process names and faces waned, we were able to use touch screen tablets as a soundboard to communicate needs.

E's mobility also waned. While she could dance for the first year and walk on her own in the second year, by the third year, our daily walks were arm-in-arm for support. Before the fourth year, E needed a walker for standing support and then a wheelchair. I continued to take E out, although wheelchair access changed our patronage options. In the fifth year, I took care of E completely in her room. Through hospice services, we were able to bring in medical equipment and a hospital bed into our home to support her caregiving.

E's overall engagement waned from year four to the end of year five. Just years before, she was a vital and savvy typist and passionate speaker. The honor of being her caregiver for those years helped me realize that life is changeable. Everyone deserves access and support to do things important to them and to engage with their loved ones. Our access needs will change over time. They could change temporarily or situationally within the next hour. They could change permanently tomorrow.

What is certain is that we all can benefit from the work of designing for all people. We can make provisions for different means that people require to meet their needs today.

The people I advocate for press me forward.

Promise

As schools, workplaces, and other physical spaces welcome greater diversity, we must be inclusive of the needs of all learners and colleagues. Equally, as the next billion users of the World Wide Web log online, creators of digital or web-based content must be prepared to design for the greatest range of variabilities. The most appropriate word I have learned to describe this calling is *kuleana*, a Hawaiian value loosely translated to mean the American English equivalent of *responsibility*.

However, the ability to respond to a need is just half of one's *kuleana*, which describes the reciprocal relationship of one's responsibility and the rights afforded by being responsible. It is as much our *kuleana* to adapt and accommodate the diverse needs and experiences of our global citizenry as it should be our expectation that other creators respond in kind. We must meet others' access needs, and they must meet our access needs situationally, temporarily, in the future, and now.

I preface accessibility discussions by encouraging people to see that we have a civil rights opportunity in accessible and inclusive design. Our mutual rights and responsibilities to provide and receive access to information is something we must hold ourselves and each other accountable to, with compassion, as we gain empathy for experiences that may not be present in our own variability.

Digital technology has made strides in providing a place where all people can engage and build a sense of digital and world belonging. The work before us is to advocate for opportunities and empower the people we meet, as well as those we may never meet. I encourage you to continue this work for as many people as possible and for your future self as well.

What You Can Do Right Away

Think about the people you've encountered throughout your life. Who would you put on your own list of people to advocate for? Who are the people you design for? Document their stories and keep them available whenever you're setting out to design a new learning experience.

6.
Intersectional Inclusion

Understanding How Dimensions of Social Identity Play Into Accessibility to Help Everyone THRIVE

Jess Jackson (she/her/they/them)
Racial Equity Strategist, TorranceLearning

When I worked in high schools, I worked predominantly with students from under-resourced school districts living in communities affected by poverty. I name these dynamics for two major reasons.

Environment
First, if my students had come from different school districts or environments, their relationship to and performance within institutions would likely be different.

One of my favorite things to share during equity, diversity, inclusion, and belonging (EDIB) training is that I was educated within and graduated from the Detroit Public Schools school system. Our early 2000s campaign, "I am DPS," still rings with pride in my ears. Well, If I am being honest, I don't know if the feeling is pride or a tinge of embarrassment as our slogan quickly became the target of jokes about underperformance and failure.

Regardless, coming from DPS had meaning in my life—so much so that when I participated in a student exchange program in the 10th grade that took students from my high school in Detroit to a school in Birmingham, Michigan, I knew it was where I came from, not who I was, that would hold me back in life.

Birmingham is in Oakland County—the most affluent county in Michigan. The campus I attended in the 10th grade was equipped with pristine facilities, new technology, a full magnet Advanced Placement and International Baccalaureate (AP/IB) curriculum, and, to my surprise, smoothie machines. The public school students in Birmingham had the opportunity to eat nutritiously, engage in technology literacy, experience academic rigor, and feel safe and valued inside their school walls.

This experience was in stark contrast to my life at DPS. At the time, my school had three AP classes to offer, a metal detector, and a pat down to start each day. The best technology we had was the antiquated and donated Dell desktops in *some* of our English Language Arts (ELA) classrooms.

These different experiences depicted a harsh reality: School districts that served students like me were not worthy of investment. And don't just take my word for it—this is by design. In the United States, we have institutionalized segregation. Many neighborhoods and the institutions within them have been kept separate, and this means they are funded differently. Take for example *redlining*, a policy used to block home loans and other financial services from communities with high concentrations of immigrants and Black people. The policy has historically blocked many folks in my community and communities like mine from receiving mortgages or home equity loans to invest in real estate. So, if public school systems receive their funding through local property taxes, and property values have been intentionally suppressed in communities of color, our school systems receive less funding. In fact, one 2019 EdBuild study found that, "nonwhite school districts get $23 billion less than white districts despite serving the same number of students."[25]

Why does this matter? *If my students had come from different school districts or environments, their relationship to and performance within institutions would likely be different.* The current institutions that exist were designed to prevent under-resourced (or, dare I say, "intentionally excluded") folks from accessing social mobility. When we uphold traditional models, we may be upholding this form of exclusion. To design for all means we must rethink institutional structures to ensure that all folks have access regardless of where they come from.

Social Identity

Second, there were and still are stark gaps in representation of the characteristics that my students shared, or what I call social identities, across most institutions that advance social mobility.

Social identity plays a key role in individual and group dynamics by creating categories or groupings for characteristics such as race, ethnicity, gender, religion, and socioeconomic background. Social identity defines who we are and how we perceive ourselves in relation to others.

Social mobility is the movement of individuals or groups within a social hierarchy. It's the ability to change our socioeconomic status, position, or occupation, and is influenced by several factors, including education, wealth, merit, and social support systems—all of which can be influenced by our social identity.

Representation matters because within systems and structures that advance social mobility, there are fewer folks who identify with historically excluded characteristics. Representation gaps create disparities in the visibility, participation, and influence of certain groups within political, media, and corporate institutions. These gaps can occur based on race, gender, sexuality, disability, and other types of social identity groups.

I am a biracial Black, queer woman from Detroit. As a professional trainer, speaker, and leader, I've navigated many contexts that have advanced my social mobility. From school systems, certification programs, professional associations, and workplaces, I am often, if not always, one of a few women of color in the room because systems and structures have historically excluded us. For example, it's hard to have a high representation of women of color in areas where we just don't live. That said, the lack of representation in these professional spaces can make it incredibly difficult to show up as my full self.

Whether it's imposter syndrome causing me to question if I belong at the tables I access, or the inherent bias that intercedes my sense of belonging, being one of a few is challenging. For example, one of my favorite ways to show up as myself is in my hair and nails. I have long acrylic nails that are always decorated. While that's common in my community and culturally appropriate, I often receive strange looks and interrogation from folks who are not used to seeing or wearing long nails.

Recently, I facilitated a live virtual workshop on EDIB. During the session, as I transitioned my slides, the audience was distracted by a clicking. The clicking kept coming up in the session until we finally realized that the sound was caused by my nails clicking the mouse and keyboard. Instead of ending the conversation about the noise, however, the audience proceeded to joke about my "aggressive" typing habits and "long nails." They made fun of an aspect of me that brings me pride and one that is normal and revered in my community. They turned me and a cultural aspect into a problem and a joke.

While it may seem harmless, this interaction reflects the bias that is pervasive within organizations that lack diverse representation. The session was mostly women, who share one identity with me, but there were few urban Black women who could understand the cultural symbolism and importance of a Black woman's nails.

This dual experience of feeling both represented by the women in the room but also excluded and ostracized because there were few women of color present is what intersectionality is all about.

Intersectionality, first coined by Kimberlé Crenshaw, professor at Columbia Law School, refers to the interconnected nature of social identity, which creates overlapping and interdependent systems of discrimination and disadvantage. In the context of accessibility, identity and intersectionality play a significant role in determining who has access to technology and how they can engage with it. And these implications are reflected in almost all institutions associated with social mobility—including access to quality education, economic opportunities, and social networks, as well as systemic barriers, such as discrimination and inequality. To truly design for all, it's essential to understand how identity, intersectionality, and representation affect people.

So, how do we design learning to be both accessible and inclusive to help all learners THRIVE?

- **T**hink for humanity.
- **R**elationships are interpersonal.
- **V**oices are everywhere.

Think for Humanity

According to the Harvard Business School Business Insights blog, human-centered design is an approach to problem solving that places people at the center of the development process.[26] This enables developers to create products and services that resonate with and are tailored to a business's real consumer needs.

The goal of human-centered design is to keep consumer wants, struggles, and desires at the forefront of every phase of the development process. As a result, you'll build more intuitive, accessible products that are likely to turn a higher profit because consumers have already vetted the solution and feel more invested in using it.

Mastering human-centered design means to consistently question the who, what, and why of a learning experience. It is an interrogative and iterative process that is centered on human needs and identities. With its focus on empathy, inclusivity, and iterative problem solving, human-centered design provides a powerful approach for addressing the complex needs of consumers from diverse and intersectional identity groups.

If designers center the experiences of individuals from historically excluded backgrounds, they can create solutions that better meet everyone's unique needs. Incorporating social identity and intersectionality throughout the design process helps challenge biases, uncover hidden perspectives, and ultimately foster greater inclusivity and equity.

When making identity-based considerations in design, it is important to include voices from people who represent those groups. Rather than engage in tokenism, move forward with real voices and feedback from underrepresented groups to avoid stereotyping or further ostracizing them.

Let's consider several strategies you can leverage to implement human-centered design in your design processes.

Empathy and User Research

Human-centered design starts with practicing empathy and actively listening to the experiences and needs of users. By engaging with individuals from diverse social identities and intersectional backgrounds, you gain deeper insights into the challenges they face and the solutions that would be most relevant and effective.

Inclusive Design Principles

Inclusive design principles guide the development of solutions that cater to a wide range of users. They involve ensuring accessibility, usability, and inclusiveness for individuals with different abilities, cultural backgrounds, and social identities. By considering the intersecting dimensions of social identity, you can create more inclusive and equitable learning experiences.

Take for example the innovations that helped develop speech recognition software that can now recognize diverse accents and languages. These advances were a direct response to accent gaps that people experienced while using the technology. According to research conducted by the *Washington Post*, there was a notable accent gap in smart-speaker speech recognition.[27] Its study found disparities in how people from different parts of the US were understood. In addition, according to *Forbes*, automated speech recognition (ASR) engine grammar (the word patterns that show ASR what to expect from human speech) needed to expand to increase diversity of pronunciations and dialects.[28] This is one way that intersectional design can affect inclusion. Although all users were speaking English, they weren't all understood because diverse dialects and pronunciations were not considered, so the software was not inclusive to a wide user base.

Co-Creation and Participation

Involving individuals from diverse social identities in the design process is essential for creating solutions that are representative and relevant. Co-creation and participation allow you to include multiple perspectives, ensuring that the needs and concerns of marginalized groups are addressed. This strategy also helps challenge biases and assumptions that may arise from your own social identity.

Iterative Design and Continuous Feedback

Human-centered design thrives on iteration and continuous feedback. Engaging with users throughout the design process, especially those from diverse social identities, helps refine solutions and ensure their effectiveness. It allows you to make adjustments based on the evolving needs and contexts of different user groups. Inclusive design practices like human-centered design require you to consider a wide range of user needs and experiences during the development process. By designing with inclusivity in mind, your design can be more accessible to all individuals, regardless of their identity.

Relationships Are Interpersonal

A critical aspect of addressing accessibility is designing with both an interpersonal and intersectional lens. For example, to address representation gaps, take proactive measures at every level within an organization—individual, institutional, and systemic. Some activities that can advance inclusion and increase representation are promoting diversity and inclusion policies, implementing affirmative action programs, providing equal educational opportunities, challenging biases and stereotypes, and fostering dialogue and collaboration among diverse groups.

However, these activities don't come without a cost. Folks within and accustomed to historically exclusionary structures may feel deprioritized as we shift focus and center identities that have been left out. Questions like "What about me?" or "How much representation is too much representation?" may arise, and this is normal. Interpersonal conflicts related to identity and diversity issues can be challenging to navigate. On the one hand, we want to make space for folks who have been excluded, but where does this space come from? With empathy, open communication, and a willingness to understand different perspectives, we can achieve resolutions.

Here are some strategies for effectively navigating these conflicts.

Cultivate Empathy and Self-Reflection

Developing empathy is crucial for understanding others' identities and experiences. L&D teams and the broader organization will need to take time to reflect on biases and privilege, and to acknowledge that everyone brings a unique set of perspectives to the table. There may need to be some training on how historical exclusion based on social identities is complex and intersecting. Above all, there needs to be a shared agreement to learn from others.

Practice Active Listening, Validation, and Microaffirmation

Teams will also need to actively listen to genuinely understand others' concerns and experiences. During dialogues, allow folks to express themselves fully without interruption or dismissal. Validate their experiences by acknowledging their emotions and demonstrating genuine empathy. This creates a safe space for open discussion.

Engage in Continuous Education and Dialogue

One of the biggest burdens of being underrepresented in the workplace is being expected to be the sole provider of education. L&D teams will need to take the initiative to educate themselves about different identities, social issues, and perspectives. This means they should seek out diverse sources of information and engage in respectful discussions to enhance their understanding and challenge their own assumptions. Doing so will foster a culture of learning and growth.

Here are some resources and strategies you can use with your team and the rest of the organization to help everyone learn about different social identities, social issues, and perspectives without relying on your diverse team members:

- **Diversity, equity, and inclusion (DEI) training.** Invest in comprehensive DEI training programs for all staff members. These programs can cover topics such as unconscious bias, cultural competency, and inclusive leadership. Encourage employees to take online courses and workshops that focus on diversity and inclusion.
- **Inclusive language training.** Offer training on using inclusive language to avoid unintentional biases. This helps create a more respectful and inclusive communication environment.
- **Reading materials.** Provide a curated list of books, articles, and research papers that address DEI. Encourage staff to read and discuss these materials to broaden their perspectives.

- **Documentaries and films.** Organize screenings of documentaries and films that explore social issues and highlight diverse voices. This can be followed by group discussions to facilitate understanding and empathy.
- **Guest speakers and experts.** Bring in guest speakers and experts to conduct workshops or talks on DEI topics. This provides firsthand insight and allows staff to engage in meaningful discussions.
- **Employee resource groups (ERGs).** Establish and support ERGs within the organization. These groups can serve as forums for employees to share experiences, discuss relevant issues, and educate one another.
- **Microlearning modules.** Develop short, targeted microlearning modules that address specific aspects of diversity and inclusion. These can be easily integrated into employees' daily routines.
- **Cultural competency assessments.** Conduct assessments to gauge employees' cultural competency and identify areas for improvement. Provide resources and support based on the assessment results.
- **Mentorship and buddy systems.** Pair employees with mentors or buddies from different backgrounds. This fosters one-on-one learning and allows for open conversations about diversity and inclusion.

Practice Respectful Communication

Using "I" statements to express yourself without making assumptions about others' intentions is key to respectful dialogue. During discussions, it is imperative that teammates avoid making personal attacks and instead focus on the issue at hand. Most importantly, everyone should be respectful in their language and tone, ensuring that words do not invalidate or discount someone else's experiences or identities.

Embrace Constructive Conflict Feedback and Resolution

Approach conflicts in perspective as opportunities for growth and understanding rather than as a win or lose situation. Express gratitude when you receive critical feedback. Find common ground and shared goals. Look for areas of overlap and identify possible solutions that promote inclusivity and harmony. Aim for compromise and collaboration, respecting diverse perspectives and finding common values.

Recognize that impact differs from intent. Even with good intentions, actions or words may have unintended consequences. Reflect on the impact caused by words and actions, and be willing to apologize and make amends when necessary. Learn from the experience and commit to personal growth. If conflicts become unproductive or escalate, consider involving a neutral third party to mediate or facilitate the conversation. This can help ensure a balanced dialogue, create a safe environment, and provide guidance for a constructive resolution.

Create Allies and Solidarity

If you are an ally to a historically excluded identity group, use your privilege to amplify their voices and advocate for their rights. Stand in solidarity and actively challenge biases and discriminatory behaviors. Promote an inclusive environment where everyone feels valued and respected.

Commit to Continuous Learning and Unlearning

Identity, intersectionality, and diversity are complex, ever-evolving topics. Commit to continuous learning and unlearning, actively challenging biases and assumptions. Engage in ongoing dialogue with a diverse range of individuals, which will help broaden your perspective and deepen understanding.

Voices Are Everywhere

The beauty of inclusive design that considers identity and intersectionality is that solutions should be collaborative. There are many ways to measure progress and effectiveness, but a key measure should be who has contributed to the design. Inclusive design invites everyone to be a part of the solution, and while this can slow down the process, it's ultimately more effective and meaningful because it is more inclusive. So, how do we standardize and measure progress on inclusive design?

User Testing and Feedback

Conduct user testing sessions with individuals who represent the target user groups. Soliciting feedback from diverse voices is crucial for creating an inclusive environment, but it's important to approach this process with sensitivity and respect and to avoid tokenizing your team members from marginalized groups.

Here are some thoughtful ways to gather feedback:

- **Be transparent and communicate intentions.** Clearly communicate the purpose of seeking feedback and emphasize the organization's commitment to inclusivity. Be transparent about how the feedback will be used to drive positive change.
- **Diversify feedback channels.** Use a variety of channels to collect feedback, including surveys, focus groups, town hall meetings, and one-on-one conversations. Ensure that marginalized individuals can choose the method that is most comfortable and accessible to them.
- **Engage in ongoing conversations.** Foster an environment of continuous dialogue rather than seeking feedback only at specific times. Create platforms for ongoing discussions, allowing marginalized individuals to share their perspectives at any time.
- **Create anonymous feedback options.** Provide anonymous channels for feedback to allow individuals to express their thoughts without fear of retribution. This can include anonymous surveys or suggestion boxes.
- **Partner with ERGs.** Collaborate with ERGs representing marginalized groups within the organization. ERGs can help facilitate communication, build trust, and provide insights on how to approach feedback collection respectfully.

- **Ensure representation in decision making.** Involve individuals from marginalized groups in the decision-making process. This goes beyond seeking feedback and demonstrates a genuine commitment to including diverse perspectives in shaping policies and practices.
- **Acknowledge and act on feedback.** Show that feedback is valued by acknowledging it and taking concrete actions based on the input received. Regularly update the organization on the progress made by the feedback.
- **Avoid tokenizing language.** Frame your requests for feedback in a way that does not tokenize individuals. Avoid using language that singles out specific people solely based on their identity. Focus on collective experiences and perspectives.
- **Use intersectional approaches.** Recognize and address the intersectionality of identities within marginalized groups. Acknowledge that individuals may have multiple aspects to their identity and experiences.
- **Offer support and resources.** Provide resources and support for individuals who may feel uncomfortable or emotionally affected by the process. This can include access to counseling services or additional support networks.
- **Periodically review and adjust practices.** Regularly evaluate your feedback collection practices and adjust them based on your continued education. Solicit feedback on the feedback process itself to ensure it remains respectful and inclusive.

By setting clear intentions and structuring feedback cycles in inclusive ways, you can gain valuable insights into accessibility, usability, and the effectiveness of inclusive design features. The key is to build trust, create ongoing dialogue, and demonstrate a genuine commitment to inclusivity and improvement based on the feedback received.

Accessibility Compliance

Ensure that design solutions comply with relevant accessibility standards and guidelines, such as the Web Content Accessibility Guidelines

(WCAG) for digital products. Conduct accessibility audits and assessments to measure the extent to which design elements adhere to these standards, identifying areas for improvement.

Inclusivity Metrics and Comparative Analysis

Develop specific metrics related to inclusivity and equity to assess the effectiveness of your design solutions. For example, metrics could include the representation of diverse user groups in user testing, the overall satisfaction and ease of use reported by different user groups, or the extent to which certain features address specific accessibility needs.

I always suggest creating some sort of diagnostic assessment or audit and comparative analysis to help design the metrics so you have a baseline for your current state and a benchmark of where to go in the future. In my comparative analysis, I often review social identity groups to discover if one group had a different, better, or worse experience than another.

User Behavior Analytics

Use analytics tools to gather data on user behavior, interactions, and engagement with the design. Analyze this data to identify any patterns or discrepancies between different user groups. By examining user behavior, you can better understand the effectiveness of inclusive design features and their influence on user experiences.

Post-Implementation Surveys

Distribute post-implementation surveys to gather feedback from users after they have interacted with the learning experience. The survey can include questions about the accessibility, usability, and inclusivity of the design, as well as participants' overall satisfaction and any suggestions for improvement.

When gathering feedback from diverse perspectives, it is important to create a sense of psychological safety for users to honestly respond. Here are some tips to facilitate psychological safety:

- **Use inclusive language.** Ensure that the language you use in the survey is inclusive and respects diverse identities. Avoid assumptions about respondents' backgrounds and use terms that are respectful and neutral. When asking demographic questions, ensure that the options are comprehensive and inclusive. Include options for gender, ethnicity, and other relevant factors that accurately represent the diversity of your audience.

- **Provide multiple-choice options like "other" and "prefer not to say."** Include a diverse set of response options for multiple-choice demographic questions to allow respondents to choose what best represents their identity. You can also allow respondents to skip questions they find uncomfortable or invasive. This gives them control over the information they choose to share and helps maintain a sense of safety.
- **Offer anonymity and confidentiality.** Clearly communicate that survey responses are anonymous or confidential. Assure respondents that their feedback will not be individually attributed, which can encourage more honest and open responses.
- **Include diverse images and examples.** Use images, examples, and case studies that represent a variety of backgrounds and experiences. This helps respondents feel seen and understood, contributing to a sense of inclusivity.
- **Test for accessibility.** Ensure that the survey is accessible to individuals with disabilities. Use accessible formats, provide alternatives for visual content, and ensure compatibility with screen readers.
- **Include inclusivity statements.** Begin the survey with a statement that emphasizes the importance of diverse perspectives and assures respondents that their input is valued. Reinforce the commitment to using feedback for positive change.
- **Pilot the survey.** Before launching the survey, conduct a pilot test with a diverse group to identify any issues with language, tone, or clarity. Use feedback from the pilot group to make necessary adjustments.
- **Ask open-ended questions.** Allow respondents to share their experiences and perspectives in their own words through

open-ended questions. This can provide valuable qualitative insights and more nuanced responses.
- **Provide supportive resources.** Include information on support resources within the survey, such as employee assistance programs or mental health services. This reinforces the organization's commitment to employee well-being.

Ultimately, post-implementation surveys can help you evaluate design solutions, processes, and culture. The feedback collected should be implemented in timely and thoughtful ways.

Collaborative Evaluation

Engage in collaborative evaluation by involving diverse stakeholders, including individuals with lived experiences related to the design goals. Conduct focus groups or interviews to gain insights into their experiences, perspectives, and suggestions for inclusivity improvements. Incorporate their feedback into the evaluation process.

Measuring the effectiveness of inclusive design is essential to ensuring that design decisions and solutions adequately address all users' needs. We can't aim to create products, services, and environments that are accessible and usable by people with diverse abilities, backgrounds, and identities without evaluating whether the design solutions meet the goals of inclusivity and enable equitable user experiences.

Intersectional Inclusion

Social identity, intersectionality, social mobility, and representation gaps are crucial contexts that influence social dynamics and subsequent priorities and performance at work. Understanding and reflecting on these concepts is essential for acknowledging the power structures and inequalities that exist, and thereby designing for all.

Intersectionality highlights the importance of recognizing and understanding the multiple dimensions of an individual's identity. It emphasizes that the experiences, challenges, and barriers faced by people accessing technology are not solely based on a single aspect of their identity but are interwoven with various social factors. For example, a person's racial background, gender, and socioeconomic status can intersect to either enable or hinder their access to technology.

Challenges faced by marginalized communities further illustrate the impact of intersectionality on accessibility. Discrimination and bias limit opportunities for individuals from underrepresented backgrounds. Without diverse representation, perspectives, and inclusion, technological advancements may not adequately cater to the needs and experiences of marginalized communities.

In my own life, I have navigated spaces that were not designed with me in mind and have been able to better understand my professional needs and the gaps in those spaces that perpetuate them. At times, this meant I needed to find a new and more supportive workplace, and other times, I cultivated networks with folks like me through identity-based employee resource and affinity groups. These networks provide unbiased support and a shared experience that makes working in less diverse environments safe for me. Regardless of the strategy, the teams and organizations that help me THRIVE are those that think for humanity, recognize that relationships are interpersonal, and include voices that are everywhere.

These approaches will enable you to design with an intersectional lens, which will empower the equitable participation of underrepresented communities, foster innovation, advance inclusive policies, and create more accessible learning for everyone.

What You Can Do Right Away

How can you begin fostering a THRIVE mindset? Consider starting with the following steps:

- **Avoid tokenism.** Recognize that just because an individual might represent a specific identity group, it does not mean that they can (or even want to) effectively represent the experience of the entire identity group. While it is important to seek feedback from diverse groups, it is just as important to only solicit feedback from individuals who are interested in providing that perspective. Consider reaching out to an employee resource

group or another internal channel designed to provide these perspectives.
- **Recognize power differentials.** Proactively recognize the power dynamics and potential biases that may exist within the design process and across leadership.
- **Prioritize diverse representation.** Ensure there's diverse representation among the design team to prevent overlooking certain perspectives.
- **Make feedback feasible to implement.** This mantra helps me manage expectations. Avoid making promises about solutions that you will not be able to effectively implement and continue to build trust even if you can't use every piece of feedback you receive. Balance honesty and transparency with the need for customization and the scalability and feasibility of solutions.

7.
Personal Discoveries
Accessible Does Not Always Mean Accessible for All

Jean Marrapodi, PhD, CPTD (she/her)
Chief Learning Architect, Applestar Productions

We've all noticed them. The signs. The ramps. The ADA push-button door openers. When President George H.W. Bush signed the Americans with Disabilities Act (ADA) in July 1990, it was intended to provide equitable access to people living with disabilities.[29]

The ADA guidelines include things like:

- **Accessible entrances.** Public and commercial buildings must provide at least one accessible entrance that is clearly marked. Accessible entrances should be free of barriers like steps, and they may have features like ramps, automatic doors, and other accommodations to ensure that people with disabilities can enter and exit the building.
- **Accessible routes.** Once inside a building, there must be an accessible route that allows people with disabilities to move through the space. This includes corridors, hallways, elevators, and other passageways.
- **Accessible restrooms.** Buildings are required to have accessible restrooms equipped with features like grab bars, lowered sinks, and sufficient space for wheelchair maneuverability.
- **Elevators and lifts.** Multistory buildings are typically required to have elevators or lifts to provide access to all levels.

- **Parking.** Accessible parking spaces should be provided and should be located close to the accessible entrance. These spaces should be marked with appropriate signage.
- **Employment.** The ADA prohibits discrimination on the basis of disability in all aspects of employment, including recruitment, hiring, promotion, training, and other terms and conditions.
- **Reasonable accommodations.** Employers are required to provide reasonable accommodations to qualified employees with disabilities, which may include modifications to the work environment, job restructuring, or other adjustments.
- **New construction and alterations.** The ADA Standards for Accessible Design provide specific requirements for new construction and alterations of buildings to ensure accessibility.[30] These standards cover everything from door widths to counter heights and more.

The responsibility for implementation is shared between the following groups:

- **Building owners and operators** are responsible for ensuring that their properties comply with ADA accessibility standards. This includes making necessary modifications to existing buildings and ensuring that new construction adheres to accessibility requirements.
- **Employers** are responsible for ensuring that their workplaces are accessible to employees with disabilities. This includes providing reasonable accommodations and making modifications as necessary.
- **Local authorities and building inspectors** are responsible for enforcing ADA requirements. They review construction plans, issue permits, and conduct inspections to ensure that buildings meet accessibility standards.

This is what the ADA supposed to do. However, reality is a bit different.

A year and a half ago, my mobility decreased so much that my physical therapist recommended I switch from using a cane to a walker. This gave me great freedom and allowed me to get around again. I'm able to heft my rollator (a wheeled mobility aid similar to a walker) into my car's trunk so I can do nearly everything I used to do. Sort of. Let me share a few stories.

Building Challenges

At the beginning of 2023, I started a new job. Many jobs have become remote since the COVID-19 pandemic, and I was delighted to be hired into a position that would be 100 percent remote. I did all my interviews virtually, so no one knew I had a mobility issue.

My orientation would be in person at the company's corporate headquarters in the Midwest. I would have a meet-and-greet session with leadership and members of my team, as well as the usual onboarding tasks and paperwork. The initial paperwork asked if I would need any special accommodation during my visit, so I disclosed my challenges with mobility.

My tickets and hotel were booked, and I arrived at the hotel without a hitch, checking into an accessible room—which had the space for a wheelchair or scooter to get around, the requisite grab bars, visual doorbell signal for the hard of hearing, and a roll-in-shower. Unfortunately, the door to access the room was incredibly heavy, with an insistent door closer mounted up top, so it took quite an effort to maneuver myself and my luggage past said entrance, but I managed. Accessible? Sort of.

The first morning, I arranged to meet my new boss in the lobby. It's always amusing to meet people in person whom you've only seen on camera from the shoulders up. He was very, very tall, which surprised me, and I was using a walker, which surprised him. (Apparently, the paperwork with the disclosure never made it to his desk.)

We ambled down the block to the corporate office, the requisite downtown marble and glass edifice, only to discover eight marble steps leading to the entrance. My boss had been there multiple times, but these steps were invisible to him because he has no challenges with them. This is an important thing to realize. *Many people don't see those stairs as a problem until they have someone with a disability in their presence.*

The corporate office was in a major metropolitan city, so I knew there were requirements for an accessible entrance, but there were no indicators as to where it was. Fortunately, there was a railing on the steps, so my boss carted my walker and I got myself up to those heavy glass doors to start our day. (To their credit, the building was equipped with an automatic door opener for that heavy glass door.)

At security, we asked about the accessible entrance, and were told it was around the other side of the building. Of course, no one told us that a locked chain was placed across the bottom of the ramp at 5 p.m., so it wasn't helpful when we tried to leave. Luckily, someone in our group realized that a screw gate carabiner attached one end of the chain to the wall, so he was able to release us before security arrived to unlock the chain. Accessible? Yes, but only during the right time. Oh, if you're wondering why there was a chain, it was intended to let customers know the branch was closed for the day.

During the day, we had to go to the HR office to contend with some additional paperwork. That required going to an adjacent building connected to the corporate office by a skywalk. My boss and I meandered through the halls and over the skywalk to be greeted by 14 steep steps to access HR and again no signage for accessible options.

We called the HR rep, who dashed down the stairs with a lot of apologies, saying if she'd known, she would have come to us. Sure, that was a workaround, but it should not have been this way in the first place. That's the point of the ADA. I asked about the accessible option to get to the HR office and was told I should go through the doors marked "Do Not Enter" to my right, which led through a mechanical room to the freight elevator, bypassing the inaccessible entrance. Once again, the issue was unseen until someone with functional needs was around.

Yes, the building has the requisite accessible bathrooms, elevators, automatic door openers, and flat access from section to section (mostly), but there were still a few wrinkles to iron out. This is a common occurrence for people with disabilities.

Job Challenges

Beyond the work I do as an instructional designer, I do a fair amount of speaking at conferences and events. As a speaker, you learn to be flexible, but now with a walker, there is an added burden for me to be successful. Fairly often, speakers have a platform to present from—usually with stairs you need to climb to get up there. It's not impossible if there is a railing and I have my cane.

I can't stand for long amounts of time anymore, so I need a stool to sit on during my presentations. I ask the meeting planner to make those arrangements, and they sometimes learn the hard way that all stools are not created equal. I'm only 5 feet tall, and on multiple occasions, I've been given a stool that was too high for me to get onto by myself.

There have also been times when I arrived at a workshop and the tables and chairs were set so close together that I couldn't get through them without moving chairs to clear a path. While I'm thrilled to be able to speak in packed rooms, this is an obstacle course for me, and like the other experiences I've shared, it's an invisible issue to those who don't have a disability. Challenges like these aren't given a second thought when things are prepared for "regular" people.

For the last conference I attended, I rented a scooter. This was great because I wasn't exhausted getting from my hotel room to the conference area. It also allowed me to do some sightseeing. However, getting in and out of the bathrooms wasn't so great. I drove my scooter into one and got stuck. Yes, stuck. There wasn't enough room to turn the scooter around, so I had to back up to the door, which I now couldn't open. I had to wait for someone else to come in so I could get out.

What You Can Do Right Away

As learning professionals, we need to practice empathy—the first step in the design thinking process. We need to put ourselves in the shoes (or chair) of someone with functional needs. Look around the places you frequent. What would it be like if you had a disability? Is there adequate signage? Think about the weight of the doors you open. Could someone with a wheelchair manage it? If you see someone with a walker, wheelchair, or cane, offer to hold the door open for them. Offer to help them with their meal if you're in a buffet line.

I think the best thing you can do is to imagine yourself in their position. If possible, try maneuvering with a walker, cane, or wheelchair on your own. Experience what it's like from a firsthand perspective. Try television without the sound, or only with the sound. Try out tools like Funkify and Silktide simulators that let you view things as if you had dyslexia, color blindness, loss of hearing, or trembling hands. It's quite astonishing.

There are several things that you can do when preparing for classes, events, and workshops. Ask the "what if" questions. What if someone comes with mobility issues? Walk the path from the entrance to your classroom, keeping an eye out for challenges including steps, raised door jams, and access to the restrooms. Think about the size of the font in your handout and slides. Is the text readable from the back of the room? For e-learning programs, try going through your course with a screen reader or without sound. Is it still cohesive? Remember to add alt tags so that individuals with visual impairments don't have to listen to "Adobe57295-6667.png" and try to determine what that image was supposed to represent.

Put on some different metaphorical shoes in your planning and think through the needs that will be invisible until they smack you in the face. Your learners will be most grateful.

8.
Understanding Neurodivergent Learners

Judy Katz (she/her)
Founder and Consultant, Neurodivergent Working

I suspected that one of my children was autistic from a very early age, and I was prepared to hear the diagnosis. I remember sitting in the doctor's office, listening to the signs that the doctor had noticed, occasionally joking that the apple didn't fall far from the tree. So many of the things the doctor was talking about were traits that I had, too, and even though it was me who had fought to get my son evaluated, parts of me wondered if some of those autistic expressions were just personality quirks he had inherited from me.

I knew that autism was inherited genetically, but it wasn't until I started reading more online that I realized my son had inherited more than personality quirks from me; he had likely inherited his autism. I was diagnosed almost two years after my son was, at the age of 40. I had learned by then that for a variety of reasons, girls aren't diagnosed in childhood with anything near the frequency that boys are, and many women only recognize their own autistic traits after their sons are diagnosed.

The emphasis on gender is important here because the diagnostic criteria for both autism and ADHD was based on boys—girls often present differently and even when girls present similarly to typical "boylike" presentations, their expressions are often interpreted differently by doctors.[31] Interpretations differ based on race and ethnicity as well, and there is a wide range of other socioeconomic conditions that can lead to lack of diagnosis until middle age—or at all.[32] And finally, there are many overlapping common traits with trauma and various types of neurodivergence, which can obscure diagnosis further, whether it is formal a diagnosis or self-diagnosis.[33]

You may be thinking, what do neurodiverse and neurodivergent mean? *Neurodivergence* is a way to describe how people may experience, interact with, and process information in a way that is not typical. This includes autism, ADHD, dyslexia, obsessive-compulsive disorder, anxiety disorders, Tourette syndrome, migraines, and other differences. *Neurodiversity* includes all brains, both neurodivergent and neurotypical.

There are many neurodiverse people who don't know they're neurodivergent while they're going to school or entering the workforce. And even after individuals are diagnosed, their neurodivergent traits may not be obvious to others, or they may spend a great deal of energy covering up—or *masking*—for increased social acceptance and career success. Neurodivergence is one category of disability that can be nonapparent, either to others or to neurodivergent individuals themselves. Don't assume there are no neurodivergent people in your target audience or that members of your target audience even know whether they are neurodivergent.

What You Can Do Right Away

Neurodivergence and other nonapparent disabilities should never be ignored as an audience characteristic; however, you also shouldn't create a separate version of learning experiences specifically for neurodivergent audiences. Start shifting your thinking to inclusive design in *every* learning experience, *every* time.

That shift should start before you develop a learning solution, before you design it, and before you pick an authoring tool; it should start with the decision about which type of learning solution to employ. As a neurodivergent person with significant sensory needs, I am much more comfortable working—and learning—from home because I can control the temperature, sounds, smells, tactile experiences, and type and level of light. I can also have greater control over my schedule and distractions, such as interactions with others. I was diagnosed with ADHD a couple of years after being diagnosed with autism, which completed the picture of why I've always been more productive working and learning from home. Again, adult diagnosis of ADHD is a common experience.

Therefore, e-learning and virtual instructor-led training are far preferable for me, as they are with many neurodiverse people, and as they are with many other audiences for whom in-person training is inconvenient or inaccessible. This book will cover how to make all types of learning experiences more accessible for neurodivergent individuals and many others, but it's worth considering that simply choosing different types of learning solutions from the outset may have benefits beyond what accommodations to in-person events can provide.

9.
The Importance of Testing With Real Users

Diane Elkins (she/her)
Co-Founder, Artisan Learning

I've spent years trying to learn the best approach to designing for accessibility—reading articles, watching webinars, talking to other practitioners, and pouring through the standards. But the best education I've ever gotten has been from having my courses tested by people who would be affected by my choices. Sure, a sighted person can catch a lot of screen reader issues through testing. But when a person who relies every day on a screen reader does the testing, the feedback is so much richer and more nuanced.

Avoiding Faulty Assumptions

I built my first fully accessible course for a major nonprofit in 2010 using Lectora, an e-learning authoring tool. I had put in a lot of work to make it accessible and was very happy with my testing. We had an accessibility link on the first page that took the learner to a slide where they could set helpful preferences, such as turning off auto-play audio. But I wanted to validate my choices. So, we hired a blind woman to take the course, and I sat down next to her and watched how she interacted with my content.

Even though that was more than a decade ago, I can still picture the library conference room in downtown Jacksonville, Florida, where we were sitting. She pulled up the course, fired up her screen reader, and blazed right past the accessibility link I was so proud of. I was gobsmacked.

Afterward, I asked her why she hadn't clicked that link. After all, I had designed it for learners just like her. She said she hadn't clicked on it because she didn't know what it would do. She sometimes ran into websites or training courses with a link that made changes that were not helpful to her or that interfered with her screen reader. So, she decided to take her chances with the course as designed. That's something many sighted testers wouldn't pick up on.

She also helped us with a solution. We discussed wording that would make it clear that the link went to a page detailing the options and letting her make choices. Adding one word, "preferences," let her know she would be given choices instead of us making the choices for her. Ever since that day, we called the link "accessibility preferences."

Addressing Ambiguity

Another subtle but important change came from a client's tester. In addition to the testing we did, the client did their own, and I was able to observe. A blind tester was going through a click-to-reveal activity. He got to the close button on the first layer. The screen reader announced, "Close," just as we wanted it to. He paused for a minute, and then asked, "Close what? Am I closing the browser, the tab, or the course?"

A tester who can see will most likely make assumptions based on what they know about the world and about how courses typically work. Even if I had tested the course with my monitor off (the best way for a sighted person to test with a screen reader), I wouldn't have caught that point of confusion. Because, in my mind's eye, I knew exactly what that pop-up screen looked like. And even if I didn't know what that specific screen looked like, I knew how click-to-reveal activities worked.

Once again, we collaborated on the best solution. I didn't want to say, "close layer," because that's the name of the feature in my software—a student doesn't know what a layer is. We decided on the term "overlay." So, now all our layer close buttons say, "close overlay."

Choosing Between Personal Preferences and Inaccessibility

Some organizations have each one of their courses tested by people with disabilities—the people who would be affected. That's the gold standard. At a minimum, I recommend having your *approach* tested by learners with disabilities. Test some representative content and make sure your methods are helpful and effective.

When working with disabled testers, keep in mind that even if they are trained in all aspects of accessibility testing, they can only use their lived experience for some aspects.

I once observed client testing for a government agency with a blind tester. This person was responsible for 100 percent of that organization's testing. He did a very thorough job testing with screen readers, but during the two-hour test, he didn't evaluate *any other access needs*, such as those that would apply to a low-vision learner (like color contrast), a deaf or hard-of-hearing learner, or a neurodivergent learner.

He also inserted a lot of his personal preferences. That's not necessarily a bad thing. If we can include simple changes that make someone else's life easier, why wouldn't we? But in this case, he was asking for very time-consuming changes to meet his preferences, even though the current approach was usable and compliant. So, whether you are doing usability testing (trying to make your designs more helpful) or compliance testing (determining if you are legally able to release a project), you and your stakeholders should decide in advance how you want to approach preference-based feedback.

What You Can Do Right Away

Accessible design requires designers and stakeholders who have the right intention, the right knowledge, and the right tools. But intentions and "book knowledge" sometimes only get us 90 percent there. When you work with the people who will be affected by your choices, you can make small changes that make a big difference.

To get started testing with real users, explore these options:
- Hire a company that uses disabled testers.
- Request feedback from employees from your own organization, but give them plenty of time—no 11th hour requests.
- Contact the office at your local university that supports students with disabilities or the county or state governmental office that supports residents with disabilities.

- Post announcements on job sites or contract work sites or look for local and national job boards designed for individuals with disabilities, such as AbilityJOBS.com.

10.
Beyond Accessibility Checklists

Integrating an Inclusive Design Mindset

Leah Holroyd (she/her)
Learning Designer and Director, White Bicycle

> "I don't even know what to say. This is what we've been advocating for, for so long. There's so much here! This is why I do what I do! This is why I work so hard to promote accessibility. This is why. Because this is important." —Steve Saylor[34]

After listening to the BBC Radio 4 program *Unplayable: Disability and the Gaming Revolution* (which explored the topic of accessibility in video games), I looked up some of the contributors.[35] That's how I came across Steve Saylor, an accessibility advocate, consultant, and content creator who posts YouTube videos as The Blind Gamer. In 2020, Saylor shared a video of himself weeping, barely able to speak, as he was overcome with emotion while reviewing the extensive accessibility features of the newly released game *The Last of Us Part II*. It included colorblind and high-contrast modes, text-to-speech functionality, fully remappable controls, and text resizing options. Saylor had been brought in as a consultant to advise on accessibility during the game's development, and to see him brought to tears by the end result was incredibly moving. It's such a powerful illustration of the difference that truly inclusive design makes to people's lives.

An Inclusive Organizational Mindset

It stands to reason that when accessibility considerations are an afterthought or considered optional, we're unlikely to create truly accessible experiences—and retrofitting accessibility tends to be challenging.

Take corporate branding, for example. If graphic designers and marketing professionals understand the importance of color contrast, they can come up with an accessible palette and color combinations. If everyone uses the brand colors in the approved combinations, they can be confident that the color contrast is sufficient to meet accessibility standards. When contrast isn't considered at this early stage, it creates accessibility issues further down the line. Either content produced adheres to the branding guidelines and is inaccessible as a result, or people try to adjust the colors to improve the contrast, resulting in additional work and likely inconsistent use of color across the company as a whole, which dilutes brand identity.

When inclusive design isn't embedded into organizational strategy, we're also likely to see accessibility initiatives that are tokenistic or misdirected, however well intentioned. In the UK in July 2023, the large retail chain Marks and Spencer proudly announced that it had created a series of greetings cards with messages in braille in collaboration with the Royal National Institute of Blind People. The news story contained a photo of two cards from the new range and explained that the cards had been created following a staff member's suggestion.[36] One card was a white square with "HAPPY BIRTHDAY" written in different colors (including yellow and pale pink), and the other was a pale pink square with "For a GREAT FRIEND" written in white text.

While it was great to see braille being incorporated into the design, I couldn't help wondering why M&S had chosen to focus purely on braille (which has an estimated 300,000 users in the UK) while ignoring the importance of color contrast and "camel case" writing (avoiding all caps and using upper and lower case letters to create words with a more recognizable shape). That consideration would have made a real difference to the estimated 1.5 million people with macular degeneration, as well as the estimated 10 percent of the UK population with dyslexia. It's my hope that with greater awareness of the broader range of accessibility issues in their greeting card designs, M&S can make their products more inclusive.

An Inclusive Project and Program Management Mindset

I find that considering accessibility at every stage of a project is a useful quality check. For example, adding alt text to images as you upload them, rather than waiting until the very end of a course build, is a great way to evaluate how useful or meaningful those images are. If I find that images are purely decorative, I might question why I'm including them; conversely, if I'm struggling to write concise alt text for a complex infographic, I might question whether it is the best way to convey the information learners need—perhaps a video or animation would be a better way to break the information up and make it easier to digest. Similarly, transcribing a video can be a useful opportunity to think critically about the video content. What value does the video add? Does the speaker express their points clearly? Humans are fallible, and speakers often stumble over their words or miss a crucial word without noticing.

Similarly, if you're organizing in-person training events, it's important to think about accessibility right from the start. It's obvious when accessibility has been an afterthought, and I've seen this lead to serious problems. On several occasions, I've witnessed trainers or event organizers wait until the start of a session—or even partway through a program—to ask about accessibility requirements. At one conference, a host was a few minutes into his welcome speech before he paused and asked, "Does anyone need me to use a microphone?" which meant that one woman in the audience had to announce to the room that she had a hearing impairment. At that point, the other hosts had to start looking around for a mic and then testing it while we all waited for the speech to continue.

A month or so into a business support program, full of workshops and networking events, one of the organizers asked me if there was anything they could do to support me, given my macular degeneration. But at that point, I felt uncomfortable asking them to redesign all their slides to ensure sufficient color contrast. Likewise, the workshop venues had already been booked, so it seemed too late to point out that there were a range of accessibility issues there too, like people at the back of the room not being able to see or hear very well or the room becoming very noisy whenever we had breakout discussions in groups. Again, these are barriers that could have been avoided—if inclusive design had been considered when planning the program.

What You Can Do Right Away

All these examples highlight the importance of integrating an inclusive design mindset into our processes right from the beginning of a project, rather than treating it as an afterthought. Accessibility can't be covered with a few cursory checks just before an online course is released or dealt with on-the-fly midway through a workshop.

A useful concept to remember is "shifting left" or "shift-left testing," which is borrowed from the software development world. I first came across it in eLaHub's excellent Designing Accessible Learning Content Programme authored by Susi Miller.[37] It's a simple idea—if you picture your development process mapped out in sequence from left to right, the point of shift-left testing is to move checks and debugging activities to an earlier stage in the process by shifting them to the left to avoid running into difficult issues in the later stages. For example, by making sure that accessibility is considered at the start of an e-learning project, you can ensure that the chosen color palette provides sufficient contrast so you'll avoid running into issues later on that might require recoloring all visual assets.

So, next time you're scoping out a new project, think about when and how to consider accessibility and ask yourself: "Could, or should, this be shifted left?"

11.
Jobs That Require a Certain Ability

Diane Elkins (she/her)
Co-Founder, Artisan Learning

Imagine you are creating a course on cardiopulmonary resuscitation, commonly known as CPR, for bystanders. Your teaching points include shouting for help, calling 9-1-1 (emergency services), and listening for breathing sounds. These steps assume the bystander can speak and listen. Some tasks require certain abilities.

Or do they? Can someone who can't speak still get someone's attention to help? Most likely. Can someone who can't hear still figure out if someone is breathing? I can't imagine why not.

When you have a set of abilities that society has traditionally been built around, it's easy to design learning from that perspective. That's why it's helpful to review your content for any potential assumptions about how to perform a given job or task.

Here are some suggestions to help with unnecessary references to specific abilities.

Use More Inclusive Language

Sometimes, you can solve a problem by using more inclusive language that doesn't reference specific abilities. For example, instead of saying, "Shout for help," you could say, "Get someone's attention." Instead of saying, "Listen for breathing sounds," you could say, "Check if the person is breathing."

However, sometimes making the language more general also makes it less clear. In that case, you can try another approach.

Provide Options

If you can't find a single phrase that would be clear to everyone, consider providing options. Instead of saying, "Check for signs of breathing," you could say, "Check for signs of breathing by listening for breath sounds or watching for the person's chest to rise and fall."

For content that heavily relies on specific abilities, consider creating branched content. For example, if you are teaching conflict management skills, you might have a lesson on how to pay attention to the other person's eye contact, tone of voice, and body language. Those are visual and auditory tasks. So, it might also be worthwhile to create alternate content specifically for learners who can't perceive those things.

Decide Whether You Can Rely on Lived Experiences

A person with a disability might still understand what you mean and can use their own lived experience to figure out how to accomplish the same thing. For example, if a person can't speak, they likely know how to get someone's attention in an emergency. They likely know how to contact emergency services. So, saying, "Call for help" might not be confusing. They'd know what to do.

However, be careful about making assumptions regarding what people can or can't figure out on their own. What if I'm wrong about whether a deaf person knows how to call 9-1-1 (while someone's life is at stake, no less)? Be careful about putting too much of the burden on the learner. You shouldn't make the learner connect the dots and figure out how to apply the CPR lesson to their abilities. If you use language like "call for help" that doesn't apply to them, they might feel excluded or "other." For these reasons, be careful about using language for "typical" abilities and relying on the learner to fill in the gaps.

Decide Whether You Can Remove the Requirement for a Certain Ability

Years ago, I was working on a course about lab safety protocols. The Web Content Accessibility Guidelines (WCAG) tester flagged one of the quiz questions because it required the learner to distinguish between colors (which is a violation of WCAG 1.4.1).[38] As it turns out, the issue wasn't the question—the issue was the job. The lab safety protocols used a color-coding system. I asked the stakeholders about it, and they said that no one who was color blind could do that job. Well, that was true, but only because they had *made* it true.

Personally, I'm a color-coding freak. It's a great tool for learning and on-the-job performance. But I've gotten to the point that if I see a color-only coding system, I cringe. It excludes so many people, and it's so easy to fix. You don't have to take away the color-coding; just supplement it with a word, letter, number, or icon.

After the client had some internal discussions, they changed the protocol so color wasn't the only way to distinguish between different items.

What You Can Do Right Away

Whether you're creating an on-the-job checklist or guide, an in-person or virtual learning experience, or even a job description, be mindful of how you're framing the tasks people need to learn or perform. Are you using inclusive language?

12.
A Proactive Approach to Inclusion
Universal Design for Learning

Sarah Mercier (she/her)
CEO, Build Capable

For many years during the early part of my career, I facilitated onboarding training for new employees. I trained thousands of people who spanned a wide range of ages, backgrounds, and abilities. Even though I learned a lot during that time about creating inclusive learning environments, it often felt like a trial-and-error experiment. I made mistakes, learned, and adjusted, but it was a reactive way to improve.

I remember a time when I facilitated an activity in a class about financial policies. It was during Halloween, a popular holiday in the US, and I invited students to create costumes out of flip chart paper to wear while presenting a group teach-back to the class. One student pulled me aside and shared that she did not celebrate Halloween for religious reasons and did not want to participate. Of course, creating a costume for the activity was not required, but at that point, it was too late. I had already alienated this learner by not providing options and alternatives at the start of the activity. I simply hadn't thought it through and instead made some assumptions about the people in my class.

This is not uncommon, and making a mistake like this is often unintentional. Usually, we don't know that we are excluding someone until it is brought to our attention. And, if you're like me, you probably don't feel too good when these mistakes happen. I often felt frustrated that I didn't know how to be more proactive in designing inclusive learning experiences.

Turns out, there is something that could have helped: Universal Design for Learning (UDL).

What Is Universal Design for Learning?

UDL is a framework to improve and optimize teaching and learning for all people based on scientific insights into how humans learn.[39] It is based on the concept of universal design, which is, "the design and composition of an environment so that it can be accessed, understood, and used to the greatest extent possible by all people regardless of their age, size, ability, or disability."[40] To put it simply, UDL reminds us that learning experiences must be designed for people, and people aren't all the same.

The UDL framework was established by the Center for Applied Special Technology (now known as CAST). Within the UDL framework, CAST also developed the UDL Guidelines (which are publicly available on CAST's website) to help us create more inclusive learning experiences. These guidelines can help you proactively identify barriers to learning, as well as ways to remove those barriers or provide alternatives.

At a high level, UDL advocates for providing multiple means of engagement, representation, and action and expression. Here is a simple breakdown of what those mean:

- **Engagement**—the "why" of learning—gets the individual interested and involved.
- **Representation**—the "what" of learning—helps the individual recognize what you want them to learn.
- **Action and expression**—the "how" of learning—helps the individual interact with information and practice.

It's important to note that, at the time of this writing, the UDL Guidelines are being revised. The revision focuses on "addressing systemic barriers that result in inequitable learning opportunities and outcomes."[41] There are several changes, including adding *identity* (the "who" of learning) and acknowledging individual, institutional, and systemic biases as barriers to learning without limits.[42]

Ultimately, the goal of UDL is to make sure we are engaging individuals in a variety of ways, providing multiple means of presenting and organizing content, and giving them different ways to practice and apply what they learn. *It's about anticipating needs, removing barriers, and providing options and alternatives.*

Honestly, much of what you'll find in the UDL Guidelines will be familiar to anyone who designs or facilitates training. As a matter of fact, you may find that you're already practicing many of them because they are research-based approaches that help a wide range of people learn. Experienced designers and facilitators will recognize the foundation of learning research throughout UDL. What UDL adds is recognizing that people are diverse, so investigate how you can design to reduce barriers and provide meaningful opportunities to learn.

A Critical View of UDL

To best explain what some critics say about UDL, I'll need to take a moment to address a widely perpetuated myth—the concept of "learning styles"—which has been debunked. There is no research to support improved educational outcomes based on a preferred style of learning.[43] You are not a visual, auditory, kinesthetic, aesthetic, or olfactory learner. I also want to acknowledge that it's possible that this is the first time you've heard this, as learning styles are commonly referenced in the teaching world. So, what does this have to do with UDL?

Because UDL emphasizes the need to provide learners with options, some have compared it to learning styles.[44] While I certainly understand the skepticism and reserve the right to change my mind if future research supports it, I believe this perspective is missing the point.

The basis of UDL is considering how you can be more inclusive to a wide range of people, including those with disabilities, in your design. This isn't about attempting to matchmake instruction with a perceived style. UDL is about designing a flexible learning environment with fewer barriers. The UDL Guidelines are grounded in evidence-based research and can provide insight into what inclusive learning experiences might look like.[45]

Instead of solely using UDL as the lens for improving learning *outcomes*, I think about it as a robust pathway to learning *access* for more people.

How Can You Use UDL?

The current UDL Guidelines are based on the principles of engagement, representation, and action and expression. My recommendation is to read through them to determine what you're doing now and what you could do differently going forward. Whether it's improving how you design learning experiences, facilitate classes, lead a team, or coach and mentor others, the guidelines are written in a way that's practical for everyone.

For example, let's say that you are responsible for facilitating an upcoming company-wide meeting and you want to ensure that you're presenting the information in a way that is inclusive to a wide audience. Head over to the representation principle and explore the options there. You'll find a wide range of suggestions, such as offering alternatives for visual information by describing images in your presentation aloud and auditory cues for key concepts and transitions.

Here's another example. If you're designing a new course and want to ensure you are being inclusive with what you provide to help participants once the course is over, in the action and expression principle, you'll find options to implement, such as providing graphic organizers as well as checklists and guides. These tools are great for many people and especially helpful for people with learning disabilities. And, while a graphic organizer may not the best tool for someone who is blind or has other visual disabilities, a checklist or guide might be a good alternative. Allow individuals to choose what tool works best for them. Also, this principle will remind you to consider the different ways that learners may physically interact with the information, such as by using a screen reader or an adapted keyboard.

If I had studied the UDL Guidelines before facilitating my Halloween classroom activity, I would have considered that I needed to make the activity relevant for a wide range of learners. A guideline under the engagement principle teaches that "it is a mistake to assume that all learners will find the same activities equally relevant or valuable to their goals" and that I should "provide options that optimize what is relevant, valuable, and meaningful to the learner."[46] That guideline also provides a list of considerations for designing a relevant, valuable, and authentic activity. Ultimately, instead of having the participants spend time on something that was in no way related to what they were learning, I should have stuck to suggesting relevant options. That doesn't mean they couldn't do something fun—I had just framed the activity around something that wasn't relevant or appropriate to the goal. There's also a guideline in the engagement principle that says I should have optimized individual choice and autonomy. Rather than requiring them to work in groups, I could have given them an alternative option to come up with their own creative ways to present the information.

It's fair to say that UDL is most useful when you have an idea of how providing multiple means of representation, action and expression, and engagement shows up in different types of learning experiences. The good news is that you'll find more stories and examples later in this book that demonstrate how UDL helps with inclusive design.

What You Can Do Right Away

When designing your next learning experience, refer to CAST's UDL Guidelines for ways to address the "why, what, and how." Pick at least two approaches for each: two means of engagement, two ways to help participants recognize what you want them to learn, and two ways to interact with the information and practice. This simple practice of "choosing two" will help you design a more accessible learning experience.

Part 2.
Designing Inclusive Digital Content

13.
Perspectives
Thinking Through Lenses

Brian Dusablon (he/him)
Consultant and Inclusive Design Advocate

When researching accessibility for a 2018 keynote, I discovered an excellent *Smashing* magazine article "Designing for Accessibility and Inclusion" by Steven Lambert. It has since become my go-to resource for teaching inclusive design. In the article, Lambert introduces 12 "lenses of accessibility," which provide a toolkit for checking assumptions and considering perspectives.[47]

> "Accessibility is solved at the design stage." —Daniel Na[48]

I love this Daniel Na quote that Lambert selected to open the article. One of the founding engineers of Etsy, Na followed the principle of "accessibility is not a feature, it's a requirement."

As we look to build Design for All into our practices, it will benefit us to share this quote with stakeholders, decision makers, and new team members. Lambert acknowledges the challenge of knowing which needs to design for, noting, "It's not that we intentionally exclude users, it's that we don't know what we don't know." We expand our awareness and empathy by analyzing our designs through lenses that provide new and varying perspectives.

Lenses help us step beyond our own worldview and consider a context different from our own. Lambert presents lenses that offer guiding questions for each stage of design. I've adapted them for learning, but I highly recommend reviewing the original article and sharing it widely.

Each lens provides a fresh vantage point on abilities and needs, enabling us to design more inclusively in a systematic way that challenges assumptions. When applied thoroughly, the lenses reveal gaps and opportunities. They prompt you to seek diverse input. Most importantly, they cultivate mindfulness about how design choices affect real people.

Lens 1. Animation and Effects

Many people love using animations in e-learning programs. I remember using Swift 3D, Flash, and some alternatives to create fancy (at the time) visual effects and animated text for web- and computer-based courses early in my career. Most of my favorite authoring tools include animations and effects as easy additions or features, but have you ever considered how flashing elements and movement could be disorienting, distracting, and potentially even deadly?

According to the Epilepsy Foundation, about 3 percent of people with epilepsy experience photosensitive epilepsy—which means exposure to flashing lights at certain intensities or certain visual patterns can trigger seizures.[49] Motion effects can also cause dizziness, vertigo, and nausea. Even something as simple as an animated GIF can be extremely disorienting or painful to some people.

Val Head shares a few key points in her excellent article "Designing Safer Web Animation for Motion Sensitivity."[50] She advises that web animation:

- **Be purposeful.** Is the effect or animation necessary? Is it adding value?
- **Provide meaningful context.** Make sure your users know what to expect. Don't surprise people with animation or effects. The A11y Project suggests using "an indicator of what movement will happen on the site when a user takes action."[51]
- **Give control to users.** Always include a toggle at the beginning of your course allowing users to turn off animations and effects throughout the course (a simple variable in most cases), along with specific toggles anywhere you've added this feature.

- **Protect your users.** Could any of these effects cause a seizure, vertigo, or dizziness?

Lens 2. Audio and Video

How many times have you dealt with autoplaying video or audio on a webpage or in a course that you couldn't figure out how to turn off? Autoplaying media can frustrate users. It also interferes with screen readers, which reduces accessibility.

Avoid using video as silent background movement. Like animated GIFs, background videos can cause dizziness, vertigo, or confusion for some users. At best, they can be distracting, and at worst, they can cause major issues.

Provide transcripts and closed captioning so your learners can choose how they want to consume your content. Remember, many folks, regardless of whether they have any kind of disability, may prefer to listen to or read the content.

Consider workspace equipment limitations too. Workstations often lack speakers and open environments may preclude headphones. Know your audience and plan for flexibility to improve accessibility.

Lens 3. Color and Contrast

Color is an essential element of design, but consider how you use color and how different people might see or interpret color. Did you know that color blindness affects roughly one in 12 men and one in 200 women?[52] Are you aware that red and green—two of the most commonly used colors to convey negative and positive meaning in most US-based e-learning programs—mean entirely different things in other countries like China?

To be inclusive when it comes to color, always include noncolor identifiers such as icons, text descriptions, labels, and patterns. Instead of relying on color alone, add a second indicator, such as the word "correct" or "incorrect" and a checkmark or "x" icon.

Noncolor Identifiers
Sarah Mercier (she/her) | CEO, Build Capable

In this simple e-learning example, you are designing feedback screens for a knowledge check question. It may seem simpler to use green for correct and red for incorrect, but those with red-green color blindness won't be able to rely on color alone (Figure 13-1 and 13-2). Instead, you could include the word "correct" or "incorrect" and a "checkmark" or "x" icon (Figure 13-3). These additional indicators ensure you aren't relying on color alone to convey meaning.

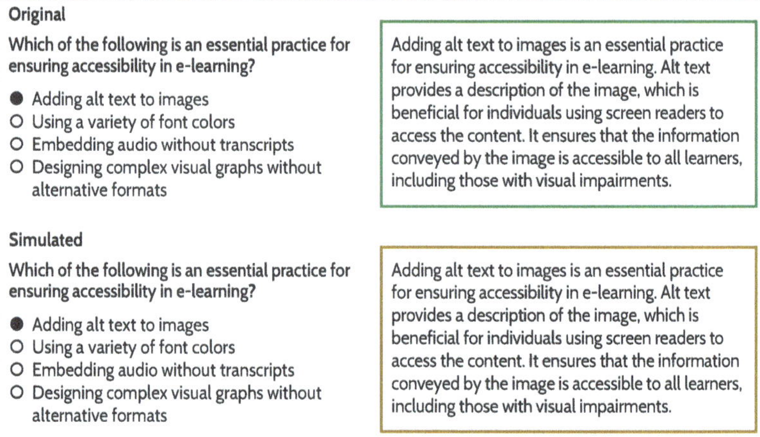

Original

Which of the following is an essential practice for ensuring accessibility in e-learning?

- ● Adding alt text to images
- ○ Using a variety of font colors
- ○ Embedding audio without transcripts
- ○ Designing complex visual graphs without alternative formats

Adding alt text to images is an essential practice for ensuring accessibility in e-learning. Alt text provides a description of the image, which is beneficial for individuals using screen readers to access the content. It ensures that the information conveyed by the image is accessible to all learners, including those with visual impairments.

Simulated

Which of the following is an essential practice for ensuring accessibility in e-learning?

- ● Adding alt text to images
- ○ Using a variety of font colors
- ○ Embedding audio without transcripts
- ○ Designing complex visual graphs without alternative formats

Adding alt text to images is an essential practice for ensuring accessibility in e-learning. Alt text provides a description of the image, which is beneficial for individuals using screen readers to access the content. It ensures that the information conveyed by the image is accessible to all learners, including those with visual impairments.

Figure 13-1. An example of how a correctly answered question would look to someone who is not colorblind and someone with red-green color blindness.

Original

Which of the following is an essential practice for ensuring accessibility in e-learning?

- ○ Adding alt text to images
- ○ Using a variety of font colors
- ● Embedding audio without transcripts
- ○ Designing complex visual graphs without alternative formats

Adding alt text to images is an essential practice for ensuring accessibility in e-learning. Alt text provides a description of the image, which is beneficial for individuals using screen readers to access the content. It ensures that the information conveyed by the image is accessible to all learners, including those with visual impairments.

Simulated

Which of the following is an essential practice for ensuring accessibility in e-learning?

- ○ Adding alt text to images
- ○ Using a variety of font colors
- ● Embedding audio without transcripts
- ○ Designing complex visual graphs without alternative formats

Adding alt text to images is an essential practice for ensuring accessibility in e-learning. Alt text provides a description of the image, which is beneficial for individuals using screen readers to access the content. It ensures that the information conveyed by the image is accessible to all learners, including those with visual impairments.

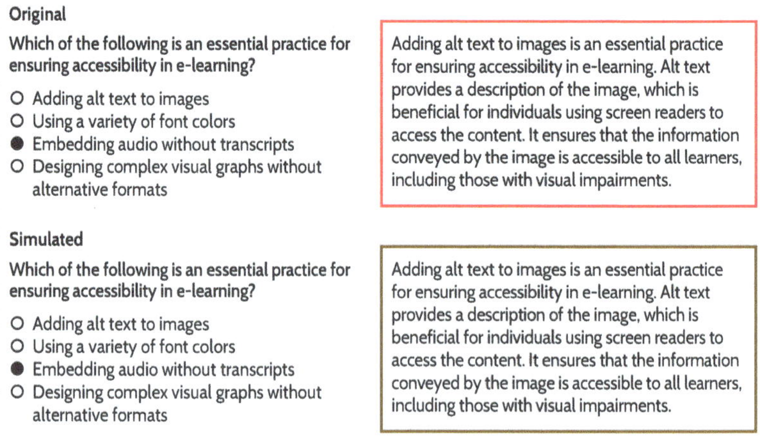

Figure 13-2. An example of how an incorrectly answered question would look to someone who is not colorblind and someone with red-green color blindness.

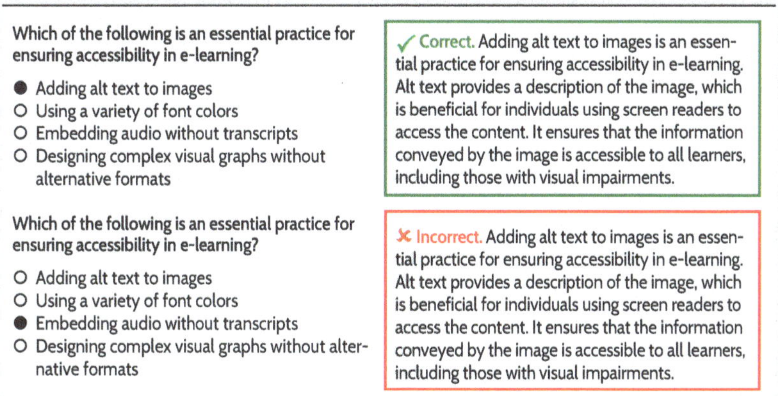

Figure 13-3. An example of correct feedback outlined in a green box with a green checkmark and the word "Correct!" added to the beginning and incorrect feedback outlined in a red box with a red x and the word "Incorrect" added to the beginning.

Lambert also notes that "Oversaturated colors, high contrasting colors, and even just the color yellow can be uncomfortable and unsettling for some users, prominently those on the autism spectrum. It's best to avoid high concentrations of these types of colors to help users remain comfortable."[53]

I began my accessibility journey after making a poor contrast design decision (which I covered in chapter 3). It's a major issue in online content, especially e-learning content, because most authoring tools lack contrast checking.

Checking contrast is straightforward. The Web Content Accessibility Guidelines (WCAG) advise following two key rules:

1. **Foreground and background colors should have a minimum 4.5:1 ratio.** This applies to text, icons, and focus indicators against the background.
2. **Links should, by default, be underlined.** Otherwise, link text requires at least 3:1 contrast to body text and a noncolor hover or focus indicator.

In addition, give control to users when possible. Allow them to adjust contrast levels, increase font sizes, and switch color modes. Use caution with text overlays on images—a common option in today's authoring tools. The overlay text may appear sharp on your screen and meet contrast standards at certain dimensions. However, it may fail when scaled to other sizes, such as on a mobile device.

Overall, your goal should be sufficient contrast for all users and situations. Use free tools to check your content early and often. Don't rely solely on how it looks to you. Plan inclusively, because abilities and contexts vary. Clear contrast benefits everyone.

Lens 4. Controls

Anything learners interact with—such as buttons, sliders, text fields, or links—are considered controls. Controls that are too small or positioned too closely together can create usability issues for many. Tiny controls may be extremely difficult to click or tap accurately, depending on the device being used. Such sizing can also cause problems for individuals with tremors or dexterity impairments, as well as for people with larger fingers. To address this, WCAG recommend a minimum size of 24 x 24 pixels for interactive control elements, with at least 32 pixels of spacing between controls.

In addition, avoid nesting controls, which make it challenging for users to select the correct one. An example of this that is used frequently in e-learning content is scrolling inside text boxes. These nested scroll areas are often difficult to navigate effectively. To improve usability, reduce excessive text or split lengthier content across multiple blocks or slides.

Controls should always include visible text labels. Screen readers require them to communicate what the control does, and it helps all users better understand the purpose of the control.

Lens 5. Fonts

Fonts are a popular design element to experiment with. The amount of time I spent early in my career on DaFont, a free fonts website, is embarrassing. I've created courses that use a dozen different fonts. Now I know better. Aim to use consistent sizing and spacing (in both headers and body text and between them), a single heading font, and a single body font. Course themes and master slides can help with this.

> "Overall, larger text, shorter line lengths, taller line heights, and increased letter spacing can help all users have a better reading experience." —Steven Lambert[54]

With the wide range of screen sizes, responsive text matters. Not just large enough—but easily readable. Avoid small, fixed fonts and limit italics. Avoid cursive and decorative styles as it is problematic for some, like those with dyslexia. Again, give control to the user whenever possible, allowing them to change the text size and font for easier readability. Remember to check the fonts on any job aids, resources, and embedded content like videos as well.

Lens 6. Images and Icons

> "They say, 'A picture is worth a thousand words.' Still, a picture you can't see is speechless, right?" —Steven Lambert[55]

Images and icons are important elements in our designs. They can convey meaning, provide context, demonstrate emotion, or help users visualize complex concepts. But for users who can't see the images, we must describe the information to them.

To do this, use alternative text (or alt text) and image descriptions. Good alt text explains the information the image contains within the context of the image, rather than simply describing what the image looks like. And good alt text is managed at the design stage. When sourcing visuals for your courses, note the reason for and meaning of the image—you can use this information later for the alt text. Doing so is also a quick check to see if the image adds value.

If an image is decorative or already described by nearby text, don't add extra information. Otherwise, describe it briefly. Include any text that appears in the image in the description as well. Keep alt text short, ideally one or two sentences, to make it easy to quickly understand.

AbilityNet shares "five golden rules for compliant alt text":[56]

1. Every <img> must have an alt= attribute.
2. Describe the information, not the picture.

3. Active images require descriptive alt text.
4. Images that contain information require descriptive alt text.
5. Decorative images should have empty or null alt text.

Note: Some authoring tools allow you to check a box to mark images as decorative. In HTML code, a null (alt="") entry will not be announced by a screen reader.

For complex images, charts, and diagrams, use a short description for the alt text, and then use the caption area or link to a different page or resource for a full text description of the content.

When using icons, make sure the meaning of the icon you use is universal or appropriate for your audience. Some symbols have significantly different meanings in different cultures. For instance, the thumbs down icon is used in many digital solutions, but in Japan, its meaning is much worse than *no* or *dislike*.

Lens 7. Keyboard

As I mentioned in chapter 3, I broke my hand in college and was very thankful that the web application I was using had keyboard accessibility. In modern authoring tools, keyboard accessibility is available, but often needs reviewing and adjusting.

You might be surprised by the number of reasons people will use a keyboard to navigate instead of a mouse. As Steven Lambert details, "Devices such as mouth sticks, switch access buttons, sip and puff buttons, and eye tracking software all require the page to be keyboard accessible."[57]

For accessible and usable focus order, put the most important user flows at the top. Remove elements that don't need to be tabbed through. It's important to check this in your authoring tool before you publish.

For example, every item you put on a slide layer in Articulate Storyline is in the focus order for the parent slide by default. This is often overlooked and can cause issues for those who use something other than a mouse to navigate your course.

Focus indicators are also important for comprehensive understanding. These visual markers highlight the currently selected element, with only one element in focus at a time. Typically, focusable elements are interactive, like form fields, links, and buttons.

For accessibility, if an element is interactive with a mouse, it should also be navigable via keyboard with a visible focus (which is also easy for screen readers to announce or describe to users who use voice-over). Many authoring tools include standard focus indicators, which may or may not be editable by the designer or developer. A clear focus helps to guide users, ensuring they recognize interactive elements and maintain a consistent design pattern.

Lens 8. Layout

The layout of your content does more than just set its visual style; it also determines how screen readers navigate your content, which can affect accessibility. When designing innovative layouts, proceed with caution to avoid disrupting user navigation.

> "By laying out elements logically and strategically, designers influence users' perceptions and guide them to desired actions." —Interaction Design Foundation[58]

Always consider the visual hierarchy of your content and how it may change on different screens. Alternating the image alignment (left and right) in consecutive "image with text" blocks in Articulate Rise may appear visually appealing on a desktop (Figure 13-4) but will stack differently on a mobile device (Figure 13-5).

Layout is also critical when translating content in languages that read left-to-right (LTR) and right-to-left (RTL). To ensure seamless and logical navigation for keyboard users, any visual layout alterations should also involve corresponding changes to the structural layout.

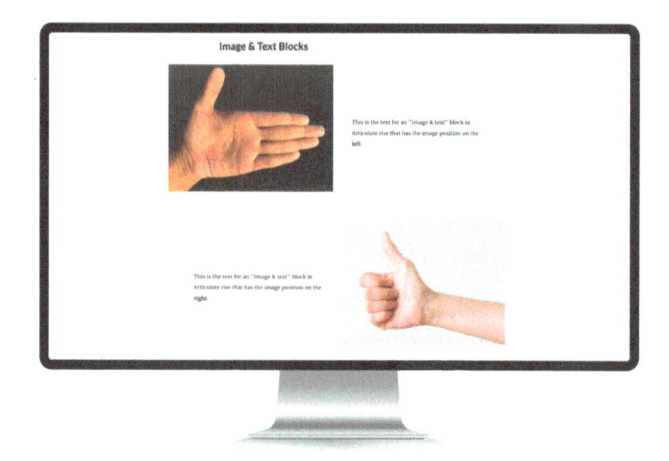

Figure 13-4. When layout works for desktop.

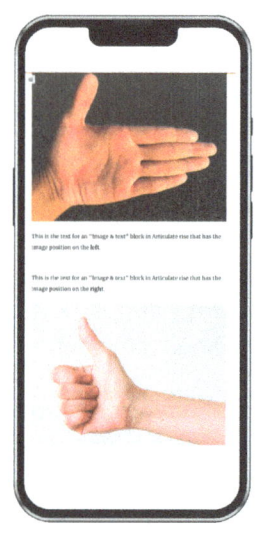

Figure 13-5. The desktop layout doesn't flow as intended when viewed on a mobile device.

Lens 9. Material Honesty

In architecture, material honesty promotes using materials in their true, unmodified form for clarity and authenticity. In digital environments, *material honesty* means that interface elements maintain their true function without masquerading. For instance, links should not resemble buttons.

Material honesty helps prevent user confusion, especially for those with disabilities. Authenticity in design promotes accessibility.

I've created courses that I now consider gimmicky—themed with intent, but using objects on the screen, such as images, as buttons. I've forced users to click areas of an image, which only worked for those without any vision impairment. I regret these design decisions and apply better standards in my current practice.

> "The starkest difference between a link and a button to me is that a link navigates the user to a new resource, taking them away from the current context. A button toggles something in the interface, like a video player, or triggers new content in that same context, like a popup menu." –Marcy Sutton[59]

Both architectural and digital design seek to balance authenticity with practical needs. Architecturally, new technologies like mass timber enable material authenticity while serving functionality. Digitally, accessibility best practices guide creation of intuitive interfaces where elements behave as expected.

Lens 10. Readability

Writing is a significant element of online learning. We write course content, performance support materials, job aids, and knowledge base articles. As instructional designers, we write a lot.

Readability should be part of your design and writing practice. Yet, how many of us were taught about readability, learning disabilities, or language barriers? Do you know what the average reading level is in corporate America? In public service? In higher education? In community services? I didn't.

The average US adult can read at the eighth-grade level. Most accessibility research says we should aim lower to be more inclusive. "WCAG defines 'lower secondary education' as seven to nine years of school. If your content is within this threshold, you're writing for accessibility. If not, look for opportunities to use simple, common words."[60]

Text readability depends on sentence length, paragraph length, and language complexity. Plain language helps all users, but especially those with cognitive disabilities or limited fluency. Each paragraph should focus on one idea for easier comprehension. Shorter sentences are also easier to understand and translate. Lines that are too long can cause users to lose focus and have difficulty moving to the next one. Lines that are too short may lead to frequent jumping, resulting in eye fatigue.

I love using writing analyzer apps or programs. They guide me as I write, highlighting the grade level of my writing, passive voice, excessive use of adverbs, and sentences that are hard to read. Some also provide word and character counts.

Lens 11. Structure

Structure looks at the foundation of a course's design instead of just how it looks. For e-learning content, the structure is usually set by HTML code. Even if instructional designers don't write HTML, thinking about it from the start is key for making designs accessible. If the structure doesn't match up with what users see, screen readers might not work correctly, leading to confusion. Setting structure from the beginning helps you organize information in a way that makes sense visually and structurally.

When we talked about how users move through digital content using their keyboard (focus order), we were touching on a part of this structure. Understanding how screen readers interact with the elements of a page or screen is essential for improving the experience of users who rely on them.

Key elements of structure include:

- **Core elements like the header, navigation area, main area, and the footer** allow a screen reader to jump to important sections in the design.
- **Headings** allow a screen reader to scan the page and get a high-level overview. Screen readers can also jump to any heading. Using manual text formatting (like increasing font size or using bold or italics instead of formal structured headings) can cause confusion for many users.
- **Unordered (bulleted) and ordered (numbered) lists** group related items together and allow a screen reader to easily jump from one item to another. Again, using nonstandard formats

like images with text or tables might be harder for some users to navigate.
- **Buttons** trigger interactions on the current page.
- **Links** navigate to or retrieve information.
- **Form labels** tell screen readers what each form input is.

While these may not all apply in your design for every learning experience, it is important to be aware of them so you also account for the systems your users experience when *accessing* your content. This includes distribution methods, such as email, learning management systems (LMSs), websites, and SharePoint portals.

Lens 12. Time

Time is an important instructional design consideration. You might choose to constrain the duration of a task for reasons like security session timeouts or time-bound assessments. However, rigid limits may disadvantage certain users who need more time. Some learners need extra exposure to grasp content. Others may be unable to perform tasks on time due to individual abilities and circumstances. Interruptions can also extend task completion.

> "The designer should assume that people will be interrupted during their activities." —Don Norman[61]

Rather than absolute constraints, aim for flexible time allotments. Provide customizable durations, save points, and options to pause progress. Constraints are sometimes unavoidable, but you can implement them with care and consideration. Allow leeway and alternatives to demonstrate respect for users' needs and abilities. With inclusive time management, designers enable all learners to engage at their own pace.

What You Can Do Right Away

The lenses presented here will not all apply to every learning experience you design. Their collective strength lies in the perspectives they provide to challenge assumptions and broaden awareness. This helps ensure a comprehensive consideration of different perspectives, situations, and abilities. This is good design. No single set of guidelines can capture all users and contexts. The lenses give a framework to assess designs for barriers that are often overlooked. They reveal opportunities to empower more people through ethical, practical, and respectful design choices.

Which of the lenses do you already apply when creating digital or online learning content? Audit your design process to determine which lenses you will consider for your next initiative.

14.
Busting Myths About Accessible Digital Content

Diane Elkins (she/her)
Co-Founder, Artisan Learning

Over the years, I've heard lots of grumbling about having to make a course accessible—as if it were a creative death sentence. Heaven forbid you can't use a drag-and-drop! I've had new-to-accessibility designers almost shut down creatively, getting in their heads about all the things they couldn't (or thought they couldn't) do in an accessible course.

However, making accessible courses is more about what you add than what you take away. As my friend Tim Slade likes to put it, you don't have to take out the stairs when you add a ramp.

Accessible courses don't have to be boring or ugly. Consider:
- There's nothing accessible or inaccessible about a great story.
- There's nothing accessible or inaccessible about a helpful scenario.
- I've never met a visual I couldn't write alt text for.
- And as for drag-and-drop questions? Sure, they can be fun. But if I think about all the things I've ever learned in my life, I would say I've learned 99.9 percent of them without dragging and dropping a thing.

I'll be honest, some of the earliest accessible courses I built weren't all that creative or engaging. But that's because I didn't know what I was doing yet. I didn't understand the true capabilities of the design tool, and I had misconceptions about what I could and couldn't do in an accessible course.

In 2020, my team at Artisan Learning had the chance to partner with the American Chemical Society (ACS) to create an authoritative and comprehensive resource to help people respond appropriately to the COVID-19 pandemic. ACS believes scientific communication should be disseminated to the widest possible audience, and, as part of this ongoing effort, they were committed to making these courses accessible. At the same time, it was important to all stakeholders that the course be highly engaging and interactive, not watered down like many accessible courses are. We worked together to stretch the limits of how engaging and interactive an accessible course could be.

To do this, we used seemingly opposite strategies: Bake accessibility in from the beginning, and design without accessibility in mind at all. How did we do that? We incorporated accessibility from the beginning by building a robust, accessible template set and getting feedback from trained accessibility testers as well as several potential learners who used assistive technologies in their daily lives. These vetted templates gave us a solid base for moving forward.

Then, our instructional design approach involved coming up with the best possible instructional strategy for everything. From there, we assessed our ideas for accessibility. If we ran into a concern, we didn't say, "You can't do that in an accessible course." Instead, we said, "How close can we get?" And in many cases, we were able to get all the way there.

We wouldn't have been able to meet our instructional goals if we had limited ourselves to simple multiple-choice questions and basic click-to-reveal activities if one of the goals of the project was to encourage critical thinking skills. There's no single, authoritative set of facts that can fully prepare people for every situation that might arise in a pandemic, epidemic, or endemic. Guidance changes as scientists learn more about active outbreaks, and best practices become more or less strict based on the current impact of any active outbreak. ACS wanted to give learners core foundational information that would help them adapt fundamental concepts to changing situations.

Because the course was designed to prepare learners to make good decisions in real-world situations, it included several scenario-based questions and other interactions. In addition to standard multiple-choice questions, it included a graphics-based multiple-choice question (Figure 14-1), branching decision tree (Figure 14-2), risk calculator (Figure 14-3), and gamified capstone scenario (Figure 14-4).

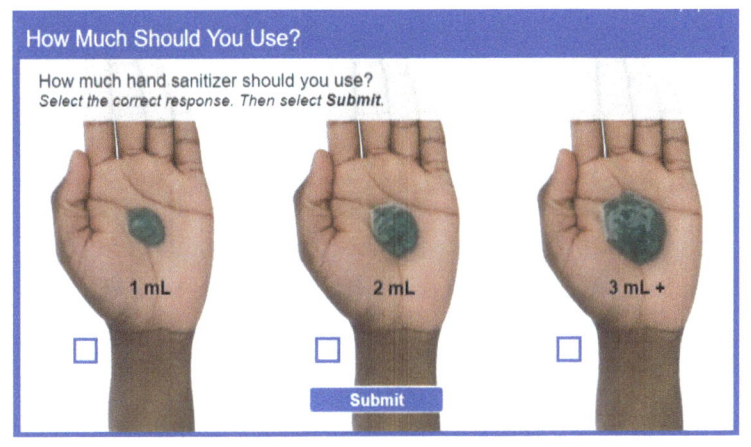

Figure 14-1. Screen capture of a multiple-choice question from the ACS e-learning course on respiratory viruses. It asks how much hand sanitizer you should use. There are photos of three hands, each holding a different amount of hand sanitizer in the palm, labeled 1 mL, 2 mL, and 3 mL+. There are checkboxes for each one. *Source: The American Chemical Society. Used with permission.*

Figure 14-2. Screen capture of an interactive decision tree from the ACS e-learning course on respiratory viruses. Learners were posed the question about whether the area was indoors. The learner chose "No," and was given feedback on what to do in that situation. There's also a start over button. *Source: The American Chemical Society. Used with permission.*

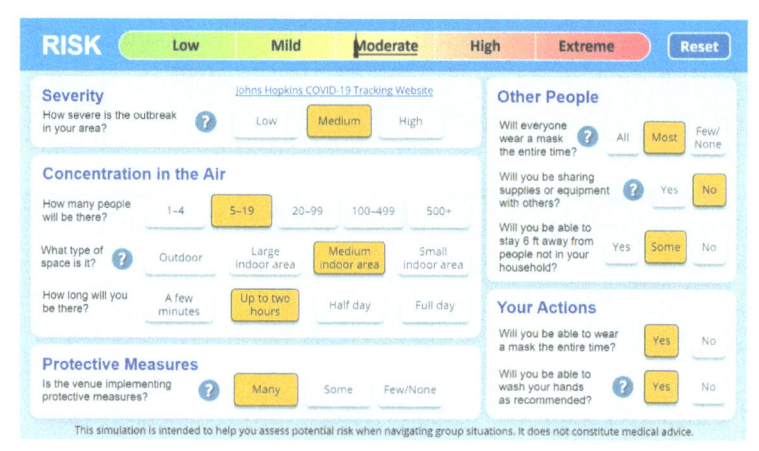

Figure 14-3. Screen capture of an interactive risk calculator from the ACS e-learning course on respiratory viruses. Learners calculate the risk of spreading or catching COVID-19 or similar illnesses by clicking buttons that describe the situation using 10 factors, such as how many people will be there, whether people will wear masks, and how severe the outbreak is. A meter across the top shows the answer on a scale from low risk to extreme risk. *Source: The American Chemical Society. Used with permission.*

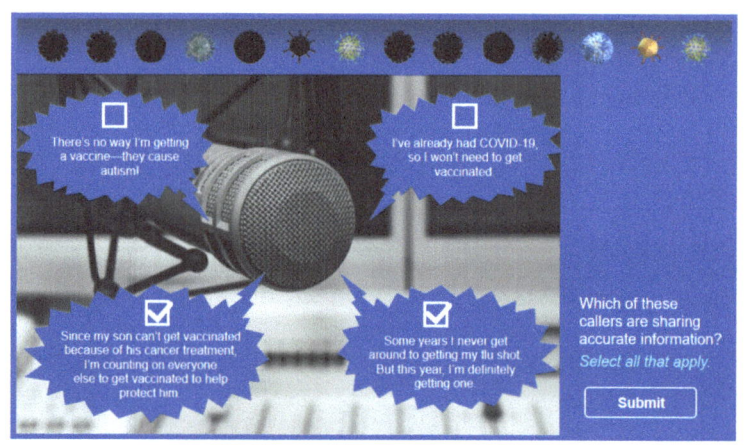

Figure 14-4. Screen capture of a gamified scenario from the ACS e-learning course on respiratory viruses. Learners are presented with four statements that people make on a call-in radio show, and the learner has to decide which ones are accurate. Across the top of the screen, there are images of virus molecules, which serve as badges. Some have been earned and some have not. *Source: The American Chemical Society. Used with permission.*

By focusing on the best possible instructional solution first, we got rid of self-limiting beliefs and assumptions about accessible design (conscious or subconscious). Then, each interaction was carefully designed and reviewed to ensure it could be completed by all target learners.

The risk calculator was the biggest challenge—or so I thought. I've done calculators and meters before, but not with as many options as we wanted. At first, I figured there was no way to make something that complex accessible. But as I thought through it, I realized that a button is just a button. A number is just a number. Tab order is tab order. The final calculator had 10 factors, about 30 links and buttons, and at least 250 triggers (I got tired of counting). The logic was hard. The math was complicated. Getting it all to fit on one screen and still be legible was really tough. But ensuring accessibility was not very hard at all.

The course was well received by learners and won a Brandon Hall Bronze Award for Best Advance in Training Programs That Require Global Accessibility Standards. The Brandon Hall award was exciting, but I think I was most excited when the course won an award at The Learning Guild's DemoFest—and that's because it wasn't just competing against other *accessible* courses.

What You Can Do Right Away

Julia Cameron's book *The Artist's Way* talks about how whitewater rafters don't focus on the rocks; they focus on where the water is flowing.[62] We can do the same with accessible design. We won't get as far if we focus on the rocks—what we *can't* do. Instead, we can focus on the flow—what we *can* do.

What's one learning solution that you've thought you couldn't design or develop because it wouldn't be accessible *and* engaging? The next time you think you're faced with this decision, shift your mindset, and ask, "How close can we get?"

15.
Keyboard Navigation, Headings, and Focus Order

Michelle Jackson (she/her)
CEO, Tilak Learning Group

Learning how to design for accessibility is an ongoing process. I recently learned how to use a screen reader. This required learning the screen reader's keyboard commands (which are different for each screen reader). I wanted to simulate the experience a screen reader user has when navigating courses built by my company. It was an insightful endeavor.

Keyboard Navigation

Keyboard navigation and mouse navigation are two different ways of interacting with a computer. *Mouse navigation* is often used for tasks that require precision and control over a cursor or other pointing device to interact with content on a screen. *Keyboard navigation* uses the keyboard to navigate through content and is essential for accessibility.

You want to ensure all individuals are included in the digital material experience. US Census statistics from 2016 found the prevalence of visual disability for men and women (ages 16 through 75+ of all races, regardless of ethnicity, with all education levels) in the US was 2.4 percent of the population. This encompasses both total or near-total blindness and "trouble seeing, even when wearing glasses or contact lenses."[63] Effective keyboard navigation allows individuals with motor disabilities, visual impairments, or those who rely on assistive technologies (such as screen readers and voice recognition software) to navigate digital material effectively and independently.

What Assistive Technologies Rely on Keyboard Navigation?

Both voice recognition and screen reader assistive technologies rely on keyboard navigation. Voice recognition assistive technology primarily uses your voice to control a device, but it also uses keyboard navigation to aid in the editing or formatting of transcribed text by navigating through menus and options. The extent to which voice recognition software relies on keyboard navigation depends on the software. Someone could use the voice recognition software to input text, or they may use a voice recognition tool such as Handsfree for Web to activate commands—such as click on link, open website, scroll down, and complete form—to navigate a page.

Screen readers are another type of assistive technology that use keyboard navigation to allow users to move through the elements on a page efficiently and effectively. They read the content displayed on a computer screen with a speech synthesizer or braille display. Here are some commonly used screen readers:

- **JAWS**—provides speech and braille output
- **NVDA**—a free open-source screen reader for Windows that provides speech and braille output
- **TalkBack**—a built-in screen reader for Android devices that provides speech output
- **VoiceOver**—a built-in screen reader for MacOS, iOS, and tvOS that provides speech and braille output

A braille display sits on the user's desk just under the front of a keyboard and electronically raises or lowers different combinations of pins in braille cells. It can show up to 80 characters from the screen (Figure 15-1). The braille display changes continuously as the user moves the cursor around the screen via command keys, screen reader commands, or routing keys.

Figure 15-1. Image shows a braille display keyboard with a strip of pins parallel to the bottom of the keyboard. The appropriate braille pins raise for the user to read as the screen reader navigates the screen.

How to Check Keyboard Navigation

Checking keyboard navigation is a manual process of using the tab, arrow, space bar, and enter keys to cycle through the interactive elements on a page to ensure they function as expected. Depending on the key (command) selected, the user can instruct the screen reader voice synthesizer to read or spell a word, read a line or full screen of text, find a string of text, or announce the location of the computer's cursor or focused item, highlighted text, text of a certain color, or an active choice in a menu, and so on.

There are three kinds of keyboard navigation: tab navigation, adaptive keyboards, and magnifiers.

Tab Navigation

The tab key is used most often to move around the interactive elements on a page, moving the focus between elements such as links, buttons, and form fields. Tab navigation uses the enter key or space bar to submit a form or open a link. The arrow keys help users navigate up and down or right to left to scroll through elements such as drop-down lists, grids, or forms. The escape key is used to cancel an action or close a dialogue box.

Adaptive Keyboards

An adaptive keyboard is used by those with unreliable hand movements, such as tremors or spastic movements (Figure 15-2). The keyboard is structured to have raised areas between the keys to allow easier typing. It also includes word-completion software that allows users to type with fewer keystrokes. The high-contrast keyboard is another type of adaptive keyboard that is specifically used by those with low vision. High-contrast keyboards have larger letters, numbers, and symbols on the keys. It may be black with yellow keys or black with white keys—both high contrast color combinations.

Figure 15-2. Adaptive keyboard.

Magnifiers

The third type of keyboard navigation is a built-in Windows 11 tool called a *magnifier*. It can be controlled through keyboard shortcuts and enlarges the screen to enhance readability for users with visual impairments. If you use a Mac, you can activate full keyboard access in the Mac Keyboard Navigator settings.

Headings

Headings add structure to content. Voice recognition software, screen readers, and braille displays rely on proper heading structure and hierarchy to help users navigate through content. When headings are properly tagged, screen reader users can move from one heading to another using keyboard shortcuts. This allows them to quickly navigate a website or e-learning module.

There are six levels of headings, with H1 being the most important heading and H6 being the least important. H1 headings contain the main subject and should only be used once on a page. The H2 heading is the next most important heading, and it's used for section titles. The H3 header is used for topics. And so forth.

If you are not already using headings, here is your call to action to begin doing so. Most content authoring tools provide automatic heading functionality so you can easily create them. This ensures that headings are tagged appropriately in any digital format, and those using assistive technologies can easily navigate the document.

How to Check Heading Structure Manually

To check your heading structure manually, you can use a screen reader to verify you have the content in the proper hierarchical order and the keyboard shortcuts function as intended. Another option is to use the outline feature to view the structure of a webpage or document. To view the outline feature in Word, select the View tab, and then select the Outline button in the View group.

If there are headings and subheadings, you will see them organized by level. If you haven't yet incorporated headings or subheadings, the outline will appear as a bulleted list with a separate bullet for each paragraph.

In most web browsers, you can check heading structure manually via the "Inspect" or "View page source" option to visually review the HTML code to ensure it is in proper hierarchical order. For example, in the Chrome web browser, you can simply open a website, right click anywhere on the page and select "Inspect." The HTML code will appear on screen allowing you to inspect it.

How to Check Heading Structure With Tools

Besides manually checking heading structure, there are also tools you can use. For example, WAVE is a tool that checks the accessibility of a webpage. It provides a report on any issues found and recommendations for improving webpage accessibility.

The HTML Headings Checker is a tool that checks a webpage's heading structure and provides recommendations to improve it. This tool also can generate a report on the usage of headings from H1 to H6. In addition, the W3C HTML Validator can check heading structure and provide recommendations for improving it.

Focus Order

Focus order, also referred to as tab order, is similar to heading structure because it helps users of assistive technologies navigate digital content in a sequential manner when using a keyboard. It is also a part of the WCAG 2.2 Success Criterion 2.4.3, which says only one element can be in focus at a time.[64]

Focus order is important because it helps the user navigate the content in the intended order. People who use screen readers often have limited mobility or attention span or memory issues, or they use advanced features not commonly used and rely on focus order to help them quickly navigate page content. If focus order is not properly set, the user will encounter content that is out of order and may not make sense or be difficult to understand.

According to W3C, the focus order should make sense to both sighted users and users with visual impairments and should not appear to either of them to jump around randomly.

When thinking about focus order, consider these six things:
- **Logical order.** Elements that are assigned a focus order should be listed in a logical order that follows the content of the page in a way that preserves meaning and operability.
- **Visual order.** The focus order should match the order in which visuals appear on a page.

- **Visible focus.** The keyboard focus indicator must be visible. In other words, as a keyboard user navigates the content, a visible border should be displayed around the content currently in focus.
- **Skip navigation links.** Always include skip navigation links to allow users to bypass repetitive elements and move to the main content on the page.
- **Keyboard traps.** Avoid creating a situation in which the user is unable to navigate away from an element on a page, thereby, trapping them so they're unable to move forward.
- **Test.** Test focus order using keyboard navigation to ensure it is logical and follows the flow of content and visuals on a page.

You should check focus order during development and again at the end of development. Many of the same tools used to check heading structure and hierarchy (such as the HTML Headings Checker, W3C HTML Validator, and WAVE) can also be used to check focus order.

To manually check focus order, use the tab key to move through the content and interactive elements. Remember, interactive elements are items such as links, buttons, and form fields. When checking them, be sure each element occurs in the order of the content on the page, rather than jumping around the page in a random fashion.

What You Can Do Right Away

To ensure anyone using keyboard navigation or a screen reader can smoothly navigate your content, assign proper headings to your content and confirm focus order is set correctly.

16.
Designing Visual Hierarchy With Headings

Judy Katz (she/her)
Founder and Consultant, Neurodivergent Working

Derek sighs in frustration as he looks at his screen. He has lost his place in an online course and can't figure out how to go back to where he was, so he'll likely have to start over at the beginning. He hopes there will be a way to skip forward to where he left off—if he can figure out where he was.

Derek has a traumatic brain injury (TBI), a common injury for veterans, among others. It negatively affects his working memory and his ability to stay focused on tasks—functions that are also negatively affected by other kinds of trauma, as well as ADHD, anxiety, depression, and a host of other conditions. And that doesn't include the additional distractions learners like him might experience when they're learning in a busy office environment, on a mobile device, or at home.

Online learning that has multiple kinds of navigation, locked-down navigation, or confusing hierarchies can be unfriendly to any learner, but especially for learners with disabilities. Although learning experience designers sometimes criticize courses with book-like menus, navigation shouldn't be a place to get creative.

Here are some of my top tips for supporting accessibility with navigation and hierarchy.

Make Navigation Consistent, Predictable, Simple, and Clear

Save your creativity for writing scenarios and designing graphics; navigation shouldn't take effort to learn and shouldn't have to be relearned with every online experience. Simple is good, but avoid minimalism. Don't remove so much detail that learners have to guess which button does what. Test your course's navigation until it's obvious for users. Courses should not require guides on how to navigate them.

Unlock Navigation as Much as Possible

Don't enforce prerequisites or staying on one slide or screen for a certain amount of time unless it's absolutely necessary. The number of use cases for this is extremely small, even in a compliance environment. Exceptions might include when a poorly written regulation requires a specific duration of training, as opposed to requiring learners to meet specific learning or performance goals. If it's essential that learners view every slide or screen, build the learning solution to track whether pages have been visited, but don't force all learners down the same linear path.

Hierarchy and Navigation

Show the course hierarchy clearly, on every slide or screen. Learners should always be able to take a (mental or physical) break and be able to identify where they are in the material when they get back. Many authoring tools have layout templates that include a menu on one side, which functions as both a display of where the learner is in the material and a way to get somewhere else. When that's not possible, consider using breadcrumb navigation, which is simply a navigation path made up of a series of links. Breadcrumb navigation is particularly useful when the material is well structured, like an outline that's several levels deep. It's usually found in the top left corner of the content area and shows the hierarchy of information, as well as links to previous levels.

So, a course on communication might have breadcrumb navigation that looks like this:

> [Interpersonal communication](#) > [Nonverbal](#) > [Facial expressions](#)

If an authoring tool doesn't make breadcrumb navigation for you or offer any other persistent way of seeing and navigating the hierarchy of content, you can create it easily using text links.

If Derek were looking at the communication example, where all the underlined words were links, he would not only be able to tell where he was at all times, but he also would be able to easily go back if he realized he'd been reading without understanding, or he forgot something foundational in the previous section.

What You Can Do Right Away

Audit an e-learning course you've recently taken or developed. What kind of navigation did it offer? If you had to stop midway through, would you be able to reorient yourself to where you left off relying only on headings and navigation features?

17.
What Frozen Shoulder Taught Me About Accessible Layout

Diane Elkins (she/her)
Co-Founder, Artisan Learning

In 2022, I had a severe case of frozen shoulder on my dominant side. There were days when I couldn't use my mouse in my right hand for more than an hour or two, so I had to switch to using my left, nondominant hand. I was working with some audio editing software that had small buttons that were close to each other. Because I wasn't very precise with my mouse, I would sometimes head toward the OK button, but then jiggle the mouse just enough to click the Cancel button instead. As a result, I then had to redo the work (with my nondominant hand, no less).

For people with a permanent disability like arthritis or a temporary disability like mine, mouse usage might be imprecise or even painful. There are a few things we can do as designers to lessen the impact.

Make Buttons Bigger and Farther Apart

I wouldn't have had an issue with the buttons in that audio editing software if they were either larger or farther apart. This is one of the easiest things you can do to make a course more accessible—and it doesn't take any extra time or money.

WCAG 2.2 introduced new guidelines in Success Criterion 2.5.8 about the recommended size and placement of buttons and other controls. Buttons either need to be at least 24 x 24 CSS pixels or have enough space between them to offset a smaller size.[65] CSS pixels are a size measurement managed within the CSS (Cascading Style Sheet) of HTML5 content. Always test to ensure sufficient button size, especially when your content may be scaled down to smaller screens like smartphones.

Include a "Submit" Button for Questions

If you add a "submit" button, you are creating an extra click instead of grading a question as soon as the learner selects an answer. That might seem like a reason *not* to have a submit button. However, it allows the learner an opportunity to change their answer. If I take a test with frozen shoulder, I could accidentally click "B" when I meant to click "A." If the question grades instantly, I will get it wrong. But if there is a submit button, I can correct my answer before submitting it.

As with many aspects of accessibility, giving learners a chance to change their answer before submitting it helps several different audiences, including learners with test anxiety or learning disabilities, as well as those who are not fully fluent in the language used in the course.

WCAG 2.0 Success Criterion 3.3.4 outlines guidance for submitting test data, among other things, noting that courses should have a way for learners to review, confirm, and correct information before finalizing their submission.[66] With a submit button, learners can do that.

Consider the Interaction Cost

Every interaction has a cost. If I walk across the room to get a piece of chocolate, it's worth the cost for me. I probably wouldn't walk a mile to get a piece of chocolate; however, I *might* walk a mile to get the best chocolate croissant in town. The benefit of the interaction needs to be worth the cost. For people with mobility disabilities, the interaction cost is higher.

Have you ever encountered a click-to-reveal activity in which the popup information was only a few words? When I come across those, I wonder why the designer went to the trouble—the revealed information could have fit on the main page. A five-button click-to-reveal with close buttons means 10 extra clicks.

Have you ever seen an Articulate Rise course where the designer got a little too excited about all the available blocks, and you ended up constantly scrolling and clicking to reveal each additional sentence? If you pulled all the information out, it would probably only fill a two-page PDF.

For me, these two designs are mildly annoying. But imagine if every click of the mouse or scroll of the mouse wheel takes a little extra time, causes fatigue that grows over the course of the day, or even causes physical pain.

I've got nothing against click-to-reveal activities or Articulate Rise courses. But the "juice needs to be worth the squeeze." If you aren't really taking advantage of an interactive medium, then don't use the medium! Make a PDF and go home.

What You Can Do Right Away

Open an e-learning course you recently designed and try to navigate the first few screens using a mouse with your nondominant hand. How much longer did it take you? Did you make any mistakes? How many clicks did you have to make? Were they all necessary?

18.
Screen Reader Overload
Considering Changes of Context When Demonstrating Assistive Technology

Yvonne Urra-Bazain (she/her)
E-Learning Developer, Briljent

I facilitate a monthly meeting called Accessibility Co-Lab. In our digital accessibility discussions, I post a guiding question and invite participants to investigate the prompt as a group. Our inaugural question was, "How accessible are your posts?"

I follow the philosophy that says experiences that elicit a response teach well. Instead of providing a dos and don'ts list about making LinkedIn posts more accessible, I structured the meeting around a tool demonstration. I sent the participants a link to download a donation-based screen reader, NonVisual Desktop Access (NVDA), and invited them to try using the screen reader on their own computers. All the participants were using Windows systems. (NVDA is not available for MacOS, but you can turn on VoiceOver as an alternative). For those who could not download NVDA, I demonstrated using Microsoft Narrator.

No one in our small group had used a screen reader before, so they asked me to demonstrate how I use it on websites. I then invited them to ask questions to guide our group investigation.

Screen Readers and Hashtags

I posed the next question for impetus, wondering aloud, "How will Microsoft Narrator read these hashtags?" *Hashtags* are prefaced by the hash symbol, also called a number or pound sign (#), and are used for indexing metadata tags for short-form social media content. To investigate how a screen reader would approach hashtags, I demonstrated tabbing into the main content field of my browser. I shared my audio so the group could hear the screen reader. We listened to #PascalCase and #camelCase compound word and phrase examples recommended for accessibility.

Pascal case requires the first letter of each word in a tag or software name to be capitalized. For example, the social media site we were browsing, LinkedIn, uses Pascal case for its name. Other examples include PowerPoint, MasterCard, and OneDrive. *Camel case* does not require the first letter to be capitalized, but the initial letter of subsequent words in a compound tag does need to be capitalized. It is often seen in coding languages, such as userName or stringName to label a field or part of a statement. Apple is known for its use of camel case in its product names, including iMac, iPod, iPhone, and iPad.

Next, we listened to a hashtag entered only in lowercase letters, which is called flat case. Microsoft Narrator slurred the words together. It seemed to have difficulty differentiating where one word stopped and another began. Tags with more than three words in flat case were the most confusing. One popular hashtag, #photooftheday, is pronounced by Microsoft Narrator as "hashtag photo off thuh·day." Another tag, #youtubecommunity, is pronounced by Microsoft Word's Read Aloud feature as "hashtag you toob·eck om·myoo·nuh·tee."

Screen Readers and Emojis

A participant then asked, "What about emojis?" I navigated to a tab of a post I had saved with emojis (or emoticons) on it. According to the Unicode Consortium, emojis are "pictographs (pictorial symbols) that are typically presented in a color form and used inline in text. They represent things such as faces, weather, vehicles and buildings, food and drink, animals and plants, or icons that represent emotions, feelings, or activities."[67] Screen readers announce the Unicode Common Locale Data Repository (CLDR) short name associated with the emoji when it reaches the image.

Table 18-1 offers some interesting emojis with their short name and Unicode.

Table 18-1. Emojis and Their Unicode Short Names

Emoji	Unicode CLDR Short Name (2023)	Unicode
😔	Pensive face	U+1F614
😪	Sleepy face	U+1F62A
😣	Persevering face	U+1F623
💢	Anger symbol	U+1F4A2
🖐	Hand with fingers splayed	U+1F590
👉	Backhand index pointing right	U+1F449
👊	Oncoming fist	U+1F44A
◾	Black medium-small square	U+25FE
👏	Clapping Hands	U+1F44F
🔥	Fire	U+1F525
🕴	Person in suit levitating	U+1F574
🎴	Flower playing cards	U+1F3B4
🔰	Japanese symbol for beginner	U+1F530

Source: The Unicode Consortium.[68]

When used sparingly, an emoji may not detract from a message. However, emojis repeated throughout a post provided the most noteworthy screen reader experience for my participants. Consider this example: "That suit 🔥🔥🔥!" may present to a screen reader as, "That suit fire fire fire!" And, "Say 👏 it 👏 louder 👏 for 👏 those 👏 in 👏 the 👏 back!" may present to a screen reader as, "Say clapping hands it clapping hands louder clapping hands for clapping hands those clapping hands in clapping hands the clapping hands back!"

Another common use of repeated emojis occurs when they replace bullets for lists, like in this example:

Five professional development opportunities to consider:
👉 Online courses and certificates
👉 Formal education and degree programs
👉 Conferences, workshops, and seminars
👉 Vocational training and mentoring
👉 Networking events and groups

This list may present to a screen reader as, "Five professional development opportunities to consider: backhand index pointing right online courses and certificates backhand index pointing right formal education and degree programs backhand index pointing right conferences, workshops, and seminars backhand index pointing right vocational training and mentoring backhand index pointing right networking events and groups."

One participant laughed and explained that she overused emojis without realizing how annoying it must sound to screen reader users. These moments of clarity were what I hoped we'd experience together through testing real-world use cases. The participants' ability to draw their own conclusions and develop an experience tied to best practices is my goal for these Co-Labs.

Screen Readers and Images

The group also explored images with succinct and descriptive alternative (alt) text. We tested screen captures of text and experienced how the information was not available to the screen reader. We discussed how adding alternative text, image descriptions, and captions, as well as including the text within the body of the post could solve these access issues.

For example, I shared an image of a hike I took with my fiancé near my island hometown (Figure 18-1). I included an image description and wrote alternative text for the photo.

Figure 18-1. Logan Dergan stands on the basalt shore of Ka'ena Point, O'ahu, Hawai'i.

Both the image description (Logan Dergan stands on the basalt shore of Ka'ena Point, O'ahu, Hawai'i) and alternative text (Man stands on volcanic shoreline of west O'ahu) will be read by screen readers. I include an image description each time I post a photo because it provides more information about an image that could benefit sighted understanding of content as well.

Screen Readers and Carousels

The group's next investigation was in response to the question, "How will Microsoft Narrator read a carousel?" We tested one example that allowed us to tab into a more accessible carousel version. LinkedIn carousels were a content posting feature that allowed you to post a series of multiple images that users could swipe or click through.

I had never tried this before. My navigation of the carousel was clunky. I used my keyboard's left- and right-facing arrows to flip through pages and found the screen reader captured only part of each page. Participants discussed that they found it to be mostly unsuccessful, and perhaps inaccessible. I made the concession that further testing may be necessary.

As of December 2023, LinkedIn discontinued user carousels from their platform.[69] The company expressed that users would be able to upload PDFs with each page functioning as a slide in a presentation. I am uncertain if accessibility was a factor in this decision.

Screen Reader Overload

I then thought it would be a good time to demonstrate how some screen reader users skim text with increased read speeds. I decided to try this in Microsoft Word because it was another program most of the participants were familiar with and had available on their computers. I minimized my browser, tabbed over to Microsoft Word, and opened a sample document. On the navigation ribbon, I selected the "Review" tab, and then "Read Aloud." The Read Aloud player overlayed to the right of my document field. I selected the settings and adjusted the speed to be closer to the maximum rate.

Something happened that I did not anticipate. One of the participants expressed that she was getting a headache from the bombardment of sounds. I paused my demonstration to give her a reprieve. I learned a valuable lesson that day about acclimation to new assistive technologies (AT). New users may need a more gradual introduction to these tools than I provided.

Limiting Automatic Changes of Context

In hindsight, I did not give enough consideration to the various changes of context I was providing during these demonstrations. These considerations reflect WCAG success criterion 3.2.5 regarding changes of context. According to W3C, changes are "major changes in the content of the Web page that, if made without user awareness, can disorient users who are not able to view the entire page simultaneously. Changes of context include changes of user agent, viewport, focus, [and] content that changes the meaning of the Web page."[70]

A change of context includes:
- Automatically opening a new window
- Shifting a focus indicator or screen viewport to a different area or component without user choice or awareness
- Opening a new page or presenting information in what appears to be a different interface
- Disrupting continuity and predictability by rearranging the position of content on a page

For example, pop-up ads provide an unwelcome change of context for many users, especially when inadvertent interaction with the ad opens a different site or window.

Not all changes of content are a change of context, however. Here are a few examples:
- Expanding a dynamic menu to access navigation options
- Expanding collapsed headings in an outline or accordion interaction to access information about a topic
- Engaging tab control to navigate to another option or section

Considerations for Acclimating People to Assistive Technology

That first Accessibility Co-Lab reminded me about the value of every user's experience. As we work to demonstrate and learn together, how can we ensure all participants' needs, disclosed or undisclosed, are met?

I recommend that AT demonstrations, especially to first-time users, could be improved with the following considerations for cognitive accessibility for all:

1. Provide advanced warning of switches between screens, software, or AT.
2. Limit presenter-only use of AT software.
3. Plan for breaks between brief demonstrations to invite discussion.

Provide Advanced Warning of Switches Between Screens, Software, or AT

There were times when I warned the group in advance of changes of context and other times when I did not consider it. Virtual presentation and demonstration of accessible practices requires us to be purposeful and considerate of all our actions. Even the unconscious act of closing or tabbing out of one program and switching to another can be visually, aurally, and cognitively jarring to some participants. Consider simplifying presentations and limiting how many different active windows must be cycled through, when possible.

Although not specified for live presentations or demonstrations, it may be valuable to reference WCAG success criteria to support uses of this practice. Take into consideration WCAG Success Criterion 2.2.2, which advises you to provide users enough time to read and use content.[71] This includes providing a mechanism for users to pause, stop, or hide nonessential moving, blinking, and scrolling media and automatic updates.

Limit Presenter-Only Use of AT Software

For some participants, the ability to control the speed of an experience is an important factor. Take into consideration WCAG Success Criteria

3.2.5, which recommends that "changes of context are initiated only by user request, or a mechanism is available to turn off such changes."[72]

However, when a participant can't control the pace of a live, virtual demonstration, the presentation can be overwhelming. Unlike a prerecorded video, the participant can't pause the demonstration if they need a break from stimulation. In that case, it's the host or facilitator's responsibility to limit the frequency of changes of context outside the participant's control. One way you can achieve this is to return control of the AT software back to participants. Allow them opportunities to view a brief demonstration of how to use the AT, and then provide them with time to use the software themselves. This allows them the ability to control how they use the software and when to pause, stop, or hide it for their comfort or needs.

Plan for Breaks Between Brief Demonstrations to Invite Discussion

This technique is directly related to the previous point and may be the simplest and most effective way to limit overstimulation. It may also support participant engagement and processing. Give participants enough time. Invite them to take notes, to share their ideas or thoughts about the demonstration in a group chat, or to unmute (if in a virtual setting) and discuss aloud. Processing time, in whatever form a participant wants or needs, is helpful for everyone. Shortening live, presenter-led demonstrations and providing space for reflection, advancement of ideas, and questions could improve the overall success of the meeting or workshop.

Take into consideration WCAG Success Criterion 2.2.1. It recommends that for each time limit that is set by the content, is under 20 hours, and is nonessential to validating the activity, the user is:[73]

- Allowed to turn off the time limit before encountering it
- Allowed to adjust the time limit to, at minimum, 10 times the default limit
- Warned before time expires and given at least 20 seconds to extend the time limit with a simple action
- Allowed to extend the time limit at least 10 times

Final Thoughts

It is a joy to meet with other people interested in improving their accessibility practices. I appreciate learning with and from my Co-Lab members. Their perspectives, experiences, and the rich problem solving I've witnessed enrich my own practice. I have the honor of setting the stage, welcoming everyone who joins, and providing a place for them to investigate, discuss, and practice skills together. I am certain to learn more about user access needs as we explore usability and accessibility topics in the months to come.

In summary, my initial Co-Lab investigation taught the group to be mindful of how we present social media posts, especially with consideration for screen reader users. We learned that hashtags written in Pascal case are most consistently read by screen readers. We learned that emojis should be pertinent and in alignment with the content message; otherwise, their overuse could send an unintended message or create a redundant experience. We realized that posts with image descriptions and alt text helped provide other ways of "seeing" images with AT. While LinkedIn is updating the presentation of an accessible alternative to carousels, they may not be accessible. I would recommend providing the carousel's content as text within the post or within a link.

Finally, my lab participants inadvertently discovered that using AT can be overwhelming, and acclimation may be needed. As is true of virtual instructor-led training programs, online team meetings, or in-person workshops, accommodating for all user needs, anticipating overstimulation with changes of context, and planning for processing breaks can help all people feel more cognitively available to gain as much as possible from each session. I encourage you to use a screen reader as both a testing tool and a means to acclimate yourself, your team, and others to become adept users.

What You Can Do Right Away

Before you design your digital content or presentation, stop to think about how the information will be received by individuals using AT and what you can do to improve accessibility. Carefully consider how and when to use elements such as hashtags, emojis, and images in your digital content.

19.
My Personal Experience With Color Contrast

Leah Holroyd (she/her)
Learning Designer and Director, White Bicycle

I have a condition called vitelliform macular dystrophy, commonly known as Best disease, which is a genetic form of macular degeneration that affects my central vision. The condition is still in the early stages, but already I'm experiencing blurring or fuzziness in the center of my vision (which is a bit like having a smudge on both lenses of a pair of glasses that you just can't get rid of). I also experience night blindness. I find the barriers I encounter in my everyday life to be very frustrating, particularly because most of the issues could be avoided if people had a better understanding of accessibility.

At workshops and presentations, even when I sit in the front row, I sometimes struggle to read the text on slides. When using e-learning authoring software, I frequently miss checkboxes and radio buttons. And on websites, I can't always spot the cross symbol that allows me to close those pesky pop-ups. I once had to contact a company for help because I couldn't fill out their online form to submit an inquiry. Each white box contained pale gray text indicating what information should be entered, and I couldn't see that text (Figure 19-1). All these issues could have been avoided with proper color contrast.

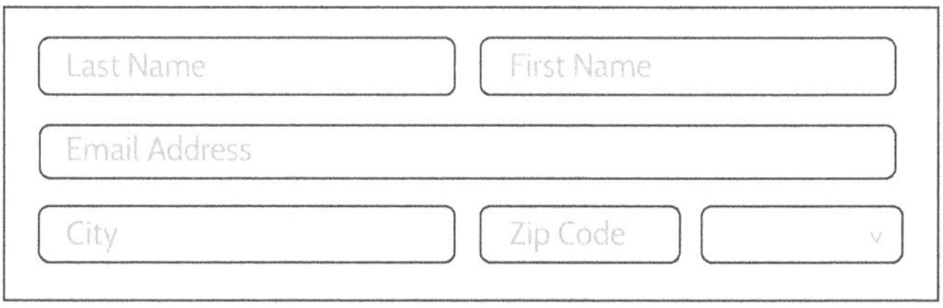

Figure 19-1. An online form with poor color contrast on form field labels.

Checking Color Contrast

Educating people about color contrast has become a personal mission of mine over the last few years. It's such an easy fix and it can have such a big impact. Good color contrast benefits everyone. It can make content more perceivable to people with sight loss or color blindness, which includes one in 12 men and one in 200 women worldwide. It can also make content more readable to people with dyslexia and reduces the likelihood of eye strain for anyone looking at a screen for long periods.

The WCAG standards set color contrast ratios for different types of elements, including normal text, large text, and buttons, as well as other user interface elements. The color contrast ratio measures the difference between the brightness of two colors, with the maximum being 21:1 for black text on a white background. Logically, it might seem that this maximum contrast would be optimal; in fact, black text on a white background, while the default in many applications, is very stark and has been found to cause eye strain.

The good news is that there are plenty of free tools available to quickly and easily check color contrast ratios. I use the WebAIM color contrast checker. By simply copying and pasting the HEX codes into the checker, you are not only able to calculate the ratio, but you will also see whether you pass or fail for the various WCAG criteria and need to adjust the lightness or darkness of your colors to find a combination that works. That means you can create an accessible color scheme within seconds. Figures 19-2 and 19-3 offer examples.

My Personal Experience With Color Contrast

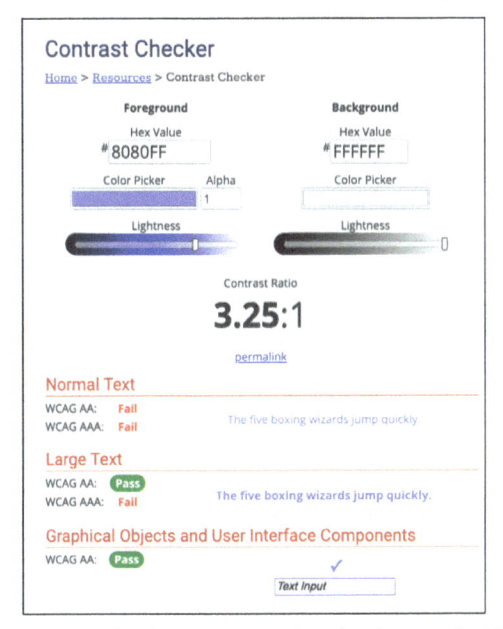

Figure 19-2. Contrast checker testing a white background with a light purple foreground. The result is that color contrast fails both WCAG AA and AAA for normal text and WCAG AAA for large text.

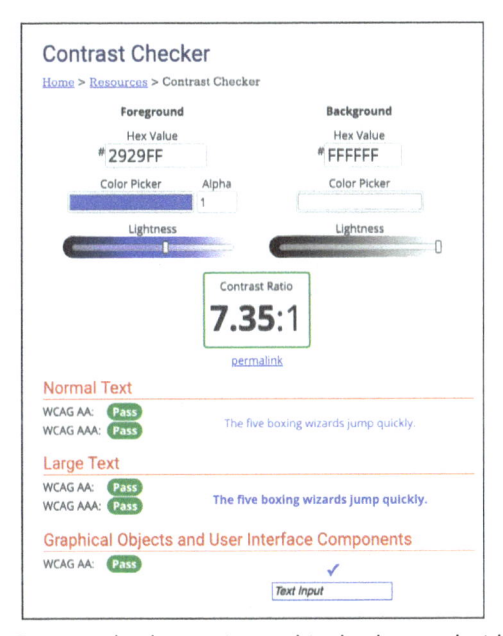

Figure 19-3. Contrast checker testing a white background with a darker purple foreground. The result is that color contrast passes both WCAG AA and AAA.

Checking Contrast of Graph Colors

In addition to considering the color contrast between elements that are in direct contrast with each other (such as the background and foreground elements), it's also important to think about the contrast between elements that a learner might need to compare, such as lines on a graph. I sometimes find it hard to distinguish between similar colors; for example, when three shades of the same color have been used on a graph or chart, it might look pretty, but it's not accessible. WCAG states that you shouldn't use color alone to convey meaning—so consider using different line styles (like dotted or dashed) in addition to different colors to help people distinguish between each category (Figure 19-4).

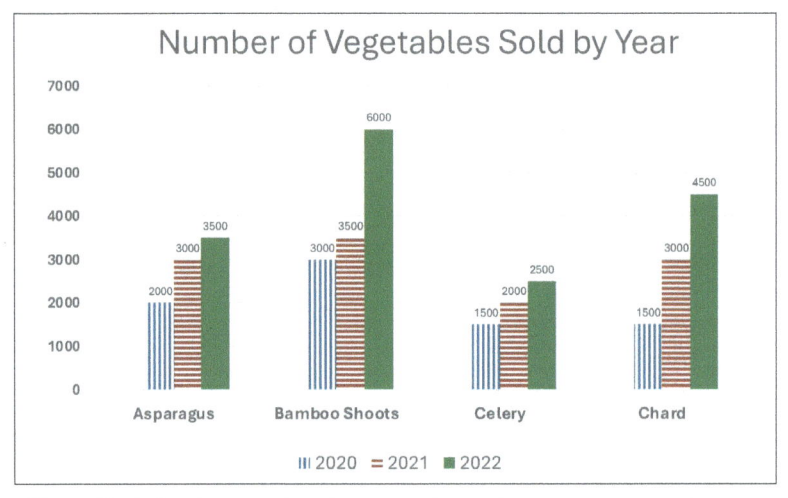

Figure 19-4. Graph example using more than color to convey meaning.

Remember that the WCAG standards apply to all states of a given element, such as a button's default, hover, active, and focus states. Note: The disabled state—or any interactive element that is not active—does not have any color contrast requirements.

The WCAG standards only apply to text and other elements that convey meaning or are designed to be operable, including infographics, progress bars, and buttons. So, if you're grappling with a limited brand color palette, you might still be able to use those colors in ways that are decorative. For example, consider using a brand color as an accent color, with a darker shade for text, buttons, and so on. Text within an organization's logo has no contrast requirements.

Checking Contrast of Text on Images

Text superimposed on images, patterned backgrounds, or color gradients can be particularly challenging. Picture the word "zebra" superimposed on a photo of a zebra. If we make the text white, the color contrast against the zebra's white stripes will be insufficient; conversely, if we make the text black, we'll run into the same issue with the black stripes.

In other words, it's difficult to ensure sufficient contrast when you're using a background that has multiple colors in it. If we adjust the color contrast of each letter, we could still run into problems when the content is displayed on different devices with different screen sizes. Additionally, if we tested the color contrast where it's lowest, text superimposed on patterns or pictures can still be distracting for people with dyslexia. I generally avoid using images as the background for text (Figure 19-5). Instead, I suggest you place the text on a colored background on top of the image.

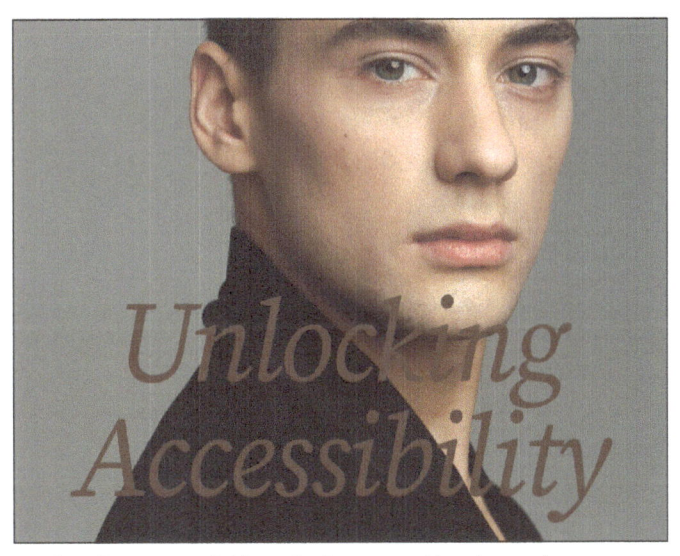

Figure 19-5. Text is overlaid on the image and has low color contrast, making it difficult to read.

What You Can Do Right Away

The British Dyslexia Association's Dyslexia Style Guide provides some further recommendations for accessible color contrast. It recommends using dark text on a light (but not white) background, such as a pastel color, but notes that individuals may have their own color preferences.[74] (You can find a link to the style guide in the Take Action Toolbox.) My local library also stocks a range of dyslexia-friendly books that are printed in blue text on cream-colored paper.

I find that color contrast is often a good starting point for discussions in the early stages of an organization's accessibility journey. While brand colors can't always be changed overnight, as this often requires input and sign-off from multiple departments, the concept of color contrast is quite straightforward and seems to be readily understandable to most people I speak to. Those who are sighted can see at a glance the difference that adjusting color contrast can make to how well text or other components stand out. Using freely available tools like WebAIM's contrast checker allows those who are new to accessibility to start making changes within clear parameters, which can help build their confidence before moving on to other steps that require more nuanced thinking, such as writing meaningful alt text for images or editing text for readability.

20.
Navigating Color Blindness in Digital Content Creation

Michelle Jackson (she/her)
CEO, Tilak Learning Group

My husband was my first conscious introduction to the world of accessibility. When we began dating, I occasionally silently questioned his wardrobe color combinations but thought to myself, "He's just not into fashion." One morning, he asked me if a certain tie matched the shirt he was wearing. I turned around, looked at him, raised my eyebrows, and said without another thought, "Are you colorblind? No, they don't go together." Imagine my surprise when he responded, "Yes, I am." I had known him for three years and been married to him for more than a year, but I had no idea that he was colorblind. It had never come up.

This knowledge answered my questions about previous wardrobe color combinations that I had just accepted as not great fashion choices. When he revealed he was colorblind, I had so many questions—what kind of color blindness, what colors he could or couldn't see, what traffic lights looked like, what he could see in nature, what paint colors in our house looked like, whether he could read websites, and so many more. He is patient when answering all my questions around his color blindness, and 18 years later, we're still married, and I still ask him questions about what he can or can't see. He is one of 350 million colorblind people in the world.[75] That is more than the entire population of the United States! Interestingly, color blindness affects more men than women—8 percent of men and 4.5 percent of women in the world are colorblind.

I consider this my awakening nearly two decades ago. I'm sure I knew people who were colorblind before meeting my husband, but no one ever stated they were. This awakening opened a whole new world of inclusive instructional design and development for me to consider. And while I know it isn't ever his job, it is a bonus to have a built-in real-life color checker for any project I am working on.

What Is Color Blindness?

People with color vision deficiency (CVD), also known as color blindness, see colors differently than people without it. They have a hard time telling the difference between certain colors. For example, they may not be able to tell how bright colors are, see the different shades of colors, or distinguish between colors.

According to the National Eye Institute, there are several different kinds of color blindness.[76] Red-green (protanomaly, protanopia, deuteranomaly, or deuteranopia), which means it's hard for someone to tell the difference between red and green colors, is the most common type of color blindness (Figure 20-1).

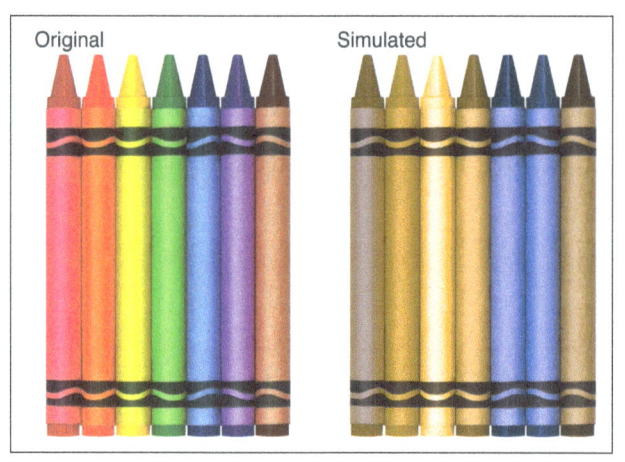

Figure 20-1. Comparison of original and red-green simulated color blindness view of crayons.

Blue-yellow (tritanomaly or tritanopia) is another type of color blindness that makes it hard to tell the difference between shades of blue and green, yellow and pink or red, and red and purple (Figure 20-2).

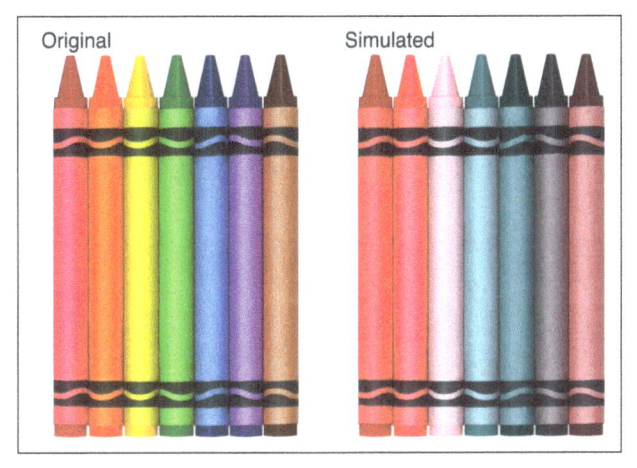

Figure 20-2. Comparison of original and blue-yellow simulated color blindness view of crayons.

Complete color blindness (monochromacy or achromatopsia) is the rarest form of color blindness (Figure 20-3). People with this type don't see colors at all.

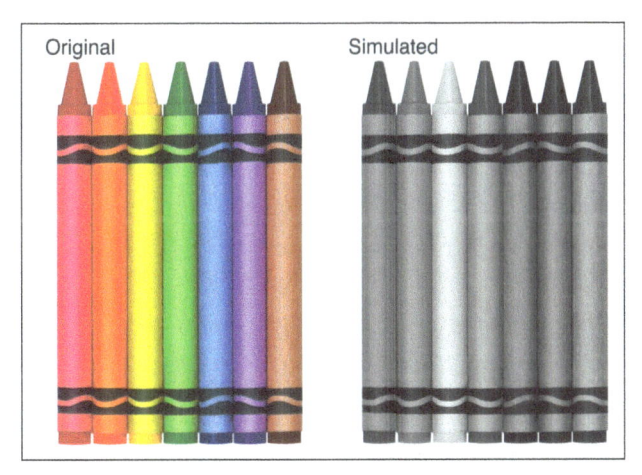

Figure 20-3. Comparison of original and complete simulated color blindness view of crayons.

Why You Should Pay Attention to Color Contrast Ratios

A key part of creating accessible content is ensuring sufficient color contrast between text and its background. The greater the difference between the foreground color and the background color, the higher the contrast ratio. A higher contrast ratio improves accessibility for those with low vision. It also makes it more readable for everyone (Figure 20-4).

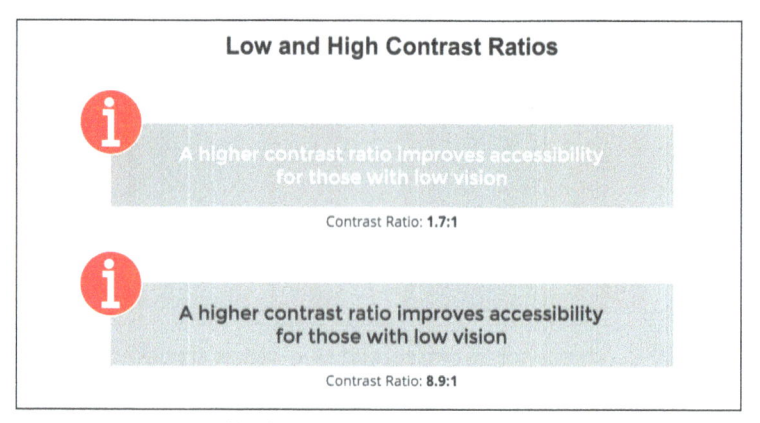

Figure 20-4. Low and high contrast ratios. *Source: Tilak Learning Group. Used with permission.*

According to the WCAG, text and images of text must have a contrast ratio of at least 4.5:1. Large scale text, text 18 pt or larger, or bold text 14 pt or larger, only needs a contrast ratio of at least 3:1. Text that is part of a logo or brand name has no contrast requirement. Some of the relevant guidelines for contrast ratio requirements established by WCAG are Success Criteria 1.3.3, 1.4.1, and 1.4.3.

Meeting color contrast ratios provides a more inclusive and accessible digital experience for a diverse range of users. Good color contrast reduces eye strain and improves readability, enhancing accessibility for everyone. And yet, the biggest challenge to meeting contrast ratios is a lack of awareness of accessibility guidelines. If designers and developers are not aware of the importance of color contrast ratios or how to achieve them, their content may not be accessible.

For example, when working with a company with strict color guidelines and a limited palette, designers and developers may have difficulty meeting color contrast ratios, especially if they are creating complex graphics. They may not be able to create enough contrast between all the elements in a graphic for a person with low vision to distinguish crucial information.

There are a couple of ways you can check for contrast ratios, including using contrast checkers and secondary cues.

Use Contrast Checkers

Color contrast checkers allow you to test different color combinations to determine if they meet WCAG accessibility standards. There are many color contrast checkers on the market, such as the WebAIM Contrast Checker, Contraste for Mac, Coolors Color Contrast Checker, Colour Contrast Analyzer, Level Access Color Contrast Checker, and Digital A11Y Color Contrast Checker.

Did you know that newer versions of Microsoft PowerPoint also have a built-in contrast checker? To see the contrast ratio in PowerPoint, select the item, right click, and choose the contrast ratio option at the bottom of the list that appears. Note, however, that PowerPoint will only display the ratio if you select a shape filled with color that has text within the shape.

Use Secondary Cues to Help Learners With Color Blindness or Low Vision

Using secondary cues—such as underlining, bolding, patterns, icons, text descriptions, and labels—differentiates text and design elements. For example, underline text or links to help identify information on a webpage or in a course. WCAG recommends using HEX #3344dd (blue) for underlined links. Apply bold or other contrast to help words stand out from other surrounding text. Use patterns such as diagonal lines or dots to help differentiate areas on a pie chart. Use icons to add meaning to elements. Use text labels to identify a chart's color coding, which helps those who are color blind understand the meaning of the colors.

What You Can Do Right Away

When designing and developing accessible content, make it easy for users to see and hear it. Be sure that color is not the only visual you're using to convey information, indicate an action, prompt a response, or distinguish a visual element. Share your knowledge with others! Many people are not aware of this simple way to improve accessibility.

21.
What Air Hockey Taught Me About Color Contrast and Alt Text

Diane Elkins (she/her)
Co-Founder, Artisan Learning

I have a friend who is legally blind. She uses a screen reader, and has a guide dog, but she still has some vision. If I were to walk into a meeting, she could probably tell it was me (especially if she expected me to be there) based on my height, weight, posture, and coloring.

We were at a social event once where there was an air hockey table (Figure 21-1). She said she had never played, so I jokingly challenged her to a match. To my surprise, she accepted. To my even bigger surprise, she beat me. Yes, a legally blind person beat me at air hockey. Boy had I made assumptions.

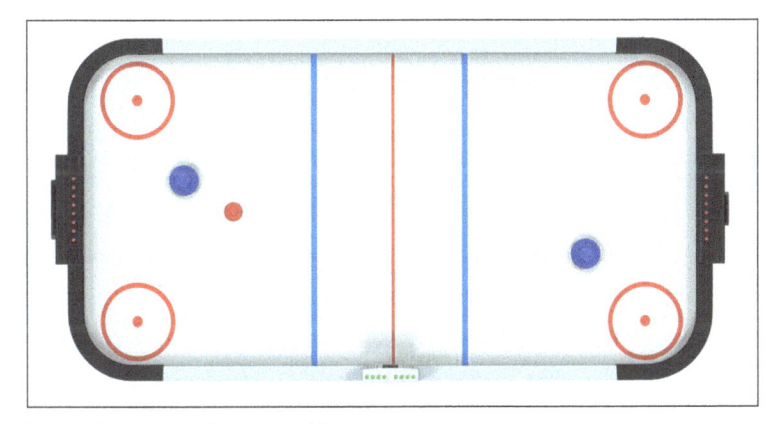

Figure 21-1. An air hockey table.

Was I really that bad at air hockey? Well, yes. But also, my friend has *some* vision. She could see the big red puck moving on a mostly solid white background. Now ping-pong—that's a different story. We decided to try, but she couldn't focus on the little white ball, especially considering the background was everything in the room—not a solid color with excellent contrast.

That experience has shaped the way I design for accessibility. We need to remember that disabilities aren't one size fits all. They can be full or partial; temporary or permanent; and static, worsening, or improving. We also need to be careful about assuming what people can or can't accomplish in their lives. I didn't expect my friend to be able to play air hockey well, just like some people assume that those with disabilities can't do a particular job.

I think about that air hockey moment when I write alt text. When an image is purely decorative, it's best to take it out of the reading order completely, meaning a screen reader or other assistive technology will ignore the image. But some images are nuanced. What about an image of a person with a lightbulb over their head? Does that count as decorative? If it is just decorative, I shouldn't waste my friend's time and mental energy having to listen to a description of it. But on the flip side, she has *some* vision and can tell there's an image there. Will she feel like she's missing out on important information if there isn't alt text?

I asked her that exact question one day, and she said she would prefer to know what the image was, but added, "Don't go on and on about it." And yet the W3C has guidance that I think conflicts with her preference. It has an alt text decision tree and tutorials for images with great advice on when to use alt text and when to mark something as decorative, and my interpretation says to err more on the side of not including alt text.[77]

Let's say you have a course on harassment prevention that says, "If you feel like you've been harassed, you can talk to the harasser, your supervisor, or the HR department." On the screen, there is a diagram with an icon for you and arrows to icons for three other people: the harasser, the supervisor, and the HR department. I wouldn't consider that type of diagram to be decorative. I'd call it *illustrative*—it's illustrating the narration. And while it adds good visual reinforcement for those who can see it, it adds no additional information.

So, what do you do? Do you describe the diagram for folks like my friend who might wonder what it shows? Or do you defer to the W3C guidance that (in my interpretation) says the existing content (the narration) already describes the diagram? And if you do use alt text, what would you write that you didn't already say in the audio? Are you wasting people's time by redescribing the process in the alt text?

This is an example of one of the many areas of accessible design where there isn't a clear-cut answer. So, in situations like this (and not just for alt text), consider whether your choice would:

- Prevent someone from navigating through the course.
- Prevent someone from understanding the content.
- Cause frustration.
- Cause someone to take one hour to go through a 20-minute course.
- Cause someone to get distracted from the learning.
- Cause someone to feel "other."

I always lead with the first two questions because if a person can't make it through the course and doesn't understand what they need to know, then what's the point of anything else? And if they can't navigate or understand, we are causing frustration and they *are* feeling "other."

What You Can Do Right Away

Guidance from the W3C, in my opinion, is extremely reliable. It has some of the best experts in the world cultivate and validate its guidance. You can trust it. But at the same time, you have your own learners with their own preferences. So, for thorny questions like when to include alt text or how much detail to provide, consider reaching out people in your specific audience and factoring their preferences into your approach. And if you really can't decide, add some alt text but keep it short and sweet. As my friend said, "Don't go on and on about it."

22.
Why Include Alt Text in Digital Learning?

Michelle Jackson (she/her)
CEO, Tilak Learning Group

In 2019, I was approached by a client to help them meet accessibility standards in their online learning programs. I thought I had a good handle on what it took to create accessible digital materials, but as I researched, I soon realized there was far more to consider. I liken that time to drinking out of a fire hose—I took every course I could find, watched every webinar, scoured websites, and networked with those "in the know."

In my research, I found something interesting about alt text, or alternative text. While including alt text was standard practice for some, writing descriptive alt text was not. I discovered some companies stuffed their alt text with business keywords to help with search engine optimization (SEO), others used a very basic nondescriptive sentence, and many simply didn't include it because they claimed they didn't have time.

The deeper I dove into learning about accessibility, the more passionate I became about the need to include well-written alt text. I learned that fewer than 1 percent of images online contain alt text or image descriptions.[78]

Alt text is now non-negotiable for me. I make sure to allocate time and budget for it to be done in every project. Alt text supports people who use a screen reader to convey an image's context and information. It is also there for those who have slower internet bandwidth, which means images may load slowly or not at all. If alt text is written poorly or not at all, you are depriving someone of the ability to gain everything an image provides.

There is an art and a science to writing good alt text. One of the best ways I have found to experience the power of alt text is with this exercise:

Read the following sentence. What image comes to mind?
Cherry trees with a snowcapped mountain and shrine.

Now, compare your mental image to the next sentence.
A shrine on the right side of the image with blossoming cherry trees in the forefront and a snowcapped solitary mountain with a sprawling city at its base in the background.

Now, compare your mental image with this sentence:
The Yasaka Shrine during spring cherry blossom season with the city of Kyoto at the base of Mount Fuji in the distance.

Which description provided the best mental picture? The answer is . . . it depends on the context of how the image is being used with the rest of the content. Each description likely evokes a different image in your mind. The first description suggests a very basic picture. You may visualize nonblooming cherry trees on the side of a mountain with some snow at the top. The second description may evoke a more complete image, because you now know there are blooming cherry trees in the foreground, a shrine on the right, a single snowcapped mountain in the background, and a sprawling city at the base of the mountains. But that description could still be considered generic, depending on the image's context and the content surrounding it. The final description provides the most descriptive text but may have too much unnecessary detail. All three descriptions could be written as the alt text for Figure 22-1, depending on the context of the image within the content you're providing.

This is the essence of alt text text. You are creating meaningful image context for those who rely on assistive technologies. Alt text can give a semantic meaning and description to the image, providing the end user with the context and function of images within the content. This is why the art and science of crafting well-written alt text is important.

Figure 22-1. The alt text for this image can be written many different ways.

Why Include Alt Text?

Ensuring proper usage of alt text tags in your digital content creation is a big first step to making accessible content. Providing alt text may help some people who have difficulty understanding the meaning of photographs, drawings, graphs, charts, animations, and other images (such as line drawings, graphic designs, paintings, and three-dimensional representations).[79] Different assistive devices can read the alt text aloud, present it visually, or even convert it to braille.

According to WCAG success criteria, all nontext content (images, video, audio, buttons, and other content that isn't conveyed by text) needs to have alt text that provides the same information found in the content unless it is a purely decorative element, such as a colored box behind some text. That box is simply for visual formatting and should be marked as decorative so assistive technologies ignore it.

What Should You Include in Alt Text?

You can ask yourself four questions to help you decide what to include in the alt text description.[80]

1. Why Is This Nontext Content Here?

If the image is conveying semantic meaning to the learner, then it needs alt text to describe what it is and how it relates to the content. Otherwise, it should be marked as "decorative." This will avoid audible clutter, which occurs when the screen reader reads items repeated on a page.

For example, four red dots are part of the visual elements on the PowerPoint slide in Figure 22-2. There is no text in the dot, and it is merely being used for visual enhancement in conjunction with the other elements and content on the slide. The red dot adds no meaning to the content and provides no additional context. Because it is decorative, it should be marked accordingly so an assistive technology such as a screen reader ignores it. If the red dot is not marked as decorative and you add "red dot" as its alt text, then the screen reader will read "red dot" every time.

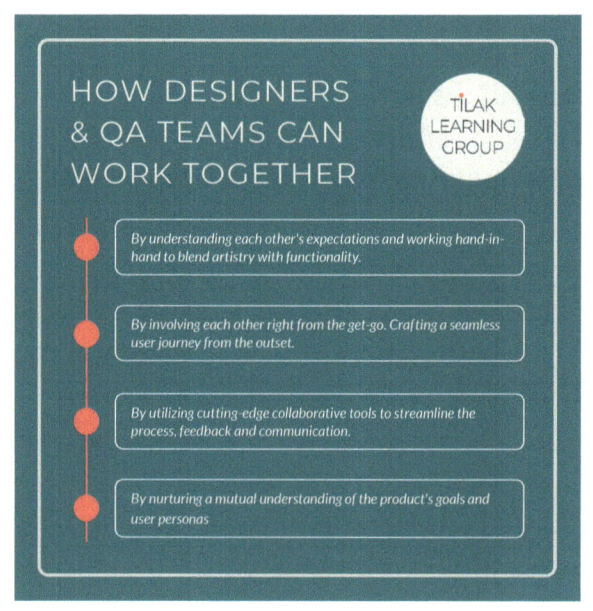

Figure 22-2. Mark visual enhancements as decorative. *Source: Tilak Learning Group. Used with permission.*

2. What Information Is It Presenting?

Look at your image. What information or meaning is being conveyed? This should be included in the alt text. Let's focus on the illustration of the three cats on the slide in Figure 22-3. The illustration conveys visual meaning accompanying the text on the right side. You could write the alt text as "illustration of three cats' faces showing the five action units at various pain levels."

Figure 22-3. Focus on what information you need to convey. *Source: Tilak Learning Group. Illustration by Paulo Steagall. Used with permission.*

3. What Purpose Does It Fulfill?

Is the image helping you convey context? If so, that information needs to be included. If the image in Figure 22-4 appears in a medical brochure discussing eye diseases, you could write, "an eye tearing," as the alt text. You don't need to describe the person or the actual eye. The image is simply conveying context for the surrounding text that discusses potential eye diseases. But, what if the image is used on a poster discussing grief? In that case, the alt text might read, "person crying," to give visual context to the topic.

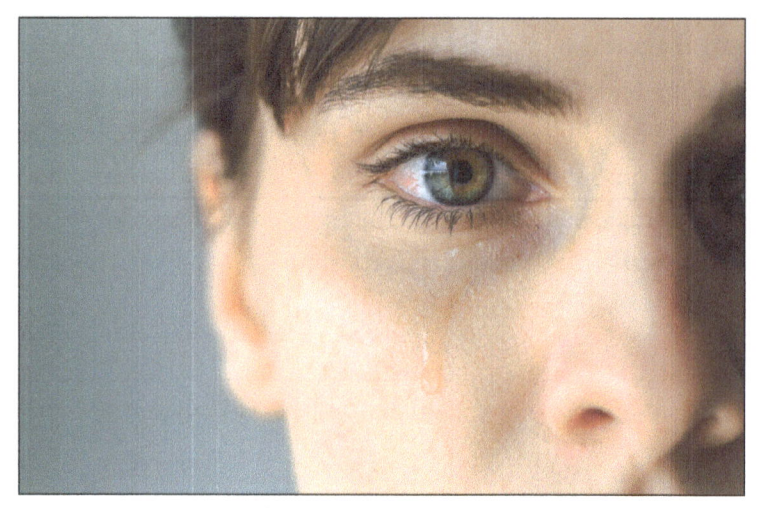

Figure 22-4. Determine the purpose or context.

4. If I Can't Use the Nontext Content, What Words Can I Use to Convey the Same Function or Information?

We want to keep alt text concise, but we also want to give a full description of what the image shows along with the context. Some screen readers may cut off longer text, so aim for 125 characters or fewer. However, if that can't be done, use a link to an outside page that contains the full text description. (This is covered more fully in the "Complex Images" section later in this chapter.) Another option is to work the description into the content rather than having the learner follow a link to another page. You need to be able to explain nontext content to the learner so they can have the full learning experience.

Don't confuse alt text with an image caption or image description. Alt text does not appear on the screen (unless the image does not load for some reason). Image captions appear just beneath an image and do not have to mirror the image exactly. An image description, however, is more detailed and can hold as much information as you want—including fuller descriptions of the image, illustration, or diagram, as well as keywords and metadata, and is often shared via a link.

Five Steps to Writing Clear Descriptive Alt Text
Now that you have determined the purpose and meaning of the non-text elements, let's turn our focus to writing clear descriptive alt text for those elements.

1. Examine the Image Closely
What meaning do you need to convey? Is the image decorative? Why is it included? Think about everything that is happening in the image. What visual information is it communicating? What would learners miss if they could not see this image?

2. Consider the Information Implied Beyond the Visuals
Does it suggest a mood, feature, or activity not mentioned or seen elsewhere on the screen?

3. Don't Start Alt Text With "Image Of"
The screen reader will automatically announce that it is an image. For example, if you add the following alt text, "This is an image of a dog running in a field," the screen reader will say, "Image. This is an image of a dog running in a field." However, you may want to describe the type of image it is. For example, if the alt text says, "A collage of various types of dogs," the screen reader will read, "Image. A collage of various types of dogs." This description creates a more complete thought in the learner's mind of what the image is. Other helpful image descriptors include illustration, infographic, headshot, or screenshot.

4. Include All Words Within the Image in the Alt Text
Screen readers will not read any words that are part of an image; instead, those words will need to be included in the alt text. The alt text in Figure 22-5, for example, could say, "A hand writing the word accessibility in black underlined in red." Alternatively, consider creating a separate text layer over the image so the screen reader can read the text.

Figure 22-5. Screen readers won't read words in an image.

5. Consider if the Layout of the Image or Graphic Is Communicating Meaning

Sometimes, the image's layout and structure is important and needs to be explained in the alt text. In Figure 22-6, the diagram of the ADDIE model itself conveys meaning and should be explained in the alt text (or through an image description if you need more than 125 characters).

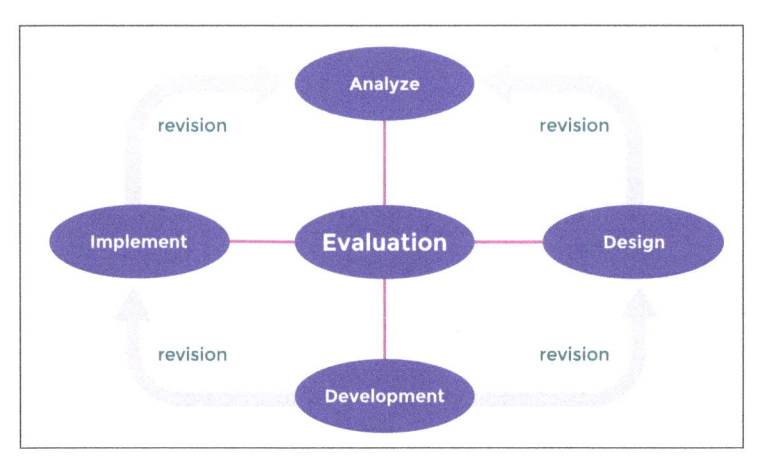

Figure 22-6. Complex images might require alt text and image description. *Source: Tilak Learning Group. Used with permission.*

For example, the alt text could read, "The ADDIE Model," and the image description could say, "A square shaped diagram of the ADDIE model depicts analyze at the top, design on the right, development at the bottom, implement on the left, and evaluation in the center with lines connecting evaluation to each of the other four steps. Arrows along the outer perimeter indicate revision, connecting analyze to design, design to development, development to implement, and implement to analyze."

Remember: When writing alt text, be sure to include the proper punctuation and end with a period. Doing this helps the screen reader read more naturally and sets a pause at the end of the sentence.

Alt Text Examples

Next, I'll apply these principles and steps to some different examples using different types of images.

Simple Image

A *simple image* can be described in 125 characters or fewer while conveying its content and purpose. How would you describe the image in Figure 22-7?

Figure 22-7. A simple image.

"Cows in a grassy field" would be the simplest description. You could also say, "Five black and white cows in a green grassy field on a clear day," or "Five Holstein-Friesian cows in the foreground in a lush green grassy field with green deciduous trees and additional jersey cows in the far background on a clear day." Which description provides the fullest explanation of the image given the context surrounding the image and the information it needs to convey?

Decorative Image

The color gradient at the bottom of the PowerPoint slide in Figure 22-8 is a decorative image. It provides no additional meaning to the slide and would be marked as decorative so a screen reader would not read "color gradient line." Additionally, if the logo in the lower right corner has been identified in a previous slide, then you may choose to mark it as a decorative image so the screen reader does not read "ATD logo" for every slide.

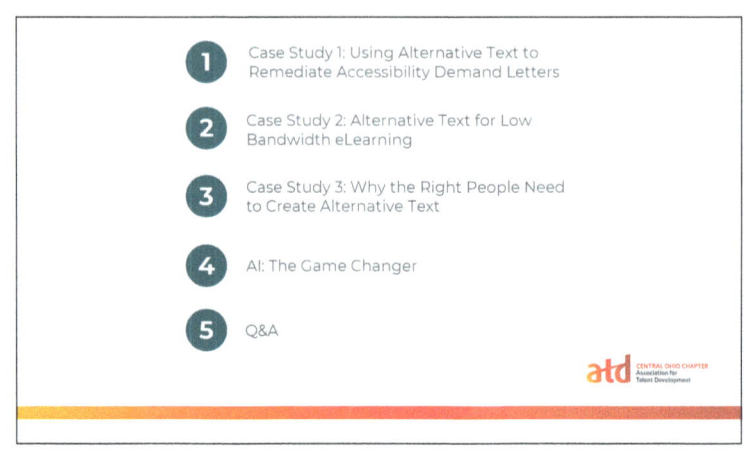

Figure 22-8. An image with decorative elements. *Source: Tilak Learning Group. Used with permission.*

Simple Diagram

The alt text tag for the diagram in Figure 22-9 could be as simple as "Cross section of a flower indicating its main parts." Now, you may be thinking, shouldn't I include the words that are in the image? Good catch. You should include them if they are not already discussed in the surrounding text. If you include them, then your alt text might be this: "Cross section of a flower indicating ovary, sepal, style, stigma, petal, anther, filament, and receptacle."

Why Include Alt Text in Digital Learning? 185

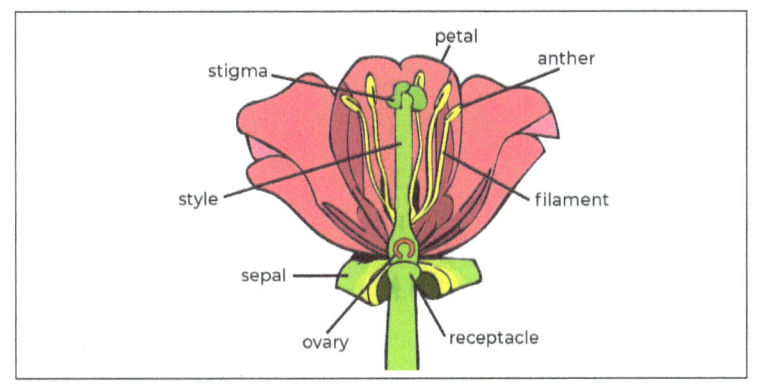

Figure 22-9. A simple diagram. *Source: Tilak Learning Group. Used with permission.*

Complex Images

Complex images require more than 125 characters to describe. They include diagrams, graphs, charts, maps, and other similar images. When describing complex images, you only need to include the pertinent information that conveys the meaning of the image in its context. The image in Figure 22-10 was part of a client presentation that we provided alt text for.

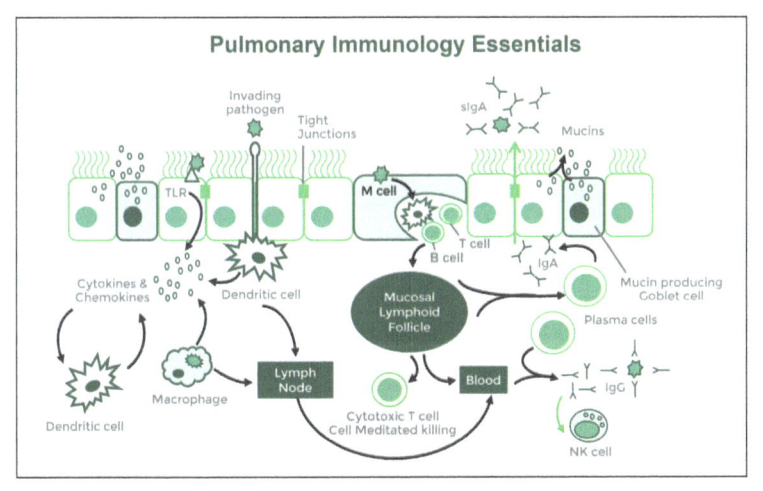

Figure 22-10. A complex diagram. *Source: Tilak Learning Group. Used with permission.*

Because the speaker would be describing much of what was in the diagram, we set the alt text as "A diagram depicting the stimulation of the lymphoid follicle (circular subepithelial in location) resulting in antibody production (Y shapes) by the plasma cells, both IgA and IgG." We described the information communicated in the complex diagram and did not describe the diagram's elements.

If a complex alt text tag can't be conveyed effectively in fewer than 125 characters or in the surrounding text, a separate document can be created to hold the full description of the image. This description may be in the form of text or a list.

The text under the image may look like this and be linked to a separate page of information: "Figure 22-10. Text description." Here is the text description on a separate page:

> This diagram represents the stimulation of the lymphoid follicle (circular subepithelial) in location resulting in antibody production (Y shapes) by the plasma cells, both IgA and IgG. It is a cut out of the middle and right part of the larger diagram. The left half of this diagram is labeled the follicle associated epithelium. It consists of three rectangles on the middle layer, two ciliated epithelial cells surrounding an M cell. The M cell rectangle has an oval removed from the bottom right corner with two circles representing T cells and B cells. In the bottom layer of the diagram from left to right is a solid rectangle labeled lymph node, a solid oval labeled mucosal lymphoid follicle, and a smaller rectangle labeled blood. The right half of this diagram has a pathogen orb surrounded with dimeric (two "Y" antibody shapes placed end to end) secretory IgA (sIgA). The middle layer of the right side has four rectangles—three representing ciliated epithelial cells and the second one from the left being a mucin producing goblet cell. The bottom right-side layer has plasma cells and IgG antibodies floating around the bottom right corner.

In that image description, we chose to include some of the elements in the diagram to create a more complete picture. Depending on the context of the presentation, the description may vary.

Whatever project you work on that involves alt text tags should always be tested at the end. Here are two ways to test:

1. Use a screen reader to determine if the alt text tags function as expected.
2. Turn off the images and read. (Each browser's settings vary for disabling images.)

Another Purpose for Alt Text: Low-Bandwidth E-Learning

An organization reached out to my company to create e-learning content that would be deployed in developing countries. Most of them had low-speed internet and some areas relied on a satellite internet connection. We were tasked to create a series of e-learning modules containing important visuals and videos, which increases the size of a module. The larger a module is, the longer it will take to download on low-bandwidth connections. How could we design for both high bandwidth and low bandwidth?

Through a lot of dialogue at the beginning of the project, we were able to better understand the parameters and what multimedia needed to be included in each module in the series. The organization wanted it to be visually engaging, but we needed to be cognizant of the file sizes so we wouldn't create problems for people who relied on satellite downloads or had intermittent internet with low bandwidth.

The obvious solution was to use low-resolution images and videos as much as possible without losing quality. But another solution was to add alt text for all images and descriptive text for each video. Why? Because alt text would replace images if the learner had a slow connection or disabled images, and descriptive text can be downloaded much faster than a video.

In the design phase, we were scrupulous in the kind of imagery we used. For each image and design element, we asked if it really needed to be included in the module. What content, context, or mood was it conveying? How large was it? For every image we chose, we included alt text.

If the learner had a slow connection, the alt text would download rather than the image, thus allowing the learner to know what the image depicted or what the video was about.

We needed to do three things to ensure the modules functioned as anticipated:

1. Identify any problematic multimedia content, such as large images or videos. Reduce their size as much as possible without sacrificing quality. Remove any unnecessary images.
2. Write concise and descriptive alt text for every image. Identify any decorative images.
3. Test the modules in a low-bandwidth environment to understand what would load, how quickly or slowly, and what it would look like.

There was a lot of discussion up front about the audience and their technological needs. Because of the care and thought taken at the beginning of the process, the project was a success.

When an Image Fails to Load
Sarah Mercier | CEO, Build Capable

Everyone can benefit from alt text—not just those who use a screen reader. For instance, Figures 22-11 and 22-12 show what happens when there is an issue loading an image (with or without alt text).

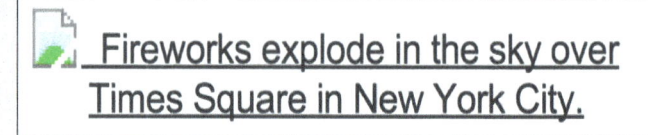

Fireworks explode in the sky over Times Square in New York City.

Figure 22-11. Alt text was entered for this image, so you can identify what the image is even though the page did not properly load.

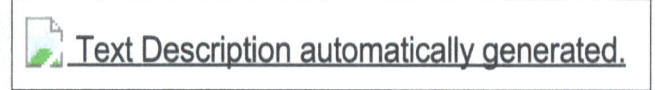

Text Description automatically generated.

Figure 22-12. Alt text was not entered for this image, so placeholder alt text is populated.

Who Should Write Alt Text?

A large organization asked my company for customized training on how to write and test alt text. It was in the process of moving the ownership of writing alt text from the IT department to the marketing and training departments. This company discovered that rather than having actual alt text tags, the IT department was *keyword stuffing*—using the company name and key brand phrases or words to increase its SEO ranking. In the HTML, they were typing in the company name instead of descriptive alt text. As a result, anyone using an assistive device would only hear "company name" for every image or illustration, rather than text that described what the image or illustration conveyed. Upon inspection of the page, you would find <img class=alt="company name">.

Using the alt text tags inappropriately meant risking legal liability under protections for individuals with disabilities because the site contained content on the internet accessed by the public every day. This was a case of assigning the wrong people to write alt text and not understanding the value and purpose of alt text. (Haley Shust covers this more in chapter 51.)

As I've stated, writing good descriptive alt text tags is a science and an art. Our solution for this company was to create a half-day training program to teach the marketing and training departments how to write alt text, including guidance on WCAG, the required criteria, why alt text is important, and so forth. Then, we put a process in place for them to check the accuracy of the alt text. They were then able to create accurate and descriptive text, as well as use assistive technology to test it for accuracy.

Is Artificial Intelligence (AI) a Potential Game Changer for Alt Text?

Working with AI has become more common, but is it a game changer for accessibility? With a few taps of the keyboard, you can direct an AI program to write alt text for an image. But will it include the context of the image in that description? Currently, as I write this, no. While AI may be able to speed up the process of writing alt text, a human still needs to review it to ensure it conveys a truly meaningful description. AI cannot exercise human judgment.

What about testing alt text tags with AI? While some automations can check whether alt text is present, AI can't read and comprehend the alt text tag to indicate if it provides a meaningful description of the image. For example, the image could be of a house and the alt text tag could say, "image of a building." The automation can indicate the alt text is there, but it can't tell if the alt text is in fact correct.

That being said, you may choose to use AI to speed up the process of checking for alt text. It can flag where alt text may be missing so you can add it. Or you can use AI to recommend alt text that you can then edit. Regardless, you will always need to read the actual alt text to ensure it conveys true information.

Ultimately, it is best to write alt text yourself rather than relying on autogenerated or AI produced alt text. In doing so, you can ensure that you consider and include the context of the content and any specific visual information.

What You Can Do Right Away

When creating any form of digital content, stop and take stock of the images you plan to include. Do you currently have alt text drafted for them? Take this opportunity to write alt text for your images. Also, go ahead and add a placeholder to your design templates, such as your storyboard template, for writing alt text as you're planning for and selecting images.

23.
Typeface, Text, and Captions
A Creative Journey in Making Digital Content Accessible

Alan Natachu (he/him)
Instructional Design and Accessibility Consultant

I am obsessed with text and typeface. I absolutely love being stuck at a train crossing when I get a good view of the passing trains. I don't get annoyed or upset because it's an opportunity for me to see the graffiti art on the side of the trains. Sometimes I can read the stylized graffiti words and characters and sometimes I can't. It's so exciting to see!

When you travel to new places, what do you take pictures of? While I do snap pictures of my family and the cool places we visit, my camera roll will be 25 to 50 percent signs and billboards. And don't get me started on how much I love animated title sequences in movies.

I decided to get a semicolon tattoo on my wrist five years ago, but I couldn't decide what font to use. It's a nearly impossible choice. (The semicolon tattoo has two meanings to me. The first is mental health. Project Semicolon is a grassroots mental health advocacy and suicide prevention nonprofit. I've battled with mental health all my life and the semicolon represents not an end, but a pause. The tattoo reminds me that there is hope even when things are dark. The second meaning for me is colon cancer. I was diagnosed with stage 3B colorectal cancer at 35. After a year of treatment, I don't have a full-sized colon anymore. I have a semicolon! Get it?)

At one point in my life, I was so enamored by text that I wanted to become a poet. I loved how characters and text were laid out across the page.

I thought it was beautiful how a poem could be so concise with so few words but be so open at the same time. I went to the Institute of American Indian Arts in Santa Fe, New Mexico, but after two years of studying, reading, and writing poetry, I found myself burntout on the genre and creative process. So, I started learning about and practicing screenwriting, playwriting, acting, directing, and video editing and video producing. I may return to poetry someday, but it's time for me to get to what all this has to do with closed captions.

Three events shaped my work ethic, and especially my views about captions.

Tales From an Ex-Poet

I learned to create closed captions manually before automation tools became widely available. In 2013, I was knee-deep in manually creating captions and starting to feel a familiar sense of burnout. What I thought of next felt like a comical slap across the face: "This is like creating poetry!"

I was delighted by this thought. When I was a poet, I was working with sentences, sentence fragments, awkward punctuation, and more. I stylized my poems to allow for empty space and the flow of words. I was working within established poetic guidelines (such as stanzas and iambic pentameter). I also broke a lot of established rules. The hardest part of poetry was creating original content. Working with captions allowed me to work with the empty space and flow of words, as well as time. But the best part was that I didn't have to create the content.

Poetry is an endless creative process with limitless possibilities. There are rules and standards that you can choose to follow or not. Captions have guidelines and best practices that aid their creation, as well as rules that should be followed. This distinction, or guardrail, became very interesting to me. I wondered, "How can I be creative within the best practices of creating captions?" New obsession unlocked: Creating the best captions possible.

Are You Sure You Can Read That?

I was watching TV shows with my two kids a few years after unlocking my new obsession. We use a Roku streaming player on our TV for our viewing needs. Some streaming channels allow you to customize caption font, font size, font color, and highlight color. My kids love to customize how their closed captions appear so the captions closely resemble a pack of Bubble Yum Bubblicious Gum—a pink background with either light or dark pink font, depending on their mood. I couldn't read their Bubblicious captions well, but my kids loved it, and I wouldn't deny them the chance to use captions or put their own spin on the formatting.

Often, something would be amiss with the captions (and no, it wasn't the custom color formatting choices). In fact, the pink color palette helped me understand timing and accuracy. It made it easier to recognize badly timed and formatted captions because it's hard to miss the Bubblicious captions taking over the bottom of the screen.

Captioned videos on Netflix and Hulu were hit or miss at the time. These major streaming platforms and major media outlets, such as NBC and Fox, have the means to create accurate captions. Their captions may have gotten better over the years, but many videos still have poorly formatted captions. I guess their inclusivity budgets are spent more on voice-overs than captions.

I'm not dissing voice-overs and additional language audio tracks. They are awesome! They provide content to more audiences and can even help with language preservation. Did you know that the 2022 Hulu movie *Prey* has a Comanche language audio track? Or that *Star Wars: Episode IV—A New Hope* was dubbed into the Navajo language? You can watch both online with these additional language tracks. (They can be found in the "Extras" section of each film.)

If you want to see some good captioning examples, you should check out PBS Kids videos. The captions are consistently well-timed, correctly formatted, and easy to read.

An Unintended, Beautiful Outcome

I've handled a lot of different caption requests in my training career. But, it wasn't until recently that I was assigned to create subtitles (foreign language captions). The video featured an English speaker, and the subtitles needed to be in Japanese.

This was the first video I worked on that would receive the subtitle treatment. It was an important one too, because it featured my company's leader. There were a few factors working against me completing these captions. First, it was during the COVID-19 pandemic, so all the help I received was via Zoom. Also, I don't speak or write in Japanese.

I have a Japanese co-worker who helped with this project, but we were worried about working on it over Zoom. Up until this point, all my collaborative caption work had been done in-person. After five minutes, however, working over Zoom proved to be a nonissue. We put the *kanji* (Japanese characters) in place. We fixed the timing. Then, we did a final screening of the video with subtitles before we made it available to the company.

She was quiet while watching the video, but then experienced some delightful moments and happy tears. She was pleased to see herself represented in the video. I put myself in her shoes and remembered how happy I was when I found out that *Finding Nemo* had a Navajo language audio track. Representation matters in all that we see and do. I, too, teared up a little with her, witnessing her joy.

I hope these stories and the tips I provide next will help you become more aware of the importance of captions. Already producing captions? I hope that I can help you create even better ones.

Captions, Subtitles, and Transcripts, Oh My!

I need to clear something up before we continue. Captions, subtitles, interactive transcripts, and text transcripts are separate items. One is not better than the other. They all provide access to a video that otherwise wouldn't be there. However, you need to know the differences between these formats.

Open Captions

Captions come in two varieties: open and closed. Have you ever watched a video with text captions you can't turn off? Those are *open captions*, and they're burned into the video. You can find examples of this in TikTok videos with animated text that act like captions. Open captions are even worse if you turn a PowerPoint slide into a video, especially if the slide is text heavy and the narrator reads the slide word for word.

Open captions are thought to be accessible, but they're not. They don't allow you to alter the text to make it easier to read (or make it "Bubblicious"). You can't change the text into another language. And, if you're adding closed captions on top of existing open captions in a video, they'll be even harder to read.

Closed Captions

Closed captions offer flexibility on how captions are displayed. You can resize and change the font, reposition them in the video player, and turn them on or off. Open captions don't have that flexibility and will always be shown the way they were formatted in the video, whether you're watching it on a smartphone or in an IMAX movie theater. Modern video players may allow you to do even more customizations. And if you don't want closed captions shown, you can select the CC (closed captions) button to toggle them off.

Avoid using open captions, and instead use closed captions. Going forward, anytime I mention "captions," I'll be talking about "closed captions" unless specified.

Subtitles

Subtitles are sometimes confused with closed captions. There are a couple distinctions, though. In the United States, *subtitles* are captions in another language and can also be open or closed. Closed subtitles are great because you can provide multiple language options for your video without having to rerecord audio voice-overs and create multiple copies of the same video in different languages.

In some countries, subtitles are called *captions*, which adds to the confusion. The subtitles or captions describe music, background noises, and other audio elements. Also, secondary foreign languages sometimes don't get captioned. For example, if someone is watching a video that has Spanish subtitles as the primary language and English as the secondary foreign language, the English parts won't be captioned.

Interactive Text Transcript

Some video players offer an interactive text transcript in addition to captions and subtitles. You often have the option to search for words in a text transcript, which makes finding specific points in a video so much quicker. Some interactive text transcripts may also allow you to download them as a .txt, .docx, or .pdf file.

Interactive text transcripts can be played back in a similar fashion to captions. But, unlike captions, which are words typically displayed in the bottom area of the video, interactive text transcripts will display words to the side of the video. This interactivity depends on the platform.

Some e-learning authoring tools allow you to add an interactive text transcript that follows along with your audio and voice-over.

Text Transcript

If you don't have access to an interactive text transcript feature in your video player or are pressed for time, you can also provide a text transcript in document form. This is a simple, extremely effective approach to providing audio alternatives to a video. There is no official text transcript format. They usually include the title of the video, who is speaking, and what they said. Remember that you'll need to make sure your text transcript is accessible.

Which Captioning File Format Should You Use?

Saving my first DIY captioning project shocked me. There were so many captioning file types to choose from. Some file types were for video editors. Some were for DVD and Blu-ray authoring. I even found a group of file types listed as "unknown." I didn't know which one to use! I'll save you the headache and tell you about the main file types you'll need for your video and e-learning content.

What Is a Captioning File Format?

All captioning file formats are essentially text files (.txt) that have a unique file extension and style formatting that contains the information needed for it to be read by a video player. You can open the caption file in a text editor and make minor edits, such as correcting misspelled words. However, I don't recommend adjusting caption timing with a text editor because the timing format is different for each caption file format. Instead, use a dedicated captioning tool to edit your caption timing. A list of captioning tools is available later in this chapter.

You can get these files from a several different sources. YouTube and Vimeo allow you to download their automatically generated captions. You can also export captions from Camtasia and Articulate Storyline (but only if you created them in the tool first).

File format types include .srt, .vtt, and .scc. When adding captions to a project, use the .srt file format first! The .vtt and .scc file types are used by popular e-learning creation tools, so use them if an .srt file doesn't work in the player you are using. You can use a caption converter to get from .srt to the right file type.

.srt—SubRip Subtitle

.srt is a universal captioning file type. Most places will accept it for closed captions. If you find a place where you can't use this file type, you can use a caption convertor to change an .srt file into a different format. Desktop and online applications like Subtitle Edit can convert caption file types for you. TranscribeFiles provides free caption conversions between 150 different file types. Here's an .srt format example:

```
1
00:00:01,981 --> 00:00:04,682
This is an example
of a .srt formatted caption.
```

```
2
00:00:05,302 --> 00:00:08,958
The numbers are the caption timecode
in hours, minutes, seconds

3
00:00:09,526 --> 00:00:11,324
and milliseconds.

4
00:00:11,423 --> 00:00:13,989
Each caption is identified
with a number.

5
00:00:14,509 --> 00:00:16,913
This number will increase
with the number of captions you create.
```

.vtt—Web Video Text Tracks (WebVTT)

.vtt is used for embedded .mp4 videos in PowerPoint, as well as with Articulate Storyline and YouTube. Here is a .vtt format example:

```
WEBVTT

00:00:05.302 --> 00:00:08.958
This is an example
of a .vtt formatted caption.

00:00:09.526 --> 00:00:11.324
The only thing this caption tracks
is the caption timecode

00:00:11.423 --> 00:00:13.989
in hours, minutes,
seconds, and milliseconds.
```

.scc—Scenarist Closed Captions

.scc is used by Adobe Captivate. Unlike other examples, .scc uses code that the video player will translate into captions. Any formatting you do will be translated in the player. You will not be able to see the formatting, paragraph breaks, or other caption details without using a player or caption editing tool.

Here is an .scc format example:

```
Scenarist_SCC V1.0

00:00:06;10 942f 942f

00:00:08;28 942c 942c 9420 9420 94ae 94ae 94f2
94f2 2020 2080 c16e 6420 6de9 ecec e973 e5e3 ef6e
6473 ae80

00:00:09;19 942f 942f
```

So, What Makes a Caption Good?

Now that you understand what captions are, let's dive into what makes good captions. I'll use the word "should" a lot in this section because these are more guidelines than absolutes. Aim for progress, not perfection, as you learn how to caption.

Synchronized

Captions should follow the speaker, meaning that they should start when the speaker speaks and stop when they stop. This seems like a no-brainer, but I can't tell you how many times I've watched videos or taken an e-learning course in which the caption timing is way off. It is almost comical how long captions would stay on the screen—sometimes for five to 10 seconds after a speaker finished talking. But the caption fail that drives me bananas is when it is very long but only onscreen for less than a second. There's no way to read it unless you pause the video. Pausing may seem easy enough; however, thinking in terms of accessibility, it may be difficult for someone who doesn't have the motor functions to quickly do so.

By the way, your captions should not look like the previous paragraph—a massive block of words. Don't be afraid to break a long sentence of dialogue into several captions. They should be short and timed with the speaker and appear onscreen for the appropriate period. There may be times when the speaker doesn't say anything. Don't add a caption saying, "The speaker is silent." Just don't add a caption for those breaks. Another important aspect of timing is including captions that identify what else is happening in the audio.

Speaker Identification and Sound

It's important to identify things other than dialogue in captions. Do you have multiple speakers doing voice-over in the video? Identify them by name or as Speaker 1 and Speaker 2. Producing a video that focuses on chainsaw safety as part of an urban forestry safety course? Identify the chainsaw when it is running. And because this is urban forestry, identify the sounds of the city landscape.

Timing these captions is just as important as timing ones that identify dialogue. They may appear onscreen between two and five seconds. I'll cover more ways to identify audio for captions and best practices later.

Accuracy

Spell-check your captions. This is especially true if you are starting your project with autogenerated captions. Be on the lookout for *missspellings*. And no, I won't correct this spelling because if it looks bad in this book, imagine how it looks in a caption. Now imagine that caption being displayed on a large movie theater screen. You can't hide that mistake.

Translations

Translations can be a faster and more budget friendly approach for your project. You can have one video with multiple language translations. Many players can support multiple subtitles. Did you know that YouTube offers more than 200 different subtitle language options? Supported languages include everything from Cherokee, Luxembourgish, Sanskrit, Tongan, and Zulu to Klingon.

Mind you, YouTube doesn't automatically translate content into these languages. Instead, it allows content creators to mark subtitles with a specific language. This makes it easier to find the language track you want to turn on when watching a video.

KISS (Keep It Super Simple)

Here's a quick checklist to run through to test if your captions are good:
- Are they synchronized?
- Is the timing accurate?
- Are they easy to read?
- Are they the right length?
- Do they capture important sounds?
- Do they look like they were inspired by a TikTok video?

If you answered yes to all but the last question, consider your captions KISS'ed!

It is very alluring to format your captions like a TikTok video with flashy highlighted words appearing when a person speaks, exotic color combinations for text, and long sentences truncated into the size of a postage stamp. Not to mention all that animation. It's enough to make you dizzy. Literally.

All that extra flash makes it hard for viewers to read the captions and understand the video. It can be a distraction for neurodivergent people and even cause physical health issues for others. WCAG addresses this issue in Success Criterion 2.3.2, Three Flashes (Level AAA), which says you can't have any flashing elements that flash more than three times a second.[81]

The goal of captions is to allow as many people as possible to view and interact with your video, not to make it even more difficult to comprehend.

A Captioning Formula

Now that you know the what and why behind good captions, let's get into the how. The following sections include optimal captioning standards. There may be times when you have to deviate from them because of issues beyond your control (like captioning a fast talker who is unavailable to rerecord). Try your best to follow these standards.

Optimal Timing

Optimal timing is usually determined by the speaker. If possible, short captions should appear onscreen for one to three seconds, and long captions for three to five seconds.

Optimal Character Length

Determining optimal character length can be tricky. It is also influenced by the speaker. If your speaker has a nice, steady pace with their voice-over, you can have a maximum of two lines of captions. You will need to caption the dialogue and identify the speaker or other audio element (such as background music) within these two lines. If possible, the captioned line shouldn't be longer than 32 characters.

If your speaker sounds like they've had one too many cups of coffee before recording, you'll need to bend the rules. You should still shoot for two lines of captions, but you can extend the number of characters beyond 32; however, don't exceed more than 50 characters per line to preserve readability.

Why Use 32 Characters?

Long story short, 32 characters was the broadcasting standard for over-the-air, cable, VHS, and DVD video captions in the United States for many years. The .scc caption file format is associated with this standard, and it's very peculiar about how many characters it allows. You can only use 32 characters per line. Modern video streaming has eased this restriction. However, you should strive for up to 32 characters per line as this is an established captioning standard to follow.

What Does 32 Characters Look Like? How Do You Measure That?

Thirty-two characters is a decent amount of space. For example:

> This line is 32 characters long.
> *(This second line of text is 32)*

Use a monospaced font (also known as a fixed-width font), such as Courier New to find out how long 32 characters is. What's unique about a fixed-width font is that the characters are equally spaced out, making it easier to see what 32 characters looks like.

Let's redo the previous example in the Courier New font:

```
This line is 32 characters long.
(This second line of text is 32)
```

Both sentences are the same size! Here are some other monospaced fonts.

- From Microsoft:
  - Lucida Sans Typewriter
  - Consolas
- From Apple:
  - Menlo
  - SF Mono
- From Google Fonts:
  - **Roboto Mono**
  - Droid Sans Mono

Breaking Up a Long Caption Line

Commas, colons, and semicolons are a good place to break a long caption line, like in this example:

```
Three people have the responsibility
of finalizing the safety report:

the manager, the safety captain,
and the employee.
```

Word modifiers, the end of a person's name or title, and conjunctions are also good places to break a line, like in this example:

```
Raphael J. Winston III
was fond of wearing

custom made red leather boots
and flashy jewelry.
```

Captioning Fast Speakers

This is one of the hardest captioning scenarios in learning and development. If possible, get a rerecording of the content. If you can't, you'll need to try to make your captions stay onscreen as long as possible. You may need to extend the character count of the captions as well, like in this example:

```
17
00:05:10,981 --> 00:05:12,682
I can't drink a lot of coffee because I get too
jittery,

18
00:05:12,683 --> 00:00:05:14,002
nauseous, sweaty, and even sometimes

19
00:05:14,003 --> 00:00:05:16,043
really, really, really depressed
after the caffeine crash.

20
00:05:16,044 --> 00:00:05:18,004
Honestly, this is my first cup
in a little over two months

21
00:05:18,005 --> 00:00:05:20,739
(takes a deep breath)
and I feel I said a lot in only 10 seconds!
```

Caption Placement and Color

You usually do not have to decide where to place your captions on the screen or mark what color they should be. The option is there for you if you need it, but it's unlikely that you will. In fact, the only times I've had to specify placement and color were when my project required open captions. This was early in my L&D career, and I had to create captioned videos but didn't know how to do closed captions effectively in the organization's learning management system (LMS) or in Macromedia Flash (now known as Adobe Flash).

In today's digital environment with modern video editing tools, it is easy to create open captions, and social media makes it seem like this is the new captioning default we should use. However, you should avoid them.

Reminder: A user can't change the font, font size, or location of an open caption. These font and location options are what make closed captions accessible. If you increase a video's size to watch it in full screen and it has open captions, the fonts can look blurry and become hard to read. If you decrease the video's size to watch it on a smartphone, the fonts can look really small and become hard to read.

For Closed Captions

Caption placement and color are usually determined by the player you use. YouTube allows you to drag the captions anywhere on the screen. Diving into the caption options will allow you to change the font, font size, font color, and many other things. Some players don't have this level of personalization and will display the captions on the bottom center of the player. However, .vtt captions allow you to code where you want the caption to appear on the screen and to use text formatting options.

For Open Captions

Because you're working with a video editor, you have way more control over how your open captions will look. Keep it simple and follow these guidelines. It is a best practice to place your captions on the bottom center of your player. This is the default for nearly all players. However, sometimes important content is blocked by the caption. The best caption placement in that scenario is the top center of the player. It's rare that you'll use the left and right sides of the player, but these areas are options if there isn't another place to put the caption.

Your player will usually take care of color for you. You'll most likely use these guidelines if you create open captions for your project. Best practice is using contrasting colored text on a black background.

How Do You Create Captions?
There are a couple ways to create captions: automatically and manually. To be more specific, you can edit automatic captions or create them from scratch.

"AutoCraptions"
Meryl Evans taught me the term "AutoCraptions" to refer to automatically generated captions, which tend to be crappy. Speech-to-text AI technology has improved over the years, but it's not to the point where we can trust the output. Many platforms have adopted automatically generated captions. Major issues include caption timing and length, spelling errors, and mistranscribed words; however, these autogenerated captions do provide a good place to start when creating your captions.

You can improve the quality of automatic captions so that you have to do less editing afterward by using the following tips.

Invest in a Good Audio Setup
Clearer audio will have a better chance of being correctly transcribed. A good audio setup will get you clearer audio. At the very least, use an external microphone to record speaking parts.

Speak Slowly
Gilmore Girls, a TV show from the 2000s, was known for its fast dialogue. The speed could reach more than 300 words per minute! If your voice-over recording sounds like an episode of *Gilmore Girls*, then your automatic captions will likely be inaccurate. The autocaptioning AI software won't know where to break your captions into different sections. You'll also increase the chance of it misinterpreting your words. So, to improve accuracy when using auto-captioning, slow down your speaking pace.

Pause Between Topics
Take a moment before moving to another topic in your recording. A momentary pause will most likely cause the autocaptioning AI software to

generate a new line, or at the very least, you'll increase the likelihood of it getting the caption right.

Work With a Script
Have a script or a transcript? Great! You can use it to verify the automatic captions when you edit them. (They're also very handy if you have to manually create captions.) You can also turn your script or transcript into an accessible transcript. A properly formatted transcript falls in line with universal design principles by providing an option for those who need content in print form.

Use Plain Language in Scripts Before Filming
Writing your video scripts in plain language can also lead to better closed captions later. Plain language isn't the oversimplification of language, or the removal of words. Take this quote from Kevin on *The Office* TV show—"Why waste time say lot word, when few word do trick?"[82] That is not plain language. Also, please don't speak like that—it is reminiscent of stereotypical portrayals of Native Americans from old Western movies and TV shows.

Plain language minimizes the use of large words, avoids jargon when possible, and is easy to understand. So, which of the following is a better example of plain language?
1. This gift is a most unexpected surprise for today! I wish you much thanks for such a wonderful memory.
2. Wow! Thank you for the gift. I will cherish it.

The second example is much easier to read and to understand. Both have positive emotion and express the same thing, but the second is direct and to the point. The first example has many large words and could potentially be difficult for those who speak English as a second language to understand.

To write in plain language, you can use a free online tool called Hemingway Editor. It will give you a grade level readability score that's based on the automated readability index. It will also mark areas in your content that could be improved, such as passive voice or hard to read sentences. According to the Hemingway Editor, the first example has a readability score of grade 4. The second example has a readability score of grade 0, which means it is very easy to read!

Manually Created Captions

Learning how to manually create captions will greatly enhance and speed up editing of your automatic captions. Some organizations may not let you use autogenerated captions if the content is proprietary. Learning how to manually create captions will allow you to create accessible content even if it is super secret.

Manually creating captions lets you control all aspects of the captioning process, including the timing and length of the captions, and, depending on the tool you use, the color and placement of the captions onscreen. There is a learning curve because captions have their own writing style. Don't let that scare you.

Think of creating manual captions as akin to writing in the American Psychological Association (APA) or the Modern Language Association (MLA) style. Students often write papers in these styles because they help provide information in a uniform and polished way. The same goes for writing captions. You want to make them look uniform and polished for the viewer. Also, as you learn how to manually create captions, you'll gain speed in recognizing what makes a caption good.

There are several tools that you can use to create and edit captions.

Free Do-It-Yourself (DIY) Captioning Tools

Whether you choose a free or paid DIY captioning tool will likely depend on your budget. I mentioned earlier that a transcript can help you create captions. You'll want to have a transcript when working with free DIY captioning tools. Otherwise, you'll have to do the transcribing as you create the captions.

CADET (PC, macOS, Linux, and Web)

CADET (Caption and Description Editing Tool) was created by the National Center for Accessible Media at PBS Boston affiliate, WGBH, for anyone to use. It is a program designed to work with all major computer operating systems and within modern web browsers. Plus, it will work without an internet connection. You will need to follow the installation instructions for CADET because the process may be different than what you're used to. Once installed, you can caption .mp4 videos and import and export various subtitle formats. CADET is also an accessible tool to use, featuring full keyboard support. Free and accessible-first design—can't go wrong with that!

Subtitle Edit (PC and Web Only)
Subtitle Edit is my personal favorite caption editor on the list! This was the program I was using when I had my epiphany about poetry and captions. Subtitle Edit shows you where you overlap your captions, if your captions are too long and need to be split, and if your captions appear onscreen too fast. It will save, export, and convert your captions across more than 300 different subtitle formats. Don't worry; you won't use all those formats. You'll probably only use the formats mentioned earlier.

Much like CADET, you'll need to follow the installation instructions closely. You can install Subtitle Edit by itself or with an accompanying video player for a more stable experience.

YouTube and Vimeo (Web)
YouTube has a tried-and-true method for creating captions and has provided free captioning tools for more than a decade. Vimeo only recently got on board with online captioning.

Once you upload your video to YouTube or Vimeo, you can let the program generate the captions for you. Then, you can use the program's caption editor to correct any mistakes. You can keep the video in YouTube or Vimeo and use their video players to display the captions, or you can delete the video after you create the captions. (Just make sure to download your captions before deleting the video.) You can then import your captions into a different video player, PowerPoint, or other program.

Clipchamp From Microsoft (Windows, Web, and iOS)
Clipchamp is a "freemium" Microsoft video editor. It can do a lot more than just create captions. Clipchamp has pro features that you can pay for

(on a monthly or yearly basis), but if you agree to have your video watermarked with Clipchamp, you can use the pro features for free.

What's cool about Clipchamp is that it borrows elements from PowerPoint and MS Teams. It can create editable autocaptions and translate them into multiple languages. It has a built-in speaker coach, can do text to speech, and has captioning language filters (which can detect a curse word and replace it with ****). You also get the standard captioning editing and file download. Microsoft has also built a set of 48 American Sign Language (ASL) motion stickers that you can add to your videos. They are animated characters using ASL to say things like "hello" and "thank you."

Paid DIY Captioning Tools

If you have the budget, you should consider a paid DIY captioning tool. More video editing programs are shipping with autotranscription and autocaptioning functions. Having these features will speed up the captioning process by providing a place to start. And paid DIY captioning tools offer one key thing that allows you to start quickly that free tools don't: increased accuracy.

TechSmith Camtasia (PC and macOS)

Camtasia is a great tool to create captions, and you may already have access to it. It can also be more cost effective when compared to other paid DIY tools. You can import and export caption files, including the .srt file type, and use the caption editing tools to create new captions or clean up autocaptions. At the time of this writing, the PC version of Camtasia can also sync captions from a script and use speech-to-text technology to create captions for you. Sorry macOS users; those two features haven't been ported over to your version of Camtasia yet.

Adobe Premiere Pro (PC and macOS)

Adobe Premiere Pro is an in-depth video editor, and the learning curve can be steep if you are new to video editing. The latest PC and macOS versions of Premiere Pro have transcribing and captioning capabilities. Adobe Premiere Pro can automatically create a transcription, allow you to edit that transcription, and convert that transcription into captions. You can then edit the captions as you see fit.

Amara (Web)

Amara is freemium online captioning solution. The free version of Amara allows you to create captions for YouTube and Vimeo videos, but they will be publicly available. Also, you can get an embed code that features the YouTube or Vimeo video with Amara's caption player. What's the benefit of this? Ever wanted to show a YouTube video but couldn't because no captions were available or the autocraptions were all over the place? This free service allows you to legally create captions for publicly available YouTube and Vimeo videos. In other words, there is no need to circumvent copyright law to create YouTube captions for videos you don't own.

Not only does Amara provide a great and free DIY captioning tool, but its team also provides captioning and translation services. Human created translation services are a paid feature. If you need a translation, it leverages native speakers to create subtitles for you in more than 50 languages. If you want a language that isn't supported, Amara will help you find someone to work with on your translation.

Upgrading to a paid account will give you a private space to create captions. You can also take advantage of project-based caption editing within a team. Need a captioning solution that's bigger than a team? They provide an enterprise-level solution as well.

Amara is unique in that it is a project of the Participatory Culture Foundation (PCF), which is working to ensure that people's stories are told and heard.

Rev

Rev has a unique subscription service called Rev Max. You can get up to 20 hours of AI transcription and AI captions each month for a monthly fee. This subscription features a five-minute turnaround time and boasts 90 percent accuracy. Rev Max also includes unlimited Zoom meeting transcription (which doesn't count toward your monthly 20-hour limit).

Captions in E-Learning Content

Everything about formatting and timing we've covered also applies to captions in e-learning content. You may have the option to incorporate additional formatting options, such as text color, text background color, and onscreen text placement. If you choose to pursue these options, follow these general accessibility guidelines in addition to the captioning guidelines:

- Captions should have white text on a black background, if possible.
- Choose a font that is easy to read. A sans serif font (such as Futura, Arial, or Helvetica) will work the best.
- Don't place captions over important areas on the screen.

Modern e-learning tools, such as Adobe Captivate and Articulate Storyline 360, have ways to create and edit captions. However, they don't have capabilities to automatically generate captions for you (at the time of this writing).

Use a transcript to create the captions. You'll be copying from the transcript and pasting into your e-learning tool's captioning editor. This is a much faster way to create the captions than transcribing and captioning at the same time.

10 Captioning Tips

Here's a captioning scenario for you: I mentioned earlier that there may be times when you have a person reading text that is already on the screen. If they're reading a presentation slide, how do you caption that? This is a common but confusing captioning situation in L&D projects. Continue on for an answer, as well as nine other tips to help with your captioning projects.

1. Onscreen Text and Captions

Sometimes, you'll encounter a video or e-learning module that includes a person reading a presentation slide verbatim (Figure 23-2). This can be advantageous for captioning.

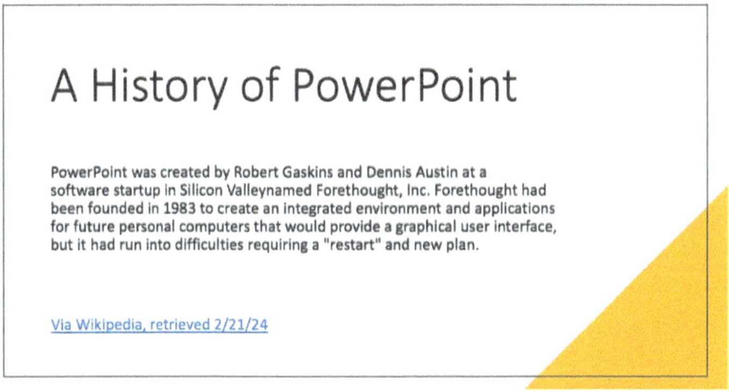

Typeface, Text, and Captions

A History of PowerPoint

PowerPoint was created by Robert Gaskins and Dennis Austin at a software startup in Silicon Valleynamed Forethought, Inc. Forethought had been founded in 1983 to create an integrated environment and applications for future personal computers that would provide a graphical user interface, but it had run into difficulties requiring a "restart" and new plan.

Via Wikipedia, retrieved 2/21/24

Figure 23-2. This PowerPoint slide has a simple white background with a yellow triangle in the corner. The text states: A History of PowerPoint— PowerPoint was created by Robert Gaskins and Dennis Austin at a software startup in Silicon Valley named Forethought, Inc. Forethought had been founded in 1983 to create an integrated environment and applications for future personal computers that would provide a graphical user interface, but it had run into difficulties requiring a "restart" and new plan. The source cited is Wikipedia, retrieved on 2/21/24.

You don't have to create captions for the presentation slide if the person is reading it verbatim. You'll need to continue the captions when the person continues speaking beyond the words on the slide. But please, exercise caution when choosing how many words to fit onto a PowerPoint slide. You are creating a presentation slide, not a novel.

2. Commas

Use commas to help the viewer break down lists, understand where breaks are in the captions, and know when a sentence is about to end. One of my favorite examples comes from a text-based internet meme:

Let's eat Grandma!
Let's eat, Grandma!

The lesson? Commas save lives.

3. Who's Talking?

There are times when a person starts talking in a video or e-learning module but we don't know who they are. You will need to identify them if there are no other onscreen clues. To identify a named speaker, place the person's name in brackets, which are important for identification. Here's an example:

```
[Susan] What we are seeing now
is photosynthesis in action.
```

Creating a caption for an unnamed person follows a similar format. You'll need to identify the person speaking in some manner, either as Narrator, Speaker 1, or Elder 1. Here's an example:

```
[Narrator] There are nine updates
in the new WCAG 2.2 guidelines.
```

4. What's That Noise!?

Just like identifying a person speaking, you need to identify music and sound effects. Use brackets with a description of the music when captioning music, like this example:

```
[background music begins]
[background music ends]
[hard rock music plays]
[indistinct opera vocals]
```

Sometimes, you'll come across the need to caption dialogue and music. Here's an example:

```
[electronic music blaring]
[Mike] I LOVE THIS SONG!
```

When captioning sound effects, use brackets with a description of the effect. Be as specific as possible, like in this example:

```
[lion roars]
[glass shattering]
[semitruck engine turns on]
```

5. Do You Use 1 or One?

In many cases, you'll use numerals when you are dealing with numbers. For example, use numerals when the number is specific:

```
More than 3,000 accidents
are prevented annually.
```

Use numerals when a date or time is involved:

```
The 20th century saw many innovations
in personal protective equipment.
```

Use numerals when referring to fractions and percentages:

```
We saw a 25% reduction
in workplace accidents.
```

Use numerals when money is mentioned:

```
We saved more than $10,000
over the course of the year.
```

Use numerals when measurements are used:

```
Mix 1 cup solution
to 1 gallon of water.
```

There are a couple exceptions to these rules and you'll need to spell out the number in some situations. For instance, spell out numbers one through 10:

```
I have three pages left to read.
```

Spell out fractions when they are attached to millions or billions:

```
More than one and a half million people
visit our museum annually.
```

Spell out numbers when they start a sentence:

```
Fifty years ago, our factory
produced its very first sprocket.
```

Lastly, don't mix numerals with spelled out numbers. Let's rewrite the previous example, but this time, we'll mix numerals with spelled out numbers:

```
Fifty years ago, our factory
produced its very 1st sprocket.
```

It doesn't look too clean, does it?

6. Using Acronyms and URLs

Acronyms should be spelled out without periods. You'll save character space by doing so, like in this example:

```
ATD provides training and resources
to learning and development professionals.
```

Websites should be written like a URL. It's best if you use the main URL of a website, such as www.td.org.

```
Visit www.td.org for more information
on becoming a member.
```

If possible, avoid using long URLs. Https://www.td.org/press-release/get-started-with-instructional-design-despite-limited-resources has 96 characters! Use your limited caption character space wisely.

You can't select URLs when they are in caption form. However, you can guide people to the URL in different ways. Place it in the video description, an email, linked in a QR code, or some other method of engagement.

7. Slang

Slang words and phrases are an important part of informal language. Different industries have different words for slang. In construction, a "New York screwdriver" refers to a very large hammer. If a doctor asks for the "guessing tube," they want the stethoscope.

Slang usually isn't scripted. It may show up in videos containing interviews. It's tempting to change slang to its a proper term. Don't. Doing so will take away the speaker's authentic voice. Take for example, "K, *skoden*!" This is a Native American slang term that means "OK, let's go then." Changing "K, *skoden*!" to "OK, let's go then," takes away the speaker's identity and background.

You must be careful when relying on autocaptions to correctly guess your slang words. They may not pick it up. For example, here's how Clipchamp's autocaptions transcribed "K, *skoden*!": "OK. Scroll down."

Last, before adding slang terms in your projects, you need to identify what they mean. Slang is a part of language, but some terms can also be derogatory.

8. Must-Follow People

Want to be a better captioner? Want to learn more about Deaf culture? These are the people to follow:

- **Meryl Evans.** I've learned a lot from Meryl on captioning. I feel like I've upped my captioning game by listening to her and following her advice.
- **Melissa "echo" Greenlee.** I love this quote from her: "The world taught me to be hearing-friendly. Now, I teach the world to be deaf-friendly." Melissa is the founder and CEO of deaffriendly.com. She speaks on Deaf culture, hospitality, and customer service.
- **Karen Lewis-Hannah.** Karen is the CEO of A Silent World Deaf Center and founder of Traveling Sign Language Camp. Her focus is community youth groups, providing Deaf education through various sign language games and activities in Jacksonville, Florida.

9. Progress Over Perfection

Meryl Evans is always talking about this, and it has become my accessibility mantra: Progress over perfection. Keep it in mind when you are creating captions and other accessible content.

10. My Secret Captioning Weapon

I found my secret weapon last year and my world has never been the same. The Described and Captioned Media Program has an in-depth resource on captioning guidelines and best practices called Captioning Key. It's a free resource on their website! And there's a printable version (but it will take approximately 70 single-sided pages to print out). You can thank me later.

What You Can Do Right Away

I gave you a lot to think about, plan for, and do in this chapter. One way to get started is to reflect on your experience with captions in your daily routine, whether watching TV shows or movies, how-to videos on YouTube, posts on social media, or content in an e-learning course. How was captioning handled? Did the captions (or their absence) enhance your experience or make it worse? Use these lessons along with the tips I've shared to turn creating the best captions possible into your newest obsession.

24.
Closed Captions
When Sound Matters

Sarah Mercier (she/her)
CEO, Build Capable

Several years ago, I was working on an e-learning course to teach police officers about de-escalation and post-traumatic stress disorder (PTSD). My team found that we needed to add captions to some videos we had curated from other sources to use in the course. I had been using a tool to transcribe the videos, but one video wasn't producing a transcript. Was something wrong with the tool or the video? Maybe there was a problem with the video upload? It was strange. I recalled that this specific video was the one that had taught me the most about PTSD—my favorite video for the course. Something was definitely wrong.

I watched it again. Sure enough, I discovered that there wasn't a transcript because there were no spoken words in the entire video. Instead, the effects of PTSD were demonstrated through sounds such as sirens, a door slamming, fireworks, and other noises that can trigger someone living with PTSD. I learned an important lesson that day—why I needed to write closed captions for sounds.

Closed captions are on-screen text that is added to a video and can be turned on or off by the viewer. They are the description of the video's audio, including spoken words and sounds where appropriate.[83] This can be particularly useful for viewers who are deaf or hard of hearing, as it allows them to understand the content of the video even if they can't hear the audio. Closed captions can also be useful for other reasons, such as helping viewers who are watching a video in a noisy environment understand the content.

What did that mean for my PTSD video? A transcription tool wasn't going to work. I needed to create closed captions that described what could be heard throughout the video, keeping in mind the relevance of those sounds to the content. For example, in one part of the video, you see a close-up of a man's face with sweat on his brow and an anxious expression. In the closed caption, I added the description of a sound in the background like this:

```
[breaking news announcement coming from a radio]
```

At another point in the video, a group of young people appear in the distance outside in a park setting, which triggered a memory that was relevant to the main character's PTSD. I added a closed caption that said:

```
[faint sounds of people talking and laughing nearby]
```

My first attempt at the closed-captioning process for this project was mostly correct, except that I originally described the sounds in brackets in all capital letters. Not long after, I learned that when you are writing closed captions to describe sounds, you should use the following format: "A description of sound effects, in brackets, should include the source of the sound. However, the source may be omitted if it can be clearly seen onscreen."[84] And it is best to avoid all caps for readability. Reserve all caps for when a speaker is shouting. Keep in mind that writing closed captions for sounds is, in many ways, an art. Practice and feedback will help you improve!

What You Can Do Right Away

This project changed my approach to creating closed captions. I now conduct a video preview dedicated solely to crafting my closed-captioning plan. To do the same, ask yourself:

1. **Does the video only have spoken words?** If so, you need to transcribe the spoken words in the video, edit for accuracy, and add anything you want to describe about the speakers' voices (such as quietly, through clenched teeth, or high pitched).

2. **Does the video have spoken words and other sounds (including music)?** If so, start with the previous step, and then add descriptions of sounds in a context that's relevant.
3. **Does the video only have sounds?** You'll have similar considerations as the previous two steps, but you will be starting with a blank transcript.

Bonus tip: When you are creating video storyboards, include both spoken words and sounds (if applicable) in the script. Then, use that script to create the closed caption file. This is a great way to begin your inclusive design practice earlier in the process, saving time and ensuring accuracy in development.

25.
The Case for Transcription

Yvonne Urra-Bazain (she/her)
E-Learning Developer, Briljent

Urgent Request

The first time I was called to assist with transcription for Briljent was in response to a time-sensitive project. A client's learning management system (LMS) no longer supported directly uploading video files. They had more than 150 .mp4 multimedia files loaded into their system and asked my team to apply a SCORM wrapper so they could use them in their LMS. In addition, the client prioritized accessibility solutions to ensure equitable access for users. We had four weeks to assist with updating their internal video training to the LMS standard.

While the client reviewed their files and pulled them into a protected file transfer service, my team came together to propose solutions. Given 20 business days, and our current resourcing pool, what could we feasibly deliver that would address their need? We needed to create an efficient process for publishing their videos in an authoring tool that could output to SCORM 1.2 standards. We also needed to test the working efficiency of our accessibility options for these videos. Because they were rich multimedia screen recordings, we needed to represent visual and audio information in a text-based transcript and select a tool that could effectively aid this process.

Transcribing the audio and video information was a non-negotiable part of our process. Before this project, I had assisted with increasing accessibility of written content for screen readers but had not written a transcript for a client before. This was a valuable opportunity to solve for other access needs.

Through that month, I learned about creating detailed transcriptions as efficiently as possible. I become more curious about transcription, so I researched it in my free time to learn more.

Why Is Transcription Non-Negotiable?

Transcription is the transfer or conversion of one form of media into a text-based format. This includes a written or printed dictation, closed-captioning, subtitling, video descriptions, and interactive or detailed transcripts. Providing text-based audio, video, and multimedia information is essential for people with disabilities and useful for everyone.

If we ask whether we should provide a transcription service, it's like asking who we should exclude. Transcribed text can serve people who are neurodivergent or have:

- Hearing loss
- Deafness
- Audio processing disorder (APD)
- Visual processing disorder (VPD)
- Blindness or vision loss
- Deaf-blindness

Without providing text versions of media, such as closed-captioning and transcripts, these people are barred access to content. How could we, with a clear conscience, justify the willful exclusion of these individuals?

Who Benefits From Closed-Captioning?

Captions are the text versions of captured audio information. *Closed-captioning* refers to the default closed state of a captioning overlay. This differs from open (or hard) captions, which are part of the video or multimedia file and can't be closed or toggled off. Closed-captioning allows a user to choose if they need or would like to engage the captioning service. The ability to toggle captioning off and on is an important consideration for people who find the text on screen distracting or have difficulty processing audio, visual, and text-based information at the same time.

People who are deaf may rely on captioning, sign language presentation, lip reading, or a combination of all three in live media content.

People who are hard of hearing or who prefer to listen to the audio may use captions to support what they may not adequately hear. And some people process auditory information in a different way from others and may use captions to follow audio with real-time delivery.

Closed-captioning also benefits people situationally in sound-sensitive environments, including quiet places such as a library or times when quiet is preferred, like early in the morning or late at night. People may also use closed-captioning in loud environments where they may not be able to hear audio well but can read what is being said. And everyone could experience temporary or situational hearing challenges, such as if they contract a cold or ear infection.

Closed-captioning can also provide clarity about what is being communicated. Background noises in news stories or films may make foreground speech difficult to discern. Some conversational language may be muffled as part of the emotional communication of a scene. Lines may be whispered to infer secrecy. Quality captioning helps capture meaning that could be lost to these and other distractions.

People who can't understand a spoken language well may benefit from having synchronized presentation of the audio. In the US, this is called subtitling. *Graphophonemic correspondence*, which is the ability to match displayed characters with language sounds, is supported by synchronized captioning over multimedia. Therefore, closed-captioning is useful for people learning to read in a language or who require visual support for processing linguistic information. It's also useful for presenting specialized vernacular, dialects, accents, or cultural idioms that may be difficult to comprehend without additional support.

Who Benefits From Access to Transcript Documents?

Because closed-captioning presents a visual overlay of audio information over a media player, it allows those with adequate vision to perceive the caption's size, legibility, and contrast at the real-time speed that sound is presented. Alternatively, transcripts can be provided as a standalone text document or alongside other media, asynchronously displayed. Some people can't focus and comprehend auditory and visual information if the visuals are changing. A descriptive transcript may better serve their needs.

A detailed transcript should be a formatted document that includes text-based descriptions of audio (which are necessary for people who have low or no hearing) and text-based descriptions of video or visuals (which are necessary for people with low or no vision). Assistive technologies (AT), such as screen readers, can present the transcript text in a usable form. People with low or no hearing can visually read the transcript, while people with low or no vision can review information without replaying the media file using their screen reader's presentation of the text. For people who are deaf-blind, or who have both low or no vision and low or no hearing, the same transcript can be presented as braille and accessed through a refreshable braille display, which is another AT.

Transcripts also serve people who may not have a disability but may want to preview an audio, video, or multimedia file before committing to watching it or listening to it. It may be more convenient for some users to read the transcript than engage in time-based media, such as watching a video or listening to a podcast. Court reporters use a stenograph to document spoken words verbatim into a written transcript, which is necessary for legal documentation.

In addition, transcripts can help users experiencing lower internet bandwidth, whether regularly or situationally. People traveling may opt to download the transcripts of multimedia files they need or want to access prior to boarding a plane. Similarly, those with mobile data constraints may also benefit from not needing to use their data to download large media files. The added benefit of a downloadable transcript is that it can be used offline or printed and easily accessed again for review.

Other Benefits of Text-Versions of Media

A national study conducted by 3PlayMedia and Oregon State University Ecampus on student use of closed captions and transcripts found a correlation between availability of text-based audio information and perceived comprehension aid.[85] In the survey, 80.9 percent of students said they did not have difficulty with hearing. When asked, "How often do you use closed captions when they were available?" 53.9 percent of respondents said they used captioning sometimes, often, or always. When asked, "How helpful were the closed captions?" 88.1 percent said captioning was moderately, very, or extremely helpful. The study concluded that both closed-captioning and transcript documents were necessary to support preferences for aiding multimedia information processing.

Podcasts and web radio, which deliver information primarily in audio format, are also improved by adding transcription to the development process. The National Public Radio (NPR) show *This American Life* has been regularly posting transcriptions of its shows one week after initial release since 2011. While providing necessary access to their content by populations who rely on text-based transcriptions, *This American Life* calculated that 7.23 percent of website visitors had engaged with the posted transcripts.[86] Of their 2 million weekly listeners, this accounts for roughly 144,600 people a week who use that service.

In addition, *This American Life* noted at the time of data collection that 4.18 percent of all unique visitors landed on a transcription page on their website. This suggests that converting their media into a text format that search engines could index and crawl helped increase the site's search engine optimization (SEO). *This American Life* found that they could attribute 6.68 percent of their search traffic to transcripts.

What does this bode for other businesses? Consumers use text to search for what they are looking for online, and text searches pull them toward what businesses are already providing. Supplying captioning and transcription of media content can increase brand awareness through increased website traffic. When a company publishes text on their website, it improves the opportunity for intended consumers to find the information or services it provides.

Aligning with access rights can also help businesses avoid litigation. Take for instance the two-year class action lawsuit filed against Netflix by The National Association of the Deaf, which led to the streaming service agreeing to caption 100 percent of its video library by 2014. The agreement cost Netflix $755,000 in legal fees and another $40,000 to roll out their agreed terms over a four-year window.[87]

People who are watching a multimedia presentation in a foreign language may benefit from toggling subtitles off and on. A benefit of including transcription in development is that transcripts can be used for translation into other languages, which is necessary for subtitling. Consumers who are searching for products and services internationally can also benefit from translation services that are enabled when media is rendered in text form.

Creating Transcripts Efficiently

If you've ever manually generated captioning, dictation, or transcription, you know that it takes a considerable amount of time listening for phrasing, writing or typing it out, and then relistening to check for accuracy. While effectively translating media into text forms is valuable, the time it takes to generate a quality transcript can be costly.

To balance time constraints with resource availability, my team looked for an efficient process that would help us generate transcripts with as few people as necessary. An instructional designer proposed that we generate transcriptions using a feature of Microsoft Word 365. Word's web-based version allows you to use the Dictate and Transcribe option on the Home ribbon to upload .mp4 videos, which the software can automatically transcribe. At the time, this option was only available in the online version of Microsoft Word and transcription was capped at 300 minutes (about five hours) of audio per month, per user. Because each member of my team had access to Microsoft 365, we could simultaneously generate audio transcriptions and use familiar Word tools to edit and format them as needed. While this process also took considerable time to refine, it gave us the option to generate multiple transcripts per day.

Although Word's Transcribe functionality provides efficient transcription, manual verification is critical. For example, there are specialized terms the automated process misrepresents in text or conversational words and phrases that might be missing or similarly mistranscribed. In addition, Word's Transcribe feature can't always identify who is speaking, so manual identification is needed. Finally, Transcribe can represent audio in text, but can't view the video to describe visuals with text descriptions.

So, to provide quality, detailed transcripts, my team viewed the videos and wrote descriptions about pertinent visuals presented in brackets. For example, one of the demonstration videos displayed an image of a system screen. In the transcript, we included a text description of the visuals, identified the speaker, and then represented their speech in text. Here's a sample of our formatting:

> [Home screen of system portal. The username and password fields are highlighted.]
>
> **Speaker's name.** Once you navigate to the home screen, ensure that you enter your username and password in these fields. Your first password will be system generated. Be sure to update your password after initial log in.

After a month of assisting with transcription and refining our process, the client recognized that only 50 of their videos needed to be reuploaded to their LMS. We were able to stay ahead of the timeline and provide transcripts of the training videos that were also checked for document accessibility within their timeframe.

Persuaded to Transcribe and Caption

I realized the impact of this client's project when I was invited to be a guest on Russell Sweep's podcast *The L&D Hot Seat*. After the interview was published, I felt responsible for publishing a text-based version of the interview. I used Word's Dictate tool to transcribe the interview, and then I listened to the transcript to fine-tune and correct it. I shared a Word version of it with Sweep and added a page to my website to host a link I could share in a LinkedIn post announcing the podcast interview.

In the transcript I created for the podcast, I included time stamps and the name of the person speaking, and I did my best to represent verbatim what was spoken aloud with written text. To capture the nature of our casual conversation, I chose to include unintentional phrasing, such as "um," and repeated phrases and words, such as "it it." Some of my audio was garbled and less clear during the podcast, so offering this access option was important for many users, including myself.

Here's a key portion of the podcast interview that I transcribed:

> **27:41 Russell Sweep**
> Oh absolutely. You wanna feel like you're being respected and you're given the sense of respect that at least the common decency to allow you to navigate something.
>
> I'm glad you brought that up. That brings us to our last question here. The idea of designing with accessibility in mind. I feel like it it does support diversity and inclusion and belonging, but how does accessibility design communicate that to other people? Like if you have an option to toggle something on or off, if you have the option to turn on closed-captioning. What does that say to your learners?
>
> **28:16 Yvonne Urra-Bazain**
> I appreciate this question. And this idea really was inspired by an image I saw online, created by Accessibility Tick of New Zealand. They are an accessibility company. Um, but they created a a a graph, and on the graph was diversity on the bottom, and then inclusion seemed to have a little more vertical superiority to diversity, and right above that was belonging.
>
> And the first time I looked at this graph, I had trouble really understanding what they were trying to communicate. Except that . . . I came to the conclusion and and we had a discussion about this in our in our kickoff collab, where diversity is having everyone in the room together. So, allowing people to join in and be invited is an example of showing diversity. So, we might do that in corporate e-learning or government e-learning by having images of people who represent different backgrounds, different modes of operation. And that's diversity.

But inclusion might go a step beyond that because it asks for and invites their feedback. It asks them: What do you think? How can we make this better for you?

And again, there's still an idea perhaps that there's a marginalized group that another group is catering. I don't know how much I believe or or agree with it. I, I think that it's, it's a solid point and I I hold it in my mind as something I teeter off and on. I, I often live in shades of gray where I'm not 100 percent sure about everything, but I, I will I'll hold an idea and consider it.

So I, I realized by reading an article they had posted about that image that when they circled belonging as something higher above, they were trying to say that if you create an environment or an experience that someone who typically or previously had difficulty accessing or being part of before, but but you create an environment where it it's like it was made for them. It was made with them in mind. Then you've created for that person a sense of belonging.

They don't have a question about was I invited to the table?

They don't have a question about will people ask me about my preferences?

Those things have been already considered. They were already designed for them.

And, they can use it as a user, as a universal user, without needing those conditional, preplanning. How do I say? They already belong. It's not a question.

31:45 Russell Sweep
That's extremely powerful, and it it definitely speaks to the idea that designing for people in mind makes them feel like they're part of something that they don't have, that they're not just an

afterthought, that they're not someone who should be maybe penciled in, but that they automatically include without having to, you know, speak up and and request that.

I feel like that's very powerful.

In hindsight, providing transcription as a means of increasing accessibility was not relegated to a procedures list I followed for clients. I internalized its value. The case for transcription became non-negotiable *for me*. Rich media content is not complete until it can be represented in multiple ways that all people can access and use, including as text captioning or transcript documents. I keep a list of incomplete media I have published that I have plans to revisit to increase its accessibility.

While my implementation of accessibility has been imperfect, I recognize that I am making progress toward being responsible for what I create and who is included in my design considerations. Meeting people who benefit from these considerations, hearing their stories, and understanding the impact a publishing procedure may have on their experience has been most powerful for me.

As I've been called and moved to design for all people, I've also developed an innate appreciation for services that give more people a seat at the table by anticipating their preferences. My attempts at improving accessibility are also my earnest efforts in being a host of content that helps others feel like they belong. For me, this is the strongest case there is.

What You Can Do Right Away

When was a time you relied on closed captions or a transcript? How would your experience with that content have varied without the ability to access it in text form? Now, think back to the last learning experience you designed that contained audio or video content. Did you provide a transcript? If not, can you use that audio or video to practice? Going forward, plan for transcription so it becomes a routine, efficient task and not an afterthought.

26.
Audio Description Versions

Diane Elkins (she/her)
Co-Founder, Artisan Learning

Let's say you have a video on the proper way for food service workers to wash their hands (Figure 26-1). It's a visual demonstration, and there's a voice-over to go along with it. As the person in the video washes their wrists, the audio says, "Be sure to go all the way up to here."

Figure 26-1. Avoid relying on visual-only information in scripts.

A blind learner won't know what "here" means. And the transcript of the audio won't help. So, what can you do?

Evaluate the Video Script

First, review the video script (or final video if you're working with existing content), and ask yourself what a learner would miss if they could only hear the audio. Consider the following questions:

- Are key points displayed visually on the screen? Do they add any extra detail or nuance that's not in the audio?
- Is there "lower third" content, such as a banner at the bottom that shows the person's name and title?

If you answered yes to either of these, you'll need a way to share that "visual only" information. If you answered no, you may not need to do anything else. For example, if you have a talking-head video with text reinforcement of what the speaker said, then you might not need to add anything else.

Revise the Video Script

If the video voice-over has not yet been recorded or can be revised, update the script to fill in the missing details. In the handwashing video example, simply changing the script from, "Be sure to go all the way to here," to, "Be sure to wash your wrists as well," solves the problem of missing visual information—and it's clearer for everyone.

Create an Audio Description Version

Sometimes, there's so much visual information you can't reasonably work it into the script without it sounding unnatural. For example, at Artisan Learning, we worked on a course for the American Chemical Society (ACS) on reducing the spread of respiratory viruses. An infectious disease specialist did a visual demonstration about how wearing gloves isn't likely to help you at the grocery store. Figure 26-2 contains a screenshot from the video. She demonstrated this by wearing gloves and touching paint to simulate the germs she might be picking up at the store. By the end of the video, there was paint all over her hands, phone, and face. While she was doing this, she was just talking about going to the grocery store. She got some milk and responded to a text from her husband about getting some more mustard. If she had stopped to say, "I now have a splotch of red paint above my eyebrow," it would have interrupted the flow of the story.

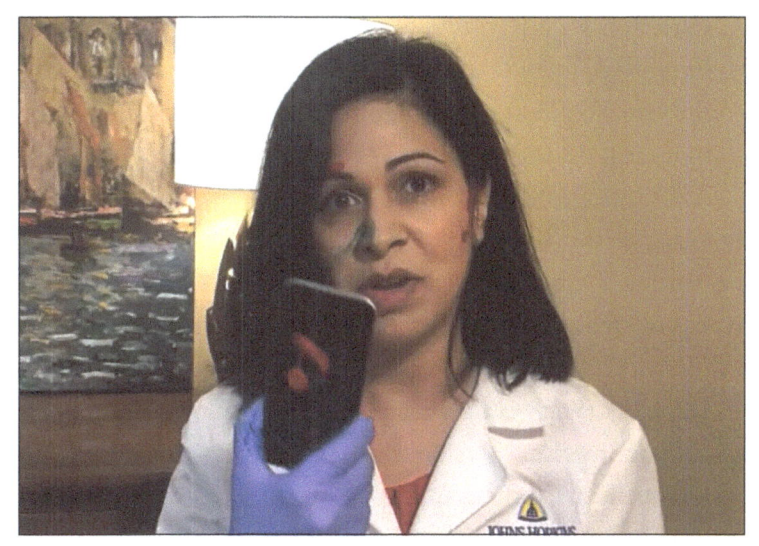

Figure 26-2. Sometimes describing action in video can disrupt flow. *Source: The American Chemical Society. Used with permission.*

For visual content like this that isn't adequately described in the audio, you can create an audio description version. It's an alternate version of the video that splices in a second voice, describing the extra visual content. You then present both options to your learners. For example, you can put the standard video on the course's main slide or page and have an "audio description" button that launches the other version (Figure 26-3).

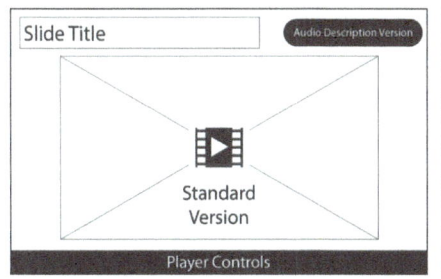

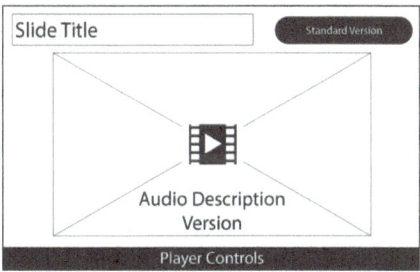

Figure 26-3. Providing options makes for a better, more accessible experience.

There are two types of audio description versions:
- **Standard.** In a standard audio description version, you add the audio describing the visual in the naturally occurring pauses in the video. This is the requirement for WCAG 2.0 AA (Success Criterion 1.2.5).[88]
- **Extended.** In an extended audio description version, you freeze the visual content to allow enough time to layer in a more thorough description. This is the requirement for WCAG 2.0 AAA (Success Criterion 1.2.7).[89]

You might be thinking, can't I just make a PDF of the transcript? The problem with this approach is that transcripts of a standard video only contain text of the *audio* content. They don't provide the missing visual information for the person who can't see.

WCAG 2.0 A (Success Criterion 1.2.3) does allow for a text version, instead of an audio-visual version, in which the descriptions of the visuals are interspersed with the transcript text.[90] Basically, it's a transcript of the extended audio description version. This is a Level A solution, which means it will be helpful to many people. But an audio description version (Level AA or AAA) can provide a richer learning experience for many individuals.

Here's an extended description sample from the grocery store simulation. It could serve as a text version for Level A or be used as the guide to create the extended audio description version for Level AAA.

> **Dr. Korpe:** And I go and then I'm going to get some milk, and I touch another shelf. And you see, I have new germs on my hands.
>
> *Visual description:* Now she has blue paint on her gloved hands.
>
> **Dr. Korpe:** And I'm going about touching the shopping cart, touching shelves. And then I get a phone call. It's my husband—he's texting to say oh, we need to pick up some mustard. So I will go get some mustard. You see, my phone is now covered in germs as well.

Visual description: She handles and types on her phone, which gets paint on it from her gloved hands.

Dr. Korpe: So I go get some mustard.
Visual description: She now has red paint on her gloved hands.

Dr. Korpe: And then oh, I want to touch my hair, and my eye is itching.
Visual description: She now has red paint on her ear and over her eye. She is still using her phone, which is getting more paint on it.

Dr. Korpe: Then I'm all ready to check out, then I have my phone, I put it back in my purse.

Now you might be wondering, what if there aren't natural pauses? One challenge with standard audio description versions is that training videos don't always have many natural pauses. Consider an action movie with a car chase or a nature video with an animal stalking its prey. There often isn't much talking during those scenes, so there's plenty of time to add audio description narration about what the cars are doing or about the animal running. But in training videos, the entire timeline is usually taken up with spoken words: either narration or dialogue. Often, there are no natural pauses for adding the extra audio. In these cases, the most accessible approach is to go to Level AAA and create an extended version, freezing the visuals for as long as needed to get all the extra information across.

What about slides that synchronize objects to audio? The WCAG standards about audio description versions don't just refer to video but rather "synchronized media." Video is a form of synchronized media, and so is a slide with animations and narration, such as a PowerPoint or Storyline slide. If you have individual elements fading in and out along the timeline of a slide, you could add alt text to the objects, but there's a problem. If objects are appearing and disappearing, the learner using a screen reader has to "chase" them. An object might disappear before they get to that portion of the slide. They never get that content, and they don't know they've missed it. Similarly, new content may appear in a portion of the slide they have already explored with their screen reader. If they don't know new content has appeared, they don't know to go back and find it. It's like asking them to play the carnival game whack-a-mole.

Instead, you might want to treat synchronized slides just like you would a video. Ask yourself what someone might miss if they could only hear the audio. If there is something, ask yourself if you can revise the script to incorporate that content without it seeming odd. And if not, consider an audio description version for those slides.

What You Can Do Right Away

Review an instructional training video—ideally one that you created. Does the video contain contextually vital visual information not captured in the audio? Or does it contain spoken cues that rely on being able to see what's happening? Follow the advice in this chapter to decide whether the script could have been revised or if it was necessary to create an audio description version to accompany the standard video. Then, consider the best approach when designing your next instructional video.

27.
Embracing Simplicity
Making a Complex Table Accessible

Yvonne Urra-Bazain (she/her)
E-Learning Developer, Briljent

Reciprocal Accessibility Mentorship

One of my first mentors in the L&D field taught me how to remediate courses created in Articulate Storyline 360 for Section 508 conformance. (This accessibility standard is discussed in chapter 51.) Together, with rounds of feedback from an accessibility testing team, we remediated 40 courses for a federally funded contract, and provided quality assurance testing for each one. My mentor offered guidance and additional resources as we built our knowledge base.

After we completed the course remediations, my next task was to author new content and publish it as documents. To prepare for this shift, I spent an hour of my personal time each evening studying document accessibility through Section508.gov. I shared a document accessibility checklist I tailored for the remediation work with my mentor. She asked if I could lead a training on document accessibility in Microsoft Word and Adobe Acrobat using what I was applying to document testing.

This was the beginning of a reciprocal mentorship between us. My mentor helped raise me to her level of knowledge so we could collaborate effectively, and I had an opportunity to share in kind what I had been putting into practice. We scheduled a two-hour workshop and I demonstrated each of the document accessibility checklist items for Microsoft Word. We then converted our accessible Word document to its final state as a PDF.

After the workshop, my mentor asked if I could show her how to make a complex table accessible. I offered to screen share a demonstration about the procedures. Instead, she asked if she could practice the procedure while I observed and offered guidance. That experience led to an important learning opportunity for us both.

Beginning With Microsoft Word

I recommended that we adjust the document for accessibility in Word first. Once we completed our accessibility checklist, and the document was good to go, we could convert the file to a PDF and continue applying accessibility adjustments in Acrobat. There are a few reasons I recommend this:

- **Word's Accessibility Checker points out accessibility issues clearly.** In addition, it offers in-application suggestions for applying fixes. This is especially useful for new practitioners.
- **Most of the basic guidelines for document accessibility can be addressed in Word using built-in features**, including applying heading styles, selecting the bulleted and numbered list buttons for creating lists, and ensuring graphic elements and textboxes are in line with the text to maintain appropriate reading order. Marking images as decorative or applying alt text is also simple in Word.
- **Word is a familiar interface for most document authors.** Fewer people have as much familiarity working in Adobe Acrobat Pro, in contrast. The Accessibility panes in Acrobat are a newer interface for most users to navigate and can be disorienting at first.
- **When an accessible Word document is converted to a PDF, most of the steps for ensuring accessibility are already completed.** Usually, only final steps and manual checks remain to finalize the document in Acrobat.

My mentor opened the accessibility checklist I presented on half of her screen and her Word document on the other half. Her document consisted of several headings followed by a complex table spanning multiple pages.

What Is a Complex Table?

There are three types of tables that could be present in a document:
1. Layout tables
2. Simple data or information tables
3. Complex data or information tables

Layout tables serve a different function than data or information tables. The purpose of a layout table is to position elements relative to each other in rows or columns while maintaining a programmatically determined reading order. This table is aptly named because it functions as a method for creating a regular layout of elements.

For example, if four images must be presented in a row, a layout table could be used to set them in relative proximity to one another. This table can be made accessible if "text wrapping" is set to "none." You can access these settings by right clicking the table and selecting "table properties." In the properties overlay, ensure "none" is selected as the text-wrapping option.

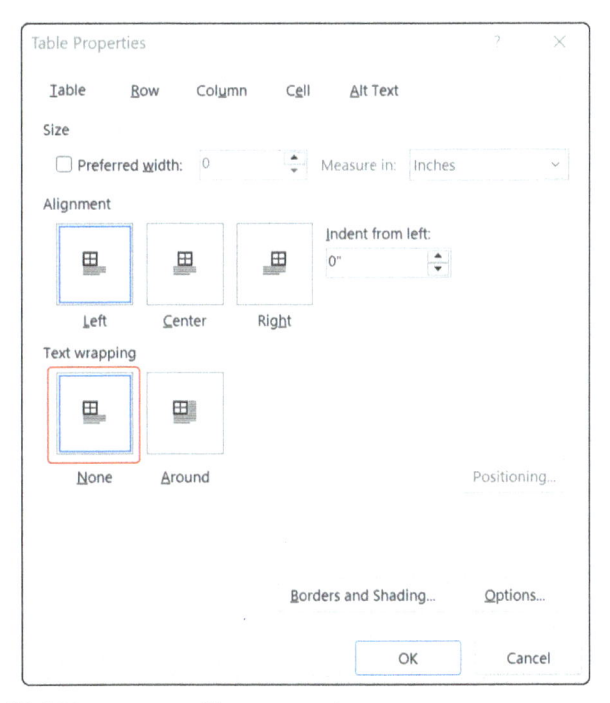

Figure 27-1. How to turn off text wrapping.

Each image's alt text can be accessed when screen reader users tab through the table row cells (Figure 27-2).

[Alt text: Snowflake to symbolize winter.]	[Alt text: Beach shoreline symbolizing summer.]	[Alt text: African daisy symbolizing spring.]	[Alt text: Assortment of pumpkins and leaves representing autumn.]

Figure 27-2. How to display images in a layout table.

If a layout table was not used, each image would still need to be placed in line with the text from the "Wrap Text Layout Options" callout box. An example of this would display each image on its own return line to ensure clear reading order. It could be presented as in Figure 27-3.

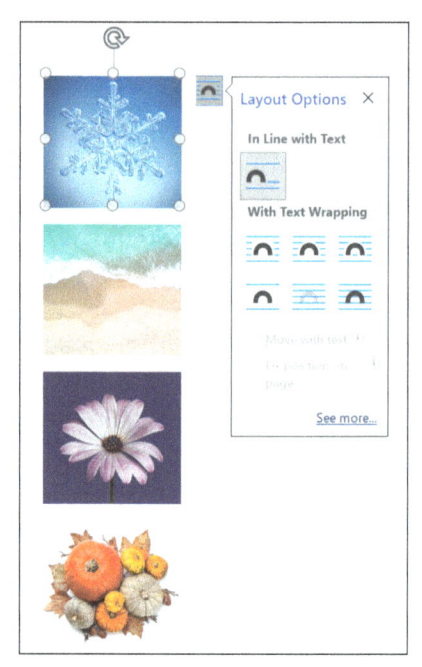

Figure 27-3. How to display images in line with text.

A *simple table* presents a clear correspondence between the table headers and table data cells. There are no split or merged cells, meaning there is a one-to-one correspondence between a header cell and a data cell.

Table 27-1 is a simple table that identifies team members on a project by their direct supervisor.

Table 27-1. An Example of a Simple Table

Instructional Design Manager	Web and Media Services Manager	Publications and Communications Lead
Instructional Designer	E-Learning Developer	Document Editor
Instructional Designer II	E-Learning Developer II	Document Editor II
Instructional Designer III	E-Learning Developer III	Document Editor III

The instructional design manager heads three rows of instructional designer roles. The web and media services manager heads three rows of e-learning developer roles. The publications and communications lead heads three rows of document editor roles.

In another version of this table, the author has added cell shading to support their intended communication—each column of headers and their corresponding data cell rows are shaded with the same color (Table 27-2). The header row consists of the three categories (or columns). All instructional designers from levels one to three report to the instructional design manager. E-Learning developers report to the web and media services manager. Document editors report to the publications and communications lead. There is a clear and direct relationship of what data or information is categorized by what header label.

Table 27-2. Using Cell Shading to Emphasize Relationships

Instructional Design Manager	Web and Media Services Manager	Publications and Communications Lead
Instructional Designer I	E-Learning Developer I	Document Editor I
Instructional Designer II	E-Learning Developer II	Document Editor II
Instructional Designer III	E-Learning Developer III	Document Editor III

In the next simple table, the author added row headers to identify two different project managers for projects 1 and 2 (Table 27-3). The data cells in each row identify which team members are assigned to each project. Shading is added to alternating rows to emphasize the relationship of the row header with the data cells in the row. As before, the direct supervisor of each team member is presented as the column header for their department. Each team member also reports to the project manager responsible for their project assignment, who is represented as the row header. Document editor II directly reports to the publications and communications lead, as well as project manager 1 regarding their specific project assignments.

Table 27-3. Adding Row Headers to Convey Extra Detail

	Instructional Design Manager	Web and Media Services Manager	Publications and Communications Lead
Project Manager 1	Instructional Designer I	E-Learning Developer III	Document Editor II
Project Manager 2	Instructional Designer II	E-Learning Developer II	Document Editor III

Layout and simple information tables appear as tiled grids. In contrast, a *complex table* does not present a clear one-to-one correspondence between data cells and headers. For example, Figure 27-4 shows the complex table in my mentor's document, which was used to organize program links for different departments.

Topic	Link
Department Name	
Program	Policy Basics
	A Brief History of Policy
	Basic Terminology and References

27-4. Complex table with multiple headings, including topic, links, department name, and program.

The first row, called the header row, signals to a reader that information will be presented in two columnar categories: topic and links. However, the table's second row disrupts the established two-column structure by merging them into one cell to create a "Department Name" subheading before returning to two-columns. Because the merged cell functions as a subheading, this table has multilevel headers, which is an indicator of complexity.

The table presents the three header levels each data cell is associated with:
1. The level that identified the column as a topic or link
2. The level that identifies what department name each topic or link is related to
3. The program a link is associated with

In addition, the "Program" row is split into three rows of hyperlinked data cells.

Assistive technology (AT) needs backend structure to present the information as the author intended. Complex tables cannot be made accessible in Microsoft Word. There is no built-in function in the table properties to define the column or row span for headers of merged or split cells.

Understandability

The "understandable" principle, which is one of the four principles that make the foundation of WCAG, sets a standard for ensuring digital content is readable, predictable, and provides input assistance for error prevention and correction. The goal of this principle is to ensure that AT users can understand information without undue effort or obstacles.

A complex table may pose a comprehension challenge for all users. However, sometimes the relationship between information is inherently complex. Authors create complex tables to convey information that may not be neatly aligned. Could a complex table be redesigned to increase understandability?

Let's use the complex table from Figure 27-4 as an example. There are several ways the information could be communicated to improve clarity. One solution is to consider removing the table entirely.

An expanded version of my mentor's table is presented in Figure 27-5.

Topic	Link
Department Name	
Program 1	Policy Basics
	A Brief History of Policy
	Basic Terminology and References
Program 2	Who Uses This Program?
	Current Changes to Program Offerings
	Future Program Expansion

Figure 27-5. Example complex table with an additional row header, program 2, displayed. The row is also split into three hyperlinked data cells.

Instead of this complex table structure, we could simply use headings and a bulleted list:

Department Name
- Program 1 links:
  - Policy Basics
  - A Brief History of Policy
  - Basic Terminology and References
- Program 2 links:
  - Who Uses This Program?
  - Current Changes to Program Offerings
  - Future Program Expansion

Let's gauge the relative understandability of this information structure by asking some questions:
- Is the same intention being communicated with this redesign?
- Is the information structured in a way AT can access?
- Is the relationship between the information clear?
- Is this format easy to understand?

Considerations for understandability benefit all users, especially those who rely on AT or modified software and people with learning or cognitive disabilities. People without known disabilities also benefit from clear communication. Understandability leads to time savings, less ambiguity, and fewer interpretation errors. It is a worthy goal and communication skill to hone.

The Cost of Complexity

Although my mentor and I discussed that there were simpler alternatives to using a complex table, she was interested in continuing forward with the process. She wanted to learn how to make a complex table understandable to AT.

It is important to note that at the time of writing this, complex tables cannot be made accessible in Microsoft Word. The Accessible Electronic Documents Community of Practice (AED COP) developed federal guidance to conform with the Section 508 standards. AED COP recommends that complex tables be made accessible by converting the .docx file to a PDF and applying adjustments in Adobe Acrobat Pro.

The table spanned six pages. My mentor and I spent two hours ensuring the cells of the complex table were correctly associated. Compare the time savings of simplifying the complex table into a bulleted list instead. Creating the table and figuring out the logic of the table's structure took time, as did formatting it. This does not include the time it took to adjust it for accessibility.

The practice of making a complex table accessible enabled us to develop a shared understanding about the value of simplicity. I realized complexity costs time and mental energy for designing, troubleshooting, and potential rework. For high-stakes or public-facing documents, undue complexity could require contracting outside consultants or planning for extra stages of review and additional revision cycles. The greatest cost of complexity is limiting access to information for populations who were not considered during development.

This experience was a key reminder to me that wherever we can simplify information delivery while retaining the author's intent, we should. This can improve communication and make content better designed for everyone.

What You Can Do Right Away

Reflect on the complexity of any tables you might include in your learning experiences or other digital content. Ask yourself, does that content need to be formatted in a table, or can it be displayed more simply, like a bulleted list? What other ways can you strive for simplicity over complexity?

28.
Accessible Documents—Why Bother?

Diane Elkins (she/her)
Co-Founder, Artisan Learning

In chapter 21, I mentioned my legally blind friend who beat me at air hockey. This same friend was once taking annual compliance training online, which was accessible. She didn't pass the test and wanted to review the policy. However, the policy document was *not* accessible, which meant she had to track down the owners of the document and ask for an accessible version. There wasn't one, but fortunately they knew how to make it accessible and were able to send it to her a day later. Unfortunately, the course had not saved her progress, so she had to take the entire course all over again.

This story haunts me—in a good way. When I have a deadline coming up to submit my slides for a speaking engagement, I might think, "Oh, that will only take me a few minutes because this is an existing presentation. I just need to update the title and closing slides and do a quick check to make sure I don't want to change anything." Now I think of my friend and take the extra time to make sure the PowerPoint slides and the PDF are accessible.

People assume that it takes too much time to make content accessible. But consider my friend and the time she wasted when she could have been doing other work. Then, multiply that by the many others who may have similar experiences.

I also learned from my friend the value of sending digital materials *before* live training events and meetings. If I provide only physical copies, someone with a visual disability might not be able to read them. If I provide them digitally at the start of the event, that person could use a screen reader to read them. However, they would have to choose between listening to their screen reader or listening to what's happening in the live event. But if I send the digital materials in advance, they can listen to them beforehand and focus on what people are saying during the live event.

What You Can Do Right Away

When you work toward making your e-learning courses, training programs, and other learning experiences accessible, you're on your way to designing for all. But don't forget about the supplemental pieces of content for those learning experiences—job aids, PDFs of presentations slides, policy documents, workbooks, marketing materials, and more. Consider auditing the external resources linked to one of your existing courses. Conduct accessibility tests using a screen reader and a color contrast checker. How accessible are they?

29.
Complex Topic, Plain Language
Harnessing Plain Language Guidelines to Support Complex Learning

Yvonne Urra-Bazain (she/her)
E-Learning Developer, Briljent

Call to Action

A client needed rapid deployment of training to reinforce unit-wide improvements and support new hires. The unit dealt directly with the complexities of enrolling a provider for federal reimbursements of services. Improper enrollment of appropriate candidates or the enrollment of a sanctioned candidate could yield high-stakes consequences, including potential civil monetary penalties. This was an urgent request for collaboration.

Over four months, our team collaborated with the unit's subject matter expert (SME) and unit supervisor to create a training roll-out that would be comprehensive and accessible. I was assigned with the technical writing and development of three of learner guides. Each one needed to provide step-by-step support for an enrollment analyst who navigated between three different system applications and validated enrollment applications with four government sites. Specialists ensured taxpayer identification aligned with the way the candidate reported their business services to the government. They also validated all fields of an application against the candidate's supporting documentation and national external records to corroborate their data.

In short, analysts had to account for a lot of data. The manuals we were developing needed to express these complex tasks and variabilities as clearly as possible. I leaned on plain language guidelines to create cognitively accessible and understandable documents to support the detailed work of the enrollment unit.

Plain Language Guidelines

The Plain Writing Act of 2010 requires federal agencies to follow plain language guidelines and use clear communication the public can understand.[91] (You can find a link to the guidelines in the Take Action Toolbox.) They include some of the following practices:

- Identify and write for one target audience.
- Organize information and use terms carefully and consistently.
- Write short sections with many useful headings.
- Use active voice, the simplest form of words, and omit unnecessary words.
- Write paragraphs that cover one topic, begin with a clear topic sentence, and use transition words to connect paragraphs.
- Clarify key points. Use examples, lists, simple tables, illustrations, and emphasis. Minimize cross-references.

The plain language guidelines represent good writing hygiene. Writing succinctly and understandably is a skill that requires repeated practice, especially for technical documents. Here's how my team followed these guidelines to deliver accessible content.

Narrow the Target Audience and Topic

Enrollment analysts were responsible for reviewing applications for more than 40 different provider types within four larger classifications. To support the enrollment specialists, we focused on one classification and one provider type throughout each guide. Our goal was to demonstrate a full yet focused enrollment process. While we received some pushback about this decision, our training lead explained the purpose of a learner guide to our stakeholders. To best support learners, we needed to demonstrate a typical enrollment process and provide succinct, step-by-step guidance to complete the task from beginning to end. This would be more feasible than creating 40 different guides for each specific provider type.

My first learner guide focused on enrolling a provider that would directly bill the government for its services. This included reviewing tax forms, business registration documents, and applicable licenses. The guide's purpose was to standardize clear document verification procedures for new and seasoned analysts, highlighting processes that applied to all provider types under the billing classification.

To demonstrate a realistic situation that resembled an analyst's experience, I referenced multiple live demonstrations of the SME's enrollment process for a common provider type. I also looked up historical enrollment information for similar providers and based my demonstration personas on those real-world examples.

After establishing foundational procedures, I introduced uncommon situations and less common provider types within the billing classification. I included reference materials to discuss different variables and unique circumstances at the end of the document. This allowed the analyst to develop background knowledge about the full process before encountering less common process steps.

Provide Guidance With Order and Term Consistency

The next decision we made was how to outline each guide. My team took a phased approach and improved the organization of our outlines as we learned more about the enrollment process.

Reaching a consensus for terms was critical to our progress. One challenge was that different sources used the same terms for different processes and different terms for the same process. With feedback from the SME and unit supervisor, we standardized terms to improve clarity.

After we set standard terms, we developed process flow charts. We based detailed outlines on these flow charts. It was critical that we standardized our organization of process names and process order. Because an analyst would eventually be responsible for enrollment of all provider types and unique circumstances, consistency of terms and continuity of practice between learner guides would limit confusion about variations in procedure. We purposefully simplified the terms to support the analysts' complex tasks.

Divide Content Into Short Sections With Useful Headings

Next, we outlined the guides using headings that defined the process steps with an active verb. We chose headings that succinctly described what tasks an analyst must accomplish and subdivided each section with headings that indicated specific steps. For example, these are the headings for one section of our learner guides:

- Analyst Review: Verifying Supporting Documentation
    - 3.1. Verifying the Bill of Sale Aligns With the Submission
    - 3.2. Verifying the W-9 Attachment Aligns With the Submission
    - 3.3. Verifying Provider License(s) Align With the Submission
    - 3.4. Verifying Other Documents Align With the Submission
    - 3.5. Verifying Signatures on the Enrollment Summary

We focused each subsection on task-specific procedures. If an analyst needed to use the learner guide as a reference, they could search for a specific task and find pertinent, focused information in the flow of their work. This structure also led use to create task-focused sections, keeping an analyst's potential uses of the guides at the forefront.

Use Active, Simple, and Necessary Words

While most of our writing choices were macrolevel decisions, plain language is also accomplished in microlevel word choices. When an analyst is processing an application and needs to make an eligibility determination, they need a guide that quickly states what to do in clear, unambiguous terms. Take for example this statement:

> The Form W-9 attachment may not be the most current, and a notation will have to be entered to document this issue.

This statement can be improved by removing redundancies and leaving only necessary words that communicate the intended message:

> The Form W-9 attachment may not be ~~the most~~ current, and a notation ~~will have to~~ must ~~be entered to~~ document this issue.

In the example, I omitted unnecessary words. "The most current" does not add any pertinent meaning. "Current" is sufficient. "Will have to" can be simplified with the word "must." Likewise, if a notation is documenting an issue, we can assume it is being entered. Indicating it "must be entered to document this issue" is not needed. We can also simplify "notation" with "note":

> The Form W-9 attachment may not be current, and a ~~notation~~ note must document this issue.

Furthermore, the statement uses passive voice. It is not clear who or what is responsible for the sentence action.

We need to align the statement with the intended communication. In this instance, we wanted to communicate how an analyst must handle an outdated Form W-9. We can achieve this by using strong verbs and focusing on what an analyst must do.

> If the Form W-9 attachment is not current, document this issue.

Compare this revised, plain language statement to the first draft. Note the difference in clarity!

We edited sentences to ensure they were written in active voice, used simple terms, and omitted redundant or unnecessary words. Clear communication reduces ambiguity and focuses on action.

Write Centralized and Connected Paragraphs

While appropriate word choice and simplified sentences are the building blocks of writing in plain language, how those sentences are grouped into paragraphs and flow from one idea to the next is equally important. Begin by opening paragraphs with a strong topic sentence. Use subsequent sentences to build on the topic by providing examples, consequences, or additional information.

In earlier drafts of the learner guide, the writing was not succinct. Sentences were long and paragraphs were not centralized. The writing skirted around the topic rather than addressing it directly.

Take for instance this first draft of a section about W-9 verification:

Verifying the Alignment of the W-9 Attachment

Some providers need to submit a Form W-9, including billing providers and group providers that bill for services provided by rendering providers. Rendering providers are not required to submit a Form W-9. Form W-9 is the shortened name for the Internal Revenue Service (IRS) Request for Taxpayer Identification Number and Certification form.

If a Form W-9 is not submitted correctly, the application may need to be returned to the provider to make changes. It is important that each field of the provider's Form W-9 submission is complete and checked for accuracy, meaning it must match what is entered in the enrollment application as well as the requirements for the enrollment type and classification.

Using the first draft example, the summary of the two paragraphs using topic sentences alone would be:

- Some providers need to submit a Form W-9, including billing providers and group providers that bill for services provided by rendering providers.
- If a Form W-9 is not submitted correctly, the application may need to be returned to the provider to make changes.

The topic sentence lays the foundation for a paragraph—the ones in this first draft hedge, or beat around the bush, instead of communicating directly. The first sentence introduces complexity that the rest of the paragraph does not address. The reader is left with questions instead of clarity. They may be wondering what a Form W-9 is; what a billing, group, or rendering provider is; and how they all differ. The second topic sentence states there is a correct way to submit the form without further explanation. The remainder of the topic sentence communicates in uncertain terms what the next step will need to be if the analyst deems the form incorrect. Do they return it to the provider or not?

This revised example from our learner guide uses concise sentences and paragraphs to express ideas that build on one another:

Verifying the W-9 Attachment Aligns With the Submission
Providers that bill for their services must submit an Internal Revenue Service (IRS) Request for Taxpayer Identification Number (TIN) and Certification form. This is called Form W-9.

This form is used to verify that the provider is enrolling under the correct legal name, TIN type, classification, and organizational structure. Successful enrollment processing depends on accurate input of the provider information on Form W-9.

Clear, strong topic sentences can summarize a passage. Using the previous example, the summary of the two paragraphs using the topic sentences alone would be:

- Providers that bill for their services must submit an Internal Revenue Service (IRS) Request for Taxpayer Identification Number (TIN) and Certification form.
- This form is used to verify that the provider is enrolling under the correct legal name, TIN type, classification, and organizational structure.

The topic of the first short paragraph is identifying what situation necessitates that a provider submits a particular form. In comparison, the first draft example said "some providers including billing providers and group providers that bill for services provided by rendering providers" needed to submit the form. While the first draft was technically accurate, it complicated the information. The revised version simplified that any provider who sends a bill for their services must submit the appropriate IRS form. The topic sentence now clearly states who must do what.

The next paragraph's topic sentence previously provided an "if, then" sentence structure without clear direction about how to know if the form was incorrect and what the next action should be. The revised topic sentence explains the purpose of the form in the enrollment process and what specific sections or fields must be verified for accuracy.

Include Screen Captures, Lists, and In-Line References

A critical element that improved the clarity of communication in the learner guides was step-by-step process lists supported by screen captures. For example, following the brief introductory sentences about verifying Form W-9, the rest of the page explained the process with numbered lists and visual references like this:

> Ensure the following information is aligned with the Form W-9 attachment (Figure 29-1):
> 1. The current Form W-9 was submitted. It should state: (Rev. October 2018).
> 2. Provider's legal name and business name aligns with the provider submission.
> 3. Organizational structure aligns with the provider submission.

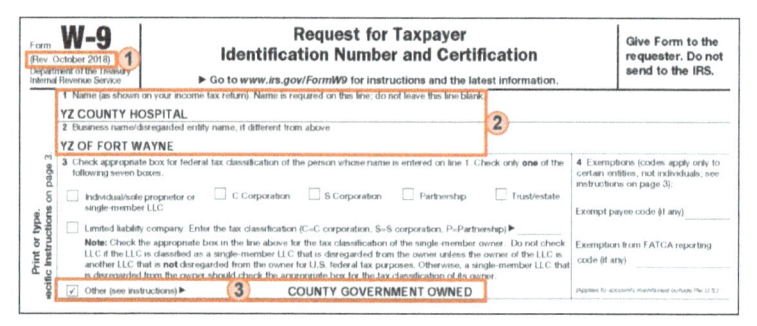

Figure 29-1. Form W-9. Verify alignment of provider name and organizational structure.

Most pages of the learner guides followed this structure. We began lists with a concise and direct lead-in sentence using active voice, and numbered each step of the process. We highlighted a screen capture with numbered markers that aligned with the listed process steps, ensuring analysts could locate specific processes and follow step-by-step directions using visual examples to support procedure standardization. This was not only important to foster between analysts, but also within each analyst's workflow processing. Numbering and demonstrating each step could help analysts complete procedures without missing an important step in any enrollment they encountered. We encouraged analysts to follow the steps and use the learner guides as references in the flow of their work.

Principles of Visual Hierarchy

In addition to the plain language guidelines, we employed visual hierarchy principles to help analysts perceive the relative importance of and relationships between headings, paragraphs, lists, and screen captures. This included using a bright orange color highlight to draw their eyes to specific information. We staggered the numbered markers on images from left to right and top to bottom, following the natural Z pattern that eyes track (which is reversed in languages that are read right to left). Where possible, we used size to create perceived hierarchy by representing big topics with larger font headings. Subsection headings were represented by increasingly smaller but readable font sizes. We also centered screen captures, which increases prominence in the perceived hierarchy of importance.

The Gestalt Principle of Similarity

Gestalt is a German word meaning "unified whole." The Gestalt principles were identified by German psychologists in the 1920s to describe the ways people process visual information as individual elements that make up a whole. They assert that the brain is more likely to consider things to be of the same group, type, or classification if they have similar features.

We leveraged the Gestalt principle of similarity to support cognitive accessibility. For example, after discussing the process steps, we displayed a fatal error message box, which explained that a mistake made within that set of steps would be considered a severe error in an audit or internal quality review.

> **Fatal error:** Processing an enrollment for the incorrect TIN type entered, either FEIN or SSN, is considered a fatal error in a quality review.

Creating a consistent icon for fatal errors created a visual cue that an error in that set of steps could be consequential. To further leverage the similarity principle, other advanced action or reference items were presented with a similar iconography and color scheme as the fatal error indicator. The following is an example of reasons an analyst would need to notate provider errors.

> **Return-to-provider:** If the TIN or TIN type is not indicated in the Form W-9 attachment, document this issue and return the application for provider corrections.

The analyst would later need to cite documentation of these errors as the reason they returned the application to the provider for corrections. Previously, they had to open a document listing fatal- and non-fatal errors. Similarly, they had to load a browser window and sign in to the system to access return-to-provider reasons. The learner guides placed pertinent enrollment process steps in one place while raising awareness of what situations would be considered an error or why to document an issue for provider correction where it would be pertinent in the analysts' workflow.

Outcome

Each of the plain language guidelines and visual principles we used seemed like small, simple improvements. Together, they helped create concise verbal and visual communication to support the understandability of complex processes.

The client's response surprised me. They thanked us for our diligence and praised the documents as easy to follow, comprehensive guides for new hires and seasoned analysts alike. The SMEs commented that they learned from the guides themselves. To this day, I am amazed that efforts to support understandability could have this kind of impact. I am now convinced of the value of clear and simple communication.

What You Can Do Right Away

When writing instruction, whether about simple or complex topics, it can be easy to equate *plain* with *boring* and *embellished* with *engaging*. But as all experienced writers know, that couldn't be further from the truth. The next time you write a learner guide, job aid, or video script, refer to the plain language guidelines and use them to keep your writing simple.

30.
Accessibility Lessons for Augmented Reality (AR)

Betty Dannewitz (she/her)
Founder, CEO, and the actual Betty of ifyouaskbetty

Over the years, accessibility in the L&D field has been a challenging topic for many practitioners. Continuously evolving accessibility requirements, a lack of understanding about the impact of accessible learning, a shortage of effective tools and resources, and failed adoption in organizations have created a steep climb for practitioners. Like so many others, I actively ignored accessibility because I did not understand what I needed to do and why—until I couldn't ignore it anymore.

I speak regularly at L&D industry conferences about augmented reality (AR), which is the technology that allows you to superimpose digital content onto the real world. I started to consistently receive the same question in my sessions: How do I make AR accessible? I had no idea.

I decided to use my podcasting platform to learn from experts and bring greater awareness about this important issue to the L&D industry. I contacted a colleague and hatched a plan to interview some people about accessibility in general, accessibility in learning, and, most importantly, what it is like to need accessible learning experiences and not get them.

Hosting these podcast episodes changed my perspective and gave me a deeper understanding of accessibility. The expert guests brought a wealth of knowledge and examples. After several hours of rich discussion, I walked away with actionable steps to apply to designing accessible AR experiences. I'd like to share my biggest takeaways from the series in the rest of this chapter.

Enhance Learning With Multiple Means of Engagement

AR provides an opportunity for an enhanced, accessible learning experience so the learner is not just reading and clicking next, but involved in the learning, often physically. This is an enhancement option that benefits many. For example, a learning experience that provides navigation directions for a building could be designed with pop-up text boxes in a linear flow. However, this design is not fully accessible to all. We could enhance the learning experience by adding an AR component that includes 360-degree images of the building with learner-led navigation to different destinations, complete with audio instructions. This dynamic enhancement provides autonomy in the learning experience, while the audio instructions present an alternative to reading many text boxes.

Add Captions to Audio and Video

Captions are easy to add in AR experiences, and they help everyone. I now add captions to all audio and video components within the AR experiences. (I don't know why I didn't before!) For example, one of the AR scavenger hunts I developed for a national conference included six AR experiences with voice-over audio narration. By adding captions for the voice-over and any videos, the experience was more accessible to those who are hard of hearing or deaf. Additionally, it enhanced the experience for everyone else, because the crowd was often so loud it was hard to hear the narration.

Eliminate Drag-and-Drop Activities

While drag and drop is not used often in AR, it can be an option for interaction. Understanding more about the physical requirements for interactions and eliminating those that may involve complex muscle movements helps to increase the accessibility of the AR experiences.

Be Mindful of Low Vision Learners

When you are in the creative mindset, it is easy to focus more on how to make the AR experience pretty and forget about making it accessible and readable for all. To help those who have low vision, you should design AR experiences using large font sizes, maximum color contrast, and additional narration of anything the learner might need to read.

What You Can Do Right Away

AR can be accessible—don't buy into the misconception that you have to sacrifice more advanced, immersive training for accessibility. Making these small adjustments has revolutionized the AR experiences I've designed and has helped me create more accessible, immersive learning for all. So, the next time you're considering whether AR might be the appropriate modality for your learning experience, make sure to factor these accessibility lessons in from the beginning.

31.
Virtual Reality
A Request for On-the-Knees Angled Training

Kristin Torrence (she/her)
Immersive Learning Engineer

Picture this: It's my first virtual reality (VR) project in my job at an extended reality (XR) company. I was the lead learning person responsible for guiding the learning design choices to create the most optimal conditions for immersive learning. It was fall 2020, the height of the COVID-19 pandemic, and remote and distributed learning was at its peak. My team partnered with a trade school that needed to provide remote and asynchronous practice opportunities to its students, because its newly adapted hybrid model limited the amount of time students had access to practice in the laboratory. VR was a perfect modality to simulate the school's lab environment. It enabled students to feel comfortable and familiar with the space and procedures before venturing on campus to practice the services in the physical lab.

We spent more than a month in the discovery phase of the project, meeting regularly with subject matter experts (SMEs) to learn about the processes involved in a series of routine heating, ventilation, and air conditioning (HVAC) services. We broke each service down into stages and steps, fully establishing both the cognitive and behavioral processes involved in the procedures. Our goal was to make this experience as realistic as possible. That's the true affordance of VR—the immersive and visceral nature of the experiences.

VR has the power to mirror authentic, real-life circumstances. We prided ourselves on the high-fidelity simulation of both environments and objects within the space, making users feel as if they were truly present in the scenery presented to them. This resonated with me because, coming from a learning sciences background, we place a high value on practice in authentic settings. In VR, practice in authentic contexts allows learners to acquire situational awareness of the task and facilitates transfer to real-life, on-the-job situations.

In the field, HVAC work is physically demanding. Much of technicians' time is spent bending, kneeling, and crouching to accomplish tasks. All the services we simulated in VR are performed kneeling in the field. So, a stakeholder had naturally assumed that the VR training would also take place kneeling. Although it hadn't initially been discussed, it seemed like a viable request—and it fell in line with the entire schema of HVAC procedures. At the very least, it was a request worth considering. If we were to make this experience as immersive and realistic as possible, kneeling was a physical aspect of the job that we couldn't ignore. How could we accomplish this in a way that was both feasible and accessible for users? It was a challenge our design team had to investigate.

The first challenge I had to wrestle with wasn't a design one, but a cognitive one. My brain felt like it was doing mental gymnastics, sifting through tidbits of learning science principles trying to figure out which ones could help me chart the way toward a design decision. Situated and embodied cognition indicated that on-the-knees training was a good idea—the physical stance of the learner while immersed and engaged in the realistic scenario would promote learning. It may also increase the experiential learning element of the entire experience. There's sound research-based support for approving an on-the-knees simulation, but my gut wasn't convinced.

Sure, in theory, it seemed like it would be okay to do an entire training on your knees because that's how it's supposed to be done in the field. Aren't we preparing learners to perform well on the job? Why wouldn't we replicate the same physical conditions they would experience in the lab or on the job? Wouldn't learning be suboptimal otherwise? How could a VR experience produce positive learning outcomes if the learner's perspective was inauthentic? What effects would this have on learners' sense of presence and immersion in the experience? All these questions raced through my mind as I attempted to ground support for on-the-knees training in literature. Meanwhile, I couldn't ignore my pragmatic side. My intuition was screaming, "There's no way this will lead to a good experience!"

My skeptical perspective likely stemmed from my personal experience spending hours in a VR headset. A one-pound headset may not seem heavy, but imagine it pressed against your forehead and cheekbones and strapped around the back of your head. The weight of it naturally tilts your head forward. Headaches, neck strain, and shoulder pain from poor posture, hunching, and rounding are common side effects of VR headset use. Knowing this firsthand, the thought of bending over to work on a simulated machine while being weighed down by a headset sounded unappealing, let alone doing so in a kneeling position.

I could theoretically argue both sides and felt conflicted. The only way to resolve this was to evolve past theory and look to empirical evidence. We had to test it out. Our small, three-person learning experience design team decided to divide and conquer. The goal was to experience virtual reality, positioned on our knees, while wearing a headset and looking downward as if we were working on an HVAC unit. We were fortunate to have a VR sandbox environment that allowed us to test this out. We tried our existing hard-skill VR modules in a kneeling position, rather than the designated seated position, and we all drew the same conclusion: The physical discomfort interfered with the experience.

Finding an appropriate spot in the home that was comfortable enough for prolonged kneeling was also a challenge. Hardwood floors were a no-go. Kneeling on carpet was an improvement, and even more so with added pillow support. Was this setup feasible for our learners? Was it too much to ask them to prepare a space with these elements for practice? Could we instead require them to use knee pads during the VR practice? What about learners who didn't have access to those supplies? The more questions we had, the less feasible on-the-knees training seemed.

Accessible supplies and physical ability are at the core of this dilemma. Even though prolonged kneeling is a requirement in the field, our learners were still in the training phase and may not yet be prepared to maintain the physicality of this stance. Deciding to go the kneeling route could potentially alienate those who were unable to meet this physical demand, preventing them from developing fundamental skills through repeated practice of the HVAC services. It seemed unfair to penalize learners for not having already developed comfort in a kneeling position. Isn't that something that would come with experience?

And that was only the knees element of the posture. We also discovered that the pressure of the headset against our facial bones and the strain on our necks at that angle was too uncomfortable to keep the headset on for even a short period. The physical discomfort was distracting and drew focused attention away from the actual experience. Sure, physical authenticity may contribute to the overall realism of the training, but at some point, pragmatism needs to come into play. All signs pointed to on-the-knees angled training as being a poor design decision.

These findings stirred a philosophical discussion about the true purpose of this VR training. We turned to the learning objectives defined at the beginning of the learning design process and used them for guidance. They centered around building proficiency and automaticity in the HVAC procedures. Therefore, the primary focus was for learners to master the steps involved in the services. This put everything else back into perspective. Physicality took a back seat to the cognitive and procedural emphasis that was required here. This gave us confidence in our ultimate decision to proceed with a seated experience.

We prioritized physical comfort to keep learners' focus on the task at hand, and not be distracted by discomfort or pain. We assumed that once the learners had mastered the steps in the comfort of a chair, they would be able to transfer this knowledge and proficiency to the field. They could then gradually acclimate to the physical demands of the job, including the kneeling posture, in their own time and at their own pace, without it being a hindrance to their learning.

We carefully designed the VR environment to mimic the actual workspace as closely as possible, and the visual and auditory cues helped learners spatially orient themselves and prepare for real-life, on-the-job scenarios. In retrospect, our initial hesitations and discussions pushed us to critically evaluate our design decisions and ensured we remained learner centric.

We've made a habit of referring to our learning objectives whenever we are unsure about a design because they help us prioritize our requirements, make decisions, and execute them. If there is a component that we are unsure about, we test it among our design team first, and then validate the design through testing with end-users and the project team.

The Pursuit of Accessibility

The largest obstacle that keeps the VR industry from releasing highly accessible experiences to the public is that, at the moment, accessibility guidelines for VR are not well established or adopted. Attempts to translate effective accessibility features from other modalities to VR have been met with certain challenges, such as the lack of universally accepted standards for alt text or object metadata. As we navigate the VR accessibility landscape, there are a few common practices among the suggested guidelines for accessibility that are worth considering.

Visual Accessibility

We must design VR experiences that can be accessed by all learners, including those with visual impairments. Learners with blurred vision, loss of peripheral vision, or light sensitivity may have difficulty reading low-contrast text or challenges identifying objects in a virtual space. Individuals with monocular vision or blind spots may have trouble navigating and perceiving events within the VR environment. Those who have color blindness may have trouble distinguishing between text and object colors.

It's no secret that VR solutions heavily rely on visual elements to facilitate experiences. Unfortunately, this coupled with the lack of compatibility with popular screen readers, makes many VR experiences nearly inaccessible for blind or low-vision learners. Mindful consideration of these factors is imperative when we are designing VR experiences.

Text and Object Size Customization

One of the most effective affordances we can provide in VR experiences is customization options, which can enable learners to tailor their experience to their specific needs and preferences. For instance, allowing learners to adjust text sizes can help improve readability, object size adjustments can increase visibility, and magnification of the screen or specific interface elements can help improve usability.

Color, Contrast, and Brightness

Appropriate levels of contrast can also make or break VR experiences. As a rule, we want to ensure that there is enough contrast between the text and the background so the text is legible and objects are visible. People with conditions such as light sensitivity may have specific needs regarding brightness and contrast levels. Allowing learners to customize those levels and edge enhancements for increased visual acuity empowers them to personalize their experience to their needs. You can provide similar options to support those with color blindness. Consider enabling learners to customize the colors they use throughout the experience or change foreground and background colors for better visual distinction. If fully customizable contrast and color features are not an option, consider providing an array of color filters to select from that vary in luminosity and color contrast levels, or including shapes or symbols alongside colors to convey meaning.

Auditory Support

Audio elements can also be added to support those with visual impairments. For example, audible menu systems can recite menu elements aloud or offer verbal descriptions of interactions, objects, and locations when prompted to assist blind or low-vision learners.

Auditory Accessibility

Audio in VR is used to communicate a wide range of elements such as instructions, location in space, interaction and feedback, ambiance, and more. As you can imagine, it would be difficult for individuals who are deaf or hard of hearing to have a high-quality experience if the VR solution relies too heavily on auditory cues. Thankfully, there are many adjustments and alternatives to auditory stimuli that we can implement in VR to create more accessible and inclusive experiences.

Stereoscopic and Monophonic Sound

As with the vision accessibility features, we should provide those who are deaf or hard of hearing with the power to control and customize auditory elements to suit their needs. One common accessibility feature is a stereo or mono audio toggle. *Stereoscopic sound*, sometimes referred to as spatialized audio, replicates a 3D soundscape, which is particularly helpful for learners with hearing difficulties because it can enhance spatial perception. The ability to control the location of spatialized audio can support learners who have hearing impairments in one ear. *Monophonic sound* means audio emanates from a single position. For learners with hearing impairments in one ear, a mono audio option can be effective for delivering equal-quality sound to both ear inputs.

Sound Controls

Auditory accessibility can also include providing volume controls for better audio comprehension. If your VR experience includes sound or music design, accessibility features can include the power to disable ambient soundscapes or minimize background noise during speech audio to enhance clarity.

Visual Support

Providing text descriptions of essential audio content can go a long way in supporting an accessible and inclusive experience in VR. Providing captions for dialogue recited in the VR experience allows learners who are deaf or hard of hearing to read what is being said. Customizable caption affordances can be further enhanced by adding subtitle options to support speakers of different languages and specifications regarding words-per-minute rates for target age or language learning groups. In addition, offering visual cues to indicate direction and the person speaking can facilitate attention and comprehension.

Physical Accessibility

Although you can certainly experience VR without interacting with the environment, most VR applications (especially those focused on knowledge and skills acquisition) will almost always require learners to act in the virtual space. Interactions can be quite challenging for those with mobility impairments, and a lack of available accessibility features can lead to suboptimal VR experiences. How can you ensure that your VR design is inclusive of those who may be experiencing mobility limitations?

While activities in the VR world can be perceived from a certain position and vantage point, that doesn't necessarily mean that a learner's physical body needs to replicate that same stance, nor does the position of the learner's body in the VR environment need to match the same position it's meant to be carried out in the physical world. Case in point, the HVAC training example from earlier in this chapter occurs in a seated position, while the on-the-job position is kneeling. To accommodate various mobility needs, you should allow several options such as seated, reclining, or stationary positions for enhanced inclusivity.

Controller Supports

VR interactions generally depend on the learner's fine motor abilities. Historically, using controllers has been a popular way to allow learners to move around in the VR space and interact with objects or people. Those with hand mobility impairments may struggle with using controllers due to the precise aim required to click targets. Learners with limited arm motor ability or fine motor ability may need larger target sizes for buttons and controls for ease of interaction. Adding elements—such as a focus indicator that visibly identifies the object of focus by the controller or an aim assistance visual that is easy to visually track on the screen where the controller is pointing—can help facilitate target interactions or sections by the learner (Figure 31-1).

Figure 31-1. Focus indicator-assisted interactions.

In this gaze assistance example, the learner's sightline is indicated by the target symbol—a white circle outline with a solid white dot at the center. When the learner gazes over a specific dialogue option's eye icon (which is located in the upper left corner), it expands to a select option button. The learner can then gaze over the select option button for a set duration of time to indicate that they want to select that dialogue option. The duration time is visually depicted by a progressive change of button color from left to right, transforming from gray to yellow along a vertical plane. When the button is completely yellow, the select option button is triggered.

Figure 31-2 shows another example of gaze and controller aim assistance. The eye icon pinpoints the text in the first bullet point that the learner is focused on, while the lasers emanating from the controllers highlight where the leaner is aiming.

Customizable elements for controllers—such as sensitivity adjustments, haptic feedback control, or signifying clear mechanisms to start and stop interactions—can help with usability. Avoid requiring multiple simultaneous actions, gestures, specific bodily movements, or button holds, as these behaviors can be extremely difficult for those with mobility limitations.

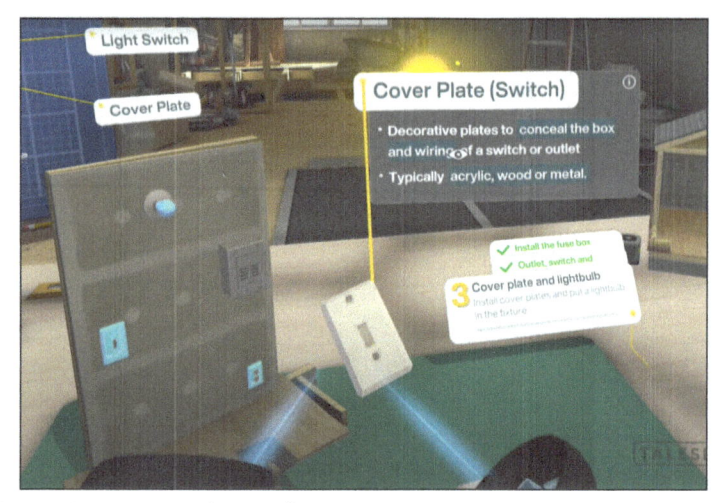

Figure 31-2. Gaze and controller aim assistance.

Alternative Controlling Options

Because controls are such an essential part of the VR experience, it's ideal if the VR application allows for multiple input devices, which can enhance interaction for those with mobility limitations. Alternatively, allowing learners to remap or reconfigure controls to buttons more suitable for their needs can support accessibility. There are also noncontroller options that can support accessibility, such as hand tracking for controller-free interaction and voice controls for navigation or selection.

It's important to also consider modifying aspects of the experience for those with mobility impairments. For instance, you can allow more time for individual interactions and overall task completion. You can also choose to automate certain actions to minimize the number of physical actions learners are required to perform.

The example in Figure 31-3 illustrates both hand tracking and automated actions. Learners can use their hands to push augmented buttons to select the specific action they want to execute. This learner is selecting the button that indicates they would like to repair the maintenance issue. They would not need to carry out the entire repair procedure; it will be fully automated for them.

Figure 31-3. Hand tracking and automated options.

The HVAC experience was semiautomated and semimanual. We opted to have hose fittings and knobs automatically animate to the end state of open or closed with a single rotation in the desired direction, when in real life, more than one rotation would be required (Figure 31-4). Learners were able to fill in the blanks between Point A of the initial twist to Point B without having to go through the tedious task of repeating the same rotating action more than five times to achieve the end open or closed state.

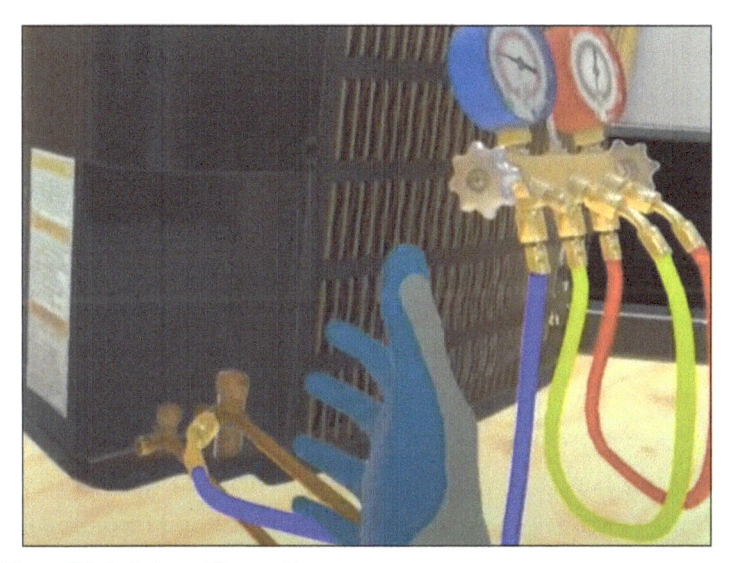

Figure 31-4. Automating motions.

User Testing Accessibility Features

As with any design decisions you make when creating your VR learning experience, you should validate the accessibility features you include. User testing was an essential and formative step in the process of creating the HVAC training, and we wouldn't have known that a seated position was the best option if we hadn't tried it ourselves. Additionally, we received user feedback from target user and project team testers during the development process that reinforced this decision. User testing is critical for ensuring that VR experiences are accessible and inclusive for all learners. Employing user testing will help you identify usability challenges, gather feedback, and refine your accessibility features.

Planning

When planning your user-testing initiative, the most important thing you can do is include individuals with disabilities among your participants. You'll want a diverse representation of folks with various disabilities, including visual, auditory, and mobility impairments. If possible, ensure you include individuals with different disabilities in representative numbers based on the target audience demographic. It will also be helpful to have a mix of participants with a range of familiarity with both VR technology and accessibility features. These folks will be able to provide valuable insight into how well your accessibility features are meeting their specific needs.

You can also engage a subset of these folks during the design phase before user testing begins. *Participatory design* involves target learners actively helping shape the direction of the design during the design and development process. Recruiting a focus group comprised of individuals who have disabilities to collaborate closely throughout the design, testing, and iteration of the VR experience leads to a more learner-focused design. In addition to representative groups, it's advantageous to include accessibility experts as user-testing participants. These key testers can provide expert insights about potential accessibility issues and recommendations for enhancing accessibility features.

During the planning phase, identify the accessibility features you want to test. The easiest way to determine what to investigate is to define the assumptions you made during the design of your VR learning experience. Design at its core is rooted in assumptions about what elements we think will lead to the most optimal experience. Reflect on the decisions that led to the accessibility features in your VR solution and what support you expect those features to serve for your target audience. Defining these research questions from the very beginning will help you be more intentional during your investigation. Use them to formulate a testing plan that outlines tasks user-testing participants will execute.

User Testing Design

Design tasks allow you to observe the ways that you expect users to navigate, interact with, and adjust settings or use features. That way, you can evaluate where their behavior matched the intended behavior and where it didn't. You should design these tasks to test the effectiveness and usability of accessibility features and gather insights into potential challenges. Refrain from making them artificial, serving only the purpose of testing. The tasks should be authentic to the environment and context of the VR learning experience to better identify how well the features support the learners' actual needs.

In some cases, it may be helpful to educate participants on how to use assistive features or shed light on specific features that are the focus of testing. However, it may be even more valuable to refrain from sharing this information until you receive some indication that explicit instructions or direction toward specific features would be useful to guide the experience.

Data Collection

There are many ways you can collect data from user testers about their experience with your VR program. Real-time observation and recording the user testing are good methods to collect rich data about how users navigated the experience, the features they used, and their interactions and behaviors. Observers can note the ease, challenges, misconceptions, points of confusion, and feedback provided during the testing session.

An effective strategy to employ to collect this data is a think-aloud protocol, which means encouraging user testers to vocalize their thoughts, actions, and reactions as they experience your VR solution. This exercise helps shed light on users' decision-making processes and identify potential areas of confusion. Think-aloud exercises typically end in a debrief for the observer and the user to discuss their experience, thoughts, feelings, and opinions. This is an excellent opportunity to home in on the perceived usability and effectiveness of the accessibility features and collect feedback and suggestions for improvement.

A less resource-intensive option for collecting data from user testers involves administering questionnaires or surveys to gather structured feedback from participants. You'll want to be very specific when formulating questions about accessibility features. Identify the accessibility features you want to validate and define the expected experience or benefit it would provide to individuals. Then, construct questions that seek to reveal whether the design worked as intended. It can be helpful to include images and descriptions so users know exactly which feature the survey item is referring to, and consider using a combination of Likert-type questions and open-ended questions to facilitate rich data collection.

There are several scales researchers use that you can use or adapt for your questionnaires. The system usability scale (SUS) is a 10 item, five-point Likert-type scale ranging from strongly disagree (1) to strongly agree (5).[92]

Some example statements for ranking include:
- I think that I would like to use this system frequently.
- I found the system unnecessarily complex.
- I thought the system was easy to use.
- I think that I would need a technical person's support to be able to use this system.
- I thought the various functions in this system were integrated well.
- I thought there was too much inconsistency in this system.
- I think that most people could learn to use this system very quickly.
- I found the system very cumbersome to use.

- I felt very confident using the system.
- I needed to learn a lot of things before I could get going with this system.

I like the usability questionnaire items that Guido Makransky and Lau Lilleholt used in their 2018 research article investigating immersive VR in education, but I adapt the language for adult end users.[93] Perceived usefulness items aim to measure the degree to which end users believe that using the platform will enhance their performance; the perceived usability question items measure the degree to which they believe that using the platform is easy or difficult. These items are measured on a five-point Likert-type scale ranging from strongly disagree (1) to strongly agree (5).

Some example statements for ranking include:

- **Perceived usefulness:**
    - Using this type of VR or computer simulation as a tool for learning will increase my learning and academic performance.
    - Using this type of VR or computer simulation will enhance the effectiveness of my learning.
    - This type of VR or computer simulation will allow me to progress at my own pace.
    - This type of VR or computer simulation supports my learning.
- **Perceived case of use:**
    - Learning to operate this type of VR or computer program is easy for me.
    - Learning how to use this type of VR or computer program is too complicated and difficult for me. (This question is reverse coded.)
    - It is easy for me to find information with the VR or computer program.
    - Overall, I think this type of VR or computer program is easy to use.

Iterative Accessibility Design

User testing accessibility features should be a continuous effort throughout the entirety of the development phase, and arguably, user data collected after deployment should inform future versions of the VR experience. While in the design and development phases, you should plan for multiple rounds of user testing with different participants. After collecting user-testing data, you should analyze it to identify consistent patterns, recurring issues, pain points, and successes related to the accessibility features. Be sure to document your findings, insights, and implications on the design of the accessibility features and disseminate these to your design and development team. Use feedback from previous rounds to inform iterative improvements to the accessibility features in your VR experience.

User testing is an essential element of VR experience design and is crucial for gaining valuable insights into the effectiveness of the VR accessibility features you employ in your experience. By observing and analyzing user testers who have diverse accessibility needs, you can further improve your accessibility features and create a more inclusive and universally usable and enjoyable VR experience.

Documenting your usability research can guide you in creating broader accessibility guidelines for your VR learning experiences, creating design tenets for both your design and development teams. By understanding the accessibility design practices that work well and scaling, while simultaneously iterating on the areas that need improvement, you'll be able to contribute to the ongoing work toward establishing industry-wide best practices.

What You Can Do Right Away

Virtual reality can be an effective and immersive learning experience. But you don't want to design and develop such an experience only to discover that some of your intended learners can't use it. If you are considering implementing VR-based training, think through the visual, auditory, and physical accessibility functionality needed to help ensure you're designing for all.

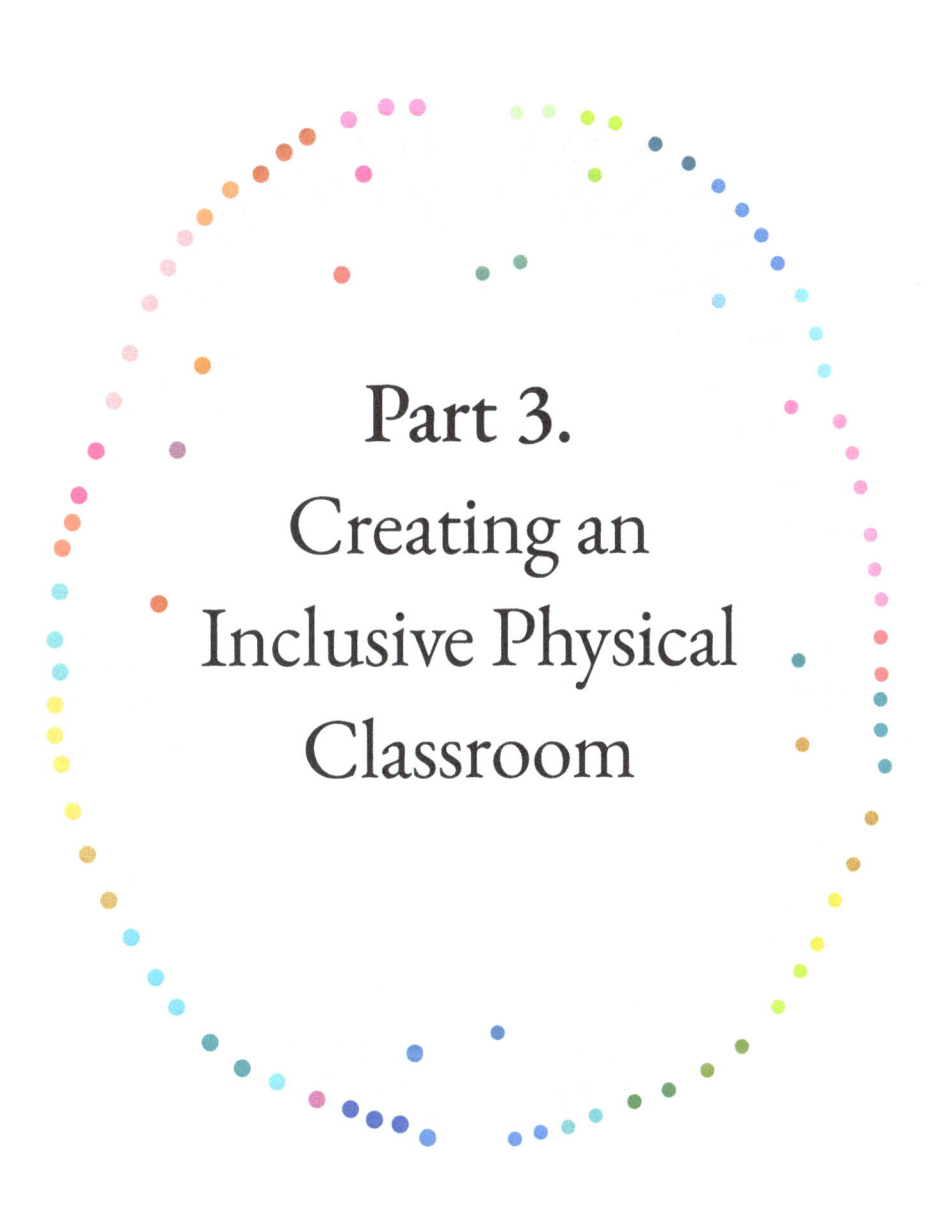

Part 3.
Creating an Inclusive Physical Classroom

32.
New to Mastery
How Applying UDL Crafted the Path to CNC Machining Careers

Cara North (she/her)
Chief Learning Consultant, The Learning Camel

The year 2021 presented peculiar and challenging circumstances. As the world grappled with the lingering effects of the COVID-19 pandemic, industries faced unprecedented disruptions, particularly in the supply chain. In the silicon manufacturing sector, where I served as a learning leader, the stakes were exceptionally high. My organization, pivotal in addressing the global semiconductor shortage, experienced rapid growth. This meant that the operations training team needed to onboard a new cohort of employees every week, despite logistical challenges.

We quickly adapted our training environment to new health protocols, converting a former research and development wing into a dedicated training space. We ensured trainees could attend in-person while adhering to strict safety measures, including wearing personal protective equipment and maintaining social distancing. The urgency to scale up production capacity amplified the pressure on every decision, from curriculum design to the pace of onboarding.

Amid the hustle of integrating new employees, leadership highlighted a critical bottleneck: While many candidates were interested in joining our team, they lacked the specific computer numerical control (CNC) machining expertise needed to immediately meet our production quotas. This skills gap threatened to exacerbate the semiconductor shortage, posing a severe risk to global supply chains. The daunting question posed to me was whether we could train individuals with no formal CNC machining background quickly enough to meet our urgent production demands.

We had to rethink traditional onboarding and training methods. We needed more than just a new curriculum or a revised training schedule; we needed a paradigm shift in how we approached skill development and workforce integration. The gravity of the situation demanded an immediate and effective solution—each day without adequate staffing worsened the global semiconductor shortage, affecting industries and consumers worldwide.

Many learning professionals who study various learning theories and models note that theory and research often get left behind in practice. The urgent and critical nature of our situation required a nimble and immediately implementable solution.

As I brainstormed, I drew on my formal education in learning design. My thoughts focused on leveraging academic insights to address our real-world crisis. If we removed the requirement of prior work experience in manufacturing and CNC machining as a job qualification, we could consider a broader range of candidates.

At the time, our plant's employees were predominantly white men. I saw this as an opportunity to create pathways to manufacturing careers for individuals who had never considered it. Traditional barriers to entry in manufacturing jobs needed reevaluation, not just to broaden our talent pool but to provide a career lifeline or change to someone in need. Hiring technically inexperienced workers required designing an inclusive onboarding process that factored in accessibility and inclusion questions previously unaddressed.

In a one-on-one meeting with my leadership, I received a verbal budget, a three-month deadline, two additional technical trainers, and a "good luck." The most challenging part of this task was that we had no machines to train on, because every machine in our plant ran 24 hours a day, 365 days a year. I started to second-guess how I would pull this off. Failure was not an option.

Designing CNC Machining Training for All

Most of the training operations team, me included, had no CNC machining expertise. Our one expert was tied up with enterprise resource planning (ERP) software training. We discussed the situation with other departments and decided to seek a partnership with a local community college to test a CNC machining class. The machinist team at Sinclair Community College in Dayton, Ohio, created a CNC overview that would give all our new hires a consistent foundation. One day down, but what next?

I committed to ensuring that whatever this program became, it could work for everyone. The Universal Design for Learning (UDL) framework aims to improve and optimize teaching and learning for all people based on scientific insights into how humans learn. As you may recall from chapter 12, UDL is built on three primary brain networks that are critical for understanding and addressing the diverse needs of learners: the affective, recognition, and strategic networks (Figure 32-1). Each network plays a crucial role in the learning process, and incorporating them into curriculum design can create more inclusive and effective learning environments.

Affective Networks	Recognition Networks	Strategic Networks
The *why* of learning	The *what* of learning	The *how* of learning
How learners get engaged and stay motivated	How learners gather facts and categorize what they see, hear, and read	How learners organize and express ideas

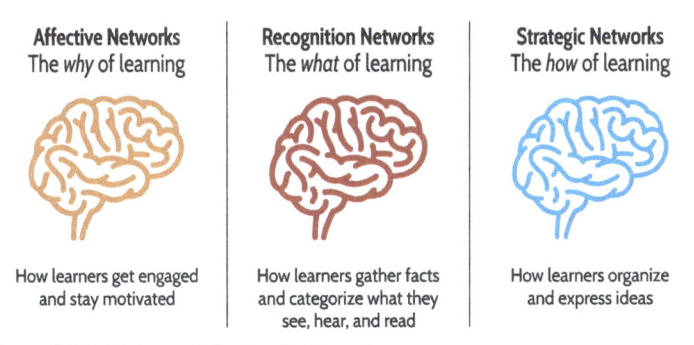

Figure 32-1. Universal design for learning.

Affective Networks: The Why of Learning

Affective networks are involved in the emotional aspects of learning. They help regulate engagement, motivation, and the overall willingness to learn. Understanding and leveraging these networks is crucial for creating an environment in which learners are motivated and eager to participate. These networks answer the question, "Why am I learning this?" The principle focuses on multiple means of *engagement*.

Because most of our candidates would have the same exposure to the primer put on by our educational partners at Sinclair Community College, it would be critical to design learning activities that had real-world scenarios and practical applications so the connection between activity and job relatedness was clear. This would help increase engagement and keep the participants focused on the tasks.

Recognition Networks: The What of Learning

Recognition networks are responsible for identifying and interpreting information, patterns, and concepts. These networks are essential for understanding what is being learned. They deal with how learners gather facts and categorize what they see, hear, and read. They answer the question, "What am I learning?" This principle focuses on providing multiple means of *representation*.

When starting to think about the variety of tasks and content needed to support a CNC machinist bootcamp, I envisioned an assessment strategy that blended formative and summative assessments as activity trackers. This gave participants and their leaders a snapshot of how they performed on various activities and tasks. It also allowed leadership to provide extra guidance in areas that were targeted for improvement.

Strategic Networks: The How of Learning

Strategic networks are involved in planning, executing, and monitoring actions and skills. They answer the question, "How am I learning?" This principle focuses on providing multiple means of action and expression. Given the complexities of the tasks in CNC machining, it was important to have multiple means of *action* and *expression* for the participants. We needed to plan for hands-on demonstrations, multiple examples, and opportunities for participants to demonstrate tasks necessary to be a CNC machinist by giving them multiple ways to do so.

By applying these UDL principles, I knew I'd be able to design a curriculum that was inclusive and effective for all learners. UDL gave me a canvas

I could build on to plan the curriculum and physical space accordingly. By understanding and leveraging the affective, recognition, and strategic networks of the brain, my team set out to design a learning experience that would keep our trainees engaged, ensure they understood what they were learning, and give them multiple ways to demonstrate their skills as they started their new career as CNC machinists.

Designing the Curriculum

Before I could start planning the physical space, I had to get alignment on the curriculum. I conducted interviews to add two seasoned CNC machinists to our operations training team as technical trainers. Once they joined, we immediately got to work. It became clear that CNC machining is complex and different in multiple settings. One of the trainers (who had previously worked with us and also had experience in glass manufacturing), stressed the nuances of CNC machining silicone in our setting. This was a key distinction that led us to circle back to our training partners at Sinclair Community College to ensure the CNC machining curriculum focused on these concerns.

It also became clear to me that I dove into the development process too quickly without focusing on what someone needs to do to be successful. With the new technical trainers and our HR partners, we did a high-level job and task analysis to determine what folks hired under this program were titled and responsible for. We came up with "CNC Machinist Level I" and identified five critical duties they would be expected to perform in our manufacturing plant. With that, we conducted interviews with folks across the plant asking what mistakes they'd observed people new to performing these tasks make or what they wished they'd known when they got started. These anecdotes became a treasure trove for building practice scenarios and brainstorming activities.

To build the curriculum, I worked with our new technical trainers to talk through the information we had collected. I started with a blank curriculum map listing each day—the full CNC bootcamp was five days long. We then determined the order of the tasks we'd want the participants to go through. Using UDL to classify and consider matching content to modalities, we worked together to brainstorm how to fulfill the needs of the curriculum along with the assessment strategy. Table 32-1 breaks down examples in each domain, along with the accompanying guidelines for access, building, and internalizing.

Some of the decisions overlapped in multiple domains, especially the assessment strategy. Every task would have formative and summative assessments that were captured in a training record. There were multiple ways trainees could scale, and depending on their performance, the trainers had less or more rigorous options. An example of a task this applied to was measuring the product. To start, they would be given basic information about appropriate instruments and scales. After gaining a basic understanding, participants would then be able to practice measuring material. Their work was then checked by trainers, and when necessary, they were debriefed. This activity could be repeated as much as needed for participants to measure and record the measures accurately. After completing the bootcamp, this record was handed over to their leadership when they joined production.

Table 32-1. UDL Alignment in Curriculum Design

	Access Networks (Provide multiple means of engagement)	Recognition Networks (Provide multiple means of representation)	Strategic Networks (Provide multiple means of action and expression)
Access	**Recruiting Interest** The mornings were structured with curriculum, but afternoon labs gave participants the opportunity to choose what tasks to practice.	**Perception** The team created multiple artifacts for the bootcamp, including physical activities, simulations, and workbooks. There were many ways for participants to receive the information.	**Physical Action** All our activities had multiple modalities in case someone requested an accommodation. We also proactively provided extra PPE and stools if necessary for participants' comfort while practicing different tasks.

Table 32-1. (Cont.)

	Access Networks (Provide multiple means of engagement)	Recognition Networks (Provide multiple means of representation)	Strategic Networks (Provide multiple means of action and expression)
Build	**Sustaining Efforts** The task analysis allowed us to create filtered, tailored experiences and curriculum that focused on the content needed to fulfill the role and be successful in production.	**Language and Symbols** The organization had its own shop talk, specifically around mathematics and measurement. So, we made sure to use the appropriate names, and did an activity with the shop talk slang once participants were familiar with it.	**Expression and Communication** We set the expectation that we wanted participants to move through the program at their own pace.
Internalize	**Self-Regulation** Many activities let participants work at their own pace. We had lab time every afternoon. If someone needed more time to practice an activity, they could. If someone mastered it quickly, trainers could give them a more rigorous challenge to continue to develop the skill.	**Comprehension** During lab time, we'd provide guidance cards to walk participants through critical work instructions if they were stuck or needed help.	**Executive Functions** The training record of all activities gave participants an indicator of their progress and showed them areas of growth and opportunity. Trainers could go over this task dashboard with participants individually, and it kept ratings and scores transparent.

Adapted from CAST.[94]

Designing the Physical Classroom

With a solid foundation, we moved forward in planning the curriculum and our training space. Knowing we couldn't access the machines for trainees to practice on, we focused on planning the curriculum and activities. I asked, "What does a successful trainee look like?" We agreed that it meant an individual could complete tasks independently and accurately by the end of the week. To achieve this, we designated each afternoon as lab time for participants to practice tasks, such as material measurement, handling, and operational procedures. This approach was crucial for determining the content and setting strong criteria for our curriculum development.

We used the employee gym for the CNC machinist bootcamp training space because it was closed due to the COVID-19 pandemic. It was critical from a planning perspective that the space be multipurpose, and we aimed to make the training as hands-on as possible while allowing time for individual and group activities. We also needed to have enough space for people to navigate the room without hitting tables or stations, because some had heavy parts on them. Working with a facilities planner, we created a computer lab in the middle of the room with plenty of space to move between desks.

Because we had no machines for the machinists to practice on, we built activities that would prepare them for their roles. For example, one critical task in production is loading a part on a rotary wheel and selecting the appropriate program for the machine to run. Our quality department informed us that parts often get damaged when being put on or removed from the wheel. We worked with multiple partners across the business, including maintenance and engineering, to build a rotary simulator. It used the screen of a training machine, had air lines hooked up so trainees could practice using pedals, and a rotary wheel to put parts on and take them off. This rotary station required mastery before trainees could move into production. If someone demonstrated mastery quickly, they could focus on other areas. If someone required extra assistance, they could practice as many times as needed.

Each station in the training room had multiple guides and challenges. For example, at the tool dressing station, activities included identifying and sorting each tool part by name, building and tearing down a tool, dressing a tool, and selecting the appropriate tool for the operation. I also tested the curriculum and instruction, eventually building and tearing down a tool without any help. We had five different stations throughout the room to practice critical tasks, and trainees needed to master these tasks by the end of the week before they could move into production.

For elements we couldn't physically build, we relied on simulations. Using 3D models, motion paths, and many layers, the training team built e-learning simulations for larger machines. By simulating the operational aspects of the machinery, we offered trainees an interactive way to familiarize themselves with the equipment's functions and processes. This method allowed for a variety of learning interactions, from visualizing the machine's components in three dimensions to executing sequences of operations that mirrored real-life tasks—all within a safe, controlled virtual environment. This involved keying in numbers, knowing what to open or close on a machine, and following the critical steps in the correct order to uphold safety standards. Assuming everyone had no prior knowledge, we built in various help steps and layers. For example, if someone didn't know what an indicator needle was, the e-learning simulation explained its purpose. This method facilitated a deeper understanding of the machinery's functions and underscored the importance of safety and precision in their operations.

Upskilling for All

Given the resource investment in the project, I knew our work needed to reach beyond just our new CNC machinists. The training team created about 30 new digital assets for the CNC machinist bootcamp, including e-learning modules, videos, and other activities. These assets, in addition to the simulations that we'd already built for some of our other efforts, could then be used for coaching, practice, and upskilling opportunities. Collaborating with IT and our communications team, we secured digital real estate on the company intranet homepage and announced that our content was available to everyone. Many employees explored what we created; some used it to upskill in areas they didn't frequently engage with, and leaders used it for practice and coaching opportunities with their teams. This also boosted company-wide confidence that individuals completing the CNC machining bootcamp would be ready to contribute to production more quickly, reducing the need for further training. Additionally, employees asked to practice in our training space when the CNC machinist bootcamp class wasn't in session, and opening our space for practice activities and upskilling strengthened partnerships across the company.

Transforming the challenges of 2021 into an opportunity to redefine corporate training with UDL principles has been one of the most rewarding projects in my learning career. Navigating the pressures of the global semiconductor shortage and the urgent need to rapidly onboard new talent, I relied on the UDL principles as my guiding stars. They led me to conceptualize and implement a CNC machinist bootcamp that not only addressed our immediate staffing needs but also innovated how we thought about and delivered training in the organization. This scenario required more than just a traditional approach to training; it demanded a shift toward a more inclusive, adaptive, and comprehensive learning strategy.

Implementing the CNC machinist bootcamp demonstrated the power of inclusive education and training in the corporate world. Designing training programs that are genuinely accessible and engaging for everyone allows us to meet immediate organizational needs while building a more diverse, skilled, and resilient workforce. I hope this experience serves as a call to action to view every training challenge as an opportunity to innovate and embrace UDL principles as tools for creating more inclusive, effective, and meaningful training solutions. By doing so, we can address the specific needs of our organizations and foster a learning environment that empowers every individual to achieve their full potential. This experience has reaffirmed my belief in the transformative potential of training designed with intention, inclusivity, and innovation at its heart.

What You Can Do Right Away

Amid the constant demands of the corporate world, trainers, instructional designers, and anyone else responsible for learning solutions can face pressure to cut corners or make assumptions about the intended audience and end up delivering experiences that might not meet accessibility standards. However, my example shows that it's possible to maintain learning principles under such pressure. Reflect on a time you might've been put in a similar position (or perhaps you're in it right now). How can you use the UDL principles and guidelines to ensure everyone benefits from your learning experience?

33.
Inclusive Design Considerations for Physical Learning Environments

Suzanne Ehrlich, EdD (she/her)
Associate Professor and Program Director, University of North Florida

Michelle Bartlett, PhD (she/her)
Assistant Professor, Old Dominion University

Morgan was excited about her trip to an annual professional development conference, especially after she noticed that the organizer advertised giving exceptional attention to providing an inclusive experience to attendees. Morgan, who uses a wheelchair, has often been met with many barriers during her travels to past conferences. However, she decided to commit to the trip based on the promise of an accessible conference experience. There, she'd meet up with her remote team, Charlie (who is a person with autism) and Ahmed (who has AMD, or age-related macular degeneration). They were excited to connect in person after much time working remotely together.

After arriving at the conference venue, however, Morgan and her team encountered obstacle after obstacle. When they entered the venue, they were immediately met with several environmental stimuli, including loud music and construction noise. Once they found the correct doors for the check-in room, they faced a broken wheelchair access push button that wouldn't open the door. The registration room itself was a windowless auditorium filled with fluorescent lighting.

When they had originally registered for the conference, they were able to request accessibility accommodations. Ahmed requested access to audio descriptions during the conference. Unfortunately, the event was supported and operated by volunteers who didn't have the knowledge of or access to the types of technology needed or being used. During check-in, Ahmed reminded the event organizers of the request. They referred him to the lead audiovisual (AV) engineer, who was not aware of the request and needed to collect the details. Despite various attempts to locate the organizers, Ahmed had to start the conference sitting next to a colleague who could relay the description of the keynote presentation and environment. Even though Ahmed also requested presentation materials prior to the event, the keynote speaker declined to make their materials shareable or accessible because they viewed the materials as their intellectual property.

In addition to lacking any clear point of contact for inquiring about accessibility needs, the venue space proved to be challenging for the team. This in turn added to their frustration, which grew as they had anticipated the event being inclusive. As the conference progressed and a great deal of time and energy was spent discussing needs with the event staff, Morgan's team eventually found themselves in a room that was designed for flexibility and inclusivity. The space was part of an experimental design project that promoted open space, windows that could be covered when too much lighting would affect occupants, adjustable and varied seating (including fidget-friendly chairs), and dedicated workspaces with USB chargers, power outlets, and an electric wheelchair charging station. The team was also able to locate a quiet room that would provide a much-needed sensory-friendly environment after a full day of social interaction.

This story about Morgan and her team's experience with lack of access and exclusion is all too common in the world today, whether it's at a conference venue, in the workplace, or in the learning environment. And yet, many of the barriers Morgan faced can be planned or designed around by adopting the right mindset and applying universal design for learning (UDL) principles.

Reducing Barriers With a UDL Mindset

The UDL framework promotes designing for all learners by reducing barriers through multiple means of engagement, representation, and action and expression regardless of learners' strengths, needs, or variability.[95] UDL is an approach that not only examines how training experiences are designed, but also how barriers within learning ecosystems, alongside the structures within organizations, are considered in designing for all learners. It provides a lens for thinking about such barriers and identifies several ways in which these changes can be identified earlier in the design or delivery process to reduce barriers for all learners.

Part of implementing UDL principles into your learning experiences is considering how you might shift your mindset within cultures of learning. How can you develop awareness for reducing barriers? How can you proactively embed accessibility as a core value from the start? How can you engage others in the development and design for learning to include all voices?

As you consider the complexities of designing for physical learning environments, the best approach is an iterative one. Shifting your thinking away from waiting and evaluating, you can begin to approach your design for learners as one of continuous improvement. This iterative process can take place at any point, whether it is just a single event or ongoing training and development at an organization.

As you may have noticed in Morgan's experience with her team, a series of events occurred at the conference that highlighted opportunities to design inclusive experiences for all in the physical environment. And while not all of what Morgan encountered is within L&D's control to fix, by embracing a UDL mindset and applying its principles and guidelines, you can work toward reducing the barriers to accessibility and inclusion.

Weaving Physical, Cultural, and Cognitive Lenses Into UDL

When building inclusive physical learning environments, you can apply UDL through the Patterns Beyond Labels model, which has three primary lenses (Figure 33-1):

- **Physical**—where learning takes place (such as spaces that invite)
- **Cultural**—who is learning (such as learning variability)
- **Cognitive**—how we think with and about learning (such as acquiring a new skill)[96]

As discussed throughout this book, barriers are not just things that prevent us from acting but can be windows into a new opportunity to change or advance our practice. By identifying barriers in all their forms, we can better engage in discussions, actions, and solutions to reduce them.

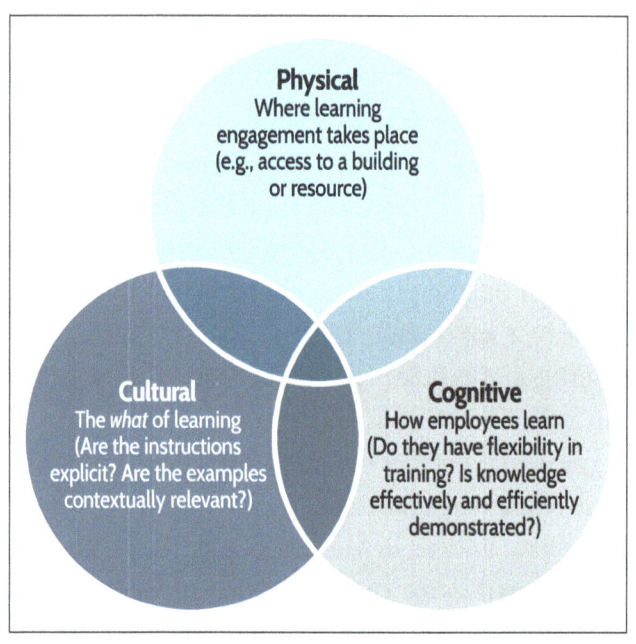

Figure 33-1. The three lenses of the Patterns Beyond Labels model. *Source: Image adapted from University of Cambridge Local Examinations Syndicate (UCLES).*[97]

By considering the three UDL principles (representation, engagement, and action and expression) with the three Patterns Beyond Labels lenses (physical, cultural, and cognitive), you can better examine physical environments for learning. Both help to move a collective conversation forward by shifting from an individual-focused lens to one that accounts for variability among learners—in how they interact with content, how they engage with the information and others, and how they show what they know. Let's now consider how these two frameworks can intersect.

UDL and the Cultural Lens

Engagement in learning spaces has undergone a cultural transformation in many ways since the COVID-19 pandemic. During the initial shift to remote work, some professionals may have adapted their home workspace to meet their needs by personalizing their desk and chair, designating a quiet space for reflection, and purchasing office equipment designed to meet their preference or needs. In addition, the presence of everyday life, including their plants and pets, made being at home both unique and personal. With the return to work in physical locations and traditional offices, employees have expected and often pushed for their organizations to create inclusive spaces to promote connection during in-person events and experiences and better reflect their remote work experiences. Returning to a collective space that was designed for an imaginary "average" is not desirable for most professionals.

By creating a welcoming and adaptable space for many, workplaces hold the key to engaging professionals in a way that shifts organizational culture. Take a moment to reflect on how you've experienced physical spaces in your organization—whether at an event or in ongoing training. Has your organization identified strategies for embracing culture and inclusive design during in-person events? Do you have methods for getting to know attendees before they arrive at an event? Is there a strategy for assessing learners' needs in a way that doesn't disclose their disability but provides an opportunity to design for a broader audience when possible? In what ways have you or your organization personalized learning spaces so attendees are welcomed into the space?

As you reflect on these questions, consider the following:
- **Language access.** Are you using interpreters and plain language in documents? Can participants access copies of all slides and documents used in the learning experience? This not only supports attendees, but other professionals such as interpreters who use the information to prepare for the event.

- **Religious needs.** Are you offering prayer spaces and flexible time expectations? Have you dedicated space for quiet needs and told attendees where to find those spaces?
- **Land acknowledgement.** Are you recognizing indigenous land? Use reputable resources to identify land occupied and share that acknowledgment verbally at the start of your class or event.[98]
- **Collective approach to learning.** Are you providing social-emotional and group-based activities? Have you evaluated the configuration of furniture in the room and how it promotes or hinders collective learning?

Take it one step further and reflect on where applying a UDL mindset through a cultural lens could positively affect in-person experiences at your organization. When your training events are planned, what mechanisms do you have in place to build culture into the experience? Do you know what your learners need? What are their values and experiences?

Consider how you can weave the cultural lens through the UDL principles of representation, engagement, and action and expression by answering these thought-provoking questions:

- **For representation and culture.** How is diversity represented in your learning content?
- **For engagement and culture.** Have you explored how taking turns may be experienced (or valued differently) by learners based on their culture?
- **For action and expression and culture.** Do you provide alternatives to group work for neurodivergent people who might not experience the assignment the same way as others?

UDL and the Physical Lens

While the three Patterns Beyond Labels lenses often overlap, this section focuses on considerations for the physical environment when designing for all learners. These considerations are limitless, so we'll provide a window into a foundational step for reflecting on and identifying physical barriers that may exist in these spaces through a UDL lens.

Examples of barriers found in the physical environment and some possible solutions include:

- **Lighting.** Traditional lighting (such as fluorescent lights) may trigger or worsen migraines.
- **Seats.** Consider providing chairs without armrests for fidgeters, seats that promote movement, and adjustable seating arrangements that accommodate left-handed individuals.
- **Flow and movement.** Accessible spaces should be mobility friendly so they're easy for people who use wheelchairs to navigate. Also, some people may need a separate space to work individually if they don't want to disclose a disability (such as a reading disability).
- Access to outlets. Some learners may need to use technology for accessibility needs (including screen readers or captioning software).

When designing your physical space, consider who is engaging in it. How do you find out who you're designing for? How are you assessing their physical needs and planning for accessibility, inclusivity, flexibility, and space for belonging? Has the learning space been designed to lessen the environmental impact on learners? Are there low-scale or cost-effective changes that you can make to the space so it's more welcoming? How is space design embedded into conversations and planning within your organization? Whose voices are in those conversations?

Take it one step further and reflect on where applying a UDL mindset and the principles of representation, engagement, and action and expression through the physical lens could positively affect in-person experiences at your organization. Consider how you'd answer these questions:

- **For representation**—How is information being shared? Is there only one modality? How can those learners with a
- visual disability interact with sticky-note activities? Do you have digital representation of all products used in physical learning environments?
- **For engagement**—Can participants continue to learn in an individual way, progressing at differing levels of expertise and

skill? For example, if someone needs more time to process and learn about a certain topic, are there opportunities for them to receive extra instruction or time without affecting others in the class?
- **For action and expression**—Pay attention to the physical barriers that may obstruct how learners participate. This may be measured by the design of the physical environment's impact on learners, perhaps through lighting, sound, temperature, and beyond.

UDL and the Cognitive Lens

The cognitive lens examines the way in which learner variability is supported in physical learning environments. UDL promotes designing for all learners in all three principles. When thinking about the cognitive lens, we can explore how engagement is fostered through authentic and relevant learning activities. We can also explore how learners process information through multiple modalities and apply authentic contexts to those modalities. And, we can promote connection to learning by creating applied learning experiences in these physical spaces by enacting the action and expression principle.

As we think of how learners engage in cognitively processing learning, we can also explore the Cognitive Apprenticeship framework, which draws on the traditional apprenticeship model of skill development with an added focus on both cognitive and physical skills that are transferred through practice that makes thinking visible.[99]

Jud Stoddard, a learning and instructional technology designer, takes this theory one step further by promoting the use of real-world scenarios to connect to workplace learning experiences and promote the visibility of decision making.[100] These frameworks not only address *why* someone performs a particular way but also *how* they effectively develop their thinking and knowledge in a newly learned skill.

For example, when working with a new employee, someone might identify how to use a session to demonstrate how decision making is fostered and developed at an organization with directed, explicit examples through reflective and mentored experiences. Our physical spaces can promote this by creating welcoming and inclusive spaces where exploration and experimentation can take place.

While you may think of visible barriers in a physical space, it's important to remember that invisible ones may also exist. An invisible barrier may be related to a visible one we have created without considering the cognitive aspect of learning. One example is anxiety. We can shift our UDL mindset to identify how physical learning spaces may create barriers for individuals who experience anxiety. Group arrangements, lack of explicit directions and agenda setting, or even environmental factors such as extraneous noise can affect people with anxiety.

By designing in-person learning experiences to adapt to learners' variability (including age, neurodivergence, disability, and preferences), we can provide the necessary space for inclusive engagement. The UDL framework provides the mindset and lens for organizations to consider how to design spaces that advance proactive thinking when designing physical learning spaces with variability in mind—including how we engage across the physical, cultural, and cognitive lenses.

Strategies for Learning Space Design

As you explore pathways for identifying the next steps in your current and future design process, consider how the outlined frameworks and examples can lead to meaningful change within your organization. The prompts we'll discuss in this section provide further reflection points to guide your exploration of how you can reduce barriers in physical learning environments.

This is not an exhaustive list; in fact, each discovery often leads to another opportunity to change. Herein lies the cyclical, interactive approach to designing physical learning spaces for all. When you engage in this work, you'll likely find more opportunities to build an accessibility-friendly space with each step forward you take. The real opportunity lies in becoming open to the potential of not only advancing learning through these strategies and beyond, but actively approaching each experience with an inclusive, UDL mindset.

In addition to the cultural, physical, and cognitive lenses, we want to acknowledge the role of community and understanding your audience in designing accessible, inclusive learning experiences.

Community Lens Prompts

Who is your audience? Discover who your audience is, but protect anonymity for those who didn't want to disclose their identity. Create an anonymous pre-event brief to check in with attendees and assess their needs. When possible, partner with accessibility professionals to lead support for those who require specific accommodations.

How can you build in community voice? Identify ways to encourage ongoing community input at different phases of learning. Create focus groups or invite subject matter experts from across the organization to share stories about their learning experiences. Also, consider how you'll assess this after an event through specific questions that elicit direct feedback about accessibility.

How can you apply empathy mapping to promote change? Try exploring learners' experiences by using empathy mapping as a tool for uncovering existing perceptions, biases, and assumptions about experiences with accessibility in learning spaces within your organization. Don't stop there. Use this tool to guide conversations by sharing and learning from participants' reflections and discoveries. (See chapter 3 for more information about empathy maps.)

Cultural Lens Prompts

Are your introductions inclusive? Ensure you're correctly pronouncing learners' names. Consider asking ahead of time or engage in an activity in which learners can share the pronunciation and history of their name. Be sure to include an alternative for those who don't know or don't want to share their history by making the story optional.

How have you designed for dietary needs? Sustenance helps maintain your participants' attention and focus, and not attending to their dietary needs may leave them feeling isolated. Instead of asking what learners need, identify diverse meal options that provide the greatest flexibility for all. Asking privately beforehand may not always capture everyone, so consider everyone from the start when possible.

Who is being represented? Learning content should incorporate media and information that is relevant to all learners. Include diverse representation in images, readings, and narratives, and ensure that diverse cultures, perspectives, and accessibility (such as closed captions) are built into all presentations, documents, and media.

Physical Lens Prompts

How are you designing for flexibility? Does your physical learning environment have flexible workspaces that support diverse learners including considerations for neuroinclusive design? Keep in mind that there is no one-size-fits-all approach, and one design will not support all neurodivergent learners. Consider using UDL strategies such as multiple modalities to train, explicit goals and agenda setting, and choice in assessments of learning.

Is your physical learning environment sensory friendly? Creating a sensory-friendly environment starts with sharing explicit expectations prior to attendee arrival, as well as what they can expect when they're in the space. Design sensory-friendly spaces by avoiding scented products and requesting attendees not wear fragrances or colognes. You can also limit harsh lighting, allow a flexible dress code, and identify a space where learners can retreat to if they need a break from stimulation in the learning experience.

Do you provide choice in modality? Offer choice through multimodality design, and include a hybrid approach when possible. Provide a quiet room option and integrate low- and high-tech engagement by creating experiences that do not require constant contact with computers, laptops, or mobile devices.

Cognitive Lens Prompts

Do you protect learners from constant focus and overload? To increase learning retention and focus, consider providing breaks (sometimes called "brain breaks") to engage learners and address cognitive overload. Breaks may be used to rest or to shift attention to aligned content to deepen connection.

Do you provide alternatives to group work? When designing activities for physical learning environments, consider how group activities may amplify anxiety—create alternatives for activities if independent work is an option.

Are your directions and goals clear and explicit? Provide an agenda to give learners clear directions and expectations for learning during the training event. Activities, directions, and goals should provide learners with a deeper understanding of how they are to engage with and explore content, as well as show you what they know.

What You Can Do Right Away

Use these questions to guide discussions and reflections and identify where growth opportunities lie within your team and work culture:

- How has leadership advocated for accessibility, inclusion, and belonging training to practice face-to-face engagement?
- How has the organization ensured the implementation of UDL practices in all learning spaces?
- How are the organization's values and mission aligned with supporting accessibility, inclusion, and belonging in shared physical spaces?
- Are the policies and practices used in learning spaces written with a UDL mindset?
- How is the organization finding growth opportunities from existing barriers associated with UDL and accessibility in face-to-face experiences?
- How can employees share their perspectives and voices to advance accessibility during in-person learning?
- How has the organization learned from past experiences?
- Have resources been allocated to support changes to create a more welcoming space?

34.
Unlocking Focus
The Vital Role of Fidget Toys in Enhancing Concentration for Neurodivergent Learners

Judy Katz (she/her)
Founder and Consultant, Neurodivergent Working

Providing fidget toys has long been a common practice in training environments, but many trainers don't know why—or how important they can be for some audiences.

Quinn loves being around people and learning new things, so they generally look forward to training events, but they also know their mind wanders in a million different directions and it can be difficult to keep it on topic. They have ADHD, a type of neurodivergence in which the brain's dopamine balance is off. Fidget toys can provide a good source of dopamine, as the physical activity can increase levels of the chemical.[101] They can also be good for *stimming*, which is short for self-stimulatory behavior, an activity that helps autistics and other neurodivergent people stay regulated. Stimming or fidgeting doesn't always mean that someone is nervous or uncomfortable, and it shouldn't be called out.

Some learners may bring their own fidget toys or have them constantly available, such as a fidget ring. Some may just fidget with their regular jewelry, hair, or clothes, or they might doodle in their notebooks (not every neurodivergent person knows that they're neurodivergent). Fidgeting and stimming has become more accepted and understood in recent years, and the market for fidget toys is booming.

But as many K–12 teachers quickly found when fidget spinners became popular, some fidget toys are loud or visible enough to distract others, making it difficult to balance distraction levels for everyone in a physical classroom. This is one reason that in-person training programs can be less ideal, as discussed in other areas of this book dealing with sensory issues. But when in-person training is required, it's a good idea to provide some quiet fidget toys.

Some examples of quiet fidget or sensory toys include puzzle balls, Pop-Its, kneadable erasers or silly putty, rubber bracelets (regular or coiled), and stretchy string. (Figures 34-1, 34-2, and 34-3 offer some examples.) Not all stores use the same names, but an internet search for classroom or therapy stores will reveal plenty of options, and many stores even have a "silent" category.

Figure 34-1. Pop-It fidget toy.

Figure 34-2. Kneadable eraser.

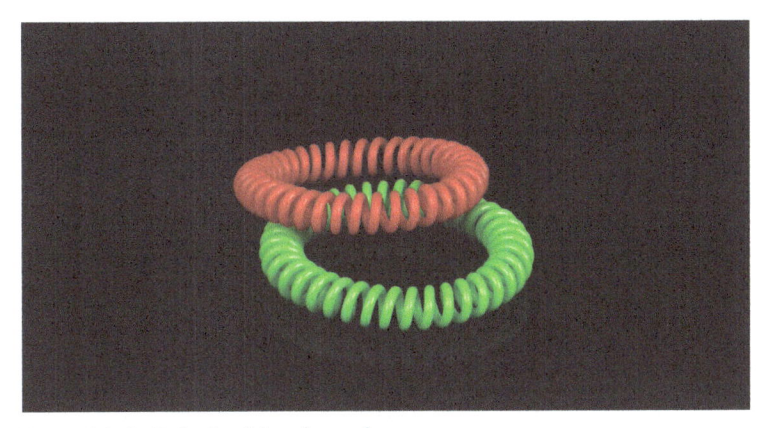

Figure 34-3. Coiled rubber bracelets.

If your budget isn't large, pipe cleaners and rubber bands will work in a pinch. And providing small notepads for doodling or colorful pieces of paper to fold can also be useful.

What You Can Do Right Away

For the next in-person learning experience you're designing or facilitating, plan to provide quiet fidget toys that learners can access without judgment. They can be a vital aid for neurodivergent learners in the program.

35.
Beyond the Rules
A Lesson in Accessibility and Empathy

Jean Marrapodi, PhD, CPTD (she/her)
Chief Learning Architect, Applestar Productions

I was teaching one of my all-time favorite workshops, Barnga by Thiagi (the master of experiential learning) at a conference for adult literacy teachers in Rhode Island. My goal was to help them understand and empathize with newcomer challenges through an experiential activity.

In Barnga, the audience is split into table groups and given a deck of cards and a version of rules for the game. For the first 10 minutes, the participants spend time learning the game and practice playing to mastery. The facilitator then announces there will be a tournament and removes the rule sheets. The game is played again, but during the tournament everyone remains silent. After each round, each table's winner moves to the table on the right, and the loser moves to the table on the left.

What the players don't realize, however, is that the rules for the game are different for each table. Aces could be high at one table and low at another. The trump suit could be hearts in one group and spades in another. As Thiagi has set up the game, there are many variations, so no group has the same rules.

When the first round is finished, the players move to their new places as instructed. When the second round begins, the two new players arrive at a table that has different rules, and their individual rules are different. You'll see lots of hand signals, knocking on the table and heads shaking as they try to play the game. By the third round, things get really mixed up and people become more animated. Sometimes they figure out they've been duped in this round, but everyone gets it by the fourth round.

In the debrief, we talk about what it was like being the *different* one and, as a group member, having someone different arrive at their table. We make the connection to cultural rules, which are unseen, and the insights pour out. Insights often include recognizing anger that "their rules aren't right," understanding that the way things are "supposed to be" is contextual, and realizing how challenging it is to sit back and remain silent when things feel wrong around you. It's a marvelous game and I always have a great time facilitating it. Teachers finally understand why their students are struggling after experiencing the challenge.

When I was teaching this workshop at the literacy conference, we had just gotten into the first round when a woman who was blind joined the class. Ordinarily, I'd have a latecomer observe the room and share their observations in the debrief. That wasn't going to work here! When I've had blind students in other settings, I can usually explain things to help them participate. That also wasn't going to work. I couldn't sit with her and explain the rules of the game or tell her what cards she had because the room had to be silent. So, I was stuck and didn't have a workaround for her. She chose to stay, which I was glad for. She participated in the discussion and shared her perspective of being the outsider in a sighted world. Even now, many years later, I don't have an option for what a workaround would be and haven't facilitated Barnga since.

What You Can Do Right Away

The lesson learned here is to remember you may have learners with different and unexpected needs in your classes. Now, when I prepare to teach a workshop, I always consider the variations of who might be in the audience so I'm ready with alternatives. In your preparation, ask yourself the "What if" questions to consider how you might adapt things to include all learners so they can participate. That way, you won't find yourself in the situation I was in and can create an environment where everyone can participate.

36.
Tailoring Group Work for Neurodivergent Learners

Judy Katz (she/her)
Founder and Consultant, Neurodivergent Working

Kara has social anxiety. She was one of those kids in school who hated group work. She would usually do the whole assignment if she could get away with it, and the other kids would let her because she often did a great job.

Now, Kara is a top performer at her job and usually breezes through learning new material. However, she dreads in-person training because there's likely to be group work. She doesn't dislike other people, but she knows she struggles with making small talk or new connections easily. She also knows from experience that people are likely to consider her awkward or standoffish. She feels like her anxiety over social interactions gets in the way of learning, but she doesn't want to be rude by asking if she can fly solo.

Sometimes, it makes sense for activities in virtual instructor-led training (vILT) and in-person training to be collaborative to better reach the program's goals. Other times, it doesn't. Group work can be difficult for learners with a variety of mental and physical conditions, even if it's not all the time and only challenging on particular days.

To better accommodate all learners, offer a version of group activities that some learners can opt to do individually. If an assignment genuinely needs to be group work, flag roles that are more geared to individual work and let learners volunteer for those at the beginning of the activity.

Let's consider two examples. Both are opportunities to allow for individual work in group activities, and these modifications can be made in both in-person and vILT training programs.

Option 1: Offer group and individual versions of the activity. The facilitator says: "Now we're going to practice having a difficult conversation with a direct report. Everyone can choose to do this activity with a partner or individually. Those in pairs will practice by role playing, and those working individually will write a script, including both the manager and the direct report's roles."

Option 2: Set up the group activity with individual roles. The facilitator says: "The next activity has specialized roles. One is a researcher, who does mostly individual work. One is a scribe. One is a presenter. There should also be one or two brainstormers in each group. It looks like we can make three groups of five. Who volunteers to be a researcher? Scribe? Presenter?"

What You Can Do Right Away

Consider a group activity that you have designed. How would it work as one of those two options? Next, consider the following questions:

- Is the activity introduction worded in a way that doesn't call out neurodivergent people or inadvertently criticize learners who choose to take the individual option?
- Does the individual version of the activity meet the same learning goals?

37.
Describe Your Visuals in Instructor-Led Programs

Diane Elkins (she/her)
Co-Founder, Artisan Learning

The first time I had a noticeably blind person in an in-person class, I became very aware of what was on my slides and how I was referring to them. Most of the time, the slides reinforce what I'm saying, so someone who couldn't see them wouldn't be missing out on anything. But sometimes, I let the slide make the point for me. Maybe it's a funny image. Maybe it's a visual I need to deconstruct.

Imagine I'm presenting a breakout session on accessibility, and I tell the following story using the slide in Figure 37-1 on the next page.

> "When I was going to my hotel in downtown Salt Lake City, Utah, last month, I was walking behind two women in motorized wheelchairs. They eventually turned, and as I kept walking straight, I encountered this. For me, it wasn't a problem—I just walked around. But when you consider everything on the left and everything on the right, those two women would have literally been stuck between a rock and a hard place."

If you could not see my slide, you would not know what I was talking about. You might get the gist of it, but why should I put you in that position?

Figure 37-1. Two scooters blocking a sidewalk.

Instead, I could say:

"As I kept walking straight, I encountered these two rental scooters parked in the middle of the sidewalk. For me, it wasn't a problem—I just walked around them. But when you consider that fence to the right of the sidewalk and the big stones to the left of it, those two women would have literally been stuck between a rock and a hard place."

That's much better and doesn't leave out context that someone who can't see the slides would need to follow along. Note how this new description can also benefit those who are fully sighted but might be positioned in a way they cannot see the slides clearly enough.

What You Can Do Right Away

Providing a version of your slides in advance with full text descriptions of the visuals can help—especially if you have complex graphics such as charts and tables. But when delivering a live presentation, sometimes just a few words can make a big difference to someone can't see your visual. Those few extra words might also add valuable clarity to others in your audience. When you use generalized language such as *this*, *that*, or *here*, it's not always clear what you are referring to, especially in a complex graphic.

38.
Improving Accessibility With Presentation Captioning

JD Dillon (he/him)
Founder and Principal, LearnGeek

I watch TV with the captions on. It has nothing to do with my hearing. Instead, I find captions helpful for other reasons. I have an old TV—circa 2007—with subpar audio. Captions help me keep up with dialogue during noisy sequences (without having to spend money on a new TV). I also sometimes struggle to understand people with accents that are different from mine—in real life and in digital content. Captions limit the number of times I feel like I'm bothering people around me by asking, "What did she just say?"

Turns out, I'm not alone. According to a 2022 survey by YPulse, 59 percent of Gen Z viewers prefer watching TV with subtitles on. Millennials are only slightly less likely to prefer subtitles at 52 percent.[102] At the same time, captions are a critical tool for 430 million people around the world with disabling hearing loss. The World Health Organization (2024) estimates nearly 2.5 billion people will experience some degree of hearing loss by 2050.[103] According to the National Council on Aging, "People with untreated hearing loss are twice as likely to be underemployed or unemployed as those with normal hearing."[104]

Captions are an essential tool for L&D professionals. With 15.5 percent of American adults experiencing hearing loss, it's almost guaranteed that someone in your audience can benefit from them. But captions are more than an accessibility requirement. They're a strategic tool we can apply to make training more equitable, personal, and engaging for everyone.

Key Definitions

Platforms like TikTok, Netflix, and YouTube have made captions an integrated part of everyday content consumption. Many of us have seen them. Most of us have used them. But before we dig into the strategic value of captions in learning, let's nail down a few key terms. The World Wide Web Consortium (W3C) defines *captions* as "a text version of the speech and non-speech audio information needed to understand the content. They are displayed within the media player and are synchronized with the audio."[105] *Closed captions* can be hidden or displayed by the viewer using options within a video player. Figure 38-1 shows an example of a media player with the closed caption option turned on.

Figure 38-1. Example media player with closed captions turned on.

Open captions are embedded within the video content and cannot be turned off. And *live captioning* is the process of adding captions to digital content in real time. This is done by a human captioner or a Communication Access Realtime Translation (CART) provider.

Some regions use the terms "caption" and "subtitles" interchangeably. While they are implemented in the same ways, *subtitles* more often refer to the text translation of spoken audio into another language. Captions may reference music included alongside spoken audio. However, they typically do not reference other audio from within the content, such as sound effects.

Educational Benefits of Captions

Captions may be leveraged within a variety of educational experiences—from synchronous classroom and online sessions to on-demand video and online courses. But do they help people learn? The Oregon State University Ecampus Research Unit partnered with 3Play Media, a captioning and transcription services provider, to conduct a survey into how 2,000 students—both with and without hearing loss—across 15 universities perceived captions within their learning experiences. They found that 90.4 percent of students with reported hearing loss found captions moderately to extremely useful.[106] At the same time, 87.7 percent of students who did not report hearing loss found captions equally useful.

When asked why they used captions while watching course videos, three-quarters of respondents reported their value as learning aids. Students cited how captions boost focus, improve information retention, and assist with vocabulary. Captions also helped viewers overcome logistical challenges like poor audio quality, speakers with heavy accents, and less audio-friendly environments, such as public places or libraries. Hearing difficulty was the sixth most-cited benefit.

Accessibility Standards and Industry Practices

Captions are more than a great idea with lots of upside for your audience. They're a non-negotiable part of content strategy for L&D teams with regional or industry accessibility standards. For example, Section 508 of the US Rehabilitation Act requires compliance with Web Content Accessibility Guidelines (WCAG).[107] This includes captions and audio descriptions for pre-recorded video along with live captioning for live video. For example, according to WCAG 2.2 Success Criterion 1.2.4, "Captions are provided for all prerecorded audio content in synchronized media, except when the media is a media alternative for text and is clearly labeled as such."[108]

Your region or industry may have additional accessibility requirements related to captions. For example, the US Federal Communications

Commission (FCC) introduced quality standards for television captioning that align with these general industry practices:
- **Accuracy.** Captions must be 99 percent accurate, relay the speaker's exact words, include background noises, and honor the speaker's original tone and intent.
- **Time synchronization.** Captions must align with the corresponding spoken words and sounds.
- **Program completeness.** Captions must be included for the full runtime of the program.
- **Placement.** Captions must be presented in a reasonably legible font size and not block important on-screen content.

There are also industry standard practices that, while not spelled out explicitly within regulatory text, will aid in the effective use of captions. Here are some examples:
- Captions may be generated automatically or input manually using a variety of file formats, including SRT (SubRip Subtitle) and WebVTT (Web Video Text Tracks format).
- The reading pace should not exceed 180 words per minute—or three words per second.
- Each caption line should not exceed 32 characters in length, with a maximum of two lines on screen at one time.
- Captions should be placed in the center bottom of the screen.

That's a quick summary of the regulatory realities of captions. Your team should consider all relevant accessibility guidelines before determining how to best apply captions within your learning experiences.

Automatic Versus Manual Captions

As recently as 2015, industry experts suggested developers add eight to 10 hours to content development timelines to account for captioning.[109] Outsourcing this process to a professional service was often considered to be prohibitively expensive, especially for content that required multiple language translations and therefore multiple versions of captions.

In 2024, it's easier than ever to add captions to live sessions, both in-person and online, as well as recorded content, including videos and e-learning modules. Automated captioning is quickly becoming a standard feature for learning authoring and delivery platforms. Many automated captioning tools can also translate spoken word into multiple languages. For example, as of this writing, Zoom can add live captions to online sessions in 30 languages, while YouTube can insert automatic captions in 14 languages. This technology not only accelerates captioning while reducing costs, but it also represents a significant leap forward in our ability to provide equitable access to learning and support resources.

Automatic speech recognition (*ASR*) applies machine learning to convert human speech to text. This is similar to the speech-to-text capabilities you use when narrating a text message or asking Amazon's Alexa to set an oven timer. ASR applies computational linguistics to transform sound into words and formatted sentences. It does not attempt to understand the audio. However, more advanced artificial intelligence (AI) capabilities, such as large language models (LLMs) and natural language processing (NLP), may be applied in the future to improve the accuracy of ASR outputs.

Sounds awesome, right? Well, there's a catch. Automatic captions do not meet accessibility requirements, including Section 508 and WCAG. Industry expectations for automated captioning are extremely high at 99 percent accuracy. Even the most advanced tools fall short of this benchmark (for now). Small caption errors can significantly alter content in embarrassing or dangerous ways. Consider the potential impact of this caption mistake:

> **Spoken audio:** "Do not exceed the recommended load of *4 to 5 kilograms.*"
>
> **Automated caption:** "Do not exceed the recommended load of *45 kilograms.*"

Technology providers continue to improve their AI models, but they're also aware of their limitations. For example, here's the disclaimer from YouTube's "Use automatic captioning" help page:

"Note: These automatic captions are generated by machine learning algorithms, so the quality of the captions may vary. We encourage creators to add professional captions first. YouTube is constantly improving its speech recognition technology. However, automatic captions might misrepresent the spoken content due to mispronunciations, accents, dialects, or background noise. You should always review automatic captions and edit any parts that haven't been properly transcribed."[110]

Automated captions have not yet reached the point of being "set and forget" solutions. Instead, they should be used to accelerate the development process by creating first drafts. A human captioner must then review and edit the captions before the content is published. This also includes translated captions, which must be reviewed by fluent speakers to ensure accuracy. If you do not have the resources to automate or review AI-generated captions, professional services are available at affordable rates. As I'm writing this, Rev.com charges $1.50 per minute while guaranteeing 99 percent accuracy.[111]

Strategic Considerations

Eventually, technology will likely take over content development processes like captioning and translation, ensuring total access to information for everyone. In the meantime, L&D must determine how to best apply our available tools to boost learning equity. Here's a short list of strategic recommendations.

Set Your Standards

Accessibility guidelines are a minimum expectation, not an ideal state. Work with your L&D peers, stakeholders, and employees to establish your organization's content standards, including the use of captions, subtitles, and translations. This should extend beyond training content to include functions like HR, communications, and marketing so employees have a consistent, equitable information experience within the workplace. Hold yourself and your team accountable to these standards across all platforms and experiences. Regularly evaluate your standards and processes as the workplace changes and technology improves.

Make Captioning a Technology Requirement

Apply your learning experience standards within your technology evaluation and procurement processes. Specify your requirements within your request for information (RFI) and request for proposal (RFP) documents. Challenge technology providers to demonstrate how they can meet your standards during demonstrations of their solutions using samples of your organization's content.

Establish Your Captioning Process

Determine how you will caption both live and recorded content. Document your standards and captioning processes to ensure they are followed by everyone. Include review requirements for automatic and manual captions, including content completed by professional service providers. Determine if and when automatic captions without review are permissible for live activities.

Stick to the Script

Scripted content is easier to manually caption than live or spontaneous content. However, this is only true if you continue to update the script as the project evolves through development and review. Make sure these materials represent the latest version of the content so they can be leveraged for captioning.

Clean Up Your Audio

Bad audio makes content harder to caption accurately, especially for automated systems. Invest in the hardware and software needed to produce clean, crisp audio for live and recorded content. Use high-quality microphones designed for voice recording instead of onboard computer audio or earbuds. Record in quiet environments to reduce background noise. Coach everyone to speak at a natural, consistent pace while properly enunciating each word during recording sessions. Capture multiple takes during each session so you have options during postproduction.

Be Consistent

Apply your captioning standards and processes consistently across learning experiences. For example, caption both live and recorded content so people have the same options regardless of format. Hold third-party content providers to the same standards so employees have consistent experiences, regardless of how content is developed. Share your standards documentation with employees so they know what to expect. Align with operational partners, such as corporate communications and HR, to foster consistent content experiences across functions.

Give People Control

Captions may be distracting for people who prefer not to use them. Opt for closed captions, which can be turned on and off, whenever possible. Ask your technology providers if their platforms allow users to turn captions on and off by default to maintain control of their learning experiences.

Budget for Captions

Once you determine your standards, make sure all project budgets include the necessary time and financial resources. If you plan to handle captions internally, dedicate time to generate and review them for recorded content. If you expect to outsource content to a service provider, identify your captioning partner and determine how much your standard content will cost to eliminate budget surprises. When you use professional services, be sure the content is finalized before sending it off for captioning to mitigate extra expenses.

Acknowledge Captioning Limits

Captioning does not automatically make your learning content accessible for all employees, including those who are deaf or have hearing loss. For example, you must also consider people with limited reading skills. Script your content so it can be easily captioned and understood by a wide spectrum of people. Consider translation options to accommodate employees with varied language preferences. Pace narration and corresponding captions so content can be easily followed by people with different educational backgrounds and reading skills.

Consider Full Transcripts

Even well-paced captions may be difficult to follow, especially in a distracting work environment. Provide the full transcript so people can easily review content segments. Evaluate technology that allows users to navigate through recorded content by clicking on sections in the transcript (similar to YouTube).

Follow Captioning Advances

Technology is quickly evolving thanks to advances in AI, especially generative AI and LLMs. This will provide new tools for promoting learning equity and accessibility, including simplified captioning and translation. Regional and industry standards are also constantly changing to meet modern workforce needs. Connect with practitioners who advocate for accessibility topics so you can stay current on the latest updates. Dedicate time and resources to experimenting with new tools and finding opportunities to improve your processes.

Don't Wait!

Equity is a difficult problem to solve, especially at the speed and scale we tend to play in L&D. Improving your strategies so every employee gets the support they need when and where they need it takes time, effort, and resources. Plus, there's often lots of red tape and distractions in our way, including conflicting priorities, budget limits, technology requirements, and differing opinions. You may not be in a position to shift resources or establish new standards within your business. However, you can still find small-but-meaningful opportunities to foster a more equitable experience for the people you support.

That's how I started captioning my sessions at industry events. I've used automated captions during online presentations and in prerecorded content for years, but I struggled to offer similar accommodations in-person. I've interacted with participants with varying accents, language preferences, and degrees of hearing loss over the years. I typically don't know exactly who will attend my sessions, so I do my best to prepare for all possible circumstances. This can be challenging when I have little-to-no control over the presentation environment.

I may be able to specify seating arrangements, but otherwise it's just me, my laptop, and a projector. Unfortunately, most events don't offer live captioning for participants. When they do, it's limited to the biggest rooms and largest audiences. In my opinion, equity shouldn't come with a minimum attendance requirement, so I went looking for a simple, affordable way to offer live captions in all my sessions—without the need for organizers' help. I quickly realized the answer was already on my laptop. Did you know PowerPoint in Microsoft 365 has automated subtitles (Figure 38-2)?

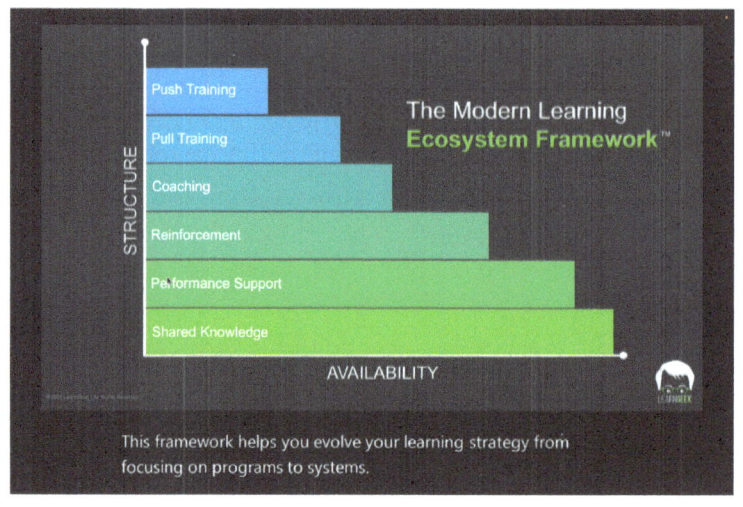

Figure 38-2. Automated subtitles in PowerPoint

PowerPoint transcribes my words as I present and displays captions on-screen in real time. I can determine where captions appear—at the top or bottom of the screen—and if they overlay onto my slide content. This option is currently available in more than 20 languages (eight are fully supported). If that wasn't cool enough, PowerPoint can also automatically translate my words into captions in more than 65 languages. All this AI-powered capability was just sitting on my laptop, waiting to be used!

I now use PowerPoint subtitles during all in-person presentations—unless organizers provide an alternative. I wear a second microphone that connects to my laptop via Bluetooth to make sure PowerPoint can always hear me as I move around the room.

It's not a perfect solution—it tends to fall short of the 99 percent industry standard for accuracy. But, for a tool that's readily available at no extra cost, it does a solid job providing an option for any participants who may benefit from captions. It's also a great conversation starter. At least one person approaches me after every session to ask how I generated them. My live captions have proven to be a great example of how I can leverage technology now to help foster a more equitable, inclusive, accessible learning environment.

What You Can Do Right Away

The next time you're preparing to deliver an in-person learning experience with presentation slides, explore options to automate captions during the presentation—don't rely on event organizers or an audio-visual team to figure this out for you. Preparing in advance allows you to control your ability to successfully support attendees.

39.
Driving Dreams
Overcoming Dyslexia With Adaptive Learning and Technology

Jean Marrapodi, PhD, CPTD (she/her)
Chief Learning Architect, Applestar Productions

I met Adrian in 2009 shortly after he was released from prison. He'd started attending a literacy program with a community agency, but they quickly realized he needed more individualized support than they were equipped to provide. So they reached out to me to see if I could help him. They were aware of my background in individualized education (which is still referred to as "special education"), and knew I could diagnose reading difficulties. It didn't take long to realize Adrian had severe dyslexia and was reading at the level of a first grader. He had some minor developmental delays but possessed a heart of gold and was eager to learn.

We met every week for several years, working on various skills, and I gradually saw some improvements. He was able to read books at the second-grade level. Even though he struggled to decode the material, he could retell everything about the story down to the smallest detail.

When Adrian turned 42, he came up with a new goal: He wanted to drive a car. In Rhode Island, as in most states, you must pass a written test before you could move on to the road test for driving. This would be quite a hurdle for him.

Adrian had ridden the bus for many years and knew the city like the back of his hand, so getting from place to place wouldn't be hard for him. He knew the rules of the road and could tell you what to do in every situation. He really wanted some independence, so we decided to work on his goal. We downloaded an app that reviewed all the rules needed for the state driver's license test, and he mastered them in short order. The app was especially helpful because it could read the questions aloud and it had illustrations.

After a couple weeks of practice with the app, I knew he was ready for the test, except for the reading it would require. I called the department of motor vehicles (DMV) to ask about an accommodation for him. I was delighted to find out that the tests were computer based, and there was a workstation in a quiet room that provided audio narration for the written questions—much like the app and our practice sessions. So, we scheduled the test.

On the test day, we arrived at the DMV, and Adrian got settled in to take the test. It took him less than 20 minutes. He came out and told the test monitor that one of the questions had the answers mixed up when read aloud, and that it should be attended to. He got a perfect score.

The Power of the Ask and Assistive Technologies

The written test could have been a showstopper for Adrian's goal. So, we had to identify what accommodations were already in place to help him (and others) be successful.

Technology enables so many things for people contending with disabilities. For example, there are apps like WeWALK and Step-Hear that provide step-by-step navigation in a city with landmarks that support independent navigation.

As trainers, we don't always know what is available, but it is always worth asking. Instead of saying no to a request like this, we need to learn to ask HMW (how might we) questions, which is a technique used in design thinking. How might we make this happen? There are untapped resources all around us. Many times, people in the disabled community are your best resources.

Adrian had the knowledge and skills to pass the test and get his driver's license. His barrier was reading, which wasn't necessarily a critical skill to be able to drive. I could have said no, but I chose to ask, "How might we?" and found a way to enable his success.

Microsoft, Google, and Adobe have ready-to-use accessibility solutions that are as simple as adding a button or making choices when building the material. Some are already incorporated into the user interface, which allows people to independently enable them. Canvas, an LMS used by many colleges, has Microsoft's Immersive Reader built right in, allowing students to enlarge the size of the text, translate it, or have it be read aloud. It also provides a dictionary that lets students look words up, right on the page.

In the classroom, whether in-person or virtually, you can add closed-captioning during a presentation by switching it on in Google Slides, Microsoft PowerPoint, and web conferencing software like Zoom and Webex. These are simple steps that provide for a need you may not even be aware of in your class.

What You Can Do Right Away

When we design for accessibility, we all win. There are often people with invisible disabilities in your audience, and having a solution incorporated from the beginning allows everyone to benefit.

What are the barriers you face with implementing accessible training? How might you leverage existing tools to be successful? Consider how you might offer assistive technology or scaffolding to English language learners, or those with low level literacy or dyslexia.

40.
Don't Forget Interpreting Needs!

Mary Henry Lightfoot, MS, NIC Advanced, CI/CT (she/her)
CEO, Interpreting Connections for ASL Interpretation, Training, and Instructional Design

Kendra is planning for an upcoming conference and has established action items, timelines, and budget. One week prior to the conference, she receives a request from a participant, asking that sign language interpreters be provided. As Kendra reviews her project plan, she discovers that she never planned for accessibility and does not know where to begin with providing interpreters. How might this situation have been avoided and what do we need to consider with providing sign language interpreters for an on-site or online event?

When preparing for an in-person or virtual event, sign language interpreting needs a place in your project plan. Here are six steps you should take.

1. Provide an Accessibility Needs Statement on Your Registration Form

This allows deaf or hard of hearing participants to identify a need for sign language interpreting services or other accessibility needs. Be sure to include a timeline for requesting the accommodation, a way to indicate the specific need, and a procedure to follow up if necessary.

2. Budget for Interpreting Needs

Sign language interpreters are communication professionals who may have advanced degrees in the pedagogy of interpreting. Nationally certified interpreters have proven a standard level of competency. They are a budget line item that must be considered. Contact local interpreting agencies to estimate cost structures in your area.

3. Understand How to Effectively Request Interpreting Services

Currently, there is more demand than supply of competent, professional interpreters. Therefore, you should request interpreters early in the process and do not expect availability of interpreters at the last minute. The National Deaf Center on Post Secondary Outcomes suggests allowing three to five weeks advance notice when requesting interpreters.[112] Use a reputable sign language interpreting service, and partner with them for any questions about providing interpreters. Because interpretation is a mentally and physically demanding profession, the industry standard is for interpreters to work in pairs, discreetly switching off at regular intervals throughout the day.

4. Understand How to Effectively Work With an Interpreting Team

Interpretation involves understanding the structure and content of the event, including the content of individual presentations. The interpretation will be more effective if you can provide enhanced information, such as the agenda with times for each section, presentation titles, presenter names, PowerPoint slides, or presentation outlines.

5. Understand How the Sign Language Interpretation Profession Works

Professional sign language interpreters operate under a code of conduct as established by a professional interpreting organization, such as the Registry of Interpreters for the Deaf. They provide communication access; they do not advise a deaf person nor speak on behalf of a deaf person. Therefore, your communication with or about a deaf person should be addressed to the person themself, not the interpreter. Certified interpreters are professionally bound to confidentiality for all assignments, including the content within the event, and can lose their certification if they break confidentiality. Therefore, any nonpublic information shared with the interpreter is held in confidence.

6. Determine the Placement of the Interpreter Within the Physical Location

Work with the interpreters (and the deaf individuals) to determine the placement of the interpreter within the physical location. This includes ensuring that there is adequate lighting to view the interpreter. For virtual sessions, it is important that the interpreters are consistently visible on screen and within a window large enough for the deaf person to access the communication. Events or meetings in which many people are visible on screen will require intentional setup so the interpreter is accessible by the deaf person. Ask the interpreter about what setup they need to provide effective services.

What You Can Do Right Away

Prepare for your next event by using these six steps. This will help ensure effective inclusion of signing deaf or hard of hearing individuals. For additional information, visit the Registry of Interpreters for the Deaf website at rid.org.

41.
Working With Sign Language Interpreters

Diane Elkins (she/her)
Co-Founder, Artisan Learning

Early in my training career, I delivered public workshops around the country on business skills. About a year in, I taught a class with a sign-language interpreter—actually, two of them. (They often work in pairs so they can swap out.)

It took a little getting used to. I could see the interpreter out of the corner of my eye, and I found it fascinating. I wanted to know what my words looked like in sign language. But I had to focus on my teaching. I also became hyperaware of how many times I started a sentence but then changed my mind and went a different direction. I wondered if that made their job harder.

I facilitated the whole day with the interpreters and never knew which learner needed the interpreter, and at the time, that felt odd. I don't even know if the learner in question showed up that day. Today, I'm more aligned with the fact that people get to choose what to disclose about themselves. Maybe the person was there—maybe they weren't. And that's OK.

Since then, I've taught other classes that were interpreted. I've also received some great advice from Mary Lightfoot, a sign-language interpreter and learning manager at Gallaudet University (which is an institution that serves deaf and hard of hearing students as well as hearing students pursuing careers related to deaf and hard of hearing people). Here are some of the tips I've learned from her about leading a training class with an interpreter. (Chapter 40 covered more about using interpreters.)

Address the Deaf or Hard of Hearing Person

When talking to a deaf or hard of hearing person through a sign-language interpreter, maintain eye contact with and address all questions and comments to the deaf or hard of hearing person, not the interpreter. Don't say things like "Tell him . . ." or "Ask her . . ." Instead, act like the interpreter isn't there. This took me a lot of focus at first. My instincts were to engage with the person speaking to me in my language. But I needed to focus my attention on the person I was really communicating with.

Manage Your Visuals Carefully

If you are explaining something with complex visual information—like charts, graphs, or computer software—hearing students can listen to you while looking at the visual. But a person using an interpreter needs to look at the interpreter to "listen" to you. This means they can't focus 100 percent of their visual attention on both the interpreter and your visuals at the same time. If your visuals are merely supporting your message, or if the graphics are simple and can be interpreted with a glance, there might not be an issue. But more complex information may need careful thought. At a minimum, pause for a little extra time before moving to the next slide or on to your next point.

I taught an Adobe Captivate course to a group that had several deaf and hard of hearing students. Typically, learners can listen to me while they choose to either look at my projected screen (a complex visual) or their own screen. In this class, I was concerned that if the students had to focus on the interpreter to get my explanation before being able to look at the screen, they might have trouble following along. As a result, I chunked the procedures into smaller pieces so they could go back and forth more easily between the interpreter and the screen without having to remember too many steps. I also worked with the stakeholders to change the timing of the course because there was a chance the process would take a little bit longer.

Manage Activities

In an instructor-led setting, you may have individual and group activities. If there is only one deaf or hard-of-hearing learner, then the interpreter can translate in the group activities and can also let them know when time is up. However, if you have more learners needing an interpreter than you have interpreters, you'll need to manage that dynamic.

In the Captivate course, many of the students were using the interpreter. I didn't have many group activities, but learners spent about half the course in individual practice time. I decided that during the practices, the interpreter would walk around with me as I checked in with each of the learners.

I also came up with a system to get everyone's attention when it was time to pause or finish the practice and "listen" again. With hearing students, I could use my voice to get their attention while they were looking at their screens. But when fully deaf students were looking at their computers, they wouldn't necessarily notice that the interpreter was signing my new instructions. Because I was training a team that worked together every day, I could ask them to let each other know by tapping someone's arm if they weren't looking when they needed to.

I also got another dose of self-awareness from this activity. Just like I realized how often I started a sentence and then changed my mind about it, I realized how often I got people started on an activity and then added a clarification on the instructions or an extra tip or comment. I was pulling everyone's attention from the task they were supposed to be working on, and it was even more disruptive for someone working with an interpreter. Now I try to be more conscious of providing all my instructions up front instead of dropping them in little pieces while people are working. Learners with ADHD likely also appreciate getting to work without my interruptions.

Check In

If the deaf or hard-of-hearing learner chooses to self-identify, check in with that person and the interpreter to find out how to have a successful session. I once taught an Articulate Storyline course with the help of an interpreter, and I was able to spend a few minutes with the interpreter and the deaf student before the class started. We talked through how I taught the class and what might work best for the learner. Normally, interpreters stand fairly close to the instructor so the learner can easily shift their focus back and forth. But in this case, we decided to try having the interpreter sit at the same table as the learner. This allowed the learner to shift focus more easily between the interpreter and their own computer screen. And it also made it easier for the interpreter to assist each time the learner did independent work. A different interpreter and learner pair might have chosen something else. The three of us checked in after the first few activities and again at lunch to make sure things were going smoothly.

What You Can Do Right Away

Communication and respect are your best tools when working with deaf learners and sign-language interpreters. Focus on the learner and what will give them a successful experience. Initiate conversations with both (if you can) to find out what will work best for them. And give yourself grace if something doesn't go well at first. Be willing to learn, grow, and improve.

42.
Creating Sensory-Smart Spaces
Strategies for Crafting Neurodivergent-Friendly Training Environments

Judy Katz (she/her)
Founder and Consultant, Neurodivergent Working

In-person training experiences can present a huge challenge for neurodivergent participants due to the sensory inputs (smell, sound, taste, touch, and visual) that they may not be able to control. When in-person training is necessary, trainers, instructional designers, and training managers and coordinators have a vital opportunity to make those sensory challenges less daunting.

Jessie is an experienced trainer who usually works in field classrooms, and she knows how stressful in-person sessions can be for a variety of conditions. Her own neurodivergence makes strong smells a particular challenge, so she started requesting that trainees avoid wearing perfumes, colognes, and body sprays when attending her training sessions. She was delighted when one of her trainees, Ethan, expressed his gratitude for the change, because strong scents tended to activate his migraines. Now her department has made the request to abstain from strong scents a standard part of their pretraining emails and treats employees who ignore the request similarly to employees who come in with strong body odor; it's a somewhat delicate issue, but not insurmountable.

Jessie also makes it a habit of visiting new training rooms beforehand to see what changes she can make (if any) to accommodate her learners' sensory needs. Sometimes there are things she has control over; other times, she needs to speak to a training manager or facilities manager to ask for customizations.

What You Can Do Right Away

What changes can you make to your organization's physical training environments to make them more sensory friendly? Start with these ideas:

- Ask trainers and trainees to refrain from wearing perfumes, colognes, and body sprays on training days.
- Unplug extra machinery and equipment in or near the training rooms, because electrical sounds can be distracting.
- Lower blinds to prevent the classroom from being uncomfortably bright.
- Turn off or lower the lights in part of the classroom so trainees can choose to limit their light exposure.
- Turn off fluorescent lights as much as possible, as the flickering and noise can cause distractions and headaches.
- Familiarize yourself with the thermostat (and ask for control if possible).
- Invite learners to bring sweaters or other warm layers if they tend to be cold in classrooms.

43.
Addressing Speech Access Needs in the Physical Classroom

Susi Miller (she/her)
Founder and Director, eLaHub

Sarah Mercier (she/her)
CEO, Build Capable

Reggie had just started a new role as a senior trainer in a large nonprofit organization. His first day consisted of a structured onboarding program he attended with a few other people who would be working in other roles across the company. The onboarding facilitator began the day's agenda with an activity: Deliver a presentation to share with the class about how their role supported the nonprofit's mission.

Sitting next to him was Nisha, the new accounting director. She appeared incredibly nervous about the activity. Reggie decided to break the ice. He leaned over to Nisha and said, "I have a couple ideas, but I'm not sure what I want to go with." After talking for a few minutes about his own choices, Reggie paused. Nisha responded slowly, as if trying to find the right words. She shared that she struggled with verbal presentations.

When she was a teenager, Nisha was in a car accident resulting in a serious head injury. Not long after, she was diagnosed with aphasia, a disorder resulting from damage to her brain from her head injury that affected her speech. She knew what she wanted to say, but it was often tough to say it. Over the years, she'd learned ways to work around the barriers she experienced with this disability, but it wasn't always easy.

Reggie reflected on this for a moment—even as an experienced trainer, he had never considered how someone with a speech disability might be in one of his classes without him even realizing it. Going forward, he knew he'd be thinking differently about his classroom activity design.

Inclusive Strategies for All Learners

Speech access needs are often overlooked when we consider including all learners in the physical classroom. Yet, according to the Mayo Clinic it's estimated that between 5 and 10 percent of people in the US have conditions that affect speech and language, including aphasia, stuttering, and vocal cord paralysis.[113]

Here are some ways you can include learners with speech access needs in the physical classroom:

- Provide the option to present with a colleague or in a group.
- Be flexible about time limits on activities wherever possible.
- Don't force learners to give feedback or lead sessions.
- Allow ample time for learners to formulate their thoughts and responses.
- Avoid rushing through discussions, which can be particularly challenging for learners with speech access needs.
- Incorporate group activities or pair learners for discussions.
- Give learners the option to ask questions or make comments in an alternative format, like a flip chart parking lot.

What You Can Do Right Away

In addition to the tips provided here, start by thinking through how much you're asking or requiring learners to speak in your training programs. What alternatives could you offer to verbal participation? Being prepared ahead of time and communicating (without judgment) how you've planned to accommodate speech access needs can help put all your learners at ease.

44.
Beyond Barriers

Creating Inclusive Learning Pathways for Nonliterate Liberian Elders in Providence

Jean Marrapodi, PhD, CPTD (she/her)
Chief Learning Architect, Applestar Productions

When I lived in Providence during the early 2000s, Rhode Island had a huge influx of Liberian refugees fleeing their homeland after their country's second civil war. The Providence school system and adult education centers suddenly had to contend with more nonliterate students.

I was the director of Christian education at a local church in the city, and we had a group of active elder Liberians arrive in our pews with a single goal: They wanted to read the Bible. They were church goers at home in Liberia, and they knew that reading the Bible is what Christians do.

Most of Liberia is English-speaking, but these seniors came from remote villages and spoke two different mother tongues. Their English was limited, but it was the only way the two groups could understand one another. As far as we could tell, they were between 70 and 85 years old, but no one really knew because they could only say things like, "I was born during the coffee crop long ago." Immigration officials had taken a best guess, giving them all January 1 birthdays in a year somewhere close to when they might have been born. It was quite interesting to consider the cultural differences.

In the early days of my career, I was an instructor for individualized education and a first-grade teacher, so I'd taught many children to read. At this point, I had been in the L&D field for years, and I was a volunteer with Literacy Volunteers, so I knew how adults generally learn and had been trained to teach them how to read. I tackled this assignment with gusto, figuring I had the methods and tools to make it work.

Trying and Testing New Approaches

The first week of our class was Palm Sunday, an event I was sure the group would be familiar with. So, I planned a learning experience story for them. I told them the story and then gave them markers to draw it on a piece of paper with the sentence, "Jesus rode into town on a donkey." The early readers I'd worked with loved this kind of activity, so I thought this would be a good way to get started. I handed everything out and they looked at me like I had two heads. I didn't know at this point that they'd never touched a pencil, book, or paper before. Markers! What was I thinking? One of the students, Martha, said, "Teacher, we haven't practiced like you have so we can't do this." OK, I needed a plan B.

The second week was Easter, another story they were familiar with. I gave them a piece of paper divided in quadrants and told the story. I drew a simple symbol in each quadrant on the board for them to copy, which they also could not do. They were still unfamiliar with how writing worked, let alone copying something from the board, which required yet another skill set. They had no idea what symbols represented, and as I learned quite a bit later, made no connections with representations of things unless they were photographs of them. What appeared to me as a seemingly simple task was inordinately complex for them. It was time for plan C.

In week three, I brought a worksheet with two columns. In the left column, I'd drawn a circle, square, and triangle for them to copy into the right one, like what I'd do with preschoolers. This was a little successful. They could draw lines if I gave them dots to create the square and triangle, but the circle was hopeless. They were very pleased with themselves and with their product, though. I wish I'd realized what an accomplishment this was at the time.

In week four, I scrapped drawing and decided to try a sight word approach. I made three cards for everyone: one with their name, one with the word "loves," and one with the word "Jesus." I placed the cards in front of each student and showed them what each one said. I touched each card, and they repeated after me what the words said in front of them. "Elizabeth loves Jesus," "Kumba loves Jesus," "Essah loves Jesus," and so on. I went up to the board with a similar set of cards and had them read, "Elizabeth loves Jesus," as I touched each word. We repeated this multiple times. Next, I told them to watch as I switched the cards for Elizabeth and Jesus, so the sentence read, "Jesus loves Elizabeth." I asked them what the sentence said now, and they all chimed in "Elizabeth loves Jesus," even though the names were on different colors and they had seen me switch the cards. I realized they had no idea that the word was attached to the card. We had a long way to go to get to reading.

Over the course of our time together, I tried many other activities. I tried phonics, giving them a letter with a key word for the sound to help them remember so they could sound out words. They had trouble remembering what the pictures were, so this didn't work. I later discovered in my research that nonliterate people will only recognize photographs of objects and have no connection between an illustration and the tangible object. I also tried the visual, auditory, kinesthetic, tactile (VAKT) method, which involved having them trace a word on a card with their fingertip, repeating the word as we worked. I tried every trick in my bag to see if I could find something that would connect with them.

Cherishing Small Wins

Eventually, we made some breakthroughs, and they began to have a sight word vocabulary of key words that were important to them. God, Jesus, Bible, and church were favorites. We worked on more drawing, and I began to see the correlation between their drawings and literacy level. The people they drew were just like the tadpole-style people that preschoolers draw, with arms and legs attached directly to the face. There is extensive research about children's cognitive development as they draw, progressing through distinct stages. My students' literacy level mirrored that of very young children, and it made sense that their drawings would also. I will never forget Elizabeth's joy when we were drawing pictures of their grandchildren and she realized she could make herself look different from the children. "Look! I can make myself fat!"

They also drew their houses here and in Liberia, and they began to understand the symbolism that drawings have, and that they were the ones who made it happen. Kumba asked if she could take some paper and markers home and returned the following week with a stack of drawings.

I continued to weave drawing with the literacy work, teaching basic words and concepts. I used word families to help make connections through repetition: cat, fat, hat, mat, sat, and so on. I'd create simple worksheets for them, with simple sentences and pictures, until one day Kumba said, "I don't want to read about the cat on the mat. No cat wears a hat. I want to read the Bible."

I switched direction and found a reproduceable Bible timeline series that had pictures of the major Bible stories in chronological order. I bought the students notebooks, and each week, I told them a story and they added the picture into their notebook. They loved these. They could bring them home and retell the stories to their grandchildren or anyone who would listen. We were making progress but not meeting their goal, which seemed impossible.

One day, I had an idea. I bought them all Bibles. I put their names in them and got special bookmarks for them. We would start our lesson by finding the place in the Bible where the story of the week could be found. I'd tell the story, and they'd add it to their notebooks, and after class, they'd march upstairs proud as peacocks carrying their Bibles into the pews. They were content to have a Bible. Eventually, they could pick out the words that they knew on a page. They also realized that the words they knew were in the lyrics to the songs we sang projected on the screen.

Overcoming Assumptions

I learned so much from them in the eight years we worked together. I learned a lot about reading, moving down to a much more granular level than I'd ever imagined. I learned about assumptions. I thought I knew how to teach reading. I did, but this group needed things I'd never done before.

I also learned how many things we take for granted that are totally foreign to someone with a different background. Try to explain a calendar to someone who's never used one. "You throw it away? Why does it start there?" They knew the days of the week, but it took a while to connect how a calendar organized the dates.

We took field trips to broaden their world. They loved the zoo and the circus and were terrified by the ocean at the beach. Heights were another scary thing. We went to the theater and one of them panicked when she saw how high we were. I was always learning something new. I got to see their deep and abiding faith in action and hear their stories from back home. It was marvelous.

You may never have the opportunity to work with a population like this, but there are still parallels for us today. In your classes, with English language learners, you may need to clarify some cultural things; for instance, idioms and customs that seem to make no sense. (The Liberians I taught were totally baffled by Halloween decorations.) How can you make it safe for them to ask questions? Don't assume everyone comes with the same schemas that are in your head.

What You Can Do Right Away

I wonder, as trainers, if we generally take our students for granted, assuming we know the right way, and have information to impart to them expecting them to listen and take it all in. Adults come with years of experience, and when it's from a place that's different from the world you've grown up in, there are lessons you can learn, as well as those you plan to teach your students. I think many times, we forget to listen and learn from them. Ask as much as you tell. They have much to give.

45.
Left in the Margins
Discover an Unexpected Accessibility Barrier

Sarah Mercier (she/her)
CEO, Build Capable

In early 2024, I was interviewing Debbie Levitt, an expert in the user experience (UX) field for some guidance on a project. During our discussion, we began talking about my work in accessibility, and she shared an interesting story with me. For her book *Delta CX: The Truth About How Valuing Customer Experience Can Transform Your Business*, she had interviewed Mike Mills, a colorblind musician, to get his thoughts on colorblind friendly designs.[114]

Debbie said she learned many things about what Mike found challenging from a color blindness perspective, including the fact that the colorblind version of the game Uno is unnecessarily complicated. (I highly recommend reading the interview in her book to learn more about color blindness and user interfaces.) However, there was one thing that stood out at the end of our conversation.

Debbie and Mike were discussing the most difficult things about being colorblind, and he said that traffic lights were probably the worst. It was around this part of the discussion that Mike mentioned being left-handed, so Debbie asked, "Which is more difficult for you based on how things are built in the real world: being left-handed or being colorblind? Mike responded, "Being left-handed is more problematic."

This reminded me of an experience very early in my career. I was teaching a class in a computer lab that had a slide-out drawer to hold the keyboard and mouse. The tray that held the keyboard was on the left, and there was a fixed mousepad on the right. But there was often someone in the room who was left-handed, which meant they would have to unplug the mouse and pull it out of the computer tray. Then, we would need to reconnect it above the desk (if the cord was long enough) and reconfigure the desk space so they could use the mouse with their left hand. This left very little space for training materials like their participant guide or notebook.

You may find it interesting that this consideration is explicitly addressed under the universal design principle, flexibility in use: accommodate right- or left-handed access and use. One study published in 2020 found that approximately 10.6 percent of people are left-handed.[115] And, yes, most people can still use their nondominant hand, but anyone who has tried this knows that it takes more time and rarely results in the same level of precision.

What You Can Do Right Away

While left-handed dominant people grow to be accustomed to operating in a right-hand dominant world, that doesn't mean you should ignore them. Some small actions in designing your learning experiences can go a long way to creating a more inclusive environment:

- **Evaluate your physical learning environment**—especially the design and workspace setup. Is there space for someone to work right- and left-handed? This often comes into play at the end of a row of desks and when computers and peripherals are present.
- **Consider your supplies and participant materials.** Do you only have right-handed scissors? Do workbooks have left spiral binding that can make it difficult for learners to write with their left hand?
- **Allow participants extra time to acclimate to interact with something that requires their right hand to operate if you can't control the design**, such as a physical device, machinery, or simulator that was designed for right-handed use.

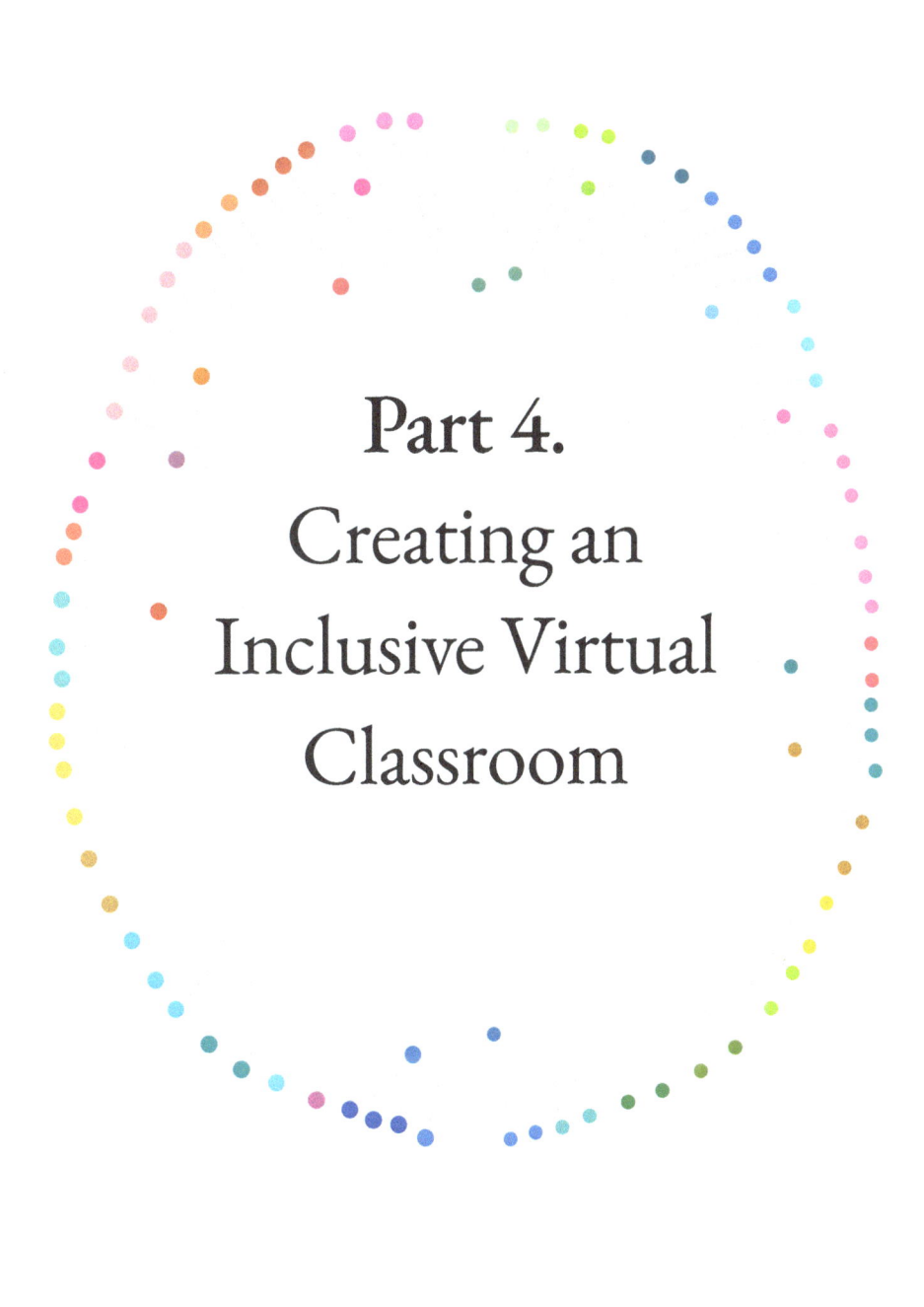

Part 4.
Creating an Inclusive Virtual Classroom

46.
Inclusive Design Considerations for a Welcoming Virtual Learning Space

Michelle Bartlett, PhD (she/her)
Assistant Professor, Old Dominion University

Suzanne Ehrlich, EdD (she/her)
Associate Professor and Program Director, University of North Florida

Virtual Workspaces and the Dynamics of Inclusivity

In recent years, many organizations have shifted to virtual workspaces. Engagement in this space offers unique opportunities—and challenges. Consider Jamie. They have worked remotely at their company for two years and, in that time, have been caring for their aging mother while being a single parent to two children. The remote work opportunity allowed them to reduce the financial and time-limiting aspects of commuting, but they still encountered barriers when participating in meetings and training. Jamie had support from in-home care; however, their environment was one that included children arriving home from school and sharing the space.

Jamie's colleague, Reese, chose a virtual position because it aligned with their need for an inclusive space and strong desire to participate as an observer and engage differently. The daily social interaction of a face-to-face position often added to Reese's anxiety and created barriers to their ability to contribute effectively, which they could do better in a virtual environment.

Jamie and Reese had a new team lead who required cameras be turned on for all meetings so they could get to know their new team. While this group valued team building, the ongoing requirement created stress among a team that had previously maneuvered a flexible and inclusive virtual practice. Once the team leader learned of these challenges through one-on-one meetings, Jamie and Reese shared ways the team could adapt to their diverse team's needs.

The team lead started engaging in small groups through breakout sessions, using technologies that allowed for input without speaking up at meetings, and providing the option for cameras to be off when not necessary for the meeting's goals. For example, it may be important for cameras to be on during a meeting if sensitive performance reviews are being discussed—seeing each other's expressions can help ensure the conversation is empathetic and clearly understood. The team lead also started using fun avatars and pictures of pets, hobbies, and pop culture, which became an activity many looked forward to sharing on Mondays.

Promoting variability and flexibility gives space for individuality to thrive. As we design virtual spaces, identifying ways to engage groups when learning virtually has become even more important. Modalities vary, but so do we. Technology has advanced in such a way that we can now freely test and adapt virtual spaces to meet participants' needs.

Practical Application of Accessibility in Virtual Learning

To consider all learners when designing a virtual space, one approach is to determine how to prepare to engage everyone. You can approach the process as a whole with the opportunity to adapt to new information or opportunities that emerge along the way. How will you present the content that people need to learn? How will you mix up different activity types? What technologies and tools will you use?

Provide Multiple Representations of Information

Virtual learning offers the flexibility to represent information in myriad ways. Whether through text, audio, video, graphics, or interactive simulations, learners benefit from multiple formats. By including tools like captions for videos, alt text for images, and transcripts for audio content, you can support accessibility for those with visual or auditory impairments.

This multimodal approach caters to diverse learning preferences (not styles), allowing learners options to access the content in a way that is most helpful to them. Consider these examples when offering support for those who prefer reading or need to refer to materials:
- A downloadable PDF with detailed notes on a topic
- Hyperlinks for further reading
- Illustrative examples

Variability in virtual spaces may also include these options:
- A podcast-style lecture complete with interviews from experts in the field is ideal for people who want to learn on-the-go.
- A recorded demonstration showing reactions in real-time with a voice-over explanation helps learners understand concepts in action.
- Infographics that visually represent information using charts, graphs, and imagery simplify complex information, making it easily digestible and memorable.

Accessibility features could also include video presentations with captions, which can assist learners whose first language is not the language of instruction and reinforce reading comprehension. In addition, alt text for images ensures that learners using screen readers get a description of the image, promoting accessibility.

These are all examples of how considering the ways in which media is *represented* in virtual spaces and how methods of content representation can ensure a more inclusive and comprehensive virtual experience.

Diversify Engagement and Activities

Traditional classroom settings might limit learners to paper-and-pencil tasks, but online platforms can incorporate forums, video responses, multimedia projects, and more. Embracing tools like voice-to-text software can further aid learners in expressing themselves. This flexibility encourages engagement and allows learners options to express their knowledge and skills. When used appropriately, incorporating a mix of self-paced modules, interactive quizzes, group activities, and gamified elements can motivate learners. Offering adjustable challenge levels or choices in topics gives learners agency over their learning journey. This personalized approach recognizes that motivation and interest can vary widely among learners.

Select Accessible Virtual Training Tools

The usability of an online platform can significantly affect a learner's experience, which means it should be intuitive to minimize the learning curve. Platforms that enable users to customize their settings like font sizes or color contrasts can improve the experience. Moreover, because many learners access content via mobile devices, a mobile-responsive design is crucial to ensure accessibility and ease of use.

In a virtual setting, consistency aids navigation and reduces cognitive load. By maintaining uniform layouts across modules and courses and adhering to consistent navigation patterns, learners can focus on the content rather than how to access it. Such predictability is especially beneficial for learners with cognitive challenges, because it minimizes potential points of confusion.

For many learners, assistive technologies like screen readers, magnifiers, or speech recognition tools are integral to their online experience. Ensuring that online platforms and content are compatible with these tools is crucial. This involves adhering to web accessibility standards and regularly testing content with various assistive technologies. Offering orientation sessions, tutorials, or help sections can ease a learner's transition into the digital classroom.

Check that additional tools (such as polling software and breakout rooms) are accessible by locating the platform's accessibility policy prior to your purchase or by contacting the company to learn more about how it considered accessibility in the design and launch of the product. Communicate to learners ahead of time what limitations the tool may have so they can plan accordingly.

Offer Opportunities for Feedback

Feedback in online learning plays a pivotal role in guiding learners' progress. Incorporating instant feedback mechanisms, such as automated quiz results with feedback, helps learners gauge their understanding immediately. Simultaneously, more detailed feedback from instructors or peers can offer insights into areas for improvement, fostering a growth mindset. Peer collaboration and feedback can also promote a sense of community in the digital realm.

Think Global

Virtual courses are commonly used to support a global audience. By offering content in multiple languages or with subtitles, you can make learning accessible to non-native speakers. Moreover, incorporating diverse examples, scenarios, and case studies that reflect multiple cultural contexts ensures the content is relatable and inclusive. Such inclusivity fosters a sense of belonging and respect among learners from various backgrounds.

Get to Know Your Audience

Empathy mapping is a technique used in training design to better understand your audience. As discussed in chapter 3, it involves creating a profile that considers their thoughts, feelings, and experiences. By exploring what the audience thinks, feels, observes, and does, you can tailor your virtual training to resonate more deeply with them, addressing their specific challenges and motivations. This approach leads to more engaged learners and effective training outcomes.

Consider How Materials Are Created and Shared

Suppose your audience includes a diverse group with varying levels of technological proficiency and access. In this case, you could create training materials in multiple formats—such as downloadable PDFs, interactive online modules, and even printed booklets—and then share them through various channels. You could use a central online platform that's accessible from different devices for digital materials, as well as provide options to mail physical copies to those who might have limited internet access or prefer hard copies. By diversifying the formats and distribution methods of your training materials, you cater to the different needs of your audience, making the training more accessible and inclusive.

Make Expectations for the Virtual Space Explicit

Provide specific guidelines for using features like chat, camera, and microphones, and clarify how and when to ask questions. Set clear norms for participation, such as engaging in polls and discussions. A clear approach to communicating expectations ensures a well-structured and respectful virtual learning environment, enabling effective engagement for all participants.

Accessibility Considerations Before, During, and After Virtual Training

We should think of learners' accessibility needs before, during, and after a virtual learning experience. The suggestions we offer here are not comprehensive, but signal ways you can easily adapt your virtual learning experiences in combination with other strategies discussed in this book.

Before:

- *Use preparation time to reduce barriers and lessen the need for participants to self-identify.* Send all documents beforehand, including an agenda, to create transparency and support understanding. By providing materials in various formats ahead of time (such as written documents, audio recordings, and visual aids), you can accommodate different learning abilities without participants having to request special accommodations or disclose personal information.
- *Proactively request any support you might need.* This could involve reaching out for technical assistance to ensure all digital platforms are fully operational, collaborating with subject matter experts for content accuracy, or arranging for additional facilitators to provide real-time assistance during the training program.
- *Use plain language in materials.* You can't assume your learners will have all the same reading and comprehension abilities.

That's why it's more accessible to use active voice, write in short sentences and paragraphs, avoid jargon (or fully explain terms if you can't), and opt for simple words over complex ones. (Refer to chapter 29 for more on using plain language.)

- *Understand the organization's culture.* If this information isn't documented, you might need to schedule a meeting with a manager or training organizer to learn more about common practices, language nuances, and the diverse backgrounds of the participants—and then document it for future use. It can help tailor the content to be culturally sensitive and inclusive, thus avoiding potential misunderstandings and fostering a more welcoming learning environment.
- *Assess current technology and any required additions.* For example, ensure your technology setup includes features like screen reader compatibility, closed-captioning for videos, and adjustable text sizes, which can preemptively address participants' needs without singling them out.
- *Deliver inclusive presentations.* Have them checked for accessibility by someone with appropriate training and experience.
- *Create a feedback mechanism.* This will allow participants to share any specific requests before the event.

During:
- *Give attendees the option to turn their cameras on or off.* Avoid making cameras required because they can be distracting for some and engaging for others. Providing an option supports a more inclusive virtual environment.
- *Reference and reshare documentation you've already shared in advance.* This reduces the need for individuals to disclose a need and request an accommodation.
- *Give flexible options for participation.* Allow participants to opt-in or observe an activity, as well as choose whether to use chat and video. Also, always include an alternative option to chat as a communication choice.

- *Use polls.* They support anonymous feedback.
- *Provide verbal descriptions of visual media.* Don't assume that all participants in a virtual environment can see the screen. Even those who don't have low vision or blindness can benefit from visual descriptions.
- *Provide breaks.* They're sometimes called brain breaks, and you can use them to address cognitive overload.

After:
- *Follow up and share recorded meetings for review.* Offer downloadable video files, audio-only versions for those who prefer to listen, and written transcripts. Some learners may be able to capture information missed due to unforeseen barriers.
- *Create an additional feedback loop.* This will allow participants to identify opportunities for improvement.

What You Can Do Right Away

While we have shared some practical applications for designing for all in a virtual space, this is also an opportunity for you to assess your current strategies for ensuring virtual learning experiences are accessible and inclusive. Design virtual learning experiences with a variability mindset to recognize the different ways in which the human side of participants can be represented and fostered for greater connection. To create a welcoming space in a virtual environment, consider how participants can personalize their virtual learning experience. Ask the questions: Who are you in a virtual space? How can a connection be created virtually? The absence of physical presence requires us to be intentional about creating safe and welcoming spaces in a meaningful virtual environment.

47.
Revolutionizing Remote Learning

A Guide to Crafting Inclusive Virtual Classrooms

Karen Hyder (she/her)
Online Event Producer and Speaker Coach

As a professional corporate trainer since the 1980s, I've used all the standard methods to reach remote learners. They usually involved some or all of us traveling. Learning time always felt crunched while travel time seemed never-ending. When desperate, I improvised and used conference calls alongside recorded video lessons and printed workbooks with Q&As posted on discussion boards. I invited participants to call in with questions. Still, I didn't always connect effectively with and support remote learners.

I quietly celebrated when virtual classroom software platforms entered into the corporate training scene. I wanted to work as a trainer, but by the late 1990s I was burned out from 10 years on the road. My clients, too, were tired of flying around the world to reach learners. One asked me to develop a train-the-trainer for virtual classrooms course. The software they chose was PlaceWare, which later became Microsoft Live Meeting.

I learned to adapt standard instructional models and methods—including verbal feedback, raising hands, handouts, and activities that started with "Turn to your neighbor and . . ." I refined my methods for handling questions and answers differently. I found ways to adapt delivery and classroom management techniques to work within PlaceWare's platform and limitations and create effective learning engagement with remote learners in a virtual classroom.

As profound as that paradigm shift was, we're now experiencing another one. Over the last several years, our industry has (belatedly) begun prioritizing the differing needs of *all* learners—particularly those whose abilities or circumstances too often left them out.

I admit to being late to the party. Even as I believed that I was supporting all learners, I realized I was underserving those most in need of support. I assumed that if it worked for me, and no one complained, everything was fine. However, when designing for and delivering training live and online, I need to think well beyond my own lived experience and those of my immediate team members. We're not a very diverse group. Personally, I don't know what it's like to be deaf or hard of hearing, or to rely on sign language interpretation, a cochlear implant, or a remote microphone to understand. I don't know what it's like to have dyslexia, ADHD, macular degeneration, photosensitivity, color blindness, neuropathy in my hands, or arthritis in my fingers.

I do know that background noise distracts me and that I can't see clearly without my glasses. My empathetic response begins here. I've been revising my approaches to better engage those who don't look like me, learn like me, or share my abilities. I invite you to join me in doing those hard things: devoting more resources to reaching all learners. We can do hard things!

Leveling the Playing Field

Until recently, I'd been feeling confident about the support I provide to learners. For example, I offer a PDF version of the session slides in advance so participants can follow along. I turn on the "everyone" chat option and invite participants to use it as a communication channel. I offer technical support to participants before, during, and between sessions. I open the session room early to attend to any last-minute needs. I prepare the facilitator in advance and analyze and optimize their audio quality. I make audio and video clips sound as clear as possible and add captions to them all. To improve accuracy, I hire a professional to caption all live sessions. I post the transcripts later, along with the recording. I believed that those steps would cover all the bases, no matter what my programs' diverse learners needed. But, by sitting down and reviewing materials—especially using a screen reader—I was shocked to discover how inadequate my approaches have been.

For one thing, I realized that my materials would not serve a low-vision or blind person. I'd actually made it more difficult for them. Sometimes I had deviated from a standard theme or template for the PowerPoint slide deck, not realizing anyone would notice or care, and had inadvertently included obstacles like too many hard returns, line breaks, or images and graphics with useless labels and text that was too small without enough contrast. I knew the challenges were real when the screen reader saw the first of many images and announced "74920192_chart.jpg" instead of relevant alt text.

Millions of working-age Americans have one or more disabilities. According to the US Bureau of Labor Statistics, "22.5 percent of people with a disability were employed—the highest recorded ratio since comparable data were first collected in 2008."[116] Further, many estimates miss workers who don't report their difficulties, says accessibility specialist Diane Elkins of Artisan Learning. If you fall and have a sore wrist, do you tell your boss? Do learners typically share details with you about their dyslexia, shoulder pain, a cut on their mousing finger, neuropathy, or migraine?

Some disabilities are situational, such as working in a noisy office or using a screen with poor contrast or glare. Needing a new mouse battery or to recharge a headset can hinder a participant. It has happened to me. How many people are participating (or attempting to participate) in my virtual classroom sessions and finding my accessibility accommodations lacking? What situations have you experienced?

If I want to continue being an effective instructional designer, trainer, and facilitator, I must commit to the effort necessary to investigate best practices and examine all the materials I develop and deliver through multiple lenses that represent the possible needs of my learners.

Some items are more obvious. For instance, I was trained to avoid font text color combinations that are problematic for those who are colorblind and to increase contrast for learners with low vision. I know that animation can be distracting and effects like flashing can even be dangerous, if misused. In screen-based learning, it's best not to change the page layout or move controls to different locations.

These things have always been important in design. However, they take on new meaning for those with disabilities operating in virtual classroom environments comprising multiple movable, sizable boxes. Only by stopping to consider things through different lenses can we ever hope to meet everyone's needs.

So, how do I proceed, and how should you? Here's how I adapt these valuable insights into the courses I design and deliver.

Start Asking Learners What They Need

Taking inspiration from my e-reader, online magazines, and language-learning apps that let me choose my own settings, I started asking participants—in a presession communication, days in advance—whether they plan to use or would welcome any of the following tools or options in the upcoming session:

- **Option for audio versus visual delivery.** Would you prefer to read the assignment in a PDF or listen to the same information in MP3 format?
- **Choice in font size and level of contrast.** Are you able to view this material in this format? Do you need to increase the font size or change the contrast?
- **Speed of audio delivery.** Do you want to be able to change the playback speed of the recording to play it faster or slower?
- **Keyboard as primary input tool, with opt in and out for mouse.** Can you participate in activities like drawing on an onscreen whiteboard? Do you require a keyboard-based alternate activity?
- **Screen-reader compatibility.** Does your screen reader convey what you need in this virtual classroom? What can I do to improve what you hear?

- **Option to choose activities that are easy, moderate, or challenging.** Would you prefer to choose the difficulty level of your assignments?

What have I learned from asking these questions? That I'm on the right path, but I have quite a way to go. Turns out that some of this work has already been done for me.

Apply WCAG in the Virtual Classroom

The WCAG (Web Content Accessibility Guidelines) are discussed throughout this book. WCAG is organized under four principles referred to as the POUR principles. (POUR stands for perceivable, operable, understandable, and robust.) I recently attended an online session from David Eifert, a learning and development senior associate at PwC with a master's degree in instructional design and technology from George Mason University.

In the session, David urged designers to regularly pause and consider POUR. So, in the virtual classroom context, pause and consider the following principles:

- **Perceivable.** Can users read the material? Have you provided a transcript? An audio recording? A summary? Is the PowerPoint handout formatted for accessibility?
- **Operable.** Will the users be able to use their keyboard's tab key to navigate the virtual classroom? Will they be able to type in chat and click to respond to polls? What alternate options are available?
- **Understandable.** Does your quantity of content serve the session's goals and your learners' needs? Does it follow a logical progression? Are the polls positioned in the same spot each time?
- **Robust.** Does the virtual classroom software support assistive technologies, such as keyboard shortcuts, tabbing, and the ability to generate captions and create transcripts? Can a standard screen reader see the menus, buttons, and features? Does a screen reader see the content? Can participants customize their preferences like resizing screens and text and displaying

in high contrast? Can they control the audio volume, webcam broadcast, and video playback?

What Challenges Do Your Learners Experience?

To ensure that my team and I started building our virtual classroom around learners' needs, I started to research those needs and identify possible ways to address them. For example, when considering the needs of learners with cognitive impairments, start with a less-is-more approach. Focus on the most important learning goals and clear all clutter out of the way.

Here are some tips for before and during the live session:

- **Before the live session.** Provide job aids for accessing the session and participating. Offer worksheets and handouts in advance. Remove extra information and digressions or relegate them to independent activities. If some learners want to know more, direct them to additional content. Tighten the focus of the live session. Simplify slides to include one question, one image, one sentence, instructions for an activity, or a few items in a numbered list. Do not include your whole script on slides. Instead, save the script text in PowerPoint Speaker notes.
- **During the live session.** Ask questions, teach participants how to respond, and then invite and encourage them to respond. Wait for responses to come in. Talk about the responses and why they are relevant. When incorrect answers are submitted, explain why a different answer is right. Suggest methods for remembering and resources to review! Encourage participants to ask questions, but set aside off-topic questions to be addressed at a more appropriate time. Be sure to define jargon and all new terminology multiple times.

Until recently, I was oblivious to how screen readers see and convey flat files like PDFs and images; I was happily distributing files that were worthless to some learners. Now that I know more, I can do better. For example, when considering the needs of learners with visual impairments, it's important to note that in virtual classrooms, neither shared applications nor shared desktops can be seen and conveyed verbally by a standard screen reader. Open and closed captions are also not seen by screen readers. That means some learners can't see or use a screen reader to access your live software demonstrations or PowerPoint slide shows. That's not accessible!

Here are some tips for before and during the live session:

- **Before the live session.** Some learners benefit from early and direct access to the native PowerPoint file with a logical tab order and concise alt text and image descriptions. Properly tagged PDF files, transcripts, and other resources in a screen-reader-friendly format can be processed in advance. Learners will be more ready to follow along and participate in the live session. Be sure to offer access to FAQs and live support.
- **During the live session.** To further include learners with visual impairments, describe everything simply! Describe yourself—what you look like and your environment. Describe the critical elements of images, charts, and video clips. Let folks in on the joke if everyone laughed at something. Read questions from participants aloud, as well as the responses others have written. Share support options and encourage everyone to ask for help when needed.

Supporting All Learners

Learners who don't have diagnosed disabilities also appreciate options. For example, be explicit with descriptions. Most participants benefit from specific, accurate language when referring to visuals. Also, avoid colloquialisms that can confuse people like, "We'll start again at half one o'clock" or idioms that might offend others.

Designing the Virtual Classroom Experience

No one stumbles into success in a virtual classroom. Good design, thoughtful planning, and careful production are critically and equally important to supporting an effective live session in which learners can learn. Rather than retrofit your course design to include accessible elements, plan for accessibility from the start. For example, discuss learning goals and accessibility concerns with learners with disabilities or their advocates. Solicit guidance and feedback on the choices you're making. Plan to check in and get feedback throughout the process. Update your design regularly.

Create Personas

Identify a few personas or fictitious characters that represent learners with common disabilities, to help inform your design decisions. I thoughtfully design and carefully test every task required to register, prepare, and participate in the course, pausing to consider how each learner persona will experience it.

Virtual Classroom Personas

Persona: Sandy (visual impairment). Sandy is a 35-year-old professional who has low vision. She uses a screen reader to access digital content and has these accessibility needs:
- Sandy relies on concise audio descriptions of visual content, well-structured slides, and accessible navigation.
- It's important that her screen reader can see the session content.
- She prefers to have the native PowerPoint file, including the alt text and speaker notes, at least a day in advance.

Persona: Alex (deaf or hard of hearing). Alex is a 15-year-old student who is deaf. He has a new cochlear implant and is developing his listening and spoken language skills. He communicates through sign language and lip-reading. Alex has these accessibility needs:
- Alex requires real-time captions for spoken content, including discussions and presentations. Providing transcripts for recorded sessions helps him review the material at his own pace.
- Offer the presenter's video in a large pod and on a strong and consistent network connection. Alex will need a good connection, too, to receive video. Lip-reading is not effective on a slow or choppy network connection.

Persona: James (mobility impairment). James is a 34-year-old professional who has limited mobility of his hands and wrists. He has these accessibility needs:

- James needs accessible materials that can be easily navigated with a keyboard. The webinar platform interface should be compatible with keyboard navigation to allow his full participation.
- James shares a high-traffic network connection that is often sluggish. The screen does not refresh new slides, videos don't play, and the presenter's full-time webcam broadcast causes audio to be choppy.

Persona: Kris (cognitive impairment). Kris is a 51-year-old individual with a cognitive impairment. She has difficulty processing complex information and has these accessibility needs:

- Kris benefits from clear and simple language, well-organized content, and limited distractions. Instructions should be straightforward, and activities should be designed to minimize cognitive overload.
- Go easy on the extra tasks. Put all resources in one place. Use single sign on, offer instruction on when and how to use tools to participate. Provide live support.

I ask myself, "Would Sandy, Alex, James, and Kris be able to register for the session, receive instructions and tutorial information, complete assignments, set up required equipment, set up specialized equipment, and access other resources? Could they log in at the correct time, control speakers, control their microphone and web camera, view captions, view the translator tool, type in the chat, respond to polls, draw on the whiteboard, drag onscreen objects, share their screen, upload and download files, follow along in the handout, participate in breakout activities, request assistance, and provide feedback?" If the answer to any of these is no, I go back and clear the learning path for each persona. I then redesign, offer an alternative, or provide support in the problem area.

Create and use personas with characteristics of common disabilities that can inform your choices. Be sure to include known disabilities in your learner population as well as common issues, such as low vision, color blindness, deafness, dyslexia, and limited use of hands.

Choose a Virtual Classroom That Supports Diverse Needs

Check out your vendor's Accessibility Conformance Report (ACR) to find out what features, options, and resources they provide. Explore the virtual classroom and meeting tools you already have available. Or, you can sign up for free software trials to test the type of activities you plan to include. Document what you find and create a list of questions to research or to ask the vendor.

Work With the Virtual Classroom's Features and Limitations

Design for the software tools you have. If you have very basic software, stick to very basic activities. Don't overcomplicate it and make producing the session difficult for the facilitator, and don't make participating difficult for the learners.

Leverage the Virtual Classroom's Live Engagement Features

Learning experiences in a physical classroom typically include most of the learning activities except for homework and small-group tasks. Lectures, discussions, and hands-on activities take place within class time. Take the pressure off having to support all content live. Instead, leverage virtual classroom sessions to support those activities that are best done live with the whole group, including interactive demonstration, role play, brainstorming, guided discussion, and application. You can use open-ended chat questions to collect responses, including opinions and recommendations. Ask poll questions to assess knowledge and encourage self-correction. Other content, such as articles, worksheets, tutorials, video clips, and recorded lectures, tests, and other assignments can be completed independently in advance or between sessions.

Script Instructions

There's a lot of pressure on the presenter to give clear, accurate instructions. Take a few minutes to write a script that includes instructions for how and when to participate using the available tools, technical troubleshooting guidance, where to go for support, and live session participation ground rules. Read when needed. I also create slides with screen captures of important menu options, instructions for each activity, and alternate activities and resources.

Plan for What You'll Need During the Live Session

As a facilitator, I know that coming up with something in the moment—like an accurate analogy, an excellent question, or an alternate activity—can be very difficult. It's much easier to plan something in advance, test it, keep it handy, and then use it when needed. My PowerPoint files often include five to 10 extra slides after the "thank you and goodbye" slide in case I need an alternate activity, if certain questions come up, or if we have extra time at the end. That way, I'm ready to skip to the slide and keep going.

Some of your learners will need accessible resources, and some will use them simply because they're available. Plan alternatives for each handout or resource. Alongside a text document, for example, create and offer a recorded audio version of the same information.

Verify Accessibility of PowerPoint Files and Other Session Materials

Check that colors conform to WCAG standards, confirm screen readers will read items in the correct sequence, and verify that each image, chart, and video includes useful alt text. If you need help designing your slides for accessibility, use the "Check Accessibility" tool in PowerPoint to identify potential issues and gain tips to improve your file. Then, manually go through the slides to be sure the best choices were made and confirm all elements are accessible, problems are corrected, and unnecessary items are removed. Also, make accessible PowerPoint and session transcripts available in advance, if possible. Include text summaries of the content you'll present and encourage participants to use immersive readers for all documents.

In addition, confirm that alt text and alternative audio tracks in videos provide visual descriptions (Figure 47-1).

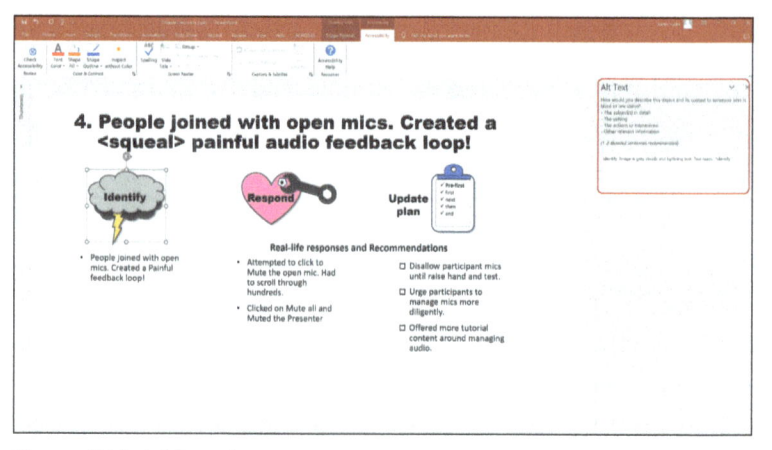

Figure 47-1. Adding alt text to images in PowerPoint.

Make Text Accessible

In PowerPoint, use an accessible theme or template with accessible colors and fonts. A PowerPoint theme provides the formatting before the text is added to the slide. Although many themes have stylized backgrounds and nonstandard fonts, I recommend selecting a clean and simple one using common fonts with clearly distinguishable characters and a heavier weight. If it's not perfect, make global adjustments to the master slides, which will adjust all slides universally.

Offer Tutorial Instructions and FAQs in Multiple Formats

Provide job aids, recordings, and user guides for participants who want to learn all they can about the virtual classroom as soon as they register. Be sure to send reminder emails to those who prepare the week before. Others will wait until the start time to think about the session. Some will have forgotten what they learned when they registered. Some are confused because they use different software at work. I recommend you open the session room early, greet participants graciously, and help them get set up and ready to start.

Pace Yourself

You might expect that you can cover more content in less time in the virtual classroom because participants complete prelearning activities beforehand, which buys you time in the live session. Classroom management is not what it was in the physical classroom; participants can respond all at once, which can also save a few minutes. That might mean you can push more content and everyone will learn.

But be careful! You might lose the entire group's attention and not notice they are gone! Also, if there's no time to participate, then why present the lesson live? Would it be more convenient to record everything and allow learners to play it back at their convenience and preferred speed without interaction? I recommend you design for interaction throughout the session instead.

Start with this: Present no more than one slide every two minutes. So, a 60-minute session would have 30 slides (including introductions and thank you slides) with questions that require an extra minute or more to tally responses and react. If you're showing short video clips or demos, double the duration of the clip to account for transitioning in and out of the activity. If you decide to show video clips twice, be sure to include that time in the calculation.

To focus attention and maintain the lesson sequence, include a PowerPoint slide as a placeholder for each question and activity (such as a demo, video clip, or breakout activity). Add open-ended questions and closed questions with possible responses. Indicate options to respond, whether it's click to the left of your answer to respond to the poll, type in the chat, click agree or disagree, or unmute your microphone and speak up (verbal).

For breakout groups, allow extra time to provide instructions, confirm setup, transition into and out of the groups, and then discuss the outcomes. Allow one minute for each group to report.

Choose the Best Video Delivery

Reserve online time for whole group activities, not watching prerecorded content. When using media to support learning, play short clips during the live session but post longer clips for participants to view beforehand. Be sure to use accurate subtitles and captions on video clips and disable auto play so individuals can control the videos.

Be Ready to Troubleshoot

At some point, participants will need assistance. Be prepared to provide technical support and instructions visually and verbally. I keep a set of tutorial slides and a text file with "pasteable" instructions that I can access to provide guidance in the moment of need.

What You Can Do Right Away

There's a lot to do to plan, prepare, and present live virtual classroom sessions that support all learners. It's easy to focus on the details and forget your objective. Above all else, we must adopt an attitude of learning, humility, and service. And we must plan ahead and budget for the work that will be involved. Designing for accessibility from day one will be easier and more efficient than trying to retrofit older programs.

We're all challenged to see improving accessibility as an ongoing process. I pledge to continuously gather feedback from learners with disabilities and make necessary adjustments to ensure an inclusive learning experience for everyone.

> "If it's not accessible, it's not finished." —Sarah Mercier, Build Capable

Here are some actions you can take to shift your mindset and approach to designing an accessible virtual classroom:

1. Pause and consider each decision point.
2. When possible, allow personalization. Let participants adjust their volume and video playback speed, change the font size and color contrast, enlarge their screen, and show and hide the tools—and teach them how to do those things.
3. Be ready to add extra support, remove obstacles, or rework activities to improve accessibility in all areas.

48.
Redefining Engagement
Designing Accessible and Inclusive Activities in Virtual Classrooms

Kassy LaBorie (she/her)
Keynote Speaker, Author, Virtual Training Pioneer

Engaging participants in the live virtual classroom is an increasingly popular topic for learning and development professionals, given the now widespread use of online meeting platforms like Zoom, Microsoft Teams, and Webex. It's also commonly accepted that lectures (or live PowerPoint slide readings), even if the presenter is appearing on camera, are simply not the most interesting or effective way to engage virtual classroom learners. This delivery creates a passive experience. Because virtual classroom tools enable a live audience to gather and collaborate, it makes sense to use those tools to involve people rather than lecture or simply read information to them. If audience interaction is not necessary, then perhaps another delivery mode like a video or an article would be more effective. Why ask people to block off their calendars and attend something at a specific date and time with others only to have them sit quietly alone and do nothing?

As a professional virtual facilitator, I want to design and deliver interactive, nonlecture-based, live virtual classroom experiences that engage participants and are accessible and inclusive for all audience members. My guiding principle for the design and delivery of all my virtual classroom training experiences is this:

> "What do I plan to say or do that I could
> let my participants say or do instead?"

It's an inclusive approach, one based on a deep desire to involve the audience in meaningful and effective ways. However, I have made the mistake of not actually including everyone or making the experience accessible to the entire audience given my lack of understanding around Universal Design for Learning (UDL). After that mistake, I began to research accessibility, inclusion, and UDL. I admit to not knowing just how much I was missing. When Sarah Mercier asked me about my experiences, I was happy to share how I am learning and broadening my understanding.

So, for this chapter, I will share how I've edited my approach to the popular "Image Connect" activity from the book I co-authored with Tom Stone, *Interact and Engage! 75+ Activities for Virtual Training, Meetings, and Webinars*.

Learning From a Mistake

Interaction in the virtual classroom is key for engagement, and, given the capabilities of the platform, it should be accessible and inclusive to all. But is it? Are the virtual platform's tools enough, and are they being used in ways that are effective for everyone? Are you preventing audience members from being able to participate or forcing them to ask you for something you should have already considered?

I was honored to be invited to speak at a well-known public learning and development industry webinar on activities for virtual training engagement. Thousands of people had registered for the event. I spent hours preparing the experience with stories, research, demonstrations, activities, materials, and, of course, as much interaction as I could create. I was prepared and rehearsed, and on the day of the webinar, we were fortunate to have no technical issues and a highly energized and engaged audience.

I'm the type of presenter to invite comments, ideas, and reactions via chat the entire time, and the audience was open to conversation. I was paying close attention to it, responding verbally as we went along. This is when I saw one person asking where they could locate the closed captions.

I verbally announced our host would assist. I privately chatted to my host to ask that they help the person sending the chat message. The chats kept coming in. And this went on until I announced and sent via chat that the closed captions were not only not available, but also, had not been enabled for the webinar because no one had requested it in advance.

I was stunned. I was ashamed. I had assumed. Where else was I also making assumptions? Where did I have more control? It was the moment I decided that I needed to know more, *and do more*, to make sure this situation would not happen again—not only regarding closed captions, but also . . . well, what else? I realized that I didn't even know the answer.

The Challenge and Assignment: Image Connect Redesign

What's an effective way to deliver accessible and inclusive experiences in the live virtual classroom when the following principles are valued?

- Limit lecture. Do not read slides, chats, and other responses word for word.
- Present interactively.
- Facilitate collaboration.
- Encourage participants to think for themselves.

With this in mind, I set out to redesign the popular "Image Connect" virtual classroom activity and materials to be inclusive for all. I chose this activity because so much of it encapsulates my engagement principle.

Image Connect asks participants to answer a question related to the topic (or respond to a request) by choosing from several images displayed on their screens (Figure 48-1). Here are some example questions:

- Which image best describes you in your current role? Using annotation, type your name on one and be prepared to unmute or use chat and explain. (This uses the images provided in Figure 48-1).
- Choose an image that looks the most like the last webinar you attended and be prepared to unmute or use chat to share why. (This version uses various weather images.)
- Which image best represents the current state of your team? Using annotation, place a stamp and be prepared to unmute or use chat and share. (This version uses images representing chaos, coordination, unhappiness, happiness, and a good leader.)

Figure 48-1. Image Connect Activity

I had to learn what participants needed before I could redesign the activity. Some of the details were obvious, as the activity was based on eyesight. I knew I needed descriptions, but I didn't want to default to the dreaded unengaging lecture—the main point of this activity is to avoid reading everything on the screen to the audience. But this presents a problem for those who are unable to see the images.

It was also important for me to understand what was incorrect, wrong, or missing from my activity's design. After speaking with several industry experts and reading through CAST's UDL guidelines, it became clear that what I needed to add to my design went beyond descriptions.

The Feedback

The changes I needed to make to the current activity affected the design, development, and delivery in several ways, including enabling closed captions, providing a downloadable file with alt text, and offering alternative response options.

Enable Closed-Captioning

It's now standard in all the virtual training, presentations, and meetings I host to enable the option for closed-captioning. Participants don't need to ask to use what is always available. While it's not a perfect feature, it is a highly useful one that helps not only those unable to hear, but participants who choose to mute the audio due to their environment. The closed-captioning feature also increases the effectiveness of a presenter's speech, smoothing over any words or inflections that may come from regional accents and dialects. No matter the accent or dialect, presenters can learn to speak clearly as a result, increasing the engagement of not only the sound of the message, but also the delivery of each of the words.

Provide a Downloadable File With Alt Text

Alternative text is read aloud by screen readers. It has the added function of displaying text in place of an image if it fails to load on a webpage. I needed to add alt text to the images in my presentation and to a handout for reference. The handout was key for my activity because I wanted to steer away from a lecture-based delivery. To avoid lecturing, I needed this additional asset for those who can't view the images to use with their screen reader applications. It was important that the file was a download because screen readers aren't always able to read from a presenter's shared screen. That way, the screen reader applications have direct access to the materials.

In this activity, the facilitator shouldn't influence the participants' responses, so they shouldn't verbally describe each image. Rather, the facilitator provides an overview of the general idea of the images, and then refers everyone to not only the screen, but also to the downloadable resource with alt text as needed. The idea for the activity is to let participants decide what each image means to them and then to answer the questions based on their own experiences.

Offer Alternative Ways to Respond

Creating alternative ways to respond using the virtual classroom's features is necessary to include everyone, but recognize that it can be confusing if not carefully and thoughtfully done. It's a paradox of choices, like when a person is in the cereal aisle at the grocery store. If there are too many choices, that can lead to the person making no choice at all! While it's important to offer alternative ways to respond, I recommend that you deliver these options with clarity and purpose, choosing to lead with one, but permitting others to be available.

Given that the Image Connect activity encourages people to actively participate in the virtual session, rather than choosing to sit back and passively watch or listen, I suggest the following instructions: Rather than saying, "Once you have chosen your image, type your name on the screen using annotation, send your answer in the chat, or raise your hand to unmute and speak—whatever way you want to respond is fine," say this instead: "Once you have chosen your image, let's use annotation to type our names on the screen. Should you prefer to share another way, please respond using chat or raise your hand and we will call on you to unmute."

The two options are not too dissimilar, but the second one suggests one clear way, and then provides options as needed.

The Outcome

The redesigned Image Connect activity that I deliver today is shown here. I still have more to learn. This is just one of many activities that I'll need to update as I continue this journey of providing accessible and engaging virtual learning using live online meeting technologies. I'm interested in pushing the limits of how we use these tools and their features to include everyone. My new template for moving forward, one in which I encourage you to adopt and use, is provided in the template following the outline of the activity.

Image Connect Activity

The instructions for the redesigned Image Connect activity are:
1. Arrange nine to 12 images on a slide and add numbers next to them for use with larger audiences (Table 48-1). Provide the same images in a downloadable document that you've set up for accessibility, including adding alt text for each image.
2. Ask participants to select the image that best describes them in their role or in their personal life.
3. If there are fewer than 20 participants, ask them to use annotation tools to type their names on the image.

4. If there are more than 20 participants, use chat and ask participants to reference the associated image number with a brief description of why they chose it.
5. Provide alternative ways to respond, as appropriate.
6. Call on participants to share over audio, or in chat, as time permits. Ask them to explain why or how. Note connections and commonalities.

Table 48-1. Onscreen Visual for Redesigned Image Connect Activity

1. Panda sitting down eating some bamboo	2. Night sky with colorful spray of large fireworks	3. Facing up from the ground looking up at a forest of tall trees with sunlight beaming down through the leaves
4. Two chairs on a beach with no people overlooking a light blue lagoon with an island mountain in the background	5. An array of hot air balloons with one more in focus and higher than the others	6. A noble tiger facing the camera walking toward it with greenery in the background

Table 48-1. (Cont.)

 7. A rocket ship with focal point on the tip orbiting around a planet	 8. A snippet of a map styled to look old with a magnifying glass looking over the Atlantic Ocean with a small compass on the table above it	 9. An assorted flower garden of tulips with a tall purple flower in center focus higher than the others

Source: Activity from Interact and Engage: 75+ Activities for Virtual Training, Meetings, and Webinars.[117] *Alt text suggestions provided by Cara North.*

Explain the question and assignment to participants. Say, "Which image best describes you in your current role? Please note the images are shown on our shared screen and within your handout (where alt text is included). Notice there are nine separate images of animals, events, places, and objects from which you may choose. I'll be quiet for the next three minutes while you decide."

When you ask participants to respond, give them the following options:
- Please use annotation to type your name on the image shared on the screen.
- Or, use chat and reference the number of the image.
- Or, raise your hand to volunteer to unmute and speak.

The Template

Use this template for the design and development of future interactive and collaborative virtual training activities that are accessible and inclusive. Note that the features of the online meeting platform are chosen as the last step in the process. This ensures the focus remains on the objective, the participant-led learning, and the inclusion of everyone. The platform features come last in the considerations to keep the focus as previously suggested and to allow for variations in feature availability, access, and function across all the current platforms in the market.

The template for virtual training success:

- **Objective.** What will the participants be able to do following their participation in this activity?
- **Social.** How or why is learning together a better experience than completing this on their own?
- **UDL.** What will make this experience accessible, inclusive, and supported by the UDL guidelines?
- **Features.** Which platform features best support the live, collaborative social gathering?

Here's how I used it to outline the Image Connect activity:

- **Objective.** Create a safe learning environment by allowing people to share and connect through stories.
- **Social.** Think creatively together and learn how others think, relate, and differ.
- **UDL:**
    - *Include alt text.* Provide alt text to describe what each image is.
    - *Provide a downloadable file.* Have an accessible PDF or document version of the image table with the alt text on each photo and as a caption below each picture.
    - *Offer alternative ways to participate:*
        - Give participants the option to share their chosen picture using the chat. (Some may not feel comfortable speaking.)
        - Alternatively, let them share the picture via their virtual background. (Some may not feel comfortable being on camera.)
        - And for more ways to be as inclusive as possible, instead of always asking for people to use the hand-raising feature, encourage them to use the chat and annotation tool.
- **Features.** Slide, handout, annotation tools, webcam, chat, audio.

What You Can Do Right Away

Whether you design virtual classroom experiences for others to facilitate, you facilitate them, or both, be mindful of the accessibility of all the elements of the experience, particularly any activities to engage participants. Use the activity template for virtual training success to begin creating an inclusive virtual classroom.

49.
Strategies to Overcome Auditory Processing Challenges

Judy Katz (she/her)
Founder and Consultant, Neurodivergent Working

Joan closes her laptop and relishes the dimness of the room. Her company, like many, went remote during the pandemic, and Joan and her colleagues have since remained on a 100 percent work-from-home schedule. She feels lucky that she can take most of her training in a self-study format, but there are still virtual instructor-led sessions from time to time. Some sessions even span half a day or more, just like in-person training.

Joan is autistic. One aspect of her neurodivergence is auditory processing disorder, a condition that makes it slower and more difficult to process audio. Complex sounds and lots of background noise can be problematic, and so can long meetings that rely heavily on relaying information via audio.

Virtual instructor-led training (vILT) is often more neurodivergent friendly than in-person training. Learners can manage their sensory inputs better because they're in their own space. Some people, like Joan, work in a home office where they can completely control their sensory inputs. Even someone who is taking vILT at work in their cubicle generally has the comfort of familiarity and more ability to control sensory inputs than in a classroom training environment. However, there still may be barriers that facilitators can help neurodivergent learners overcome.

Joan's favorite virtual instructor, Maya, is sensitive to the needs of learners with audio processing disorder and many other disabilities. Maya uses a wired internet connection for good audio quality and conducts training sessions from a private space so there's no background noise. She asks participants to keep their audio off when they're not speaking to eliminate further distractions. She doesn't rely solely on talking; instead, she uses well-planned and clear visuals to convey information. Maya sends her slides with descriptive text out ahead of time to accommodate learners with visual disabilities. She stays focused on the training program's goals and doesn't require everyone to be on video. Joan appreciates this because it can be distracting and make her feel like she's on the spot. Maya also reminds participants that auto captions are available and shares how to use them.

The use of auto captions is controversial, and rightly so due to the imprecision of current technological capabilities. However, for people with audio processing disorder, captioning errors don't pose as big of a problem as they can for deaf and hard of hearing learners. Learners with audio processing disorder can hear, which makes it easier to overcome mistakes made by auto captions. There are also separate dictation tools that learners might prefer over the auto captions built into a particular teleconference tool, so those can be used in a separate window or on a separate device.

What You Can Do Right Away

How can you be more like Maya as an inclusive-oriented virtual instructor? Think about the audio experience of your virtual learning programs. Does the audio quality, background noises, or distractions impede the participant's ability to process the information? What alternative options do learners have if they can't hear the audio? Start putting this into practice by investigating the captioning options in the teleconference software that you use and auditing your vILT practices according to the information in this and other chapters.

50.
Optimizing Virtual Training Accessibility
Addressing Speech Access Needs

Susi Miller (she/her)
Founder and Director, eLaHub

When I first became interested in accessibility, one of the things I found most confusing about the Web Content Accessibility Guidelines (WCAG) was the POUR principles. After a while, I realized that each of the letters in the acronym stood for one of the four principles that the WCAG standards are divided into: perceivable, operable, understandable, and robust.

Unfortunately, understanding what the acronym meant didn't help me to make sense of the standards or apply them practically. When I got started with creating accessible learning content, I found things much easier to understand and process if I focused instead on the access needs the standards were aimed toward. These digital access needs are very often divided into four categories: vision, hearing, motor, and cognitive.

An important access need that is commonly missed from this list, however, is speech. Common disabilities and conditions that can affect speech include stammer or stutter, Tourette syndrome, and dysarthria (conditions that lead to speech being slow, slurred, or difficult to understand).

One of the reasons speech access needs are overlooked by learning practitioners is because there are currently no WCAG standards aimed at including these learners in digital learning content created with authoring tools. However, it's vital that we take them into consideration in virtual (and face-to-face) training sessions.

Early in my accessibility career, I overlooked speech access needs in a virtual, instructor-led training (vILT) session. It was a valuable reminder that it can be difficult to get things right all the time. I'd always been very mindful of being accessible and inclusive in my vILT sessions. One way I did this was to remind participants that they could use the chat rather than their microphone to communicate for any reason, such as being in a noisy environment or having a speech access need. But I never considered that I needed to remind people about this before breakout sessions.

In the virtual training event where I got things wrong, I was the moderator of a breakout room. I was concerned that one of the participants didn't seem to be engaged and wasn't contributing to the activity, so I asked them if they could open their microphone and answer a question. After an uncomfortable pause, they began speaking. They explained that they had a stammer, which made them very reluctant to contribute in this way. I was absolutely horrified that I'd put them in a position where they had to declare an access need in front of the rest of the group.

To this day, it still makes me uncomfortable to think about how I made the learner in that breakout session feel. Although my first reaction after the event was to try and forget that it had ever happened, I eventually realized what a valuable opportunity it was to learn from.

When I thought more about what had gone wrong, I realized that I was a lot less confident about how to include learners with speech access needs in my learning solutions than I was for the other four categories (vision, hearing, motor, and cognitive). As a result, I found out as much as I could about some of the different conditions associated with speech access needs, and things I needed to be mindful of.

What You Can Do Right Away

The following recommendations are the results of that research. They are actions that you can take to make sure you include learners with speech access needs in your virtual training sessions:

- **Always use presession communication** to make sure that attendees have the opportunity to advise you of their access needs.

- **Encourage attendees to use the direct messaging option in virtual sessions** to advise you of their access needs if for any reason they have not been able to do so prior to the session.
- **Let learners know about alternative ways to participate and communicate in the session,** such as the chat functionality. Make sure you do this for both the main session and for activities in breakout rooms!
- **Consider using alternative methods of communication,** such as icons and reaction emojis. For example, using the cross and tick or check icons is a great way to quickly check in with all attendees and include those with speech access needs.
- **In larger sessions, use breakout rooms** to facilitate smaller group discussions. This can reduce anxiety for participants with speech access needs and make it easier for them to contribute verbally.
- **Be flexible with timing and avoid rushing through discussions.** Give attendees enough time to express their thoughts without feeling pressured.
- **Don't force attendees to give feedback.** Allow breakout groups to choose someone who feels comfortable presenting to the wider group.

Part 5.
A Primer on Accessibility Standards

51.
Interpreting Accessibility Standards

Haley Shust (she/her)
Accessibility Specialist and Instructional Designer

Determining Where to Start

Coaching is my favorite part of my role as an accessibility specialist. Not only do I get to connect with my peers, but I get a glimpse into how they work. Whether as a designer, a facilitator, or a technology analyst, I've learned a great deal about process and priorities in different parts of Salesforce. Even if we're all working toward a common goal, there will always be variations in how individuals contribute toward that goal. That is especially true for how people understand and apply accessibility practices.

When I begin a coaching program, I like to have my participants define *accessibility* in their own words. Oftentimes I structure this as a game of word association: "When you hear the word *accessibility*, what do you think of?" An unofficial ranking of the most common responses includes *disability*, *equality*, *inclusion*, *screen reader*, and *alternative text*.

By asking someone to associate terms or define accessibility in their own words, I get a glimpse into their depth of understanding. For example, if they mention only visible disabilities (like blindness or physical impairments), then it's possible they're overlooking invisible disabilities (such as cognitive or psychological ones).

Sometimes—but not frequently—a participant will reference a law, policy, guideline, or other regulation related to accessibility. This cues me for the follow-up question, "How do you apply [*insert accessibility standard*] in your role?" In my experience, nine times out of 10, participants

indicate that they are loosely familiar with an accessibility standard, but haven't examined it in depth for one or several of the following reasons:
- The standards are difficult to understand.
- They aren't sure which standards to apply.
- They don't see any commonality between their actions and the standards.
- Their organization has not chosen standards to align to.
- Their organization already has an accessibility checklist that is based off standards.
- They assume their technology meets minimum standards.

There's no shame in any of these responses. Accessibility standards *are* difficult to understand, especially the laws and policies that are written in legalese and resemble a terms and conditions document.

For most L&D practitioners, it is important to understand the standards; however, there's no need to start your journey with them. You can be an accessibility champion without memorizing policies and guidelines.

Defining Accessibility Standards

Generally, accessibility standards are used to measure compliance. Some standards speak to architecture, focusing on the physical accessibility of a facility or a building. Others focus on services, such as transportation or communication. These standards aim to provide equal access to individuals with disabilities.

Because you're reading this book, you are also learning just how important it is to understand accessibility standards related to information technology, or digital experiences, are in your own work. Trainers and facilitators use technology, such as slide decks, polling, and live transcription. Through the internet, we can communicate, access learning, and share information online. The benefits are tremendous; however, this evolution has posed challenges for people with disabilities. Processes that were once in-person have transitioned online.

Let's use paying bills as an example. In the past, individuals had to deliver or mail a check. But thanks to online banking, bills can be paid directly from an account without using any physical materials. For most, this transition was revolutionary. Yet, this created a gap for those with disabilities. Sometimes the digital option isn't accessible. Maybe it doesn't play nicely with assistive technology. Or a site can't be navigated with a keyboard alone. Long story short, there is a tremendous need for accessibility standards related to technology and digital experiences.

Many countries have digital accessibility laws and regulations in place, but plenty do not. Some of those laws and regulations require all organizations—private or public—to comply. Other countries have accessibility standards in place for only federal departments. Needless to say, the rate at which technology is evolving is faster than the creation of accessibility standards. That's where the mantra "progress over perfection" aligns perfectly with accessibility efforts.

Understanding Types of Accessibility Standards

One of the most challenging aspects of understanding accessibility standards is categorizing them. There are standards that exist as conventions, treaties, declarations, laws, policies, regulations, charters, acts, and guidelines. The following list is a short primer of accessibility standards:

- **Web Content Accessibility Guidelines (WCAG)**
    - *Type:* Standards
    - *Published:* World Wide Web Consortium (W3C) ongoing publications; version 2.1 published in September 2023
    - *Description:* The Web Content Accessibility Guidelines offer testable success criteria for making web content more accessible. They are not regulated by a country or organization but are often used to assess compliance. WCAG is considered the universal standard for how to create accessible content for all devices and online experiences. In fact, many other standards in this list are based on WCAG.
- **International Standards Organization and International Electrotechnical Commission 40500:2012 (ISO/IEC 40500:12)**
    - *Type:* Standards
    - *Published:* International Standards Organization and International Electrotechnical Commission in 2012

- *Description:* ISO/IEC 40500:12 is identical to WCAG 2.0, which is an older version of the guidelines. The primary difference is that some ISO/IEC 40500:12 standards are mandatory, while none of the guidelines are mandatory. Some countries prefer to use ISO/IEC 40500:12 because of these mandatory standards.
- **Section 508**
  - *Type:* Section of a law
  - *Published:* United States of America in 1998
  - *Description:* Section 508 is a part of the US Rehabilitation Act, which requires federal agencies and departments to ensure any electronic information is accessible to people with disabilities. This applies to both individuals working for the federal government and people the government serves. Failure to comply to Section 508 can result in complaints and civil lawsuits.
- **Americans with Disability Act (ADA)**
  - *Type:* Civil rights law
  - *Published:* United States of America in 1990
  - *Description:* The Americans with Disabilities Act aims to prohibit discrimination against people with disabilities. The law is made up of many titles that aim for disability equality in employment, transportation, education, communications, and information technology. Nonprofits, businesses, and local and state governments are expected to meet ADA guidelines.
- **European Union Web Accessibility Directive (EN 301 549)**
  - *Type:* Directive with standards
  - *Published:* European Union in 2018
  - *Description:* The European Union Web Accessibility Directive requires all public sector websites and applications to implement, maintain, and enforce fines or legal penalties related to accessibility. Within this directive, the EU outlines standards (EN 301 549) to make websites and applications more accessible. Unsurprisingly, EN 301 549 is based on WCAG.

- **European Accessibility Act**
    - *Type:* Directive
    - *Published:* European Union in 2019
    - *Description:* The European Accessibility Act mandates that products and services, especially digital ones, are accessible to people with disabilities. This act is widely beneficial because it standardizes expectations across European countries by removing the need for country-specific requirements. All businesses—private and public—are expected to become compliant by June 2025.
- **Web Accessibility Initiative—Accessible Rich Internet Applications Suite (WAI-ARIA)**
    - *Type:* Technical specification
    - *Published:* World Wide Web Consortium (W3C) in 2014
    - *Description:* This initiative was designed to provide guidance on how to use Accessible Rich Internet Applications (ARIA) to design accessible digital experiences. Like HTML, JavaScript, and CSS, ARIA is a web language. Specifically, it is used to make digital interactions accessible to people who use assistive technology. ARIA is typically used with HTML5 but can also be used with XHTML and HTML4. WAI-ARIA was published to share best practices for web developers.
- **Japanese Industrial Standards X 8341 (JIS X 8341)**
    - *Type:* Standards
    - *Published:* Japan in 2004
    - *Description:* JIS X 8341 standards aim to make websites accessible for elderly and disabled people across Japan. Created by the Japan Web Accessibility Consortium (JWAC), these standards align with WCAG and are updated every five years. They must be met by private and public organizations.
- **Accessibility for Ontarians With Disabilities Act (AODA)**
    - *Type:* Law
    - *Published:* Ontario, Canada, in 2005

- *Description:* The AODA's purpose is to improve accessibility for Ontarians with disabilities by 2025. The scope includes public and private organizations and addresses the accessibility of information and communications, employment, transportation, and more. Compliance deadlines vary by sector and institution size; however, the government and other large institutions have already begun taking steps toward more accessible products and services.
- **Marrakesh Treaty**
  - *Type:* Treaty
  - *Published:* World Intellectual Property Organization (WIPO) in 2013
  - *Description:* The Marrakesh Treaty was administered by the WIPO and first adopted in Marrakesh, Morocco. The purpose of the treaty is to make print materials more accessible to blind and visually impaired people. At the time, these populations were experiencing a "book famine" in which few books were formatted or printed in a way that made them accessible. Thanks to the Marrakesh Treaty, there are copyright exceptions to facilitate the creation of accessible books. As of the writing of this book, 120 countries have signed the treaty.

Now, I want to be clear that you don't need to memorize accessibility standards to be effective. You should, however, learn how to interpret them so they translate to your line of work. As you begin to explore them, you'll find that some are specific to web developers or architects, while others can apply to any role. No matter what you do, the very foundation of these standards is the same: Make experiences more accessible for people with disabilities.

Making Sense of Accessibility Standards

With so many standards, which ones do you need to learn? Should you prioritize the ones specific to your country? Or will universal standards, like WCAG or ISO/IEC 40500:12 suffice? Where do you need to start?

I don't advise exploring the standards until you've determined your scope. Your responsibilities as an accessibility champion depend heavily on your role. If you're a web developer responsible for coding websites and apps, you'll need to understand assistive technology and ARIA. If you're a learning designer, you must ensure deliverables function with assistive technologies. If you're a trainer, you require knowledge of accessibility accommodations. If you're a manager, you'll need to identify methods and tools that your employees can use to access information and do their job.

A foolproof way to get started is to search "accessibility best practices for [*your role*]." Then it's time to weed through the many results, including blogs, articles, podcasts, webinars, and courses. Find commonalities in your search results. What topics seem to be emphasized? What are some keywords among the results? Use that information to inform more specific research.

Speaking from my own experience as a learning designer, there is one article that demystified accessibility above all others: Steven Lambert's 2018 Smashing magazine article, "Designing for Accessibility and Inclusion."[118] I've referenced and shared this article hundreds of times in my career. Brian Dusablon has also adapted Steven's approach in chapter 13, focusing on designing learning experiences.

Early in my accessibility journey, I would reference Steven's article as my accessibility checklist. Over time, I began to memorize the questions and master the practices. I knew I was ready to increase my rigor when I became responsible for auditing the accessibility of my peer's content. I began to create checklists based on the WCAG success criteria.

My first checklists were not user friendly. They were wordy, like the guidelines themselves, and did not include examples. And while they were comprehensive and thorough, they provided no feedback for how to fix the accessibility issues. It was a simple binary indication of "met" or "did not meet" a particular standard. That approach is just fine if your audience knows WCAG backward and forward. But that's rarely the case.

There are a few actions that I conduct at least once a month or on a project-by-project basis. I've included questions that I ask myself at each step. Use this list as a starting point to create your own routine for staying current with accessibility:

1. **Set expectations.** Determine which accessibility standards matter in your organization.
   - What expectations does your organization have related to the application of accessibility?
   - What standards are you expected to meet?
2. **Identify relevant standards.** Determine which ones relate to the scope of your role or project.
   - How does accessibility apply to your role?
   - Which accessibility standards are most relevant to your role?
   - What does compliance look like?
3. **Explore technology.** Determine the accessibility compliance of the tools you use.
   - What types of assistive technology might your audience use?
   - How does your suite of tools comply with accessibility standards?
   - What settings need to be enabled to ensure an experience can be navigated with assistive technology?
4. **Elicit change.** Teach back what you know about accessibility.
   - How can you elicit change to improve accessibility in your organization?
   - How can you share what you've learned about accessibility?
5. **Expand knowledge.** Learn about accessibility standards and practices in other domains.
   - What other accessibility standards exist?
   - How do they compare to the standards you use?
   - Are there any useful standards that you aren't currently considering?

We must start somewhere. Some of us will learn ADA before WCAG. Some of us will prioritize closed captions before alternative text. There is much to learn in the domain of accessibility, so give yourself time to focus on the aspects that relate to your role first.

Whether you're beginning your accessibility journey or are already an expert, there will always be new standards, technology, and best practices.

It can be challenging to keep up, but it's important that you make space for upskilling and reskilling.

Applying Accessibility Standards

When I reflect on my own accessibility journey, I can't help but cringe at the many mistakes I made early on. But those mistakes fueled my pursuit to learn more. Today, I'm at the point where I can look at a website or e-learning content, identify inaccessibilities, and align them to WCAG criteria. I've only reached this level of rigor because I'm passionate about the domain of accessibility—so much that I made a career out of it.

At Salesforce, we aim to create products that are WCAG 2.2 Level AA compliant, meaning they are usable and understandable for a wide range of people, with and without disabilities. The same goes for the training we create for internal employees. A significant amount of my time goes toward supporting learning designers in building accessible experiences. Depending on the project, I might be involved as early as kickoff when we're assessing technology. Other times, learning designers rely on self-service resources I've created; they'll reach out to me only when they have questions.

In the library of resources I've created, there's one that stands out: WCAG in simple language. This resource is a simple spreadsheet but has the highest usage of any of my accessibility resources. It does exactly what the title suggests; it lists each WCAG success criterion and describes it in easy-to-understand terms. I've also included a column to indicate if a criterion relates to a specific domain, such as text, audio, video, images, or interactives.

Table 51-1 illustrates the organization for one criterion.

Table 51-1. Sample Success Criterion From One of My Accessibility Resources

Principle	Guideline	Success Criterion	Level	Description	Relates to
Perceivable	Time-based media	1.2.2. Captions (Prerecorded)	A	The audio in videos should be captioned.	Video

Initially, I thought about including that resource in this book, but I've since changed my mind. Instead, I want to challenge you to build your own. Reading WCAG and rewriting each criterion in your own words is a powerful practice. It forces you to interpret the standards and begin to commit them to memory. The deeper you understand accessibility standards, the easier it becomes to apply them. But if you're just starting on your accessibility journey, hold off on this exercise. The standards are undoubtedly important, but they are not the best place to start.

Expanding Your Knowledge

To reach mastery of anything, you must first learn the fundamental skills. For sports, it's running, throwing, or jumping. For cooking, it's dicing, braising, and roasting. For accessibility, it's understanding types of disabilities and building empathy for those who have them.

I began building these accessibility skills in 2016 when I was designing digital curriculum for primary school science classes. I received an email from a frustrated teacher who indicated a blind student could not access any of the images with their screen reader. At the time, I had no idea what a screen reader was. So, I downloaded one, which ended up being NVDA, and started testing.

Practicing with assistive technology is an act of empathy. You put yourself in the perspective of someone with a disability to understand how they navigate virtual experiences. I think anyone—regardless of their career—can benefit from activities like testing with a screen reader, using a one-hand keyboard, or watching a video with closed captions and no audio. People with disabilities do not inherently know how to use these technologies. They must adapt to using them, so we must adapt to designing for them.

It took me time to realize that assistive technology compliance is just one aspect of accessible design. There are many challenges to solve for because there are many types of disabilities. After pursuing medicine in my undergraduate studies, I assumed I was aware of most disabilities. I didn't recognize my own ignorance until I learned about permanent, temporary, and situational impairments. The realization struck me: Anyone can have a disability or impairment, which means everyone can benefit from accessible design. It's seemingly so obvious, but somehow can still be overlooked.

I've learned a great deal about disabilities through books, podcasts, and blogs. Listening to personal essays and reflections has led me to cry, laugh, and feel angry or disgusted. In addition to the one you're reading now, here are a few books I recommend:

- *About Us: Essays From the Disability Series of the New York Times* by Peter Catapano and Rosemarie Garland-Thomson
- *Disability Visibility: First-Person Stories From the Twenty-First Century* edited by Alice Wong
- *Being Heumann: An Unrepentant Memoir of a Disability Rights Activist* by Judy Heumann

Studying for the Certified Professional in Accessibility Core Competencies (CPACC) exam, issued by the International Association of Accessibility Professionals (IAAP), also helped me build empathy and knowledge. While I don't believe this certification is required to be an accessibility advocate, I think there's merit in exploring the topics covered in the exam. The CPACC Body of Knowledge document is a fabulous resource to start with, and it's publicly available on IAAP's website.

What You Can Do Right Away

Sure, there's a lot to keep up with. The landscape is ever-changing with new tools, laws, and standards, but it's worth doing. That said, you may not want to start your accessibility journey by opening the fire hose of content and trying to keep up. It's better to understand your role, the learning experience products and services you provide, and what standards most apply to it.

With practice, accessible design will come naturally. One day, you'll find yourself auditing your own content to improve color contrast or reduce language complexity. Then perhaps you'll help improve someone else's content or coach others on interpreting WCAG. No matter where your career takes you, bring your Design for All mentality.

52.
Practically Applying WCAG Standards to Learning Content

Susi Miller (she/her)
Founder and Director, eLaHub

One of the main reasons I wanted to write my book *Designing Accessible Learning Content* was to spare other learning practitioners from the frustrating and lengthy journey I went through trying to understand the WCAG standards and how to apply them to my learning resources. The experience I had when I was writing the book, however, was limited only to my own practice and that of a handful of colleagues. It wasn't until I started auditing learning content and delivering training and consultancy for organizations, that I fully realized just how many complexities and ambiguities there were when it came to interpreting the standards and practically applying them to learning content.

Since writing the book, I've supported more than 60 organizations and helped them make their learning content compliant with the WCAG standards. My clients are global and have spanned the private, public, and charity sectors. In addition, they've included higher and further education institutions. My experience has also covered a wide range of different types of learning content and subject areas.

The insights I've gained from this experience not only enhanced my ability to make my own learning content accessible, but they've also helped me better support my clients to achieve WCAG conformance in their learning content. In the words of Maya Angelou, "Do the best you can until you know better. Then when you know better, do better." The following points are my key takeaways from this experience. I hope they help make the process of applying WCAG standards easier for everyone who is committed to making their learning content as accessible as possible.

WCAG Standards: Versions and Levels

Often, the first challenge encountered when organizations start practically applying WCAG success criteria or standards is understanding the different versions and levels involved.

WCAG Versions

Since the WCAG Version 1.0 standards were first released in 1999, they have been continuously updated. WCAG Version 2.0 was released in 2008, and Version 2.1 in 2018. The most recent version, WCAG 2.2, was finally confirmed in fall 2023. Although the continuous updates help ensure that the standards keep pace with technological advancements, they can lead to confusion. This is particularly the case when it comes to meeting legislative requirements because legislation often lags significantly behind the latest WCAG version updates.

It's worth being aware, therefore, that most current international legislation requires that organizations meet WCAG Version 2.1. Even if this is not a legal requirement, it is increasingly considered best practice. Another important consideration is that although it will likely take several months, if not years, for some legislation to catch up with WCAG Version 2.2, again, it's considered best practice for organizations to meet the requirements of this version as quickly as possible.

WCAG Levels

The WCAG standards are divided into three levels: A, AA, and AAA. Organizations are sometimes confused about which level they should be trying to meet for legal requirements or for best practice. Most current global regulations require that organizations meet WCAG Level AA requirements, which includes meeting all WCAG Level A and AA standards. Several organizations I've worked with have interpreted the need to be Level AA compliant to mean they only need to meet WCAG Level AA requirements, but that is incorrect.

Another area of confusion I've often encountered surrounds the impact that meeting the standards has on learners. I find that this is because the three WCAG levels are often classified in the following way:

- **Level A**—basic standards
- **Level AA**—intermediate standards
- **Level AAA**—advanced standards

The main problem with this classification is that it can be easily misinterpreted and often creates the wrong impression about the impact that meeting standards at each of the levels has on learners—especially with Level A because these standards are frequently labelled as "basic." In my experience, practitioners often interpret this to mean that not meeting Level A standards will only have a basic or low impact on their learners, but this is not the case. This confusion prompted me to develop my own definitions of the WCAG levels.

Level A

Level A standards are the most important to meet to ensure that learners with disabilities and access needs have an equal learning experience. **These standards have the most severe impact on learners' experience of content if they are not met.** In some cases, not meeting Level A requirements can result in learners with disabilities not being able to access certain aspects of the learning content at all.

Take WCAG Success Criterion 1.1.1 Non-Text Content—Level A, for example. One of the requirements of this standard is that you provide a description of any images that add meaning to your learning content. This allows learners who use screen readers (because they are blind or have low vision) to have an equivalent experience to sighted learners. If you don't meet this Level A standard and provide alternative text, these learners are denied the ability to learn from the images you use in your learning content.

Level AA

Meeting Level AA standards is often thought to cover more types of disabilities and a broader range of assistive technologies. These standards have slightly less impact on learners with disabilities and access needs if they are not met. In most cases, not meeting these standards will not prevent someone from accessing content altogether. It may, however, prevent learners from having a positive learning experience equal to that of other learners.

For example, consider WCAG Success Criterion 1.4.3 Contrast Minimum—Level AA. It requires a contrast ratio of at least 4.5:1 between the text and the background it appears on depending on the size and weight of the text. If you don't meet this requirement, it might make it more difficult for learners with a range of vision access needs to read the content, but it rarely stops learners from being able to access it completely.

Level AAA

Meeting Level AAA standards makes learning content accessible to the widest range of people with disabilities and access needs. Level AAA standards also contribute significantly to a positive learner experience for these learners. There is often a significant overlap between the requirements of these standards and the principles of usability and inclusive design.

For example, WCAG Success Criterion 2.4.10 Section Headings—Level AAA requires that section headings are used to organize content. Using proper hierarchy, clear labeling, and consistency in headings throughout learning resources makes the content more usable for everyone. But it has a particularly significant positive impact on learners with cognitive access needs that affect processing and memory skills.

* * *

Understanding the ever-evolving landscape of WCAG versions and the impact of applying standards at different levels on learners with access needs is a crucial first step in getting started with successfully applying WCAG standards to learning content. However, there are many more considerations that practitioners need to be aware of. We'll explore these in more detail now.

WCAG Level AAA Compliance: What's Different About E-Learning?

Although we touched on the different WCAG levels in the previous section, it's worth focusing in more detail on Level AAA compliance. I've found it's another area where practitioners are often not entirely confident when it comes to applying the WCAG standards. The most common issue regarding the Level AAA requirements concerns organizations that are legally obliged or have made a strategic decision to meet WCAG Level AAA conformance. It's important to keep in mind that it can be extremely difficult to meet all these standards for learning content. Even the World Wide Web Consortium (W3C) concedes that "it is not recommended that Level AAA conformance is required as a general policy for all sites because it is not possible to satisfy all Level AAA criteria for some content."[119]

A good example to demonstrate this is WCAG Success Criterion 3.1.5 Reading Level—Level AAA. It requires that you provide an easily readable alternative or supplementary content if the language used in the learning program is too difficult for someone with a lower secondary education reading level (that is, someone with between seven and nine years of education) to understand. The challenge with this standard for learning practitioners is that it doesn't account for the varying educational levels that different types of learning content may need. For many organizations, creating an alternative, easy-read version of their learning materials is not logistically feasible. At eLaHub, our pragmatic approach to meeting this standard is to use language that is as straightforward and clear as possible, tailored to the specific audience of the learning resource. But this means that, like many organizations, we are not always able to meet the standard.

Another issue concerning Level AAA requirements is that they may be overlooked by practitioners because of the sheer number of standards there are to achieve. For WCAG Version 2.1, for example, there are 78 standards altogether; it's been increased to 86 in Version 2.2. It is not surprising therefore that practitioners will often focus on Level

A and AA standards, with Level AAA requirements being overlooked. Unfortunately, some of the Level AAA standards have a significant impact on improving the experience for all learners, including those with disabilities and access needs. This is best demonstrated by two standards: 2.4.8 Location—Level AAA and 2.4.9 Link Purpose (Link Only)—Level AAA.

WCAG Success Criterion 2.4.8 Location—Level AAA

WCAG Success Criterion 2.4.8 Location—Level AAA requires that "information about the user's location within a set of Web pages is available."[120] This standard may not have a significant impact on a user's experience if it is applied to a website, which is probably why it has been assigned the AAA level. But for learning content, it is extremely beneficial for learners to be aware of their location and their progress in the learner journey. This can be achieved simply by displaying the specific page or lesson that learners are currently on within the resource; for example, "11|24" to indicate you are on page 11 of 24. Some authoring tools also allow practitioners to add a progress bar to inform learners on how much of the learning content they have completed and how much is left. These indicators benefit everyone, but they are particularly important for learners with cognitive access needs.

WCAG Success Criterion 2.4.9 Link Purpose (Link Only)—Level AAA

Another good example of a Level AAA standard that has a beneficial impact on all learners but is particularly helpful for people with a disability or access need is WCAG Success Criterion 2.4.9 Link Purpose (Link Only)—Level AAA. It requires you to add the destination of a link to the text of the link itself, rather than giving information about the destination of the link in the text surrounding it. For example:

- **Don't do this:** This article from the British Association of Teachers of Deaf Children provides more information about conductive hearing loss. Find out more.
- **Do this instead:** Find out more about conductive hearing loss from the British Association of Teachers of Deaf Children.

This standard makes links clearer and easier to follow for all learners, but it is vitally important for screen reader users who navigate using the screen reader's elements list functionality, which allows them to navigate easily by presenting content such as links or headings in a list. If practitioners only meet the Level AA standard, which allows them to provide information about the link's destination in the surrounding text, the only information that would be read out in the elements list from our examples would be "Find out more." If the destination of the link is included in the text of the link itself, however, the screen reader would read out, "Find out more about conductive hearing loss from the British Association of Teachers of Deaf Children." This is another useful example of how important it is not to overlook Level AAA requirements.

In addition, standards 2.4.8 Location—Level AAA and 2.4.9 Link Purpose (Link Only)—Level AAA are very helpful in tackling the misconception that all Level AAA standards are complex and difficult to achieve, which is another common reason why they may be overlooked by practitioners. Ensuring that your learning resources provide clear information about a learner's location and progress, as well as using meaningful text for links, are both excellent examples of how Level AAA standards can be straightforward to implement and significantly improve the learning experience for everyone.

Accessibility Statements

I hope these examples serve as a good indication both of why it can be a challenge for organizations to meet Level AAA standards, but also of the potential pitfalls of overlooking them. The approach we use at eLaHub is to aim to meet Level AA conformance as standard. However, we also try to achieve any of the Level AAA standards that we believe have a significant impact on learners with disabilities and access needs. For transparency and to help learners, we document this approach in an accessibility statement.

Accessibility statements are a legal requirement for some organizations; for example, in the UK, they've been mandatory for public sector organizations since 2018. However, even if they are not a legal requirement, they provide practitioners with a helpful way to document any accessibility features and explain any accessibility limitations. The following excerpts from eLaHub's accessibility statement for our online self-directed Designing Accessible Learning Content Programme demonstrate how we address the issues surrounding level conformance and a sample issue.

> **How accessible is this module?** Wherever possible the content in this module conforms to the WCAG Version 2.1 Level A and AA standards and the new WCAG Version 2.2 Level A and AA standards released in Autumn 2023. In addition, the content also conforms to any Level AAA standards that have a significant impact on improving the learner experience for learners with disabilities and access needs.
>
> **Example issue:** Some of the videos in this module do not have audio description and therefore fail WCAG Success Criterion 1.2.5 Audio Description (Prerecorded)—Level AA. If videos do not have audio description, we have provided descriptive transcripts which detail all important visual information.

Exceptions to WCAG Standards

Another important issue that is sometimes overlooked when trying to practically apply WCAG requirements is that many of the standards have exceptions. You should be aware of these exceptions because they might mean that the standards don't apply to the learning content you are creating. Not being aware of them can lead to a lot of wasted time and effort.

A memorable example from our consultancy work took place when a client wasn't aware of the exceptions that applied to WCAG Success Criterion 1.4.11 Non-text Contrast—Level AA. This standard requires a contrast ratio of at least 3:1 for navigation buttons and the background they appear on.

Our client was having difficulty finding a range of colors that met both their brand guidelines and the contrast ratio requirement for every state of their navigation buttons, including the inactive state. Unfortunately, they didn't know an exception to this standard says that the contrast requirement does not apply to inactive navigation buttons. Although the exception solved the issue for the client, they were frustrated by the extra time and effort they had wasted. It's a useful reminder of why you need to be familiar with not only the WCAG standards themselves, but also of the exceptions that apply to them.

Open to Interpretation: Not Designed for Learning Content

As you're probably now aware, the WCAG standards weren't written for learning content created using digital authoring tools. They were primarily designed for developers creating websites or mobile applications, which use programming code. So, although some of the standards are universally relevant to all digital content including learning resources, it certainly isn't the case for all of them. This issue is best demonstrated by the WCAG standards that apply to errors.

The WCAG standards around errors (3.3.1 Error Correction—Level A, 3.3.3 Error Suggestion—Level AA, and 3.3.4 Error Prevention—Level AA) are specifically relevant to filling in details on web forms. They refer to errors such as not entering data into mandatory fields or entering data in the wrong format, such as not using @ in an email address. Yet, the errors people typically make in learning content happen when they answer questions incorrectly. The WCAG standards make no reference to this scenario.

For example, 3.3.3 Error Suggestion—Level AA requires that we suggest a correction if users make an error. This makes sense if they enter their telephone number in the wrong format on a web form, but what about in a learning resource? If they get the answer to a quiz question wrong, should we always suggest a correction, giving them the correct answer? While many practitioners might consider giving the correct answer good instructional design that reinforces learning, what happens if a learner makes an error in a knowledge check question of a compliance test in which learners are deliberately not given the correct answer? Does this example fail WCAG Success Criterion 3.3.3 Error Suggestion—Level A? Or do we decide that this standard isn't applicable to learning content because it is designed for web forms?

Because there is no consensus from the L&D industry about how to tackle standards that aren't designed for learning content, individual practitioners are left having to interpret and apply the standards as best they can.

Open to Interpretation: Complex Language

I believe another reason learning practitioners are sometimes forced to make their own interpretations of the standards is because the language that is used to describe them can be complex and confusing. This is best demonstrated by some of the WCAG standards about audio and video content, or as W3C calls it, "time-based media." Trying to make sense of these standards was, without a doubt, one of the most challenging aspects of writing my book *Designing Accessible Learning Content*. It remains the area that causes the most confusion and standard fails in the audits we carry out at eLaHub.

One of the problematic areas is around the need to provide audio description, extended audio description, or include a media alternative for videos with sound that contain important visual content that would be missed by blind or partially sighted learners.

If you are not familiar with these, I have included an explanation of the relevant standards here:

- **1.2.5 Audio Description (Prerecorded)—Level AA** requires that you provide audio description for prerecorded videos with sound. This is a verbal description of the important visual details in video content for people who are blind or have low vision. It typically describes key visual details such as on-screen text, settings, character actions, and scene transitions.
- **1.2.7 Extended Audio Description (Prerecorded)—Level AAA** requires that you provide extended audio description for prerecorded videos with sound. This is provided when there is not enough time in the pauses between the dialogue and the action to give a verbal description of the important visual details. This means that the video is frozen to extend the pauses and add enough time for the verbal description.

- **1.2.3 Audio Description or Media Alternative (Prerecorded)—Level A** requires that you provide audio description or a media alternative for prerecorded videos with sound. A *media alternative* is a text version of everything that happens in the video. It's essentially a text description of all the important visual details that add meaning, as well as the dialogue and narration. It's very similar to a detailed script for a film. At eLaHub, we call this a "descriptive transcript." W3C also calls it a "full-text alternative."
- **1.2.8 Media Alternative (Prerecorded)—Level AAA** requires that you provide a media alternative for prerecorded videos with sound.

Many organizations we work with struggle to understand why there are so many requirements, and what they need to provide to meet the different WCAG levels they want to achieve. Unfortunately, the W3C guidance provided in the "Understanding SC 1.2.8: Media Alternative (Prerecorded) (Level AAA)" information doesn't help very much. It's a good example of the complexity of the language that practitioners are sometimes required to interpret:

> For 1.2.3, 1.2.5, and 1.2.7, if all of the information in the video track is already provided in the audio track, no audio description is necessary.
>
> 1.2.3, 1.2.5, and 1.2.8 overlap somewhat with each other. This is to give the author some choice at the minimum conformance level, and to provide additional requirements at higher levels. At Level A in Success Criterion 1.2.3, authors do have the choice of providing either an audio description or a full text alternative. If they wish to conform at Level AA, under Success Criterion 1.2.5 authors must provide an audio description—a requirement already met if they chose that alternative for 1.2.3, otherwise an additional requirement. At Level AAA under Success Criterion 1.2.8 they must

provide an extended text description. This is an additional requirement if both 1.2.3 and 1.2.5 were met by providing an audio description only. If 1.2.3 was met, however, by providing a text description, and the 1.2.5 requirement for an audio description was met, then 1.2.8 does not add new requirements.[121]

eLaHub's pragmatic interpretation of this information is as follows:
- **Level A.** To meet Level A requirements, you must provide either audio description or a descriptive transcript. This meets 1.2.3 Audio Description or Media Alternative (Prerecorded)—Level A.
- **Level AA.** To meet Level AA requirements, you must provide audio description. This meets 1.2.5 Audio Description (Prerecorded)—Level AA. Note: At eLaHub, we recommend if there is not enough time in the pauses between the dialogue and the action to give a verbal description of the important visual details, then you should provide extended audio description (freezing the video to extend the pauses for the verbal description). We also recommend that if it is not possible to provide audio description for logistical reasons, then it is essential to provide a descriptive transcript.
- **Level AAA.** To meet Level AAA requirements, you must provide:
  - *Extended audio description.* This meets 1.2.7 Extended Audio Description (Prerecorded)—Level AAA.
  - *A descriptive transcript in addition to audio description.* This meets 1.2.8 Media Alternative (Prerecorded)—Level AAA.

This is the interpretation we work toward at eLaHub and that we recommend to the organizations we work with. However, there is no consensus in the L&D industry about whether this interpretation is correct. We are very aware that it is possible that some practitioners, accessibility experts, and auditors may disagree with us.

Practically Applying WCAG Standards: A Case Study

When I first started creating and auditing accessible learning content, I believed that I struggled to make sense of the WCAG standards and apply them effectively because I wasn't experienced and didn't know enough about them. My lightbulb moment came when I began working with accessibility experts while carrying out research for my book. I realized that even my collaborators, who had specialized in web accessibility and auditing for many years, frequently disagreed about how to interpret and apply the WCAG standards. It made me realize that these guidelines are not the clear-cut, unambiguous, pass-or-fail standards that many people believe they are. The experience I gained working with numerous organizations also proved just how complex it could be to apply the standards to different types of learning content.

This gave me the confidence to adopt a practical "progress over perfection" approach when I design and develop learning content for eLaHub. Although I adhere to the guidelines as closely as possible, I adopt a pragmatic approach to overcoming any ambiguities I encounter. Although I cannot be 100 percent sure that everyone will agree with me, my decisions are always governed by what I believe to be my learners' best interests. If I make any decisions that have relied on a judgement call based on my interpretation of a WCAG standard, I make this clear in an accessibility statement. At eLaHub, we also adopt the same approach to the decisions we make in our auditing work.

To demonstrate this approach in action, I'll focus on my interpretation of the WCAG Success Criterion 2.4.5 Multiple Ways—Level AA and how I tackle it in my own learning content and auditing work.

WCAG Success Criterion 2.4.5 Multiple Ways—Level AA

WCAG Success Criterion 2.4.5 Multiple Ways—Level AA requires that "more than one way is available to locate a Web page within a set of Web pages."[122] This can be through a breadcrumb trail, a menu, a search facility, interactive page numbers, and other methods that allow people to access content in the way that suits them best. This standard benefits the access needs and preferences of learners, so it's something I always try to achieve in my learning resources. But what if the learning content I'm designing needs my learners to follow a particular learner journey? What about things like compliance training? The learner journey is deliberately locked so participants can't progress to the next lesson until they have completed the previous one. If I don't allow my learners to access the learning content in multiple ways, does it fail WCAG Success Criterion 2.4.5 Multiple Ways—Level AA?

My interpretation is that it doesn't—there is an exception to this standard that means it doesn't apply if the web page is "a step in a process." As you might have guessed, the example given by W3C to clarify this exception is relevant for websites, not learning content. The guidance refers to a process (like transferring funds on a website) that needs to be completed in a sequential order and therefore can't allow users multiple ways to access the pages on the site. I believe, however, that it's possible to apply this interpretation to learning content that has a fixed learner journey and needs to be completed in a sequential order. Nevertheless, I always provide multiple ways and open access to the learning after learners have completed the original learner journey so they can go back and revisit the content again.

The following excerpt from eLaHub's accessibility statement for our online self-directed Designing Accessible Learning Content Programme demonstrates how we address this issue:

> The learning content in this resource is "step locked." This means that you can only progress to the next topic if you have completed the previous one. This is because the content only makes sense if it is accessed in this order. Once you have completed the learning in the required sequence, you will have free access to revisit the content using the menu, back and forward links, and the search facility. Although the WCAG Success Criterion 2.4.5 Multiple Ways—Level AA requires that learners are given multiple ways to access content, an exception to this applies to "steps in a process." At eLaHub, we believe this exception is relevant to a learner journey that needs to be completed in a required sequence. But we provide multiple ways

to access the learning content after it has been completed in this initial sequence.

Note: Not all accessibility experts or auditors may agree with this interpretation.

What You Can Do Right Away

My key takeaway for applying WCAG standards to learning content comes from a memorable quote I once heard in an accessibility webinar delivered by Dafydd Henke-Reed from AbilityNet in the UK. During his presentation, Henke-Reed explained that "being honest about inaccessibility is a form of accessibility in itself." What struck me so powerfully about this quote was the word *honesty*. It made me reflect on my own approach to interpreting and applying the WCAG standards. I realized how important it was to be open and honest about the complexities and ambiguities that surround the WCAG standards, particularly when applying them to learning content.

This change in mindset has had a transformational impact on my work. When I began my accessibility journey, I was often too influenced by imposter syndrome to be entirely honest about how difficult it was to make sense of the standards and apply them. My practical approach now is to be transparent if any of the decisions I make in my own learning content or in my auditing work are based on judgment calls guided by my interpretation of the standards. I explain why my interpretation is in the best interest of my learners and acknowledge that not everyone will agree with me. My hope is that exploring these complexities in more detail and outlining my approach to them will help open up discussion and debate in the L&D field. It might even finally lead to consensus in our industry about how these, sometimes infuriating, standards can be interpreted to best serve our learners and practitioners.

Whether you're ready to apply the WCAG standards to your learning content, or still in your learning phase, you can always start by asking yourself, "In what ways can I be more honest and transparent with learners about known inaccessibility in my learning experiences?"

53.
Testing WCAG Standards

Susi Miller (she/her)
Founder and Director, eLaHub

The testing of WCAG standards is another important area where there is lack of consensus and standardization in the L&D industry. It's my belief that this is another significant factor that hinders organizations when they are working to make their learning content accessible. Our eLaHub consultancy work demonstrated that this is very often due to lack of confidence and the belief that accessibility testing is a complex technical task that can only be carried out by experts. This mindset often leads to a situation in which accessibility checks are not carried out until after learning resources have been completed.

Having the privilege of helping many organizations overcome this issue allowed me to develop a testing matrix that I hope can help simplify accessibility testing and show how responsibility can be shifted to everyone in an L&D team.

Traditional Learning Content Development and Testing Process

The traditional development and testing workflow for learning content begins with analysis, proceeds through design and development, and transitions to technical testing and quality assurance, before ending with the launch. The infographic in Figure 53-1 shows this typical six-step process, with horizontal arrows starting on the left with analysis and ending on the right with launch.

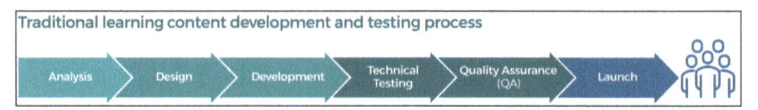

Figure 53-1. The traditional process for developing and testing learning content.

For many organizations, technical testing and quality assurance (QA) take place when the analysis, design, and development phases for learning content are complete—often just before a resource is launched. Because accessibility testing most often takes place in the technical testing or QA stage, it typically happens after the resource has been completed. But, if accessibility issues are found after the resource has been fully developed, they're much more complex and expensive to fix than if they were discovered early on. So, what can we do to make sure this doesn't happen? An approach that works brilliantly in software development is to move accessibility testing earlier in the process. In other words, to shift it left.

Shifting Learning Content Accessibility Testing Left

Figure 53-2 demonstrates how you can apply the shifting left principle to creating learning content. In this case, the process comprises seven steps instead of six: analyze, design, develop global elements and templates, develop the first section, extend the build, undergo final QA and accessibility testing, and launch. Whereas in Figure 53-1, the process (and arrows) flowed linearly from analysis to launch, now there are three points where, if you're following the process, you should loop back and check for accessibility.

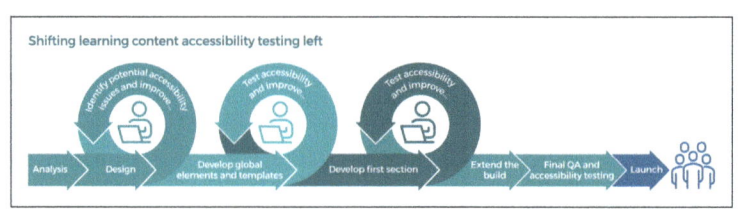

Figure 53-2. Moving accessibility testing to earlier in the development process.

Before completing the design step, you should identify potential accessibility issues and improve. Before completing the develop global elements and templates step, you should test accessibility and improve. And, before completing the develop first section step, you should test accessibility and improve. Then, you can carry on to the remaining steps of extending the build, conducting final QA and accessibility testing, and launching the content to learners.

The infographic shows that the optimal time to start identifying and improving accessibility is after the initial analysis and design phases. This allows you to resolve any potential issues before global elements—such as templates and master pages—are repeatedly used or copied throughout the resource. To keep up the good work, you should test for accessibility again after the first section of the resource is completed, and again after the build is extended (or more content is added to the resource). This should ensure that very few accessibility issues are found in the final testing and QA stage. Or better still—none at all!

This approach works so well because it moves the responsibility from a few highly specialized technical experts to everyone on the team. At eLaHub, we've found that with the right support, anyone on an L&D team can be given the confidence to become an effective accessibility tester.

Practical Accessibility Testing

So, how do you start shifting your accessibility testing strategy left? To empower practitioners to become confident accessibility testers, it's important to begin with comprehensive training about the WCAG standards. I also recommend ensuring that practitioners understand the complexities of applying the WCAG standards that I've outlined in chapter 52 of this book.

Another useful step is to develop a strategy for testing the standards. Some of the organizations we work with divide accessibility testing tasks among the members of a team, while others prefer to have one dedicated tester. Whichever strategy works best for your team, a useful starting point is to break down the standards into categories depending on the best way to test them.

To support our clients, I developed an eLaHub learning content accessibility testing matrix (Figure 53-3).

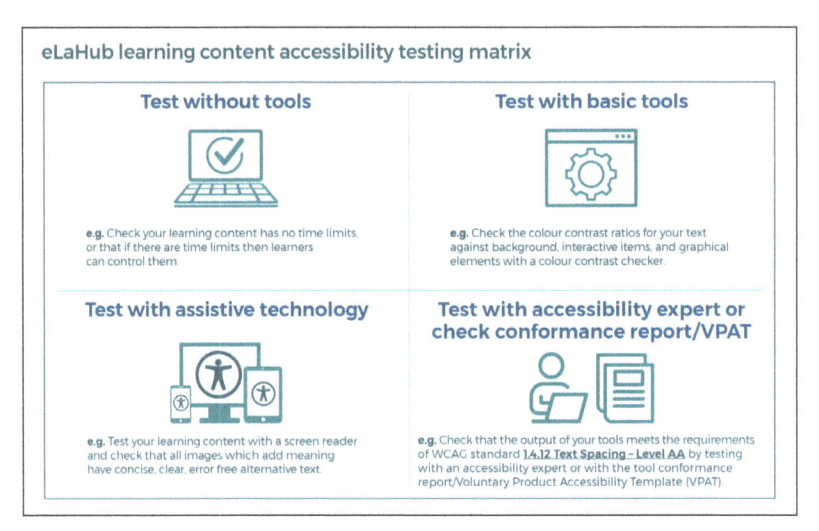

eLaHub learning content accessibility testing matrix

Test without tools	Test with basic tools
e.g. Check your learning content has no time limits, or that if there are time limits then learners can control them.	e.g. Check the colour contrast ratios for your text against background, interactive items, and graphical elements with a colour contrast checker.
Test with assistive technology	**Test with accessibility expert or check conformance report/VPAT**
e.g. Test your learning content with a screen reader and check that all images which add meaning have concise, clear, error free alternative text.	e.g. Check that the output of your tools meets the requirements of WCAG standard 1.4.12 Text Spacing – Level AA by testing with an accessibility expert or with the tool conformance report/Voluntary Product Accessibility Template (VPAT).

Figure 53-3. eLaHub Learning Content Accessibility Testing Matrix.

This matrix divides the WCAG standards into four different sections depending on the best way to test them:

1. **Test without tools (top left quadrant).** For example, confirm your learning content has no time limits, or if there are time limits, that learners can control them.
2. **Test with basic tools (top right quadrant).** This refers to tools that are readily available to practitioners, such as a color contrast checker, web browser's zoom functionality, and grayscale filter. For example, check the color contrast ratios for your text against the background, interactive items, and graphical elements with a color contrast checker.
3. **Test with assistive technology (bottom left quadrant).** This refers to tools such as screen readers, screen magnifiers, and third-party browser extensions to customize text. For example, test your learning content with a screen reader and ensure that all images that add meaning have concise, clear, error-free alternative text.

4. **Test with accessibility experts or check the conformance report (bottom right quadrant).** Standards to check within this category are the more complex technical ones often reliant on underlying coding. Because most learning practitioners don't have the technical expertise to test these standards, I recommend using an accessibility expert's services or referring to a voluntary product accessibility template (VPAT; more on that later). For example, check that the output of your tool meets the requirements of WCAG Success Criterion 1.4.12 Text Spacing—Level AA by testing with an accessibility expert or with the tool's conformance report or VPAT.

Of course, not all the WCAG standards fit neatly into the four testing categories in eLaHub's matrix. But for the organizations we've worked with, just the simple process of dividing the standards into different testable categories has proved beneficial. It has allowed them to begin identifying testing tasks they can complete as resources are being designed and developed, not just at the end of the process. It has also helped them begin thinking about practical strategies for assigning testing tasks to different roles on a team.

Accessibility Testing Considerations

Although I strongly believe that testing can become the responsibility of a whole team and should not be left in the hands of a few experts, there are some important considerations to be aware of before you embark on implementing an accessibility testing strategy at your organization.

Screen Reader Testing

At eLaHub, we recommend that as many practitioners as possible learn to carry out basic screen reader testing. It's a great way to test standards like 1.1.1 Non-Text Content—Level A and 1.3.2 Meaningful Sequence—Level A. It's also a great way to proofread your content! Although you can learn a lot from your own screen reader testing, I always recommend supplementing this with testing by an experienced assistive technology user who has a lived experience with a disability. This has been transformational for us at eLaHub. It means not only that someone is double-checking our results, but we also get a usability perspective. It helps us check that our learning content is inclusive by providing a usable and engaging learning experience for assistive technology users.

Test With an Accessibility Expert or Check the Conformance Report or VPAT

Some of the WCAG standards are achieved by underlying coding. To test standards like 1.3.1 Info and Relationships—Level A and 4.1.2 Name, Role, Value—Level A, you need technical expertise that many L&D practitioners don't usually have. As a result, there are two ways I recommend you test these requirements:

1. **Work with technical accessibility coding experts.** Sometimes, this expertise will already exist and be available within an organization. Another option is to work with external experts or auditors.
2. **Use the information provided by the authoring tool provider in a conformance report or a VPAT.** You can find a good example for the CourseArc authoring tool on its website at coursearc.com/vpat. Articulate also provides comprehensive accessibility conformance reports (ACRs) for both Storyline and Rise. Any authoring tool provider that is committed to accessibility should provide an up-to-date conformance report or VPAT. One of the advantages of using these reports is that everyone can check the WCAG requirements related to complex technical coding standards without having to rely solely on accessibility experts. (Note: Because conformance reports or VPATs are often self-administered, and because the WCAG standards are open to interpretation, they aren't always considered to be 100 percent accurate. Despite this, they're still an important first step in helping learning practitioners check complex WCAG coding accessibility standards.)

Accessibility Standards and Neurodivergence
Judy Katz (she/her) | Founder and Consultant, Neurodivergent Working

Accessibility guidelines that benefit neurodivergent people aren't necessarily obvious in the way standards for some disabilities, such as color blindness and deafness, are, and many of them are slightly more open to interpretation. For instance, they may call for controls having a clear purpose or for navigation to be consistent, rather than the more objective standard of requiring color contrast to be at least 4.5:1.

Another challenge in creating design standards for neurodivergence is that it's a huge category of disability, including not only autism and ADHD (which are perhaps the most closely associated in people's minds), but also trauma, learning disabilities, and psychological disabilities. Neurodivergence itself is not a medically recognized category. It arose from disability (particularly autistic) activism and is meant to encompass any brain difference from the typical; however, not everyone uses the intended definition. Complicating matters further, there is a lack of understanding that individuals can be neurodivergent without having significant support needs or intellectual disabilities.

The good news is that there are many ways that designing to accommodate one disability can also accommodate other disabilities; for example, closed captions benefit both Deaf and hard of hearing learners and learners with audio-processing disorder, which is common among autistic people. Giving learners options and making delivery simple and clear in every way possible goes a long way toward accessibility and usability for all.

What You Can Do Right Away
In her book *Accessibility for Everyone*, Laura Kalbag states, "Accessibility is often presented as something that should be left to experts. We do need experts for their specialized knowledge and guidance, but there aren't enough accessibility experts in the world to leave the task of building an accessible web in their hands alone."[123]

I strongly agree that we have no hope of making accessibility mainstream if we continue to leave it in the hands of a few experts. This applies to the websites Kalbag refers to, but it is just as relevant to learning content. I believe that by sharing the approaches to testing WCAG standards that we use at eLaHub and with our clients, we can help to democratize accessibility.

Have you put off accessibility testing and improvements because you're not an accessibility expert? A better approach is to consider what steps you can take to create learning content that is accessible as the default. Begin by shifting accessibility testing earlier in your development process and conducting testing at multiple points.

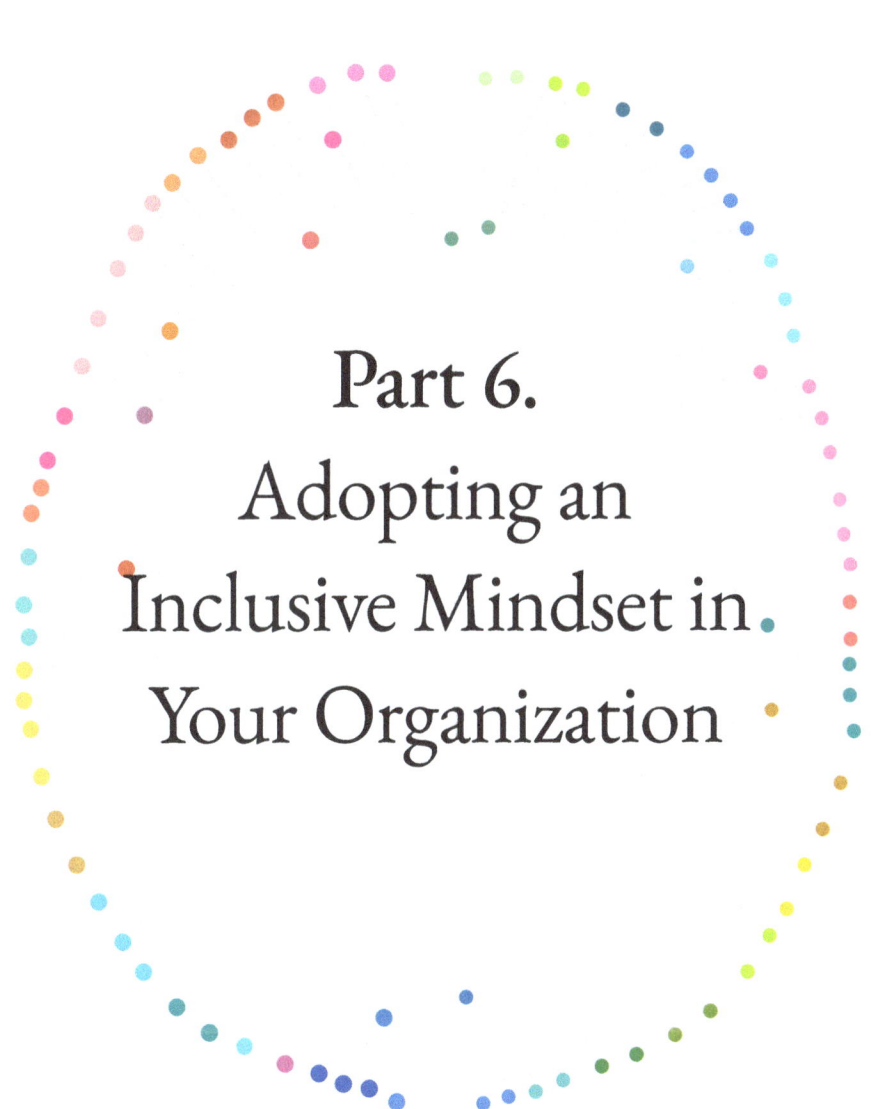

Part 6.
Adopting an Inclusive Mindset in Your Organization

54.
The Invisible Why

Daron Moore (he/him)
Founder and Principal, The Re:Connect

"What does your momma call you?" This casual question from my chief human resources officer (CHRO) came from a genuine place of curiosity. Yet, it was one of the most profound questions I had ever been asked. It was a question that led to an internal awakening I didn't even know was dormant. This question led me to uncovering my invisible "Y."

You see, my name is Daron (pronounced "day-ron") but for more than two decades—almost all of my professional career—I pronounced my name like Darren (or "dare-in"). I interviewed, introduced myself, and responded to work questions as Darren. When I clocked out and went home with the people I cared about the most, I was Daron.

I hadn't realized it, but Darren had become my alter ego. In professional circles, he was the confident, capable version of myself. Interviews, speeches, and high-stakes interactions all belonged to Darren. However, Daron, the empathetic, passionate real me, retreated backstage. Who would listen to the opinion of someone called Daron? How could Daron get an interview or his resume looked at? I didn't think it was possible and convinced myself that I had to go by Darren if I wanted to be successful.

My mother *never* called me Darren. Frankly, she hated that I allowed others to do so. "As long as my checks cleared," I would say, I didn't care what they called me. But that was a lie.

The mask I wore as Darren was both my cloak and my camouflage. It covered my insecurities and helped me blend in with the crowd. I'd worn that Darren mask for so long that I even forgot I was wearing it. So, when I was asked what my mother calls me, I was able to take off my mask for the first time in my adult life. I explained to my CHRO that my family calls me Daron but everyone at work calls me Darren. The mispronunciation was understandable, and I dismissed it as no big deal.

"Well, if your mother calls you Daron," she said. "I'm calling you Daron." I smiled, accepted her stance and had to admit to myself it felt good. It felt good to hear my name. It felt good to have a conversation as Daron instead of Darren. It felt good to be seen, heard, and valued as me by someone I respected, revered, and appreciated. But, it felt awkward when she corrected people on my behalf, whether I was in the room or not. After three years and two promotions at the company, explaining what my real name was made me uncomfortable. Then, after the first couple dozen times explaining why, the discomfort turned to a snowball of curiosity—why was I *really* uncomfortable telling people my name was Daron? Why didn't I want to introduce complete strangers to Daron instead of only my family and close friends? How could a stranger advocate for me even when I was unwilling to advocate for myself?

In unravelling all those questions around the invisible "Y" in the correct pronunciation of my name, I learned that Darren knew the right words to say, but Daron knew the right questions to ask. I've been committed to freeing the knots from my intertwined reality (and helping others do the same) ever since.

In the tapestry of our lives, each thread is colored by the names we are given and the ones we choose to accept. For years, I allowed fear to weave a narrative that wasn't mine, answering to Darren when my true identity was Daron—a difference that represented so much. It was the invisible "why" behind my invisible "Y," and a silent plea for acceptance in a world where authenticity often feels like a risk rather than a right.

But what about you? Have you ever dimmed your light or altered the hue of your true colors for fear of standing out? Have you ever changed the pronunciation of your name or hesitated to share your story because you were worried that the uniqueness of your thread might unravel the fabric of your workplace?

The power of authenticity is not just in being true to ourselves but in creating spaces where others feel empowered to do the same. Inclusion is not about erasing our differences but about embracing them, weaving a richer tapestry where every Y is visible, every why is understood, and every voice is heard.

May we all commit to doing our part in creating spaces where the invisible becomes visible.

Curious to Courageous

Today, I teach new leaders to not bury the lede. Time is precious. Get to the point. Put your "bottom line up front" (BLUF). So, here's my BLUF: *The most lucrative investment an organization can make is in resources that ensure employees have space to be heard, seen, and valued*. Period.

Think about that—the most valuable benefit an organization can offer its employees is the opportunity to be heard, seen, and valued. Not a salary. Not benefits. Not unlimited paid time off. The jobs that we've loved in the companies we've hated to leave were because of the people we worked with. There is no better bottom line to any organization's success.

Unfortunately, the sentiment—being seen, heard, and valued—has been truncated and abbreviated under DEIB (diversity, equity, inclusion, and belonging) and reduced to a popular trend for some organizations. There are other organizations that are genuinely looking for ways to bridge the gap between their organization and the people who make them great. Despite the implementation of DEIB programs, however, organizations are still having trouble making real progress.

Understandably so—DEIB is nuanced, complex, and involves many touchy-feely things we've learned to keep out of work. You can't copy and paste what other companies have done or use ChatGPT to find a plug-and-play solution. This ongoing journey of learning and unlearning will uproot some deep-seated behaviors. And it will be as exhausting as it is rewarding and as meaningful as it is revealing. Anyone can embark on this journey if they have the courage.

If you are ready to take the leap from curious to courageous, whether you are part of a large team or a team of one, there are strategic ways to transform or renovate your workplace culture.

Focus on Your Efforts on Inclusion, Not Diversity

Prioritizing a diverse culture involves focusing your efforts on the makeup of your workforce (including age, gender, and race). Inclusive cultures, however, focus on the "how." It's the creation of a work environment that enables all employees to contribute and thrive. Inclusion goes beyond representation and examines how different groups of people are valued. Remember: *Diversity is a byproduct of inclusive culture.*

In recent years, many organizations have made tremendous strides in improving their diversity—with recruiting efforts, employee and leadership training on unconscious bias, company emails, and holiday calendars, for example—but few have reported significant or sustainable change in productivity, morale, or retention. Why? Because there were no inclusion practices in place to help employees thrive in their workplace culture.

Diversity without inclusion may undermine the good intentions you're after, because now you have a bunch of diverse people feeling isolated and unable to connect on the levels needed to do meaningful work.

Get Your DEIB Key Ingredients

No matter the focus of your DEIB efforts, there are some key ingredients to consider. You don't have to have everything before you start, but you'll eventually need them all along the way.

Data

Collecting and analyzing data related to diversity, equity, inclusion, and belonging is crucial. It helps organizations understand their current state, identify gaps, and track progress over time. Data informs decision making and ensures accountability.

Start small. One or two attention-grabbing data points will be all you need to open the door to more in-depth data mining. One organization I worked with highlighted its lack of data as a data point. Glassdoor reviews and scores (what employees and candidates see) and marketing material (what your customers see) are solid places to start your data collection.

Directives
Clear directives from leadership are essential. When leaders communicate a commitment to DEIB, it sets the tone for the entire organization. These directives not only guide policies but give others permission to support them.

I recommend identifying your sponsors and champions. *Sponsors* are usually executives or senior leaders. Your sponsor has the authority and influence to make things happen. They can approve budgets, define priorities, and provide valuable insight. *Champions* may not have the same title or authority as a sponsor, but they often have the influence necessary to help lead your initiatives.

Deadlines
Setting deadlines ensures that DEIB efforts remain a priority. Without them, initiatives can lose momentum. Timelines create urgency and hold teams accountable. Try breaking your DEIB initiative into multiyear, annual, and quarterly milestones. Work on smaller tasks in two-week sprints and share your progress with your champions and sponsors.

Education
Continuous learning and education are vital. Training programs, workshops, and awareness campaigns help employees understand biases, stereotypes, and systemic issues. Education fosters empathy and drives behavior change.

Environment
Creating an inclusive culture involves both physical and cultural aspects. Organizations must design spaces that accommodate diverse needs and promote psychological safety to foster an inclusive culture. They should do so in their policies, ceremonies, and language they use.

I once led an off-site team building exercise for a newly formed executive team following an unexpected merger. I had each leader complete a user manual, but instead of sharing meaningless fun facts and favorite quotes, I asked them to describe their work behaviors, how they communicated best, and their expectations of one another. We talked as a group about how those dynamics would affect the business and how to use those findings to draft an executive team charter.

Endurance

DEIB work is ongoing. It requires persistence and resilience. Organizations must commit to long-term efforts, even when faced with challenges or setbacks. Endurance ensures sustained progress.

Incentive

Providing incentives encourages participation in DEIB initiatives. An incentive must be recognized at the individual (recognition), team (retention), and enterprise (revenue) levels if you have any interest in sustaining momentum. Incentives reinforce the importance of DEIB. Recognition at the individual level can come in the form of a digital badge, intranet newsletter, or title and compensation changes. Also, be sure to show how your efforts affect employee and customer retention. For example, starting a scholarship for single mothers may resonate with many.

Intersectionality

Recognizing that individuals have multiple identities (such as their race, gender, disability, or sexual orientation) is crucial. Intersectionality acknowledges that experiences vary based on these intersecting factors, and effective DEIB initiatives consider these complexities. This can be tricky and speaks directly to my earlier point about prioritizing inclusion instead of diversity. When positioned correctly, you'll help your organization see differences as assets. Consider joint campaigns in which marginalized groups can work side-by-side.

Intercommunication

Communication across all levels of the organization is key. Regular updates, transparent discussions, and feedback channels foster understanding and alignment. Intercommunication ensures everyone is informed and engaged. If you have an intranet, communication hub, or learning management system (LMS), have a single source of truth to point your employees to.

Budget

Allocating financial resources to DEIB initiatives demonstrates commitment. If there isn't a line item on the budget for DEIB, it's not a priority. Budgets fund training, events, and programs, and adequate funding ensures sustainability. Maybe your organization funds a company inclusion assessment, an unconscious bias training for leaders, or a new internship program.

The amount of the budget isn't as important as being able to demonstrate the financial impacts of your DEIB initiative to the organization. If you are fortunate enough to have a line item in your budget for DEIB, do your best to maximize the return on investment.

Backup

It's essential to have leadership and ally support. When challenges arise, having a strong network of allies, aides, and advocates provides backup:

- **Allies** amplify voices and champion DEIB efforts. They are in the background, supporting your DEIB efforts by not getting in the way. They, for whatever reason, aren't in a position to stand alongside or lead your cause.
- **Aides** stand side-by-side with you. They are willing to roll up their sleeves and help, even if it's only in a limited capacity.
- **Advocates** are out front, willing to make sacrifices to support DEIB initiatives. You can count on them as respected partners.

Buy-In

Securing buy-in from all stakeholders—leadership, employees, and external partners—is critical. When everyone believes in the value of DEIB, progress accelerates. Buy-in drives collective action. Put your sponsors, champions, allies, aides, and advocates into a DEIB task force, which is a great way to create momentum and awareness of your initiative.

Remember, these components are interconnected, and a holistic approach is necessary for an effective DEIB program. Organizations that prioritize diversity, equity, inclusion, and belonging create better workplaces and drive positive societal change.

What You Can Do Right Away

In the journey toward fostering an inclusive culture, the questions we ask ourselves and others are not just inquiries—they are the compass that guides us through the complex terrain of the human experience. I implore you to start getting good at asking yourself these three questions:

1. **What do I want?** This question is the starting point of introspection. It prompts you to identify your personal aspirations within the context of inclusivity. By asking yourself what you truly desire, you can uncover your motivations for championing diversity, equity, inclusion, and belonging. It's a question that encourages you to envision the kind of environment you want to cultivate—where every individual feels valued and heard.

2. **Where are we going?** This question shifts your gaze from the individual to the collective journey. It's a call to align your personal goals with the broader objectives of your organization or community. By asking where you're headed, you can set a direction for your inclusion efforts and ensure that every step you take is a stride toward a shared vision of equity and unity.

3. **How can I help?** The final question transforms intention into action. It's an offer of service and a willingness to contribute to inclusion in tangible ways. By asking how you can help, you open yourself up to opportunities for collaboration, learning, and growth. It's a question that embodies the spirit of allyship and underscores the importance of active participation in creating a culture of inclusion.

Together, these questions form a powerful framework for driving change. They compel us to:

- Reflect on our personal commitment to inclusion.

- Align our actions with the collective mission of our organizations.
- Engage actively in the process of building a culture that celebrates diversity.

By consistently asking yourself, "What do I want?" "Where are we going?" and "How can I help?" you maintain a dynamic and responsive approach to the evolving needs of an inclusive culture. These questions are not just a reflection of your intent; they are the seeds from which the fruits of change will grow.

55.
Breaking the "Serving One" Mentality

Belo Miguel Cipriani, EdD (he/him)
Digital Inclusion Strategist, Oleb Media

An Urgent, All-Too-Familiar Request

On a warm Minneapolis morning in 2019, I was answering emails on my patio when a message came through that said, "We have an emergency with an employee with a disability!" landed in my inbox. The email was from an HR manager at a prestigious university who thought an employee was asking for accommodations that were not appropriate for their condition.

While I get many messages about this topic, what made this particular plea for help different was that the employee's requests seemed standard. Clearly they had received these support services before and just wanted to ensure they continued with this job. I set my assumptions aside and met with the HR manager a few days later.

Under the white patio umbrella on my deck, I listened to the HR manager share her side of the story. The employee, a residence hall director, was an alumnus of the institution. "He was the little darling of the college," she said, "but now he's changed. We simply cannot provide this level of support. It's the real world and he needs to figure it out."

I explained to her that the video transcripts he was requesting were standard. In fact, they are mandatory if an organization wants to comply with Web Content Accessibility Guidelines (WCAG). But no matter how many benefits of video transcripts I presented to her, she kept insisting that the university chose to only offer captions for employees. So, I was not surprised when she scoffed at my quote, which didn't just include my consulting fees but also the price of adding video transcripts to their entire library of employee training materials.

In the end, she was looking for someone to validate the university's decision to only offer captions. She wasn't going to invest the money on one employee—no matter who that employee was—she said multiple times.

I got off the phone and began to rock back and forth in my patio chair. While not getting a client is a common experience of running a business, the journey of being treated differently as a student and an employee by the same institution was familiar to me. In fact, I would say that some of the worst experiences I've had as a worker with a disability have been in learning environments.

Frustration Leads to an Opportunity to Help

The leaves began to fall. I could hear them move across the patio, signaling that a change was coming. Snow soon fell and I was forced back into my office. The COVID-19 pandemic struck, and I even found myself working with a mask out on my patio after the ice melted. I was enjoying the warmth of the sun on my arms when I heard my screen reader announce an email through my headset. An attorney wanted to talk to me about a quote I had provided to his client a year prior. A few Zoom meetings later, I was working with the university—the same one with the HR manager who thought the cost of digital accessibility was too high for her institution. My role was to provide training to a group of employees on creating video transcripts, captions, audio descriptions, and writing alt text. The HR manager was no longer with the university. I also learned that the institution had settled out of court for more than a million dollars.

In 2023, I was rehired by the institution to help them purchase a new learning management system (LMS). Because the LMS they were using didn't have any built-in accessibility features, we ended up creating a lot of workarounds for the employee training materials. For example, we offered staff the option of choosing between two videos: one with accessibility features and one without. The video with accessibility features included captions, transcripts, and an audio description (AD) when necessary.

One thing worth mentioning is that audio description, which provides visual details about a video to a blind person, is not always needed—if the content can be understood without the additional details from the AD, then it's not required. An example of a video that does not need AD is of a poet reading a poem—the author's name and title of work could be the title of the video. Moreover, describing what the poet is wearing will not help someone better understand the poem.

We also opted to offer transcripts as downloadable PDFs because the LMS didn't offer a place to display a transcript next to the video. To the HR director's surprise, about 40 percent of people taking the training course were downloading the transcript. Moreover, 55 percent of employees accessing the training were doing so with the accessible version of the video.

What Happens When You Make Accessibility a Priority?

The university now had evidence that the accessibility features were not only being used by the employee who had filed the complaint, but by more than half of the workers reviewing the training materials. Thus, it was important for the university's LMS to include build-in access features so it could present a better user experience to its teams.

When I asked the university's director of online learning if they were considering a specific LMS, he confessed that he was overwhelmed by the idea of reviewing hundreds of options. "There are so many products out there," he sighed. I pointed out to him that while there are many LMSs and authoring tools available for educators, many of them don't make accessibility a priority. "Accessibility is purposeful," I said while we perused the site of an LMS a colleague had recommended. In about two hours, we trimmed the list of 40 options down to five. The leading factor that let us eliminate contenders from the list was whether the company had clear information on their product's accessibility features.

In my experience, as I told this client, if a product does not have information on its site about its accessibility features, that means it doesn't have them. And, no matter how much a salesperson promises that the features will be added in the future, what matters is that they aren't available now, and a tool without a current accessibility offering is not worth investing in.

It has been four years since I began working with this client. I have seen many staff members come and go. However, the accessibility and digital inclusion experience has only improved with time. This is because the university made the decision to operationalize accessibility across the entire institution. When I see employees present at accessibility panels and conferences, I smile.

What You Can Do Right Away

Think about how your L&D team designs learning programs and your broader organization's accessibility policies and processes (or lack thereof). Are similar "serving one" biases present in decisions about whether to make the experience accessible and inclusive for all learners, employees, or customers? How might you break from that mentality, recognizing that everyone can benefit when you make accessibility a priority?

56.
Accessibility Advocacy in Corporate Environments

Haley Shust (she/her)
Accessibility Specialist and Instructional Designer

Section 1. Forming an Accessibility Committee

Finding Knowledge Gaps

Have you noticed that onboarding becomes increasingly difficult with the complexity of the organization? Large corporations tend to rely on a "drinking from the fire hose" approach, bombarding new hires with new information every day. As a learning designer, I can't say this method is very effective. However, I also recognize that onboarding is a complicated process. It requires a delicate balance between learning, application, assessment, and team building. It's a time for transferring knowledge, building relationships, and asking questions—a lot of questions if you're like me.

I began onboarding into the learning experience designer role at Salesforce on October 18, 2021. Initially, my list of questions was standard for a new hire. Most of them took the form of "What should I do if X happens?" or "Who should I reach out to in the event of X?" But when I began the onboarding curriculum for my role, my list of questions grew from a single page to several. Most of them related to a single course: "Accessibility in Enablement Content."

The course had four learning assets:
1. A high-level overview of accessibility and its importance
2. A video demonstrating a screen reader with no context about what a screen reader is

3. An overview of closed captions, their function, and a reminder to designers that automated captions are rarely accurate
4. Guidance on alternative text and with a practice exercise

Frankly, I was disappointed with how shallow the course was. Accessibility is a broad topic. Why narrow the learning content to screen readers, closed captions, and alternative text when there's so much more to discuss?

Rather than dwelling on it, I spent my time jotting down questions to ask my manager: "Which level of WCAG standards are we expected to design for?" "Who's responsible for conducting accessibility audits with a screen reader?" Thankfully, I had a manager who knew most of the answers. And if she didn't have an answer, she'd do whatever was needed to find it. As I began running down my list of questions, it quickly became evident that there wasn't ownership around accessibility. Each designer was expected to create accessible content, but no one was checking for it.

A few days later, my manager shared the name of a learning designer I ought to connect with: Pauli Evanson. Pauli was preparing to pitch the creation of an accessibility subcommittee to our leadership team. Minutes after reading my manager's message, I scheduled time to connect with her.

Pitching an Initiative

Pauli and I had no pauses in our first conversation. After we commiserated over the lack of accessibility training, I shared my desire to support the subcommittee initiative. Pauli shared the slide deck that she was pitching to the leadership team and invited me to make comments. I put aside my onboarding curriculum and dug in.

The pitch began with identifying the problem: Learning designers were creating interactive, yet inaccessible content. There weren't enough resources to support them in learning how to make their content more accessible. Designers also expected the authoring technology they used to be inherently accessible.

The proposed solution had three objectives:
1. Create a self-service inclusive design checklist that could be used to assess a learning experience before its launch.

2. Develop and launch an accessibility curriculum that scales with experience.
3. Offer coaching and office hours using a Slack channel managed by the accessibility subcommittee. (Note: Slack is the communication platform at Salesforce.)

Keep in mind, I was barely a month into working at the company. I only had a faint idea of which authoring tools we used, how our learning management system worked, and the leadership organizational structure. As I reviewed Pauli's slide deck, I had nothing to add. I simply said, "I will do absolutely anything to help you make this a reality."

Finding Time

Let's fast forward to December 2021. I was three months into my role. Pauli's accessibility initiative had been approved. The first meeting had a date, a time, and an agenda. It was really happening! But I was unable to attend. By this point, I'd been assigned to work on the account executive onboarding team. The team was wonderful and the work was interesting, but my days were filled with stakeholder interviews, collaboration sessions, and storyboarding. It just so happened that we had a big design review at the same time as the subcommittee meeting. And, as one of the newest designers, I certainly wasn't going to request to skip it.

Missing that first meeting led to an important revelation about working in a corporation: You are solely responsible for allocating time toward extracurriculars like subcommittees, equality groups, and volunteering. There is always work to be done. Some of the work has aggressive timelines and some is flexible. If there's an activity, event, or meeting you're passionate about, it's on you to put that time aside.

After that revelation, I began blocking time on my calendar to support the subcommittee. Pauli, myself, and a few other designers would divide up various tasks, and I'd spend a few hours a week thinking about the accessibility curriculum or designing support resources. I even hosted a few meetings.

Knowing When It's Time to Quit

Within a year, the subcommittee was dissolved. Participation was decreasing. There was little engagement in the Slack channel. Meeting attendance ranged from five to 20 designers, but it was mostly the same few folks (who were already well-versed in accessibility). Leaders, like Pauli and me, struggled to find the balance between our assigned work, our outside lives, and this passion project.

But this isn't a tragedy. In its year of existence, the subcommittee accomplished all of its original objectives. We created an inclusive design checklist that agile teams were using to assess their content. Every learning designer was assigned the "Accessible Visual and Audio Elements" course, which led to an uptick in the creation of alternative text and closed captions. We formed partnerships with two Salesforce organizations: the Office of Accessibility and the Office of Ethics and Integrity. There was much to celebrate.

I've spent a lot of time reflecting on the subcommittee's journey and realized it was the first time I felt like I was championing something. It's a fantastic feeling that I'm continuing to chase. I hope more learning professionals feel the drive to do the same, especially if it spreads the word about Design for All practices.

Forming Your Own Subcommittee

I now want to share some advice for establishing an accessibility initiative. By following these six practices, your initiative will have a solid foundation. Accessibility initiatives can take on many forms, such as committees, clubs, task forces, surveys, courses, checklists, training programs, and campaigns. No matter the form, each one has a similar goal of prioritizing accessibility in design and development processes. That's worth pursuing in any organization.

1. Conduct Discovery

Discovery means researching a problem by gathering information. It's closely aligned with user experience design methodology but applies to many domains. Selling a product or service? Conduct discovery on your prospective customer. Planning a trip? Asking friends for advice is a form of discovery. You should apply the same process if you're forming an accessibility committee or task force.

There are three primary objectives when conducting discovery:
1. Define the intended audience.
2. Identify the problems that need to be solved.
3. Propose a vision for the future.

Discovery can take different forms. It can be synchronous via meetings or conversations, and it can be asynchronous through surveys or chat messages. You can ask general questions like, "How do you prioritize accessibility during a design project?" or specific questions like, "How many times do you reference the accessibility checklist each month?" Using both methods can reach a larger audience and result in more data.

In the world of accessibility, there is both qualitative and quantitative data. *Qualitative data* is descriptive and helps us understand the why, how, and what of behaviors. For instance, the question, "How do you assess your content for accessibility?" will yield qualitative data. Some individuals may begin discussing accessibility during the design phase, while others conduct an audit just before launch. Inversely, *quantitative data* is measurable because it's based on numbers. It aligns with questions that begin with "How many . . ." "How much . . ." or "How often . . .?" If you have an accessibility checklist, you might be able to quantify how many views it gets each month or how many times each criterion has been checked off. Moreover, you can quantify the number of learners who have reported accessibility issues in learning experiences.

After collecting both quantitative and qualitative data, analyze it to look for trends, which will tell a story that reveals core problems. Once you've identified the core problems, you can begin thinking about solutions. How will the subcommittee drive change and provide value? What are the long-term implications? What does success look like? Summarize the answers into a vision statement.

2. Get Leadership Buy-In

No matter the size of the organization, leadership buy-in is imperative. The benefits go beyond simply receiving approval. Leaders are well connected and have high visibility. They play a crucial role in building awareness and excitement. And let's not forget about their ownership of that sweet, sweet budget.

Accessibility initiatives seem like an easy sell, right? Who would argue against more inclusive learning? No matter how obvious it may seem, you have to prepare. Leaders will want to know who, what, when, and why. More importantly, they want to understand the impact. View this effort as a sales pitch. You'll need to define your audience's priorities, practice your delivery, and prepare for challenging questions. How will this initiative help the organization meet key performance indicators? Why focus on accessibility to drive efficiency? Which metrics will improve because of this initiative? What does success look like?

Remember that you are suggesting an initiative and not defending accessibility. There's no questioning that content and experiences should be accessible. If a leader doesn't approve of your initiative, it doesn't mean they're insensitive. It could be an issue of timing or access to resources. Don't fret. Simply apply what you learned from your leader and redefine the scope.

3. Gather Interest

Thankfully, the discovery process will get your audience thinking about accessibility. This is the first step toward gathering interest. But it's only the first step. Launching an initiative, like a subcommittee, requires a marketing strategy, just like goods and services. "Coming soon" banners and teaser trailers might not be necessary, but you'll certainly want to build hype. Introduce a guest speaker. Share a schedule of anticipated events. Post flyers around an office space. No matter the format, you'll need to convince your audience why they should be a part of this accessibility initiative.

Lead with telling people what's in it for them. This is integral. Remember, you're driving the initiative, so it likely feels like the most important thing in the world to you. But to everyone else, it's another thing that can eat up their workday. Speak from their perspective and not your own. Be clear about the time commitment, the value, and the greater impact.

Candidly, I've always struggled with this part. To me, accessibility is obvious. It ought to be a requirement. Yet, I must remind myself that everyone has their own priorities and sometimes the desire for professional development isn't there. Or maybe it's an issue with timing or capacity.

However, I've noticed that the best learning designers have a shared quality: We're all learner-focused. We live for positive learner feedback. We swoon upon hearing, "This training was a good use of my time." By positioning the accessibility initiative as a way to better serve learners, you pique the interest of the L&D audience. Accessible learning is equitable. That's something we can all get behind.

4. Collaborate

As Helen Keller is famously quoted as saying, "Alone we can do so little; together we can do so much." Collaboration improves any initiative. Not just for the delegation of tasks, but for innovation. When you collaborate, you invite an expansion of perspectives. In turn, that leads to a larger network, new ideas, and ultimately a better experience for you and your audience.

Pauli knew this. Before I joined her effort, she was collaborating with two other learning designers in building a case for the accessibility subcommittee. I stepped in just as those designers were assigned other projects. Perfect timing, I suppose. Both continued to contribute to the effort by reviewing resources, schedules, and communications.

Thanks to an introduction from my manager, we were able to secure our first guest speaker, a leader of the Salesforce neurodiversity equality group. Soon after that, a director advertised our committee during an organization-wide call. Then, peers shared our announcements to relevant internal channels. Although Pauli and I hosted the meetings, we had many allies. We wouldn't have been successful without them.

The core message here is to form partnerships. Even if you own the effort, there are tremendous benefits to collaboration. It enhances problem solving by harnessing collective knowledge and expertise and combining efforts. It fosters a sense of community.

5. Be Adaptable

As your initiative takes shape, prepare for challenges. Conduct an exercise to identify the worst-case scenarios. For an accessibility subcommittee, that might look like low attendance at meetings or no adoption of practices. Create a plan for adapting. Whenever possible, offer several solutions. Trial and error may be required to determine the best course of action. Allow me to use an example to clarify.

Beginning in December 2022, there was a noticeable drop-off in attendance at our subcommittee meetings. That's normal as the holidays approached. January was also a packed month because designers were preparing content for a company kickoff in February. Pauli and I realized that attendance would continue to decline.

Our solution? Host an asynchronous meeting. We used our Slack channel to achieve this. In a series of posts, we shared updates and news, offered things to try, and conducted polls using emoji reactions. Our audience was delighted to have one less meeting on their calendar. We managed to meet our metrics for sharing accessibility resources.

Adaptation is crucial to the success of any initiative. There are some events you simply can't forecast, such as massive layoffs or product acquisitions. At the end of the day, everyone will prioritize their own work over a subcommittee (and they should!). Just like collaboration, adaptation fosters innovation. It's a key factor in ensuring your initiative stays relevant in a dynamic environment.

6. Have an Exit Strategy

You might be thinking, "With all the effort I'm putting into this initiative, why would I want to think about disassociating with it?" If so, hear me out. Things change. Maybe you'll switch to a different team, be assigned to a time-consuming project, or accept a new role elsewhere. Maybe you're burnt out because you haven't met your attendance goals in months.

Maybe a leader wants to dissolve the initiative. No matter the circumstances, you'll need an exit strategy. It's insurance that the initiative will live on and continue to have a meaningful impact. It's a promise that the organization will remain committed to inclusive design best practices.

This is another reason why collaboration is essential. With more people involved, there's a greater likelihood of keeping the initiative alive. That's less likely if you're working in a silo. If you have the luxury of forecasting your exit, you can select and onboard the next initiative leader. In some cases, it might be an obvious, easy choice. Other times, you might need to do some searching. Invite dedicated audience members to take on more responsibilities. And remember, it's OK to have a few individuals share a leadership role!

Documentation will make your exit easier. Maintain one document as a single source of truth from the time of inception. Include the initiative's vision and definition for success, relevant metrics, and stakeholders. Keep a log of meeting topics, participant feedback, and ideas for future efforts. With this documentation, a new initiative leader will have centralized, aggregated information. They can gather insight into what the initiative aims to do, who's been involved, and what has been accomplished so far.

Sometimes, leading an initiative can feel like another job. A quality exit strategy ensures that you leave the initiative on good terms and without regret. Instead of being caught in the trap of thinking, "I could have done more," you'll focus on the positive influence. It might be time to move on, but it doesn't mean you've lost your Design for All mentality.

What Can You Do Right Away

Forming an accessibility committee within your organization is not for the faint of heart, but there are small steps you can take to begin. As I shared in the Conduct Discovery section, you can start by identifying how your organization handles accessibility issues. Or, to start even smaller, you can focus on your own department or team. Once you've done that, you can structure the committee around any gaps and go from there.

Section 2. Creating an Accessibility Role

Increasing Awareness

Around the same time that participation fell off for the Salesforce accessibility subcommittee (as detailed in section 1 of this chapter), a new initiative began: a diversity, equity, inclusion, and accessibility (DEIA) task force. In some ways, this was the next generation of the subcommittee. The entire global enablement organization was invited to participate, extending outreach beyond learning designers to facilitators, program managers, editors, and more. The scope expanded from accessible courses to accessible experiences.

The DEIA task force was divided into five pillars: events, talents, communications, storytelling, and inclusive enablement. Each pillar had its own leader and set of responsibilities. I joined the inclusive enablement pillar as one of eight members. Our primary responsibility was to conduct audits of required enablement using an accessibility checklist—the very one that our former accessibility subcommittee had created.

We set up a nice process for this. Agile teams would submit an intake request for an audit. Our pillar leader would scope the request, and then share it with the pillar members. Each of us would take turns reviewing the experiences using the checklist, and then share the report with the agile teams. Then, they would make the necessary edits to improve content accessibility before launch. Seamless, right? It would have been if every pillar member had a foundational understanding of inclusive design practices. Unfortunately—as was bound to happen at a large organization full of well-intentioned people wanting to make an impact—that wasn't the case here. So, while every pillar member was willing to learn, the lack of knowledge caused a rocky start.

Our answer to this problem was accessibility checklist training. Although I wasn't the pillar leader, I led this training because I was familiar with WCAG and quality assurance processes. During each meeting, we allocated 15 to 30 minutes toward interpreting WCAG standards, as well as how they ought to appear in learning experiences. I taught pillar members how to check for alternative text, generate an audio transcript, and use a screen reader.

After several meetings, pillar members had enough confidence to begin performing some of the audits. It was delightful to hear success stories of how they helped a designer write quality alternative text. Or how they reminded the communications team to limit their use of flashing emojis. One of my favorite moments was receiving a message that stated, "I think I'm getting the hang of using NVDA [a screen reader]. I found some focus order issues in that last simulation!"

Thinking Bigger

Alongside the DEIA task force efforts, I was still supporting the account executive onboarding design team. We were in the midst of a major revision, and I was struggling to find balance. While I found the onboarding work to be interesting, my heart wasn't in it as much as the inclusive design effort. Yet, I had no choice but to pour my time and energy into onboarding because that's the work I was hired to do. Anything DEIA-related was ancillary.

As time went on, the inclusive design pillar began feeling like the subcommittee all over again. Participation and meeting attendance were low. I conducted most of the audits. It's not that people didn't care anymore; they just had other priorities. It might sound like a "woe is me" situation, but rather, I enjoyed it. I loved helping design teams improve their user experience for the betterment of all learners. Any time I could talk about accessibility or coach a peer was time well spent.

After sharing this sentiment with my manager, she challenged me to think bigger. Could I create an entire accessibility curriculum for the global enablement organization? How much time would it take to conduct audits of optional training? Were there opportunities to partner with our facilitation teams? How could we build an accessibility checklist into our LMS?

Fireworks went off in my brain. The more I thought about the possibilities, the more I saw potential. Subcommittees and task forces weren't cutting it. Someone needed to own the accessibility of our internal learning ecosystem. This could be a whole role. I imagined myself handing out business cards that said, "Haley Shust, Accessibility Specialist, Salesforce." I opened a new tab and typed, "How to build a business case for a new role," into my search engine. The journey began.

Conducting Discovery

I read blogs. Looked at examples. I reached out to people on LinkedIn. There was a lot to learn. First, I realized that there's no right or wrong way to format your business case. Some people write in paragraphs, while others provide bulleted sections. Next, I learned that, at its core, a business case is a justification for a project or effort. It needs to provide the who, what, when, why, and how. Finally, I noticed the importance of data and metrics. Stakeholders love metrics because they tell a story at a glance. A "90 percent reduction in accessibility cases" is better than "fewer people are complaining about closed captions."

With my discovery completed, I began to design my business case. I used Miro—a visual workspace that works like a digital whiteboard and can be used for diagramming, mapping, note-taking, and organizing ideas. I chose Miro because it functions like a dynamic canvas that evolves as you begin to shape an idea. Sticky notes captured the thoughts that popped into my head. I used different shapes or colors to represent different categories of problems or solutions. Miro also provides space that documents and slide decks can't offer. But this is the way I like to work, and preferences vary.

It took me about two weeks to create the business case. Given the limited time in my workday, I spent my evenings organizing ideas and perfecting the layout. Honestly, I'm not sure if this is a normal timeline, but to me, it was worth prioritizing. Not to mention, I wanted to get the ideas out of my head and onto my Miro board before they were replaced with recipes and memes.

Building Your Business Case

My business case was organized into eight sections. Here's an overview of each section's purpose:

1. **Problem statement.** Write one or two sentences that summarize the problems or gaps that an accessibility specialist can solve. Make sure this statement speaks to widespread challenges that affect a large audience. If the audience is too narrow, your case may be insufficient to support a role.
2. **Strategic goals.** Cite several strategic goals related to the problem. Use exact language. Prioritize goals from executives, leaders, or the entire organization. In addition to goals, reference mission statements and company visions or values.
3. **Current programs and efforts.** List programs, initiatives, and other efforts that either aim to address the problem (from the problem statements) or support a strategic goal. You might want to use arrows or color coding to show connections between programs and the goals they align to. Add relevant details, such as stakeholders, objectives, or mission statements.
4. **Challenges encountered.** For each of the programs or efforts, share related challenges or blockers. Limit the list to two or three and expect to repeat the same challenges for different programs. Again, it might be useful to use arrows or color coding to show relationships from goals to programs to challenges.
5. **Challenges by category (optional).** Add this section if you want to provide an at-a-glance summary. Sort the challenges from the prior section into categories and include a brief summary of each. Example categories include budget, communications, sponsorship, training, awareness, strategy, process, and consistency. If this seems redundant, I hear you. I didn't initially include this section, but added it in when a stakeholder asked for an organized view of common challenges.
6. **About this role.** Write the job description and requirements. Reference job postings for similar roles if you need inspiration. This is your opportunity to describe your vision for the role. Be explicit about what services this role will provide. If possible, categorize them into types of services, such as self-service,

coaching, and full-service. Keep in mind that this section should not communicate how you'll address challenges—that's what the next section is for!
7. **Actionable solutions.** Communicate how the role will solve the aforementioned challenges. Each solution should be an action statement. Use bullets to communicate specific details, such as intended audience or metrics.
8. **Business impacts.** Summarize how creating this role will affect the business. Use simple language and formulaic statements that indicate behavior changes. Cite specific metrics and KPIs. Depending on the scope, you may be able to categorize business impacts based on the audience, such as learner impacts, organizational impacts, or budget impacts.

Refining Your Business Case

The formatting and section headings of your business case may differ. You might include other details like timing, budget, and even a cost benefit analysis. Some business cases offer a variety of options to solve a problem, and then weigh the pros and cons of each option. Point to data where it makes sense but be cautious when making estimations.

Relevant data is challenging to find for accessibility initiatives because organizations would never (and should never) publish statistics on how many employees have a disability or impairment. It's also impossible to quantify how many individuals have temporary or situational impairments. So, it's unlikely you'll be able to point to a metric and say something like, "By prioritizing accessibility, we'll improve the learning experience for this many learners."

Instead, quantify the number of learners in your entire audience and use that number in your business case. Remember that the best learning experiences are ones that everyone can access and benefit from. Accessible learning affects your entire audience, even if they don't acknowledge it. However, when Design for All is done right, your audience won't realize it. It's just quality learning with no blockers.

As you write your business case, you'll also need to balance concision with elaboration. Remember that leaders are busy. Ten pages of paragraph-style explanation is awfully verbose. In that instance, you should write an executive summary. Alternatively, a list of bullet point items might not convey enough valuable information. So think of your business case like a movie trailer—it tells a story but in a short period of time.

Once you've put together your first draft, request reviews from stakeholders, managers, and peers. Practice speaking to your business case as well. Expect to iterate on it several times. Feedback will make your business case stronger—and the stronger your business case, the more likely your leadership will approve it.

Submitting Your Business Case

When you've finalized your business case, you'll need to determine your strategy for submitting it. If you're lucky, there may already be a formal process for this. If not, you'll need to conduct discovery to determine the best method for communicating with your leaders. Maybe it's an email or a video message. Personally, I've found that many prefer you book time on their calendar. In that case, you'll want to be prepared to present your case.

I was fortunate enough to have my business case delivered for me. One of my stakeholders, a director, was an accessibility ally who had sponsored a few initiatives, including the subcommittee. She reviewed the case and shared a clear understanding of my objectives with her manager, who was the vice president of my organization. Honestly, I didn't know whether to feel elated or disappointed, but I was glad to have one less thing occupying space in my mind. Please don't expect the same outcome if you create a business case. It is best to practice your pitch repeatedly and have a power suit ironed and ready.

I submitted my business case in late November 2022, and it was presented in early December. I heard it went well, but there were two stipulations. First, nothing was to be actioned on until the new fiscal year, which began in February. Second, conversations were ongoing about the new role. In the meantime, I was to continue supporting the DEIA task force by conducting accessibility audits of mandatory training. That sounded like a win to me!

Waiting Your Turn

Patience is key when you submit a business case. Remind yourself that it's not a personal matter or that your suggestion isn't solid; it's just that priorities are fluid. Sometimes, an organization has to be reactive instead of proactive, and leaders often have other considerations when making decisions. Every day, they have to assess their to-do list to determine which questions or efforts take priority. Then, there are emergencies that require immediate attention or last-minute meetings from executives. Realistically, your business case will sit on your leader's to-do list for some time.

So, when I tell you that it took about four months for the accessibility specialist role to be approved, I say it with no resentment. In fact, it was one of the happiest moments in my career. My dream came to fruition. Leadership saw the value of the role and believed that I could elicit change. Finally, I had the opportunity to narrow my focus to the accessibility of our learning ecosystem.

At the time of writing this, I'm about two months into this role and loving it. Rather than living in the design cycle, I'm able to coach, mentor, audit, collaborate, write, develop, and support. Each day offers something different, and each day brings the global enablement organization a little closer to applying Design for All.

What You Can Do Right Away

Whether you're interested in creating an accessibility-focused role within your company or adding accessibility responsibilities to your current position, prepare to pitch to your manager and other decision-makers by building a business case. Use the outline I provided to collect your own thoughts and conduct your own discovery about what metrics or goals will matter most to your business.

Section 3. Operationalizing Accessibility to Measure Impact

Defining Operationalization

The Oxford Dictionary defines *operationalize* as "to put into operation or use." You have to love a definition that includes part of the word you're defining, right? I have historically avoided this word because I'm never confident that I'm using it correctly. If I start my dishwasher, am I operationalizing it? For a long while, I wasn't sure.

Since I started at Salesforce, I hear "operationalize" on a weekly basis, maybe even daily. "Product owners need a detailed plan to operationalize the project's milestones." "We're trying to operationalize a culture of innovation to stay competitive." "Let's operationalize learner feedback into concrete next steps."

One day it clicked. It all starts with something abstract or ambiguous, like a mission statement. That abstract concept is operationalized when you apply processes, tasks, and associated measurable variables. In other words, we create a method to achieve measurable results.

Describing Operationalization

Often the term operationalize is aligned with building a business. What begins as an idea, a vision, or a mission eventually requires processes, policies, and procedures—all of which need to be standardized and documented using manual or automated means. With a firm process in place, we can quantify the duration of each step in the process. Later, we can gauge the effectiveness of a solution through surveys. Then, we can compare those two data points to determine how to provide the greatest amount of value in the shortest amount of time. This is when the phrase "time is money" applies.

Corporations, like Salesforce, rely on data to illustrate impact. If the process exists, it's going to be tracked. The resulting data is turned into a report, and then maybe a dashboard. Once a few months of data has been collected, you can calculate averages. At an organization with around 80,000 employees, these averages are used to set goals.

Over time, goal metrics are scaled to increase rigor. If you meet your metrics, you're doing fine. Exceed your metrics, and you're a high performer. Fail to meet your metrics? You should have a good explanation for why.

Operationalizing Accessibility

When learning experiences are designed well, there's no indication that accessibility has been baked in. It's inherent. As a result, you'll drastically reduce the occurrence of *accessibility blockers*, which are any instances when a user can't progress through a digital experience due to inaccessible features. For example, if a video doesn't have closed captions, someone who is deaf would be blocked from accessing that content.

Tracking blockers is vital because it reveals design flaws, which can inform accessibility training opportunities. But maybe your design team prioritizes accessibility, so there are rarely any blockers and you're missing an important dataset. In that case, you'll need to find other methods for collecting accessibility data. Perhaps you could create a digital display that tracks the number of days since someone has encountered a blocker. That's data, right?

If you work in a corporate setting, you'll need to operationalize accessibility in some capacity. I have been tasked with this. On one hand, I get it. I need to prove the value of my role by demonstrating impact. My leaders want to point to a piece of data and exclaim, "Our accessibility specialist reduced learning blockers by 203 percent!" (And yes, that's an exaggeration.)

On the other hand, accessibility wins are best shared through stories. They can be enhanced with data—qualitative and quantitative—to show impact. Sometimes, you have to know where someone started to truly appreciate where they've ended up.

As accessibility allies, we're in the business of touching lives through inclusive experiences, yet we can't quantify the number of lives we've touched. And that's for good reason—it's illegal (and unethical) to ask employees to disclose a disability or impairment. Therefore, you should never, ever ask learners to disclose their disability or impairment.

Even if the individual openly discloses their disability, you don't have the green light to exploit them for their disability. For instance, if a learner shares that they are neurodivergent, they don't automatically become your subject matter expert. The same goes for individuals who use screen readers. Don't send them a PDF and ask them to test it with their screen reader.

The challenge of operationalizing accessibility is finding the "before" data that can be used to make comparisons and prove positive impact. You want to be able to say that an accessibility initiative changed a behavior, and the only way you can prove that change is if you have data about that behavior from before and after the initiative.

This is the situation I currently find myself in. Basically, I'm trying to prove that my role is essential because I'm improving the learner experience for individuals with disabilities. But there's a limited amount of relevant data I can reference from before my role existed. My options include learner survey responses, support cases, and completion of accessibility courses. That might sound like plenty of data sources, but I assure you it's not—especially when you consider that our proprietary LMS has existed for only three years.

Telling Accessibility Stories With Data

In the global enablement organization, I'm the pioneer for measuring the impact of accessibility, and I've implemented some methods to operationalize my efforts. Before I share them, I want to preface this section by stating that each of these methods is still in its infancy. I can't yet speak to their effectiveness or the data story they tell.

1. Measure the Adoption of a Self-Service Accessibility Checklist

First things first, you need a self-service accessibility checklist. If your organization already has one, that's great! You get to skip a step. The next step is to simply survey how many teams and individuals are using it. That's your starting dataset. If your organization doesn't have an accessibility checklist, you must create one. There are countless examples online and in this book that offer a quality starting point, but you should tailor it to your organization and audience.

The good news about this scenario is that your starting dataset is zero. Any adoption of the checklist is a net positive result. For this method, your objective is simple: Increase the adoption of the accessibility checklist. In theory, the more individuals using the checklist, the less likely that learners will encounter a blocker or inaccessible element.

Whenever I audit a learning experience, I reference the checklist to remind myself of the criteria I'm looking for. Although I am not the target audience for the checklist, I still count my uses in the overall dataset. No matter your role or amount of experience with accessibility, a checklist is an insurance policy that no accessibility standard will go unchecked.

Promoting the adoption of the checklist can take many forms, such as:
- Advertise the checklist in an organization-wide channel.
- Reach out to individuals or attend team meetings.
- Create mandatory training around how to use the checklist.
- Foster competition by creating a leaderboard of checklist uses. (Adding some kind of incentive always seems to help, whether it be a public shout out or a prize.)

After promoting the checklist, re-evaluate how many people are using it and compare the results against the starting data set. Ideally, you'll find that more individuals or teams are using it.

2. Log Inaccessibilities From Audits

This strategy is extremely effective if you have a system for conducting quality control checks. At Salesforce, mandatory training materials are expected to undergo an editorial and accessibility review before they go live. This process has been widely accepted by design teams throughout the global enablement organization.

Presently, I am the only individual responsible for conducting formal accessibility audits. I use a template to generate a report of my findings, which I share with the design team.

After I conduct my review and share the report, I log the common inaccessibilities using a Google Form. Before I move on, I want to clarify that you can use any form or survey tool as a log. Salesforce uses Google Workspace, so that's the most convenient option for me. Your log can be a simple spreadsheet or you can use tools like Airtable, Tally, SurveyMonkey, or ClickUp. Using a basic checklist format, I note all the issues I find in the learning experience. I repeat this process for every learning asset I review.

Over time, this log helps me gather data that will inform the types of accessibility training I develop. Maybe I notice that learning designers are failing to add audio transcripts to their videos. That cues me to reach out to our video production team and collaborate on a refresher course.

In essence, the inaccessibility log reveals strengths and weaknesses in our content design. When I evaluate the data, I look for trends and decide if additional training or upskilling is needed. Sometimes, I organize coaching sessions, like a lunch & learn. Other times, I create e-learning courses to assess and practice the application of accessible design. When design teams are busy, I might even address a common weakness in a communication post to a public channel in Slack, our messaging app.

If my training and remediation efforts are effective, I should observe a wider adoption of inclusive, accessible design. I'll log fewer inaccessible elements and spend more time upskilling my peers. If not, then I'll need to conduct some discovery. There may be other nontraining variables that are influencing processes or tools. It's a wonderful feedback loop that operationalizes education around accessibility.

3. Create a Process for Reporting Accessibility Blockers

Products and services rely on customers submitting support cases to identify issues. A similar process can be put in place within a learning ecosystem. You'll want to apply this process anywhere that learning occurs, such as a LMS or a video hosting platform.

The objective of this method is to collect data about accessibility blockers. Unlike the log from audits, this information is provided by learners and should reveal inaccessibilities with the learning ecosystem itself in addition to specific content. Obviously, we hope the audit will catch any inaccessibilities before the content is live, but this will give learners a way to report any blockers they encounter. This method is challenging to implement, especially in a large organization with disparate learning systems. It may be best to start with one or two of the larger systems, which is what I've done.

Salesforce uses a proprietary LMS, which offers a built-in support functionality that learners can use to report system inaccuracies, issues, or bugs. A group of support agents manage these cases and unblock learners from completing their coursework. Typically, it takes less than 24 hours for a case to be solved. Unless, of course, the blocker is unsolvable because the LMS is incompatible with an assistive technology.

That was the case for a few learners who couldn't complete courses because they were unable to navigate them using their assistive technology. It's a brutal example of inequitable learning, but it's also a reality that many learners face. Assistive technologies are evolving like everything else. Ideally, learning systems would evolve with them (and for them), but that's not always possible.

My solution to this issue was to create a new support category titled "Accessibility Blocker" and route the cases to my personal queue. Whenever a case was logged, I would receive a notification so I could immediately unblock the learner by pulling content out of the LMS and into a document. If the blocker happened to be caused by a learning asset, I would work directly with the design team to remove the inaccessible interaction.

This process allows me to operationalize accessibility by creating associations between functionalities and blockers. An increase in cases indicates something in our learning ecosystem that doesn't operate properly with assistive technology. If I can identify the core issue and fix it, the number of cases should decrease—and that's evidence the process works.

Unfortunately, that's not what has transpired since I've implemented this support process. "Accessibility Blocker" is too vague of a category. Instead of receiving messages from assistive technology users, the vast majority of my cases report simple access issues. Things like, "This link didn't work," or "The e-learning timed out and won't reload." While it's certainly data, it's not telling the story I had hoped for. To address that, I'm reimagining the user-facing support form so it provides more precise tagging. The user will be able to call out specific blockers, like "I can't use my assistive technology" instead of more general blockers, like "I can't access this content." Consequently, this will allow me to filter for cases specific to accessibility issues.

I'm also working with the technology team to add new functionality to event registration. My hope is that learners will be able to request accommodations for in-person and virtual events, which are then forwarded to the facilitators. It's another step forward in creating a more equitable learning ecosystem.

What You Can Do Right Away

Accessibility should be operationalized in an organizational setting. Not necessarily for the sake of measuring the impact of a role or initiative, but to apply a data-driven approach to improving accessibility practices. Through audits, you can identify inaccessible elements. By tracking those elements, you can determine where you're falling short in designing accessible content. Through support cases, you can find accessibility blockers. By monitoring those cases, you can make a strong case for investing in more accessible technology. By monitoring the completion of accessibility courses and curriculum, you can tell a story about an organization that's committed to Design for All. That's the story I hope to tell.

57.
Hiring an Accessibility Consultant

Belo Miguel Cipriani, EdD (he/him)
Digital Inclusion Strategist, Oleb Media

People in the L&D field always want to know: "Did you get into the accessibility field to make a change for the disability community?" My response usually puzzles them. "I became an accessibility consultant," I answer, "because I was forced into it."

In 2008, I was living in San Francisco, California, and was newly blind. A tech company came into the blind center where I was learning to use JAWS and read braille, and they asked for people to test their website. A group of my classmates jumped at the opportunity, but I didn't. I felt like we should be getting paid by the tech giant and stayed behind with my cooking teacher. As I chopped onions, he lectured me on how hard it is for blind people to get jobs and said that doing this little project was something I could add to my resume. As a former recruiter in Silicon Valley, I knew he was on to something. I bit my lip and joined the rest of the group in the computer room.

After losing my sight, I tried many career paths. However, they all came to a roaring end because of accessibility issues. Tech companies were using project management tools I couldn't access. My journalism career ended when newspapers and radio stations began to lose advertisement money to tech companies and switched to hiring mostly contractors. As a freelancer, they didn't have to accommodate me, so I couldn't get support with photo editing or slide show design for social media. My university teaching career also went nowhere. I couldn't even interview for the roles that required me to teach online due to their inaccessible learning management system (LMS).

For four years, I applied to jobs. I was eventually contacted—not for the role I had applied to, but to talk about the one accessibility testing project I had on my resume. So, I sighed and decided to make accessibility my new path. It seemed like everyone was pushing me in that direction.

Fast forward 14 years, and I now run a digital inclusion firm. Accessibility is a field, and I'm even teaching courses on accessibility as part of degree programs. In my opinion, accessibility is a core aspect of any business, like accounting and marketing. There are things you can do on your own, but sometimes it's best to hire a professional.

Distinguishing Between an Accessibility Consultant and a Natural User

I've been working in the accessibility space for more than a decade. I have hired hundreds of individuals for different types of accessibility projects, from testing major brands' corporate websites to consulting for film and tech startups. I have hired consultants with accessibility certificates and some without. But, no matter what level of training they possess, I think that a consultant should be able to do three things:

1. Point out an issue.
2. Articulate the type of problem.
3. Hypothesize a solution.

Sometimes, however, an accessibility consultant may not be able to do all three for every type of access problem. I'll use myself as an example. Because I am blind, I'm not able to test for color contrast. However, I have developed ways to work around this problem by hiring someone on my team with a design background to be my color tester.

I'm often asked to fix or alter an accessibility problem that was handled by an employee. In many cases, it was an employee who was a natural user of assistive technology and based on a solution to something from an accessibility blog. As a result, their solution was not based on accessibility best practices, but a workaround that was later forgotten, and consequently, the original access problem wasn't fixed. For example, a workaround might be a company allowing a blind employee to email their timecard instead of reporting the problem to the payroll company. Or, a company might only provide training accommodation to one employee, and accessibility goes away when that employee leaves the organization. In both scenarios, the team members were natural users of assistive technology. So, while they could point out problems, they lacked the training to document and report the issue to the proper stakeholder.

By the way, the example of the blind employee and the timecard issue is a real situation from my career experience. I learned that the employee called the payroll company's customer service department to report the issue. However, the representative told him that there wasn't a payroll option for the blind. When a second blind employee joined and refused to email her timesheet because she didn't want her personal information stored in emails, I was brought in to help. In four weeks, I was able to report the code issue to the engineering manager at the payroll company and offer them solutions on how to fix the issue. While the consumer in me wanted to complain to the customer service rep, I knew that the issue would only get fixed if I talked to the engineering manager—and if I offered a clear solution to the problem.

Deciding When to Do It Yourself and When to Hire Out

I would break up my clients into two groups. One group comes to me because of a legal judgement. They are being forced to change because, for an array of reasons, they didn't make accessibility a priority. The second group includes accessibility coordinators, managers, and directors from organizations that are launching a new service or product and want help to ensure a smooth launch. They contact me months, sometimes even a year, before their course, website, or mobile app reaches their audiences.

When deciding if your organization should tackle an accessibility project or hire a professional, it all comes down to time. In some cases, time may be determined by a grant deadline, a letter from a judge, or a product or event launch date. Whichever it may be, if your organization has less than three months to add accessibility features to a learning product, I recommend you hire a consultant. While this will be a more costly route, it will ensure that access elements are created correctly and to the highest industry standards. Ultimately, if your accessibility needs are time sensitive, save yourself some stress and find an accessibility consultant. Learning accessibility best practices will take longer to master than a couple months.

If time is on your side (say you have six months to a year before the big release of your new training program), I recommend doing some work yourself while collaborating with a trained professional. By handling some of the accessibility work yourself, and then having an accessibility consultant double-check it, you will keep costs down by reducing the consultant's workload. You can also learn from the accessibility professional by seeing how they solve problems and ask questions about your specific project. In the end, working with a professional will elevate your own skill set, while ensuring that your project gets the best access level possible.

Growing Your Own Internal Resources

One of the most overlooked aspects of accessibility is maintenance. You can't simply add access features and forget about them. Technology updates can easily render a course inaccessible. In fact, I once had a client go from meeting WCAG Level AAA requirements, the gold standard in accessibility, down to Level A when their LMS was bought out by another tech company that decided to merge its tech and drop some access features. Because this organization hadn't grown internal resources that could help monitor or recreate what was lost, it needed to start from scratch with a consultant.

To maintain accessibility levels, organizations need to invest in training their teams. A common trend is to assign accessibility tasks to one person; however, I recommend that an entire team be tasked with accessibility so there are no interruptions to access if an employee goes on vacation or moves to another company. My clients have had great success by assigning accessibility to either their marketing, HR, or IT teams.

As I stated earlier, technology changes quickly. Aside from lack of training, updates are the biggest foe for accessibility. As a result, many accessibility blogs and videos can become obsolete after a few months. So, while free resources are always a good place to start, the latest information on accessibility for a tool will often come directly from a professional. I suggest creating a list of accessibility consultants and following their work. Don't just connect with them on social media, but also attend training programs they may offer.

Interviewing an Accessibility Consultant

Whether you are short on time or simply want to ensure quality for your project, hiring an accessibility consultant may seem like a daunting task. After all, how can you ask them questions about a subject you're not comfortable with?

When reviewing accessibility experience, it really comes down to product consumption—meaning, how many people have used the digital property, and what are the reviews like for it?

I once received a resume from an accessibility consultant who was applying for the lead role in my film and TV division. This is the group that handles the projects from TV networks. As I typed the names of their projects into my web browser, I noticed that they had terrible reviews, including one from a customer who said that the audio description was terrible. So, it was easy for me to pass on that specific candidate.

Another consideration when interviewing accessibility consultants is to match industry experience to your project. Thus, if you create art training, and the consultant has worked with helping arts organizations with accessibility projects, then the odds of them being the right match are high.

I believe that both training and experience are important. While a course on accessibility will help someone understand how to fix a problem, it's the experience of doing something for a long time that will help them come up with multiple solutions to the problem. At my firm, I don't hire any testers for our entry-level positions unless they have a course and three projects under their belt. In addition, I look for people who like mysteries and being focused on a single problem, because that's a big part of being an accessibility consultant. We must find what is wrong and we can't move on until that issue is solved. There used to be a time when accessibility training could only be obtained through certificates. Now, that's changed, and there are consultants who received their training through a degree program or by doing an apprenticeship in an accessibility consulting firm. The most important thing to inquire about is how they received their accessibility training and what they do to maintain their skills. Simply asking, "Where did you get your accessibility training," or "How do you stay up to date with accessibility trends?" will give you a wide glimpse into the consultant's skill set.

What You Can Do Right Away

I never thought I would become an accessibility professional. But now, I can't imagine doing anything else. It's become my passion, and I'm glad that it's now recognized as a field of study. But just like you'll click with some doctors, lawyers, and accountants and avoid working with others, the same applies to accessibility professionals. I wish you all the best with finding the right access partner for your project or organization.

Where you start depends on your current need. If you're reading this chapter (and book) because you're in the middle of creating a learning experience and need help with accessibility testing, prioritize hiring an accessibility consultant—and sooner rather than later; as with any consultant, they will have ongoing projects to manage. But if you're mapping what skills to develop (for yourself or your team), you can complement your own growth with outside help.

58.
Incorporating Accessibility in Development
Guidance for Quality Assurance

David Lindenberg (he/him)
Senior Technical Learning and Development Specialist, SAS

The course was done! I had that sense of excitement and relief. I felt good. All that was left was sending it to our accessibility team for an audit. I was new to the company and had never worked somewhere with an accessibility team. I didn't think it would take long or that it would be a big deal. However, it was quite humbling to receive the audit results for my shiny, new, inaccessible course. This is where my journey to designing more inclusive learning experiences began.

From an accessibility standpoint, the course was a mess. The audit was well organized, but I found myself repeatedly asking the accessibility team for clarification. How do I write alt text? What is focus order and why does it matter? I didn't know what I didn't know. The accessibility audit was a lesson in quality control. I left out alt text for images, the color contrast was poor, and the keyboard navigation was all over the place. Oh, and the two videos in the course didn't have closed captions or transcripts. Thankfully, we performed the audit before the course was released.

In addition to improving my own accessibility and inclusive design practice, I realized the importance of adding accessibility to the list of items to check in my quality control review. Examining the results of the accessibility audit also made me realize the number and scope of inaccessible items that needed to be addressed. This is where having a well-defined quality assurance process can help.

Quality Assurance and Quality Control

So, what's the difference between quality assurance and quality control? *Quality assurance (QA)* is the overall process you use to make sure what you're building (such as an e-learning course) meets industry and company standards for a quality product. For QA, you'll consider:

- What steps do you take to ensure quality?
- What procedures do you follow?
- What templates do you use?
- Do you include certain standards for every course?
- Are these standards documented?

Quality control (QC) is an event in the QA process. Often referred to as "testing your course," it often happens at the end of the development process and is frequently a one-time occurrence. When you perform a QC test, you're getting into the specifics of a particular course. For QC, you'll check for the following:

- Is the course working as designed?
- Does the navigation work properly?
- Are there any misspelled words or formatting errors?
- Is the audio narration understandable and loud enough?
- Do the hyperlinks work and are they pointing to the correct locations?
- Do videos work as expected?

I like to think of QA as a timeline for development (Figure 58-1). You want a usable, quality-infused product (in this case, training content), so you should think about quality standards from the beginning to the end of the design and development timeline. Furthermore, you should follow the standards at each step of the timeline. A QC event is a designated checkpoint on the QA timeline where you verify that what you're building is conforming to your standard of quality.

```
        QUALITY                        QUALITY
        CONTROL                        CONTROL
   |-------●----------------------------●-------|
                   QUALITY ASSURANCE
```

Figure 58-1. Quality assurance as a timeline for development.

Quality Assurance Recommendations

QA is a shared process that applies to everyone in your organization and should be communicated across teams and built into everything you do. To put it simply, QA is everyone's responsibility. The QC checks test that the QA process is being followed and is working. Accessibility and inclusive design should be integrated into the standards that guide your full QA process. Therefore, they should also be included in every QC test.

Including accessibility and inclusive design in your QA process from the start makes the QC testing easier and faster. Let's say that a QA standard states that all images should have alt text. If you automatically add alt text to an image when you load it into your content, the person testing the course in a QC review won't have to stop and document each instance of missing alt text. You also make it easier on yourself because you won't have to track down the location of each image to add the missing alt text. This saves you and the tester time.

Let's take that a step further back in the process. What if you modified your templates (such as design documents and storyboards) to include a place to add alt text in your design? If you've already planned for alt text in the design phase, you just have to copy and paste it into the alt text field for that image during development.

Similarly, think about color contrast. It's much easier to be deliberate about choosing colors for readability and low vision at the beginning of the development process, rather than finding out in a QC review that the text color fails a basic color contrast test. This can be a nightmare to fix after the fact. For example, if you haven't used a template with theme colors, you may need to update every slide or page of your project. The worst-case scenario may require checking every object on every slide or page.

Here are a few suggestions to incorporate into your QA process to address accessibility:

- If your storyboards contain images, add a placeholder to document the alt text for those images.
- Set up templates with theme colors and test color contrast *before* development.
- Maintain tidy file management. Keep your video and closed caption files in the same folder. Store audio files and script documents in the same folder. Use a consistent file naming system to keep media assets organized.

Quality Control Checklist

If you've made it this far in the book, you know that there are a lot of things to think about when designing inclusive learning experiences. The good news is that testing for most common accessibility issues isn't as hard as you may think.

What should you include in a QC test for accessibility? Start by including everything I've listed here, but don't limit yourself. Remember, by adding items to your QA standards, the QC test will be faster and easier.

Alternative (alt) text
- ☐ Alt text is present.
- ☐ It's meaningful and appropriate.
- ☐ It's error-free (correct spelling and grammar).
- ☐ Decorative images are tagged appropriately by placing "" in the alt text area or using the authoring tool's function to mark an image as decorative.
- ☐ Full image descriptions are also included where appropriate.

Keyboard navigation
- ☐ You can successfully navigate the course or content using only the keyboard.
- ☐ It follows an accurate progression, meaning items on screen typically progress from left to right and top to bottom (this varies in some regions and languages).

- ☐ Note any keyboard traps where the user gets stuck and can't advance to the next item.

Screen readers
- ☐ You can successfully use screen reader software to navigate the course or content.
- ☐ Items are read in the correct order.
- ☐ They are labeled correctly. For example, are buttons designated as buttons? A screen reader will read out items, such as "Button, start," so the user knows they are on the start button.
- ☐ Note any point where you get stuck or advance before you've reviewed all the content.

Color and contrast
- ☐ The text and background colors pass color contrast testing.
- ☐ Text overlays on images pass color contrast testing.
- ☐ Different states of hyperlinks and buttons pass color contrast testing.
- ☐ Color is not the only indicator used. Additional context (such as text and icons) is added.

Closed captions
- ☐ All videos include closed captions.
- ☐ Closed captions are accurate.
- ☐ They're synced correctly with the video.
- ☐ They can be turned on and off.
- ☐ Music, background noises, and sounds are described in the captions as appropriate.

Transcript
- ☐ A transcript is available.
- ☐ It's accurate.
- ☐ Music, background noises, and sounds are described in the transcript as appropriate.
- ☐ Visual information is described where appropriate.

This list highlights the most common items that are missing in QC testing. Pay special attention to including them in all projects or courses.

It's a good starting point, but like any example template, you will need to adapt it for your own organization.

What You Can Do Right Away

It's important that you work with your team and others throughout the organization to establish processes and strategies for QA *and* QC testing. Take time to revisit the processes you set up to ensure they are being implemented consistently. Edit and update your testing processes as necessary. Be aware of updates to vendor software or accessibility guidelines that might affect how and what you test. By doing these things, you can ensure the best inclusive and accessible learning experiences for your end users.

59.
Keeping Neurodivergent Learners in the Flow With Quality Content

Judy Katz (she/her)
Founder and Consultant, Neurodivergent Working

Erica has been taking courses to become a certified nursing assistant. While she has great background experience and most of the content is easy for her, she became frustrated with the imprecise and poor-quality digital content in her e-learning courses and assessments. Furthermore, due to an anxiety disorder, she can't seem to brush it off the way some learners would.

When she found something like the example in Figure 59-1 on an assessment, she lost faith in the content and her own ability to pass the course.

Question 2 *of 25* **INCORRECT**

_____ involves signs and fingerspelling.

✗ **Your answer:**
Oral communication

Correct answer:
Oral communication

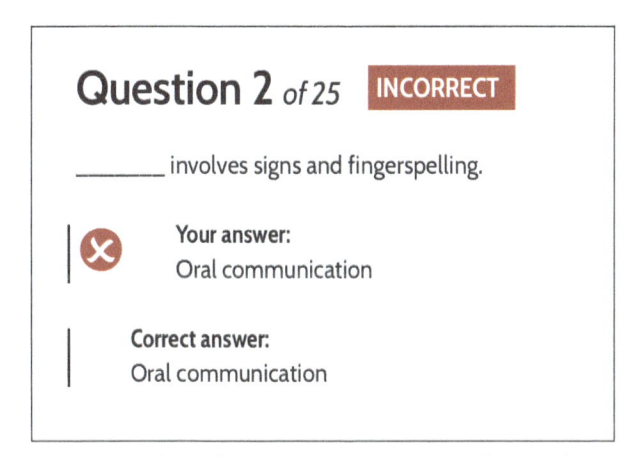

Figure 59-1. Screenshot of an assessment question that reads, "Question 2 of 25. [blank] involves signs and fingerspelling." The learner has answered, "Oral Communication." The answer is marked incorrect, but the feedback says the correct answer is "Oral Communication."

In this real example, Erica couldn't tell whether she answered correctly or not. She asked her manager for the correct answer and was told not to worry about it because she passed the quiz. Many neurodivergent people—including those with anxiety, OCD, and depression—can have perfectionistic tendencies.[124] Therefore, errors like this are particularly distressing. Furthermore, Erica wants to make sure she's doing the best job she can, and it's frustrating to be told not to worry about it.

What You Can Do Right Away

It's worth doing a quality control check to make sure learners aren't potentially disadvantaged by poor-quality content. Aside from perfectionism, this kind of error might also be distracting for learners who are very detail-oriented, such as many (but not all) autistic people. So, making sure digital content is high quality isn't just an accommodation; it's a way to keep neurodivergent workers able and willing to use their superpowers for your organization and for you to communicate to them that those traits are valued.

You can start improving your designs now by making sure your project plans allow for adequate time and resources to test your learning experiences and make necessary revisions. If you don't already have a process in place for quality control, start by allocating an additional 10 percent of the development time for testing and revisions. You can adjust your project plans as you refine the process.

60.
Accessibility Is Better When You're in It Together

Sarah Mercier (she/her)
CEO, Build Capable

I was recently speaking with a colleague about her team's accessibility initiative in a large, decentralized organization. They work with numerous systems, many of which are internal, proprietary platforms.

In a recent project, she was tasked with creating guidance documentation for one of those platforms. She has access to an accessibility review team, so she sent the documentation to them for feedback. One part of the feedback she received was particularly challenging: *"The buttons in your screenshots don't pass color contrast."* Why was this challenging? The buttons in the screenshots didn't pass color contrast because the buttons *in the platform* didn't pass color contrast. So, the only way to truly correct the issue was to fix the color contrast in the system's user interface.

Accessibility expands beyond one person, or even one team. To be successful in our accessibility efforts, other teams must also be in the loop. For instance, what happens when images and other assets from the marketing team have poor color contrast or lack diverse representation? Or, what if the communications team includes a teaser for an upcoming training event in the newsletter, unknowingly including language that is offensive to individuals with disabilities? What happens when IT works with procurement to purchase a fancy new performance support system, but no one checks whether the new vendor has documentation and regular reporting on accessibility conformance?

It is nearly impossible for a company to foster a culture of inclusion when they assume that one person, or even a small team of people, can take care of everything for the entire organization. Many DEI efforts have failed for this very reason.[125]

However, it is possible to advocate for accessibility across your organization's functions. As a matter of fact, most organizational learning functions have the unique opportunity to work across the entire organization, so you may be able to have a broader influence than other roles.

What You Can Do Right Away

Seek high-level leadership that can and will support and champion these efforts company-wide. This includes allocating resources for formal training and skill development, accessibility consulting, and sometimes even new tools and platforms. Build relationships with individuals on other teams who can advocate for accessibility with their peers. Share resources that have helped you and your team. And, perhaps most importantly, find champions who are dedicated to supporting efforts long term. Improving accessibility can range from a shift in mindset to dismantling and rebuilding entire systems and processes. This takes time, money, effort, patience, and commitment—but the results are worth it!

Part 7. Taking Action

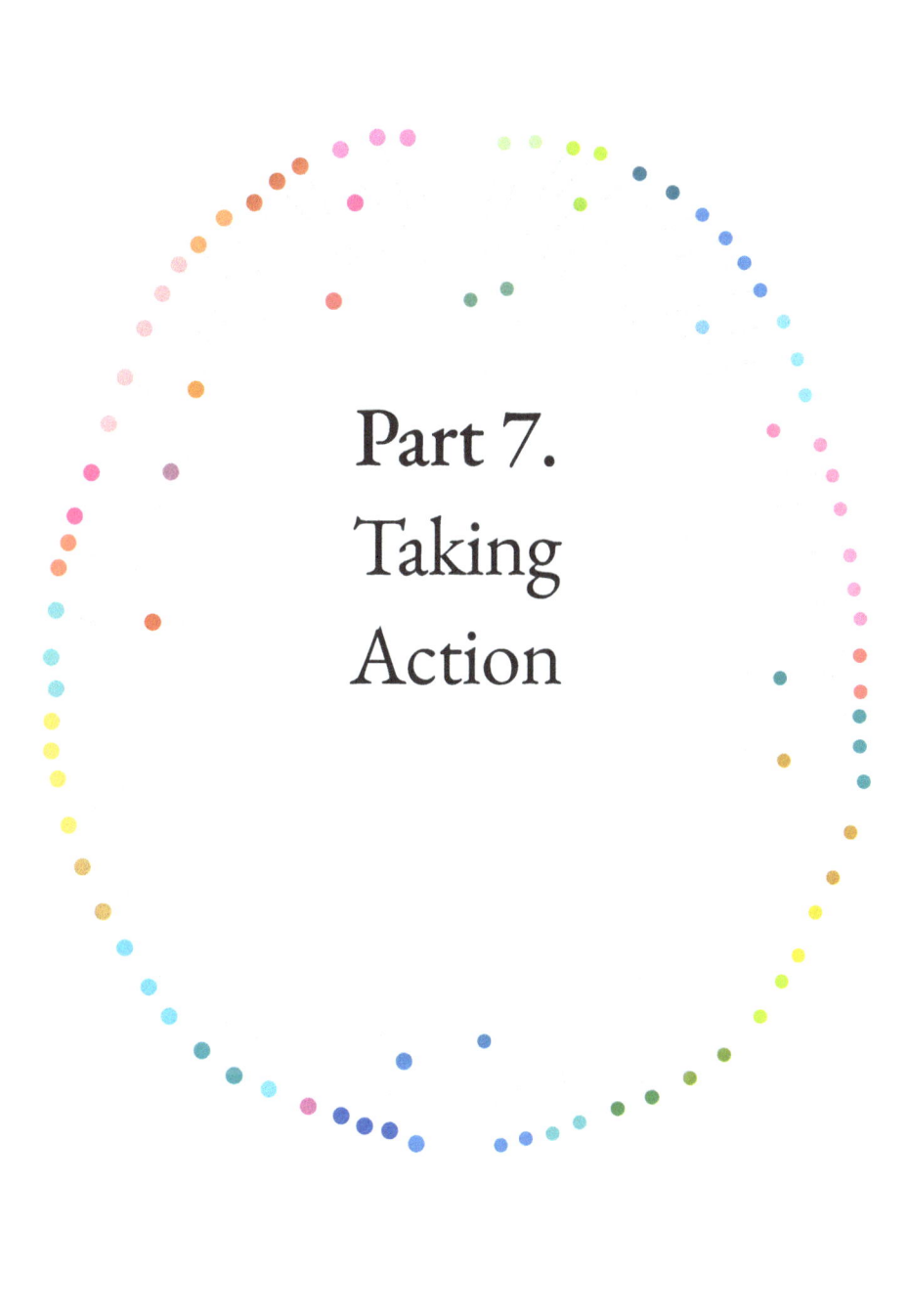

61.
When Efforts to Be Inclusive Don't Go as Planned

Todd Cummings (he/him)
COO, ELB Learning

In the L&D world, ELB Learning has consistently aimed to be at the forefront of innovation and engagement for all learners. We firmly believe that *diversity* is not a buzzword, but a reflection of the real world, and that the inclusion of individuals with disabilities is a crucial part of our mission.

I'd like to share a story that demonstrates part of our journey to become more accessible and inclusive in our work processes. Specifically, I'd like to recall one of our missteps, which led to a wonderful learning experience that will help us as we move forward.

The Photo Shoot

In 2009, ELB Learning began by specializing in selling stock images and templates for e-learning developers. Over the years, we expanded to offer additional software, services, and strategy. Based on internal audits and public feedback, we recognized a need to diversify our image portfolio and improve our offerings by including people with disabilities.

Media plays a pivotal role in shaping perceptions and influencing societal change. Our commitment to addressing the representation gap was more than just a public relations move; it was a genuine desire to affect change.

As we began the process to diversify our image portfolio, we wanted to find the right people to help. We sent out messages to work colleagues, friends, community groups, and others putting out a call for people to join the many faces of ELB Learning. We found most were connected through relationships with our existing employees, adding more importance and meaning to the initiative.

Once we selected our group of five models, we arranged a photo shoot. These individuals were excited to be part of an initiative to increase awareness and opportunities for individuals with disabilities. For them, it was a chance to contribute in ways that they may not have envisioned. One model mentioned that it was like becoming a movie star. Each photograph would tell a story—they were helping to break stereotypes and providing a more authentic representation of people with disabilities.

Our team was driven not only by the desire to create change but also by the knowledge that we were part of something meaningful. This project was a testament to the fact that our workforce embraced a commitment to inclusivity, from the top down. No words needed to be shared; no emails were sent or posters put up inside the office to indicate the commitment felt toward inclusivity and diversity. For employees, the act and production of creating a diverse portfolio of individuals for our templates was a sign for everyone that our organization was taking a step forward. It made this step even more meaningful that friends and family members were able to contribute and take part.

With the photo shoots completed, we created a representative image set featuring one shot from each of the individuals who had taken part (Figure 61-1).

Before production and publishing, we asked the individuals to review and approve their photo sets. They asked when and where the images would be shared and how they would be used. Once again, the responses from the participants were positive. They were all in regarding how they were being represented in the images.

When Efforts to Be Inclusive Don't Go as Planned

Figure 61-1. ELB's announcement of their new, more inclusive stock characters. The image heading says, "More Inclusive Characters to Amp Up Your Learning." There are four white male individuals in different poses. One man's left arm is amputated just below the elbow, and he is shown twice in two different poses. There is another man in a wheelchair. The remaining two characters do not appear to have any visible disability.

The Reaction

To be transparent and to inspire others, we decided to share this new image set on LinkedIn. It was a conscious choice because we wanted to reach an audience that had the power to influence change. While our intentions were sincere, some of the feedback we received was very different from what we had anticipated. The comments and criticism from several individuals online pointed out our shortfalls and even labeled our efforts as "mediocre." These comments, although initially hard to digest, were accurate.

We had fallen short in several areas:
- We didn't include any women in our photo shoot.
- All four men were white.
- The staged look (everyone smiling and having fun) wasn't perceived to be a true reflection of diversity. We determined that we would include more natural looks as well.
- We were accused of initiating the photo shoot as part of a broader business strategy versus trying to do the right thing.

It's hard to argue against these perspectives, so we decided to invite dialogue and try to move forward.

Next Steps

We took the criticism to heart and acknowledged that we had an opportunity for growth. These comments, however tough they might have been, were the voices we needed to hear. They were the reminders that our journey was far from over. It was a moment when our commitment to diversity and accessibility was put to the test.

Instead of becoming disheartened by the feedback, we decided to embrace it. We were grateful for the insights and knew that the road to inclusivity would be fraught with challenges. As a result, we set out to learn and improve, and that's the message we communicated to our audience.

The first step in our response was to express our gratitude for the feedback. We wanted the responders to know that their voices had been heard. We were genuinely thankful that they took the time to engage with us and provide their insights. I personally reached out and extended an open and specific invitation for further feedback and conversations, not just from those who shared thoughts, but from everyone. We believed in turning criticism into an opportunity for growth, and we wanted to learn how to do better.

In an era when the world is increasingly interconnected through digital platforms, we recognized the value of opening a dialogue. Our invitation was not merely a formality; it was an earnest request for collaboration. We wanted to engage with everyone who shared our vision of a more inclusive world.

What followed was an insightful lesson for our company. Several in the accessibility community reposted our LinkedIn thread, and we were grateful for their comments and support. However, some comments under the reposts were critical of our efforts. We initially reached out to those commenters to create dialogue, but their responses were limited. While it was initially disappointing, we've come to view this experience as a valuable learning opportunity. We realized that the absence of further suggestions didn't signify a roadblock, but rather a prompt for us to take the initiative in our journey toward improvement.

We are now more determined than ever to delve deeper into the insights we received. This situation has spurred us into action, pushing us to explore new avenues and strategies to address the shortcomings identified. We began immediate efforts to publish new and more diverse templates and images (Figure 61-2).

Figure 61-2. ELB Learning's more diverse stock image library.

We also began evaluating our own tools and software to make them more accessible, and we sponsored an internal forum on accessibility and encouraged many of our staff and friends to write articles or run podcasts that we shared through our internal marketing and communication channels. The internal response was incredible, encouraging us to reach out and partner with our competitors to create a working group called Inspire Accessibility.

This experience was a catalyst for enhancing our internal processes for feedback and dialogue. We continue to explore ways to encourage more sustained and constructive engagement in the future, recognizing the value of diverse perspectives in our growth. What we have learned has been pivotal in reinforcing our resolve. Far from deterring us, it has strengthened our commitment to self-improvement and progress. We are not just waiting for external guidance; we are proactively seeking out ways to evolve and improve. Our journey has been one of positive effort and negative feedback, highlighting missed opportunities for improvement. But, most importantly, it underscores our continued focus on moving forward. We are committed to learning and growing from this experience.

What You Can Do Right Away

ELB Learning turned a negative response to inclusion efforts into a learning experience. You too can learn from it—and ideally avoid it yourself. First, when embarking on any accessibility effort, pause and reflect on the diversity of the group leading the effort. Are diverse voices present? This pause can help you realize you might be acting on behalf of the accessibility community, rather than using it as an opportunity to involve them in the change. Second, if you find yourself having committed a similar misstep and encountering valid but perhaps critical feedback, pause and reflect before acting. Avoid getting defensive and instead shift your mindset into one of learning and improvement.

62.
Progress Over Perfection

Meryl K. Evans (she/her)
Speaker, Trainer, and Consultant in Marketing and Accessibility, Meryl.net

Disability Language and Etiquette

When I first publicly shared a story about messing up disability language, I was embarrassed. Nonetheless, I shared it to show that people who are passionate and care about accessibility and inclusion make mistakes too. I don't just talk about accessibility and inclusion. I work to live it and show it through actions.

I slip up from time to time. When I do, I'm hard on myself. It takes me a long time to get over it. And it takes longer to get over it when accessibility allies send strongly worded messages about my mistake. They will do that in response to incorrect language use, the lack of accessibility, or accessibility that's not good enough.

Allow me to share three examples of my own mistakes. The first one occurred in an airport bathroom. I was at the front of the line for the bathroom. A door opened and I was about to enter when I noticed it was an accessible bathroom. There was no sign on the door. Usually, they're in the back of the bathroom. This was the front.

"Oops. This is the handicapped bathroom," I muttered to myself. No one heard, but that's not the point. Right away, I caught my mistake. I questioned myself trying to figure out why I said that when I wouldn't normally. I've trained myself to say accessible bathroom, accessible parking, and so on. I didn't have an answer. It wasn't unconscious bias.

Handicapped was an uncomfortable word for me at one time, and it's a hot button for many disabled people. There's a popular misconception that the word originated from the phrase "hand in cap" or "cap in hand," and that this referred to a disabled person begging for money. Yet, this was not the case, and after researching its entomology, I learned the history of the word was indeed a myth. To make a long story short, it was incorrect information that went viral long before the internet existed. *Handicap* does not come from "hand in cap" or "cap in hand."[126]

I posted about it on LinkedIn. The comments were respectful. The commenters and I educated each other. We shared our problems with the term and its definition, and I came out of the conversation with greater understanding. Despite softening my stance on the word, I believe *accessible* is a better word for accessible parking and accessible bathrooms. *Handicapped* is an outdated term referring to an individual's condition or identity. On the flip side, *accessible* indicates the state of being. A parking spot is accessible, but it doesn't indicate the identity of the individual using the parking spot.

The second instance happened at a conference. Someone had a cool crutch with a picture on it. I took a closer look at the image. My hand accidentally touched the picture on the crutch, but the picture was part of the person's assistive device. It's good etiquette to avoid touching anyone's assistive device without their permission. Think of it as an extension of themselves. Would you want someone to touch you without your permission? It's the same for wheelchairs, crutches, service animals, and white canes.

I immediately apologized. They said it was no problem. Despite this, the mistake bugged me for a long time after it happened. I told you I'm hard on myself.

The third instance was on a LinkedIn audio call hosted by fellow accessibility advocate, Catarina Rivera. I was talking about the progress over perfection approach. I said it makes accessibility less daunting and prevents [gulps] "analysis paralysis."

After I finished speaking, Catarina asked me to confirm that's what I'd said. As soon as I finished answering, I realized my mistake and that I should have found a different phrase. I appreciated that she asked me to verify what I'd said. Then, she went on to explain the problem with that phrase in a calm and educational way. (She had a progress over perfection attitude.)

The easiest way to explain it is that inclusive language avoids using any disability-related terms in a phrase not related to a disability. While some don't see that phrase as concerning, I prefer to take a more considerate approach and avoid it. English has many other available words and phrases.

These incidents stick with me and I hope to never make these mistakes again. Even the biggest allies can mess up, and the best way to respond to mistakes is to educate, not berate.

I was prepared for angry comments when I first shared my mistakes, but not one single comment was angry. In fact, they had a progress over perfection mindset. The people commenting said we're human and we make mistakes. They advised me to give myself grace as I was still struggling with them. So, how about extending grace to others who make mistakes—or simply don't know what they don't know?

That's the other challenge. People who work in accessibility advocacy think about disability and accessibility often. They may keep up with disability language, but others may not. Of course, there are instances that call for forceful words, and often those of us with disabilities can be frustrated and overwhelmed. However, even though I have a disability and I'm not the intended recipient, angry public messages about accessibility and disability can make me feel bad.

The Progress Over Perfection Approach in Accessibility

People feel overwhelmed in getting started with accessibility, digital and physical. It's daunting. When it comes to accessibility, I encourage focusing on progress over perfection. Take that first step. No matter how small it is, it's a step forward. Don't wait until you get the website, product, or whatever just right.

Instead, get started and learn from successes and mistakes. Accept that sometimes progress goes backward. That's OK. It doesn't mean progress has stopped. Progress isn't always a straight line. The key is to keep trying. (Of course, take time to rest too. There's a reason airlines tell us to put the oxygen masks on ourselves before helping others. We're not good to anyone if we pass out.)

Start on the journey and stay the course. For example, if you plan to launch a redesigned website built with accessibility in mind, don't wait until the it goes live. Get started by making all new content accessible.

The next time you publish a new blog post, make sure it has proper headings and alt text for any images. The next time you create a video, add captions and audio descriptions. The next time you post an audio file or podcast, add a well-formatted transcript with speaker identification. The next time you create a graphic, check the color contrast to ensure it's strong enough between overlapping colors. The next time you create a graph or chart, confirm that it doesn't rely on color alone to convey the message.

For accessibility professionals and disability allies, progress over perfection means educating, not berating. It means forgiving mistakes and being flexible. It also means that sometimes there is no right or wrong answer, especially with disability language. Besides, we can always use more kindness.

Consider this example: When you're referring to people with hearing disabilities, the current recommendation—which could change tomorrow—is to use *deaf* or *hard of hearing*. *Hearing impaired* has fallen out of favor. However, quite a few people still self-identify as hearing impaired.

One friend, who self-identifies as hearing impaired, mentioned this on social media in a comment. A fellow deaf person wrote a long response saying hearing impaired was offensive. I was not the subject of the comment, but it was painful reading it and watching my friend be the target. It didn't matter that my friend's comments actually supported the Deaf and Hard of Hearing community. Her simply identifying as hearing impaired caused the person to rant and say upsetting things. This isn't a progress over perfection mindset.

Here's an example of the progress over perfection way: Someone says "hearing impaired" in a comment. Another person responds explaining why deaf and hard of hearing are the preferred terms. The first person reconsiders and edits their comment to change "hearing impaired" to "hard of hearing." No berating. Just kindness and education.

Progress over perfection is a mindset that makes us more open to respectful conversations and willing to make changes. It's a kinder way of communicating. We may not always agree, but we can do it respectfully.

Progress Over Perfection Is a Growth Mindset

Progress over perfection isn't just applicable to accessibility. *In Mindset: The New Psychology of Success*, Carol S. Dweck talks about a *growth mindset*—the "belief that your basic qualities are things you can cultivate through your efforts, your strategies, and help from others."[127] On the opposite spectrum, the *fixed mindset* is the idea that a person's intelligence and abilities can't change. This mindset can cause a person to stay within their boundaries, so they don't try new things, take risks, and do other actions that will help them grow.

Having a growth mindset means I approach interactions to connect with others. Sometimes, I learn something new, but, other times, I have the opportunity to share information. Of course, it doesn't always work, and there will always be people who get upset or angry.

Progress Over Perfection for Accessibility Advocates

Here are some considerations for applying progress over perfection.

Even Accessibility Advocates Make Mistakes

Despite making it a habit, I've accidentally shared an image without alt text. Someone called me out. I'm human—maybe I was multitasking or tired. Who knows? Believe me, when I realize I forget an image description or alt text, I get mad at myself and fix it.

Sometimes people search for a quick fix and consider accessibility overlays as a solution. For those who don't know, websites using an overlay typically have the accessibility icon as a button (Figure 62-1). When you select the button, it opens a range of accessibility options.

Figure 62-1. The accessibility icon commonly used online.

In general, accessibility overlays tend to break any accessibility that was built in with good coding practices. Overlays disrupt navigation and cause people to spend more time working around the overlay instead of using the product. In some cases, the overlay hides important functions from screen readers, such as "Add to cart" and "Check out" (Figure 62-2).

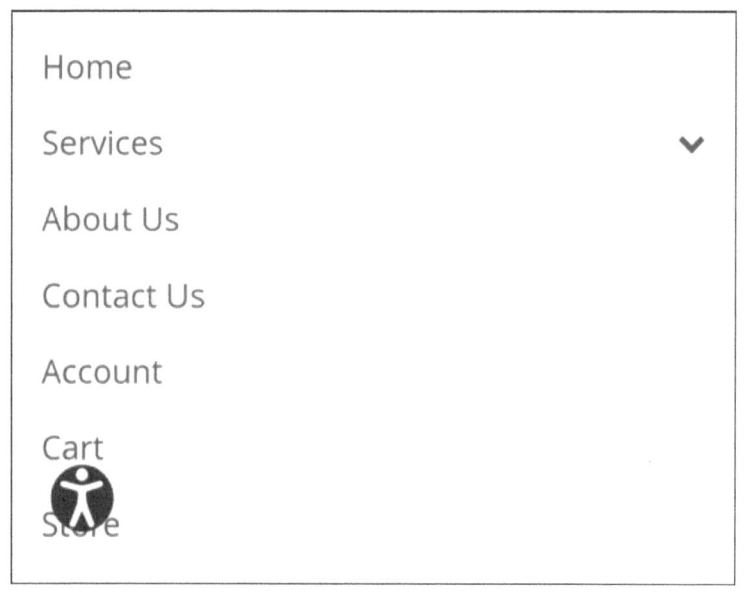

Figure 62-2. In this screenshot of a website menu, the accessibility icon is overlayed on top of the menu items.

Does any business want to miss out on a purchase because a potential customer can't add an item to their shopping cart and pay for it? That's what can happen to a business using an accessibility overlay. In addition, an accessibility overlay won't protect a company from a lawsuit. (Note: This is not progress over perfection in action. Quite the opposite. For more information, visit overlayfactsheet.com.)

Accessibility overlays are triggering for a lot of folks. Some overlay companies have unethical marketing practices and take advantage of the lack of awareness about accessibility. They promise they can quickly and easily solve your website's accessibility compliance problems with a line of code.

When anyone mentions adding an overlay to a website or how cool they are, it can lead to a big backlash. This is why I preach progress over perfection so much. It applies to disability and accessibility supporters—and it's about educating instead of scolding.

Here's a good example of a hostile reaction that didn't have to happen. A self-employed person with a disability shared a social media post about how excited they were to add an accessibility overlay to their website. They thought it was a quick and easy first step toward accessibility. This is a progress over perfection attitude.

It didn't take long before the backlash started in the comments. Shortly after, the person removed the overlay. They simply didn't know the accessibility overlay didn't work. Ultimately, that person edited their post to change their stance, admitting their mistake. However, they didn't deserve the verbal attack. They simply needed an education. I reached out to them privately and explained the problem with accessibility overlays. But, even after admitting their mistake multiple times and fixing it, it didn't erase the horrible feeling that came from reading all the comments. It's not easy to shake that off—it can take me days to get over a nastygram.

Here's another example: My friend posted images on social media that provided excellent accessibility tips. However, the images did not have a strong enough contrast. We happened to get on a video call, and I educated her on the need for strong color contrast for accessibility. I told her about a free tool that makes it easy to know if the color pairing passes the contrast ratio.

My friend's designer had worked with her brand colors, which also didn't have a strong contrast. Both are learning about accessibility as they go, and my friend shared the color contrast checker tool with her graphic designer. This friend is a big supporter of accessibility and inclusion—she's always pushing for it.

Well, an accessibility advocate saw the images my friend had originally posted on social media and responded with a harsh message. It upset my friend. (Of course, she felt awful. She's one of the kindest people I know.) Fortunately, this didn't deter her from continuing to push for accessibility and learning more about it.

Consider a different example: Someone on a social media platform shared an image of an amazing ad on a bus stop window that said:

> "Dear entertainment industry, there's no diversity, equity, and inclusion without disability. Disability is diversity.com. Designed by an all-disabled creative team and powered by Inevitable Foundation."

The person who shared the photo did not add alternative text or an image description. In this case, the comments about the missing alt text were either kind or talking about the irony of posting about accessibility without providing accessibility for the image. The person sharing the image is a supporter of people with disabilities and a diversity, equity, and inclusion professional. They thanked the accessibility supporters for their help and added the alt text. Educating people goes a long way and leads to change. The next person may not respond that way. Insensitive words can have the opposite effect. It may cause someone to not bother with accessibility if it means they'll be reprimanded for every mistake.

Consider this example of "not good enough" accessibility: My client posted an image on social media that contained alt text, but an accessibility ally complained about it. They said the alt text wasn't good enough and a company specializing in accessibility should know better. I didn't say anything to the ally, but my thinking is that they were nitpicking. There is no one right way to write alt text. Besides, many posts don't contain alt text at all.

When I see a video not following captioning best practices, I don't complain. Why? Because they proactively added captions when many don't. I don't want to criticize captions unless someone asks for my feedback. People don't always respond well to unsolicited feedback, and the last thing I want to do is cause them to stop captioning altogether.

How to Communicate and Advocate for Accessibility

There are many topics related to accessibility and people with disabilities. We can't know it all, yet many people in the accessibility community harshly call out someone for an accessibility mistake. For example, don't criticize a company for using automatic captions for live video events and then human captions for recorded videos. Although I depend on high-quality, accurate captions, I don't always get upset when the captions aren't helpful. (There are exceptions, like captioning companies that repeatedly produce poor-quality captions.) There are too many videos that don't have captions at all. At least, the company is doing something. Its team is making progress.

Although some of the captioning options on Instagram and Facebook could be better, I view it as progress. It's my hope that the built-in captions compel creators to make captioning part of their video creation process—just like editing is part of the writing process.

When I see captioned videos that could be better, I never provide feedback unless asked. Again, providing criticism and negative feedback could have the opposite effect, causing someone to give up because they think there's no point in trying. We never know how someone will handle feedback, and while some value it as a growth tool, others view it as an insult.

I work harder when someone says I'm doing a good job or gives me advice on how to take it to the next level; however, I become upset with myself when someone gives me negatively worded feedback. I value all feedback, good and bad. But people who come across as angry bother me. It takes me a long time to shake it off.

It takes a lot of practice for something to become a habit. In the early days of adding alternative text, I'd forget every other photo. Now, I rarely do. So, please educate. Don't berate. Even a simple, "Stop doing this!" can negatively affect people. Try educating them first and see what happens. Ask, "Did you know doing this will help more people access your content?" You just might find yourself a new ally.

Here's how I educated my city's government. One day, I went to dinner at the boardwalk in my adult hometown of Plano, Texas. (I'm also proud of my childhood hometown, which is Fort Worth, Texas!) The boardwalk has restaurants with indoor and outdoor seating. Most have TVs, but one restaurant did not have captions on while the others did.

I later saw that the mayor of Boston, Massachusetts, signed an order into law requiring bars and restaurants with TVs to have closed-captioning on. The ordinance applies to any public-facing TVs in public places, including those on city property (such as gyms and banks). This compelled me to contact the city manager and mayor of Plano. I shared my experience along with an article about Boston's ordinance. It costs nothing to turn on captions.

Mark Israelson, the city manager, replied right away. This demonstrated good practice—it's important to acknowledge someone's accessibility question, feedback, or request as soon as possible. You don't need to have answers yet. The key is to acknowledge it by saying you've received the message, you're working on it, and you'll reply when you have answers. That's exactly what he did. He said he'd have his team look into it. Soon after I contacted Mark, I found out that Seattle, Washington, had a similar policy, so I shared that too.

A few months later, I'd forgotten about the request until I received an email from Mark. He said the city council would consider a resolution on captioning at their next meeting.[128] This was an opportunity for me and my friend Dylan M. Rafaty to speak in front of the mayor and city council. They unanimously passed the resolution requiring all city-owned facilities to turn on closed captions on TVs in places of public accommodation, and encouraging businesses to do the same.

While a resolution is not a law, it's progress! The next step is to educate businesses. Dylan and I would like to see more cities across the US adopt a similar ordinance or resolution. We are already working with other Texas cities to do the same. Not long after this happened, Allen, a nearby city, issued a similar resolution for closed captions.

While you work to address accessibility in your own work or team, it's possible to "go big" beyond your team to help make your entire organization more inclusive. Contact senior leadership with a suggestion. Add support for the suggestion by sharing resources and explaining the benefit to the company. Start with something doable to make progress.

What do you wish your organization would make accessible? What do you wish people not familiar with accessibility would stop doing? What do you wish they would start doing? What do you wish they knew? Use the TEACH feedback method to request a change.

TEACH: Steps to the Progress Over Perfection Way of Communicating

Applying progress over perfection in my everyday life makes a difference. If I find myself writing an unfriendly message or making a request for a change, I stop and remind myself, "TEACH." The person on the receiving end may not know what they don't know. This is the approach I used when requesting public-facing TVs to have captions turned on in my city.

Because progress over perfection is about education, this acronym, TEACH, helps me remember how to communicate with a progress over perfection mindset.

- **Thank** them or start with something positive.
- **Educate** them and explain why.
- **Advocate** for action to make change.
- **Calmly communicate** to keep their attention.
- **High note:** End it on a high note with hope for a positive response.

If I'm upset or angry, then I wait until I've calmed down. Or, I write the message while it's fresh in my head, but I don't send it. Instead, I'll wait at least 24 hours and reread it to ensure it's respectful. Remember, some folks simply don't know what they don't know. While many accessibility advocates think about disability and accessibility every day, other people do not think about accessibility much or at all.

What Can We Learn From the Capitol Crawl?

A friend had an ethical and moral dilemma and reached out for my thoughts. She had been invited to do a podcast on accessibility and inclusion. However, it was a small, independent podcast with no funds for a transcript. So, should she do the podcast and educate people? Or, should she ask them to reach out when they could add transcripts?

When advocating for accessibility and disability inclusion, progress over perfection helps push for change. It applies to people in organizations, teams, or departments just starting on their journeys. It's a mindset that works in everyday life. It means talking like you're teaching, rather than coming across as angry. Of course, there are a few situations that warrant anger, but these are usually after someone or a company has not listened.

It also means not waiting until something is perfect to move forward. Accessibility isn't all or nothing. Apple exemplified a progress over perfection mindset when it released live captions for iOS in beta. Knowing the feature was in beta made it easier to be forgiving of problems with it. Yet, it also made me grateful to have it sooner rather than later.

Some advocates won't speak at an inaccessible event or do a podcast that doesn't provide a transcript. A few were angry when they said no organization should celebrate Global Accessibility Awareness Day if their [*fill in the blank*] is inaccessible. But these are the very audiences that need the message the most. Often, it's because of my speaking or appearing on a podcast that an organization starts making an effort with accessibility.

Not doing the event at all rarely compels people to change. The famous Capitol Crawl of 1990 had people crawling up the inaccessible steps in front of the US Capitol.[129] Soon after, Congress passed the ADA. Imagine if the protesters had said, "Oh, we can't protest until they make it accessible and add ramps first." Nothing would have changed if they weren't at the Capitol. The presence of people with disabilities crawling up the stairs provided a visual demonstration of the inaccessibility of the Capitol. No one could ignore it.

The problem isn't the lack of accessibility. The real problem is *not making an effort* to make progress with accessibility. It takes time to make systemic changes.

Accessibility Paradox (Schrödinger's a11y cat)

It's impossible to achieve 100 percent accessibility. You'll eventually run into, as Christopher Patnoe says, the "accessibility paradox," or as I like to call it, "Schrödinger's a11y cat." By the way, there are 11 letters between A and Y in accessibility, hence "a11y."

In case you're not familiar with Schrödinger's cat, the phrase is used to reference something as a paradox. It means something working against itself. Therefore, Schrödinger's a11y cat means that something you do for accessibility could create an accessibility problem for someone else.

The simplest example is dark and light modes. Many websites, operating systems, browsers, apps, and mobile devices offer dark and light modes, which affect how the interface looks. With light mode, the interface has a light background and dark text. The most common is a white background with black text. Dark mode is the opposite—the interface has a dark background and light text.

Some people find light mode too bright or harsh. Or they may struggle to read the text. To fix this, they switch to dark mode. I'm one of those people. I find white and bright lights hard to look at. My spouse turns up the brightness on their phone while I keep mine low. Whenever they show me something on their phone, I instinctively back away because the brightness bothers my eyes.

At first, I thought dark mode was a universal solution that most people would prefer. However, I found out friends of mine have trouble with dark mode and prefer light mode.

Fortunately, there are technical solutions to including both dark and light modes as options, but it's not always possible. For example, what do you choose when giving a presentation with slides? It's hard to find color pairings that will work for everyone.

Do you think all deaf and hard of hearing people prefer captions over transcripts? Think again. I've met a couple of hard of hearing folks who do better with transcripts, but I can't use transcripts in live events and meetings. They are overwhelming and make it hard to keep my place while reading.

Even though you can't achieve 100 percent accessibility, universal design is very powerful. This design approach works toward creating experiences for the greatest number of people, and goes beyond accessibility.

A good example of universal design is the automatic sliding doors at grocery stores. Anyone can go through them without using a body part. Parents carrying children won't have to adjust to open the doors or use their body. People who use wheelchairs can go right through the doors. So can children, people carrying groceries, people with service animals, and people with assistive devices.

Another example is from a cartoon from Michael F. Giangreco, a university distinguished professor emeritus of special education at the University of Vermont.[130] In it people are outside a building where there's a lot of snow on the ground. An employee is shoveling the stairs. Someone who uses a wheelchair asks them to shovel the ramp. The employee responds that everyone is waiting for the stairs. They will clear the ramp after they finish the stairs. The person replies that if they shovel the ramp instead, everyone can get in including the walkers and the people using wheelchairs and other assistive devices. Baking accessibility into an organization and training clears the path for everyone. Not having accessibility is like shoveling the stairs instead of the ramp.

The Value of Progress Over Perfection

What happens when you adopt a progress over perfection mindset?

1. **You communicate more effectively.** Effective communication involves listening actively, opening yourself to learning, and being flexible. It leads to more inclusive and accessible interactions. You catch more flies with honey than vinegar—meaning, people respond better when you're nice.
2. **You encourage a growth mindset.** A growth mindset to advocacy means you're helping other people grow. When someone faces backlash, they're not going to grow. Instead,

they'll likely fall into a fixed mindset thinking nothing will change.

3. **You are more flexible.** The progress over perfection approach emphasizes learning, adapting, and growing. It means accepting you may not have all the answers and viewing mistakes as opportunities for improvement. The approach encourages taking risks, experimenting, and collaborating to find better solutions. It's a reminder to focus on the journey rather than the destination. Every step toward progress matters.

4. **You celebrate progress.** No matter how small the progress is, it's worth celebrating. By doing this, people will feel excited and motivated to keep iterating and improving. If a company adds automatic captioning and advocates complain that there's no way to edit the captions, they may undermine the company's efforts to improve. Celebrate instead. When the company sees that people like the progress it's made, it will be inspired to keep going. You can even say, "Great job adding automatic captions. I hope you take it to the next level by adding editing capabilities."

5. **You respond to differences with respect and civility.** At a Leadership Plano program I attended, LaShon Ross gave a talk, "Respect Is Respect," that stuck with me. She advises responding, but not defending. Discuss, don't fight. You can empathize without agreeing, and you can disagree without disrespect. Respect and civility come naturally when you communicate more effectively, encourage a growth mindset, and are flexible. It's possible to disagree with someone while maintaining respect and civility.

Getting Started With Accessibility

I was scheduled to participate in a half marathon. Just as I was about to start training, I ended up in the hospital where I underwent an appendectomy. Once the doctor gave me the approval to start working out again, do you think I ran 13.1 miles on the first day? Not even close. I walked. I couldn't even walk a mile, and that's usually a breeze for me. Every day, I got faster, and my endurance improved. It paid off and was my best half marathon time at 1:55. Yes, I'm proud I completed the half marathon in under two hours. It's called sub-2.

Progress is often tiny or slow. It's rarely big, and sometimes, it goes backward. The key is to keep at it. Accessibility is more than checklists. However, creating processes and checklists will go a long way to prevent skipping or forgetting a step.

Here are some suggestions to get you started on your next accessibility habit:

- Ensure captions are available for every video meeting.
- Check forms to verify you give people choices about what contact information they share.
- Ask people about their preferred contact methods.
- Make it a habit to always have a second way to communicate in case the default doesn't work. If someone doesn't understand you, be gracious and offer another way to communicate. (Hint: Your cell phone can communicate in many ways!)
- Put away your mouse for the day and navigate using only your keyboard. Use the Tab key to move around. Use Shift+Tab to go backward. Use the space bar or Enter keys to activate a link or a button.
- Add closed captions to all videos going forward.
- Create a transcript for your most important podcast or audio clip.
- Say, "This is [*your name*]" each time you speak on a call with more than two people. (Not everyone sees the video or hears or recognizes voices.)
- Include an image description for images you post on a blog or social media.
- Try the screen reader on your phone by switching it on in the accessibility settings.
- Ask participants for their communication preferences for synchronous (live) and asynchronous communications.
- Have a text messaging conversation with a friend in a restaurant or with colleagues at a networking event. Texting is great for

noisy settings! And people can use their phone in their preferred way whether that's typing or using speech-to-text. That's the beauty of texting. Devices give us multiple ways to enter text.

- Apply headings instead of individual styles in your next document or blog post.
- Describe the images in your class presentations and materials.
- Ensure your presentations and class materials have a strong color contrast.

Pick one. Work on it. When you feel like you've mastered it or learned from it, pick another one. Work to clear the ramp before the stairs.

We don't know everything. That includes accessibility advocates. Accessibility is huge! What may be obvious to you may not be obvious to someone else. Besides, we're human. We make mistakes. I'm self-employed, wearing many hats and serving clients. Any work that I do for my business, myself, and meryl.net is the last thing I do. Despite making it a habit to make accessibility part of my processes, sometimes I get distracted or I'm plumb tired and skip a step.

I wouldn't feel as awful if the people who caught my mistake said something like: "Hey, Meryl! You forgot the alt text." Or, if they don't know me and my accessibility background, "Hey, Meryl. In case you don't know, adding alt text helps those using screen readers. It'd be great if you could add it."

I'm always learning. I don't know how to do everything in accessibility. Far from it. Web Content Accessibility Guidelines (WCAG) are challenging for me to understand. And while I don't understand the Accessible Rich Internet Applications Suite (WAI-ARIA), I do know one rule: No ARIA is better than bad ARIA. I struggle to explain ARIA in plain language. So, I asked ChatGPT, and it gave me the best answer:

> "WAI-ARIA is like a special language that computers use to help people who can't see or hear very well. It's like a magic spell that makes websites easier to understand and use for everyone, even if they can't see the pictures or hear the sounds. It's kind of like when you use bigger letters or different colors to help someone

who has trouble reading. WAI-ARIA helps websites talk to people in a way they can understand, no matter what their abilities are."

That's why I push for progress over perfection. It's a kinder approach. And we must keep in mind that someone may not know what they don't know, and they need a gentle education.

What You Can Do Right Away

Creating a culture inclusive of people with disabilities is an ongoing journey. Your product or website may be accessible today, but tomorrow someone might forget something and make it inaccessible. Thus, accessibility is everyone's job. It takes time to learn and bake into your processes. Don't stress over perfection. Accessibility matters because it gives everyone access regardless of the circumstances. It matters because it gives people choices. Accessibility is rewarding. It takes all of us to make it happen.

Acknowledgments

I am deeply grateful to each contributor. You were vulnerable in sharing your experiences. You also dedicated your time and energy to make sure this book made it into the world. I don't think I'll ever be able to articulate how much you've inspired me—what I've learned from you has changed me forever. Thank you.

To my mom, Brenda Mercier: Aimee and I are fortunate that you showed us how to treat people with dignity and respect. I'm grateful to have been raised with these values when I know not every household was like ours. And to my Aunt Shannon, thank you for teaching me how to be reliable and supportive without expecting anything in return.

Christian, Ian, Nathaniel, and Megan—you inspire me. I'm so grateful that you are caring, empathetic adults. You taught me to tell my friends I love them when I talk to them on the phone. You give me hope that your generation will make progress fixing what is broken.

I want to thank Brian Dusablon for inspiring me and supporting me in my own professional journey to Design for All. If it wasn't for the chain of events that started with your accessibility keynote, I don't think this book would exist today. You are an amazing human, partner, and friend. The world needs more people like you.

Julie Dirksen, Jennifer Solberg, Steve Howard, Bianca Woods, Koreen Pagano, Teresa Dussault, Brian Womack, and Lucette Alphonse—you are there for me when I need it most. It is rare to be close to so many incredibly talented and knowledgeable people, even when we are staying connected virtually. Thank you for making me better.

To Justin Brusino and Alexandria Clapp: After all these years, we finally did it! Thank you for your passion and support for this book.

And, to my family and community of friends and colleagues that have listened to me emphatically go on and on about this book for the last year—thank you for your feedback and support. It is a gift to know you and be part of your lives.

Take Action Toolbox

Are you ready to take action? Here, you'll find tools and curated resources from authors throughout the book to practice Design for All. You can also find these and more at DesignForAllBook.com.

Part 1.
Exploring an Inclusive Mindset

Resources

- Microsoft's "Inclusive 101 Design Guidebook" is an introduction to inclusive design. Leah Holroyd recommends checking out the persona spectrum on page 42. To learn more, visit inclusive.microsoft.design.
- The "Disability Language Style Guide" from The National Center on Disability and Journalism is a list of guidelines that can help you make better, more inclusive word choices. To learn more, visit ncdj.org/style-guide.
- Dyslexia friendly style guide from the British Dyslexia Association. To learn more, visit bdadyslexia.org.uk/advice/employers/creating-a-dyslexia-friendly-workplace/dyslexia-friendly-style-guide.
- "Disability Impacts All" is an infographic created by the Centers for Disease Control and Prevention detailing disability statistics in the US. To learn more, visit cdc.gov/ncbddd/disabilityandhealth/infographic-disability-impacts-all.html.
- W3C's "Web Accessibility Perspectives Videos" demonstrate how accessibility is essential for people with disabilities, but useful for everyone. To learn more, visit w3.org/WAI/perspective-videos.
- Harvard's Implicit Association Test (IAT) is a tool to help individuals uncover unconscious biases. To learn more, visit implicit.harvard.edu/implicit/takeatest.html.
- Project Implicit offers a variety of Implicit Association Tests (IATs) to measure implicit biases. To learn more, visit projectimplicit.net.

Tool 1-1. Persona Pitfalls and How to Avoid Them

Use these tips to avoid four common learner persona pitfalls.

Too General (Personas Represent the Average Learner)
- Ensure the descriptions included in your learner personas are based on data you've collected from learners and periphery personnel.
- Ensure your learner personas highlight specific characteristics gathered from nuanced trends in the data rather than generalized traits.
- Ensure your learner personas are clear and detailed enough to represent distinct individuals.

Too Narrow (Personas Don't Represent the Range of Learners)
- Identify the meaningful subgroups within your target learner population (such as categories based on role, experience level, and context).
- Ensure you've created learner personas to represent each of the subgroups.

Stereotypical (Personas Include Biases, Social Judgments, or Invalid Assumptions)
- Conduct a thorough review and correct any biased assumptions or stereotypes in your learner personas, including but not limited to race, gender, culture, age, disability, socioeconomic status, and education level.
- Validate learner persona attributes with real learners to ensure accuracy and cultural sensitivity,
- Hire a sensitivity reader to help identify instances of stereotyping (optional).

Fixed (Personas Not Updated to Evolve Over Time)

- Plan for regular reviews to update your collection of learner personas based on new information gathered from learners or needs of the learning solution.
- Validate the collection of learner personas with learners and peripheral personnel to ensure the range of learner personas is still relevant and create additional learner personas if the need arises.

Tool 1-2. Testing With Real Users

To get started testing with real users, explore these options:
- Hire a company that uses disabled testers.
- Request feedback from employees in your own organization, but give them plenty of time—no 11th hour requests.
- Contact the office at your local university that supports students with disabilities or the county or state governmental office that supports residents with disabilities.
- Post announcements on job sites or contract work sites or look for local and national job boards designed for individuals with disabilities, such as AbilityJOBS.com.

Part 2.
Designing Inclusive Digital Content

Resources

- WebAIM's "WCAG Checklist" presents recommendations for implementing common accessibility principles and techniques. To learn more, visit webaim.org/standards/wcag/checklist.
- W3C's How to Meet WCAG quick reference is a customizable resource to help you check success criteria. To learn more, visit w3.org/WAI/WCAG22/quickref.
- Disability:IN's GAAD Toolkit provides guidelines for creating accessible social media content. To learn more, visit disabilityin.org/resource/creating-accessible-social-media-content.
- Unicode's emoji list identifies how an emoji will be read by a screen reader. To learn more, visit unicode.org/emoji/charts/full-emoji-list.html.
- WebAIM's Color Contrast Checker allows you to select a foreground and background color to check the level of color contrast. To learn more, visit webaim.org/resources/contrastchecker.
- Colorblind Guide's Colorblindness Simulator allows you to upload an image and filter by different types of colorblindness. To learn more, visit colorblindguide.com/color-blindness-simulator.
- W3C's "Alt Decision Tree" helps you make decisions about alt text in a variety of situations. To learn more, visit w3.org/WAI/tutorials/images/decision-tree.

- Perkins School for the Blind maintains a resource for how to write alt text and image descriptions. To learn more, visit perkins.org/resource/how-write-alt-text-and-image-descriptions-visually-impaired.
- "The Complete Guide to Captioned Videos" is a page full of captioning guidance from Meryl Evans. To learn more, visit meryl.net/captioned-videos-complete-guide.
- DCMP's "Captioning Key" contains guidelines and best practices for captioning educational videos. To learn more, visit dcmp.org/learn/captioningkey.
- "How to Add Closed Captions to Your Videos" is a step-by-step process for adding closed captions to a video. To learn more, visit buildcapable.com/how-to-add-closed-captions-to-your-videos.
- W3C's Transcripts page helps you understand and create transcripts. To learn more, visit w3.org/WAI/media/av/transcripts/#creating-transcripts.
- W3C's Transcribing Audio to Text page provides guidance on transcribing audio to text for captions and transcripts. To learn more, visit w3.org/WAI/media/av/transcribing.
- DCMP's Description Key provides guidelines for creating audio descriptions. To learn more, visit dcmp.org/learn/descriptionkey/624.
- Federal Plain Language Guidelines is a US government resource containing guidelines to help you write clearly. To learn more, visit plainlanguage.gov/guidelines.
- Adobe's accessibility features page includes guidelines for setting accessibility in Acrobat. To learn more, visit helpx.adobe.com/reader/using/accessibility-features.html.
- The University of South Carolina's "Virtual Environments Accessibility Guidelines" assist with designing more inclusive and accessible extended reality (XR) environments, which include virtual reality (VR), augmented reality (AR), and mixed reality (MR). To learn more, visit sc.edu/about/offices_and_divisions/cte/teaching_resources/virtual_environments/ve_accessibility_guidelines/index.php.

Tool 2-1. Lenses of Accessibility Questions

Use these questions adapted from Steven Lambert's article "Design for Accessibility and Inclusion" to check assumptions and consider perspectives.

Animation and Effects
- Are these elements necessary? Are they adding value? Are they distracting?
- Could any of these elements cause a seizure?
- Could any of these elements produce vertigo or dizziness?
- Can you provide controls to stop, hide, or change the speed of these elements?

Audio and Video
- Do you have transcripts?
- Do you have subtitles and closed captioning?
- If you have anything autoplaying, have you given control to the user?

Color and Contrast
- If color was removed, would meaning be lost?
- How can you provide meaning without using color?
- Are any of the colors you've selected oversaturated or high contrast?
- Do all your elements meet the minimum 4.5:1 contrast ratio?
- Do all your links have noncolor indicators and meet the minimum 3:1 contrast ratio with surrounding text?

Controls
- Are all your controls large enough (24px) and spaced far enough apart (32px)?
- Do you have any nested controls?
- Do all controls have visible text labels?

Fonts
- Do you have a responsive design? Do your fonts adjust automatically?
- Can users increase or decrease the font size?
- Is your font style easy to read?

Images and Icons
- Do you need an image? Does it add value?
- How can you provide this information in a nonvisual way?
- Are you using universal designs and symbols for your icons?

Keyboard
- What keyboard navigation order (focus order) makes the most sense?
- How can you allow keyboard users to get to what they want or need as fast as possible?
- Have you checked the focus indicator colors to ensure they are distinct against the different colors you use in the course?
- Have you tested your content by trying to navigate it using only a keyboard?

Layout
- Does the layout follow a logical and meaningful sequence?
- How does the layout adapt when viewed on a small screen or when zoomed in to 200 percent? 400 percent?
- Are related contents or elements that change due to user interaction positioned close to one another?
- What is a logical focus order?
- How will this look if mirrored for RTL (right-to-left) language translation?

Material Honesty
- Is the design honest to the user?
- Do any elements mimic the appearance, behavior, or function of other elements?
- Are there components merging different behaviors? If so, does this compromise their material honesty?

Readability
- Do you know your audience's reading level?
- Can you write more clearly and concisely to ensure you're being inclusive?
- What is the Flesch readability score of your content?

Structure
- Can you outline a rough HTML structure or visual hierarchy of your design? If not, can you review the outcome on different screen sizes?
- How can you structure the design to better help someone using a screen reader understand the content or find the content they want?
- How can you help the person who will implement the design understand the intended structure? Did you provide appropriate annotation of the desired structure?

Time
- Do you need to constrain users by time?
- Is it possible to provide controls to adjust or remove time limits?
- What would happen if a user was interrupted during this interaction?
- Are you being respectful of the user's time?

Part 3.
Creating an Inclusive Physical Classroom

Resources
- CAST's Universal Design for Learning Guidelines. To learn more, visit udlguidelines.cast.org.
- NCHPAD's "A Guide to Creating Access and Inclusion in All Events" is an inclusive event toolkit. To learn more, visit nchpad.org/fppics/Discover%20Inclusive%20Events.pdf.
- ASHE's "Land Acknowledgements" page has resources and recommendations for creating land acknowledgements. To learn more, visit ashe.ws/landacknowledgements.
- Steelcase's "Work Better: Learning Spaces" page contains design ideas for learning spaces. To learn more, visit steelcase.com/asia-en/spaces/work-better/learning-spaces.
- The Registry of Interpreters for the Deaf (RID) maintains a search page for certified interpreters. To learn more, visit myaccount.rid.org/Public/Search/Member.aspx.
- The National Deaf Center (NDC) maintains a resource page for hiring qualified interpreters. To learn more, visit nationaldeafcenter.org/resources/access-accommodations/coordinating-services/interpreting/hiring-qualified-interpreters.

Tool 3-1. Reflection Prompts for In-Person Learning Spaces

Use this organized list to guide discussions and reflections to identify growth opportunities within your own teams and work culture.

At the Organizational Level
- How has leadership advocated for accessibility, inclusion, and belonging training to practice face-to-face engagement?
- How has the organization ensured the implementation of UDL practices in all learning spaces?

From the Values Perspective
- How are the organization's values and mission aligned with supporting accessibility, inclusion, and belonging in shared physical spaces?
- Are policies and practices used in learning spaces written with a UDL mindset?

From an Opportunity Approach
- How is the organization finding growth opportunities from existing barriers associated with UDL and accessibility in face-to-face experiences?
- How can employees share their perspectives and voices to advance accessibility in in-person learning?

From Theory, to Practice, to Support
- How has the organization learned from past experiences?
- Have resources been allocated to support changes that create a more welcoming space?

Tool 3-2. Tips for Working With Sign Language Interpreters

Follow these tips when working with sign language interpreters:

1. Address the deaf or hard of hearing person, not their interpreter.
2. Manage your visuals carefully.
3. Manage activities.
4. Check in.

Tool 3-3. Sensory Accommodations Checklist

Use these tips to make your physical training environments more sensory friendly:

- ☐ Ask trainers and trainees to refrain from wearing perfumes, colognes, and body sprays on training days.
- ☐ Unplug extra machinery and equipment in or near the training rooms, as electrical sounds can be distracting.
- ☐ Lower blinds to prevent the classroom from being uncomfortably bright.
- ☐ Turn off or lower lights in part of the classroom so trainees can choose to limit their light exposure.
- ☐ Turn off fluorescent lights as much as possible, because the flickering and noise can cause distractions and headaches.
- ☐ Familiarize yourself with the thermostat (and ask for control if possible).
- ☐ Invite learners to bring sweaters or other warm layers if they tend to be cold in classrooms.

Tool 3-4. Ways to Include Learners With Speech Access Needs

Use these tips to include learners with speech access needs in the physical classroom:

- Give learners the option to present with a colleague or in a group.
- Be flexible about time limits on activities wherever possible.
- Don't force learners to give feedback or lead sessions.
- Allow ample time for learners to formulate their thoughts and responses.
- Avoid rushing through discussions, because that can be particularly challenging for learners with speech access needs.
- Incorporate group activities or pair learners for discussions.
- Give learners the option to ask questions or make comments in an alternative format, like a flip chart parking lot or some other method.

Part 4.
Creating an Inclusive Virtual Classroom

Resources

- Revisiting Camera Use in Live Remote Teaching: Considerations for Learning and Equity. To learn more, visit er.educause.edu/articles/2022/3/revisiting-camera-use-in-live-remote-teaching-considerations-for-learning-and-equity.
- Zoom's accessibility frequently asked questions page. To learn more, visit explore.zoom.us/en/accessibility/faq.
- Adobe Connect's accessibility features. To learn more, visit helpx.adobe.com/adobe-connect/using/accessibility-features.html.

Tool 4-1. Reflection Prompts for Inclusive Virtual Learning Spaces

Use this organized list to guide discussions and reflections to identify growth opportunities within your own teams and work culture.

At the Organizational Level
- How has leadership advocated for engagement in virtual spaces that promote accessibility, inclusion, and belonging practice?
- How has the organizational community ensured the implementation of practices to include all in virtual spaces?

From the Values Perspective
- How are the organization's values and mission aligned with supporting accessibility, inclusion, and belonging in shared virtual environments?
- Are policies and practices written in ways that promote virtual flexibility and inclusion?

From an Opportunity Approach
- How is the organization finding growth opportunities from existing barriers associated with accessibility in virtual experiences?
- How can employees share their perspectives and voices to advance accessibility in virtual experiences?

From Theory, to Practice, to Support
- How has the organization learned from past experiences?
- Have resources been allocated to support changes to create more welcoming virtual spaces?

Tool 4-2. Virtual Classroom Shopping List for Platform Accessibility Features

Look for these features and tools when you're shopping for virtual classroom software. Test everything in advance to be sure it works as promised. Regularly re-evaluate your options because software is updated and vendors offer new products.

- Live, in-session caption functionality and autocaptions
- Recordings with captions
- Keyboard shortcuts
- High-contrast setting
- Scalable text size
- Resizable screens
- Translation support
- Supports screen readers (note that shared slides and uploaded files are not usually readable)
- Transfer files (such as handouts, presentation slides, and participant assignments)
- Access to support materials, troubleshooting steps, FAQs, and live chat
- What else is important to you?

Tool 4-3. Virtual Event Marketing Materials Checklist

Use these tips to prioritize accessibility in marketing materials and website design to ensure participants know that you are serious about supporting their learning needs.

Start With Accessibility in Mind
- ☐ Design marketing materials and websites with accessibility as a foundational consideration.
- ☐ Employ standards and tools to ensure quality and consistency testing to confirm compliance.
- ☐ Post an accessibility statement identifying the available tools and resources.
- ☐ Craft content using plain language and short sentences.
- ☐ Maintain uniformity by adjusting templates and ensuring consistent page layout.
- ☐ Select readable font sizes, colors with high contrast, and bold text for on-screen buttons.
- ☐ Use a contrast checker for color choices.

Accessibility for Alternate Inputs
- ☐ Ensure keyboard navigation and functionality for all screen functions.
- ☐ Confirm keyboard tabbing advances through content in a logical order.
- ☐ Make URLs descriptive.

Accessibility and Session Information
- ☐ Display session times in declared time zones and include language accessibility details.
- ☐ Offer comprehensive guidance and resources before and after live sessions.
- ☐ Declare which language will be used for voice, captions, and sign language interpretation.

Tools and Support Accessibility

- ☐ Post software system requirements, guidelines, assignments, technical tests, recommendations for equipment, and other resources somewhere participants can easily access.
- ☐ Provide tutorials for software tools and additional support beyond the virtual classroom's capabilities.
- ☐ Incorporate features like time conversion widgets and alerts for daylight saving time changes.
- ☐ Integrate participant need surveys and post-session feedback to improve support.

Accessibility in Support Services

- ☐ Offer various support channels, such as FAQs, email, live chat, direct messaging, and teletypewriter (TTY) where available.
- ☐ Direct participants to accessibility tools within the virtual classroom environment, such as full-screen view, magnification, font size and color modifications, contrast settings, and keyboard shortcuts.

Tool 4-4. Example Presession Attendee Survey to Determine Needs

Presession surveys gather information that can help create connections. You can customize and format this example survey for your purposes.

1. Name.
2. What name do you prefer to be called (nickname)?
3. What pronouns do you use?
4. Are you comfortable participating in English? What is your preferred language?
5. Which time zone are you joining from?
6. Is there anything that might make it difficult to attend?
7. What is your job role? [*Provide attendees with a poll or ask for a text response.*]
8. What experience do you have with the subject matter? [*Ask attendees to provide a rating or a text response.*]
9. What do you hope to learn?
10. Which of the listed objectives is the most important for you to learn? (Choose all that apply.)
11. How will you apply what you learn?
12. Is there anything you'd like me to know about you?
13. What types of support do you need before the session? (Select all that apply.)
    - Visual support (a screen reader or accessible handout files)
    - In what other ways can I support your learning? [*Provide an open text entry box for attendees to respond.*]
14. What types of support do you need during the session? (Select all that apply.)
    - Auditory support (sign language interpretation or a dial in number)
    - Physical support (alternate activities or keyboard shortcuts)
    - Real-time support (access to help, FAQs, and live chat)
    - Process support (extra time, reminders, or a learning guide)
    - In what other ways can I support your learning? [*Provide an open text entry box for attendees to respond.*]

15. Before the session, are you able and ready to do the following? (Select all that apply.)
    - Prepare a quiet place to sit during the live session.
    - Access a computer that's set up and ready to support the live session.
    - Access a microphone that's connected and tested for quality sound.
    - Connect with the microphone, speaker, headset, and camera.
    - Access a strong and consistent internet connection. [*Add speed requirements for attendees.*]
    - Log in to the live session.
16. During the session, are you able and ready to do the following? (Select all that apply.)
    - Speak up using a microphone.
    - Show webcam video.
    - View webcam video.
    - Type in the chat.
    - Click to respond to poll responses.
    - Use status menu to display agree, disagree, and raise hand.
    - Contribute to breakout group activities.
    - Draw on the whiteboard.
    - Share your screen.

Tool 4-5. Facilitator and Producer Setup Checklists

Use these lists to prepare facilitators and producers before and during a virtual learning experience.

Presession Preparations

Workstation setup for accessibility:
- ☐ Arrange a quiet, ergonomic workstation with two monitors, if possible, to extend your screen space.
- ☐ Reduce noise and distractions.
- ☐ Pause and consider the needs of the personas you created to represent your learners.
- ☐ Test learner-facing resources using adaptive tools such as a screen reader.

Announcing and adjusting for accessibility:
- ☐ Adapt instructions and scripts as needed. Simplify your messages to focus on what is most important.
- ☐ Alert participants about available resources such as closed captions.
- ☐ Encourage requests for support.
- ☐ Ensure that all participant materials are accessible.

Scheduling and technical setup:
- ☐ Schedule early log in time to finalize setups with the facilitator and accommodate accessibility support, such as closed caption writers and sign language interpreters.
- ☐ Assess and select the best network connection.

Hardware and software accessibility:
- ☐ Select for the best hardware options, prioritizing laptops or desktops for enhanced features. Phones and tablets are useful as backups, but functionality is limited.
- ☐ Use the best headset and microphone available. Built-in mics are noisy and prone to causing echoes and other distractions.

- [ ] Update the virtual classroom software regularly. Install the newest version of the virtual classroom application on any devices you'll use to log in. Explore the changes and be ready to adapt procedures and instructions.

Producer tasks:
- [ ] Confirm you have host access for comprehensive control and accessibility management.
- [ ] Review presentation slides for accessibility, ensuring all elements are clear and functional.
- [ ] Create interactive elements considering accessibility needs.
- [ ] Prepare a technical support document with responses to common technical issues. Be ready to paste into the chat or email, or even read aloud, as needed.

Day of the Live Session
Accessibility-centric session initiation:
- [ ] Before you log in, reboot your computer or shut down unnecessary applications. Open only the files and applications you need for the session.
- [ ] Provide clear instructions for accessing tools and resources. Open the session 15–20 minutes before the start time, offering technical assistance.
- [ ] Ensure there are multiple methods for participants to access support during the live session.

Inclusive session delivery:
- [ ] Announce that the session will be recorded and start the recording.
- [ ] Welcome everyone and state the title of the session.
- [ ] Introduce the facilitator and producer. Describe your physical characteristics.
- [ ] State your role and intentions for the session and how you will achieve the expected outcomes. Invite contribution and requests for assistance.

- ☐ Guide participants on software features and accessible communication methods.
- ☐ Create a safe and inclusive space by acknowledging territory and declaring the session to be safe for all learners. For example, "I (we) respectfully acknowledge that the territory where I sit today as the ancestral unceded homelands of the Five Nations, comprising the Seneca, Cayuga, Onondaga, Oneida, and Mohawk, united in confederation about the year AD 1200. This unification took place under the 'Great Tree of Peace,' and each nation gave its pledge to not war with the other members of the confederation."[131]
- ☐ List ground rules for respectful interactions and best practices for participation.
- ☐ Encourage active participation, providing downloadable materials and alternate content resources for accessibility.

Accessible presentation techniques:
- ☐ Narrate relevant information aloud, describing visual content.
- ☐ Offer standard and alternate methods of participation.
- ☐ Verbally highlight messages in the chat and summarize responses to poll questions.
- ☐ Transition between demonstration screens and video clips smoothly and avoid potentially disorienting movements.
- ☐ Direct attention to specific locations within shared materials, allowing ample time for processing and comprehension.
- ☐ Regularly invite feedback and suggestions for improvement, emphasizing inclusivity and continuous enhancement of accessibility features.

Tool 4-6. Recipe for Successful Virtual Training Activities

Use this template for virtual training success:
- **Objective.** What will the participants be able to do following their participation in this activity?
- **Social.** How or why is learning together a better experience than completing this on their own?
- **UDL.** What will make this experience accessible, inclusive, and supported by the UDL guidelines?
- **Features.** Which platform features best support the live, collaborative social gathering?

Part 5.
A Primer on Accessibility Standards

Resources

- IAAP's Certified Professional in Accessibility Core Competencies (CPACC) Body of Knowledge document outlines the knowledge and skills expected of candidates seeking to obtain the CPACC credential. To learn more, visit accessibilityassociation.org/resource/CPACC_BoK_Oct2023.
- W3C's Web Accessibility Laws and Policies page lists governmental policies related to web accessibility. It's selectable by country, but it is not a comprehensive or definitive listing. To learn more, visit w3.org/WAI/policies.
- W3C's Web Content Accessibility Guidelines (WCAG). To learn more, visit w3.org/WAI/standards-guidelines/wcag.
- CAST's Universal Design for Learning (UDL) Guidelines. To learn more, visit udlguidelines.cast.org.
- World Intellectual Property Organization (WIPO) manages an informational page on the Marrakesh Treaty. To learn more, visit wipo.int/marrakesh_treaty/en.

Part 6. Adopting an Inclusive Mindset in Your Organization

Resources

- "Costs and Benefits of Accommodation" is a report from the Job Accommodation Network (JAN) on current accommodation data in the US. To learn more, visit askjan.org/topics/costs.cfm.
- The "Diversity, Equity, and Inclusion Resource Guide" is a comprehensive list of articles, reports, and tools on workplace DEI. To learn more, visit thebestandbrightest.com/racial-justice-resources.

Tool 6-1. Accessibility Specialist Business Case Example Outline

Note: This business case is a high level. It's meant to demonstrate structure and share example content. You can adapt it to your specific needs.

New Role
Accessibility Specialist

Problem Statement
Global enablement aspires to prioritize accessibility but is unable to carry out the training and quality assurance required to ensure content meets accessibility standards. As a result, we perpetuate the delivery of inaccessible learning content that fails to meet the needs of all learners.

Strategic Goals
Salesforce Core Value of Equality: Everyone deserves equal opportunities. We believe everyone should be seen, heard, valued, and empowered to succeed. Hearing diverse perspectives fuels innovation, which drives business and makes Salesforce a better company.

Current Programs and Efforts
- *Program*: Accessibility Subcommittee
  - Lead by Hayley Judd and Faith Fuqua-Lesser
  - Objective: Most managers don't have best practices related to accessibility and inclusive design topics.
- *Effort*: Adoption of the Accessibility and Inclusive Design QA Checklist
  - Lead by Deb Dannen, David De Camp, and Hayley Judd
  - Objective: Not all teams use the QA checklist to evaluate learner experiences for accessibility and inclusion.

Challenges Encountered
- Related to Accessibility Subcommittee:
    - Inconsistent meetings
    - Inconsistent attendance
    - Limited outreach
- Related to the adoption of the Accessibility and Inclusive Design QA Checklist:
    - Not adopted due to competing with other checklists
    - Checklist is challenging to use without prior knowledge of Web Content Accessibility Guidelines (WCAG)

Challenges by Category
- *Awareness*: The learning experience designer onboarding program has little content around accessibility and expectations.
- *Strategy and process*: Without a mature strategy, learning experiences may contain inaccessibilities that create learning blockers.

About the Accessibility Specialist Role
- *Job responsibilities*:
    - Conduct quality assurance (QA) tests to identify accessibility issues.
    - Develop training to ensure compliance with WCAG 2.1.
    - Guide teams in accessible design, development, and implementation.
- *Job requirements*:
    - Bachelor's degree in computer science, information systems, or related fields
    - Minimum of two years of experience in accessibility testing
    - Accessibility-related certifications preferred (e.g., IAAP's CPACC)
- *Self-service*:
    - Inclusive design curriculum
    - Accessibility trailhead modules

- *Coaching*:
  - Slack channel
  - Accessibility office hours
- *Full service*:
  - Intake requests
  - Accessibility audits

Actionable Solutions

Conduct accessibility QA:

- Partner with QE testers for Agile teams to request accessibility support.
- Create AMA (Ask me Anything) sessions and prepare for a short "appetite" talk with Agile teams that includes solutions to inaccessible design.
- Refine QA checklist for easy reference and to communicate the process.
- Test all new technologies in a staging or testing tool for accessibility compliance.

Business Impacts

- *Learner impact*: Fewer learning blockers leads to higher completion rates (metrics target: 100 percent).
- *Global enablement impact*:
  - Increased learner sentiment DEI initiatives (improves insights survey scores; category: diversity and inclusion).
  - Less budget spent on revisions to retroactively fix inaccessibilities.

Tool 6-2. Accessibility Audit Report Example

Use this report as an example of what you could share with your design team after an accessibility audit.

Course title: [*Name*]
Reviewer: [*Name*]
Asset reviewed: [*Linked asset title*]
Date reviewed: [*Date*]
Assessed with assistive technology? [*Yes or No*]
Assistive technology: [*Names and versions*]

Location	Inaccessible Element	How to Fix It	Rationale
Homepage			
Navigation buttons	The "next" arrow button is missing a label. The screen reader only announced "button."	Add a text-based label to the button.	Users with visual impairments will be unable to determine how to navigate to the first lesson.
Lesson 1			
Throughout: Graphics	Decorative images have alternative text (example: dividers).	Assess your graphics against the alt text decision tree to determine if they require alternative text. For all decorative graphics, mark the alt text as null.	Decorative graphics do not offer any context, so they do not require alternative text. Note: Failure to mark the graphics as null will cause the screen reader to announce the image file name.

Location	Inaccessible Element	How to Fix It	Rationale
Lesson 1			
Interactive chart	This interactive chart is not accessible with a screen reader or screen magnifier. Additionally, the chart uses color to convey meaning.	Summarize the chart in a text-based format. Create a key to indicate that red shows a decrease in revenue and green shows an increase in revenue.	Color alone should not be used to convey meaning because it can create challenges for users with color blindness. Additionally, color has different meanings in difficult cultures.

Tool 6-3. Inaccessibility Log Example

Use this inaccessibility log example as a starting point for noting all the issues you find in a learning experience:

- ☐ Issues with hierarchy (headings)
- ☐ Illogical content flow
- ☐ Walls of text
- ☐ Reading level too high
- ☐ Missing instructions
- ☐ Acronyms, idioms, adages, and jargon
- ☐ Text formatting (such as not enough line space or font is difficult to read)
- ☐ Inconsistent navigation
- ☐ Issues with material honesty
- ☐ Inaccessible interactions (drag and drop)
- ☐ Does not function with keyboard navigation or screen reader
- ☐ Does not magnify (cannot resize text)
- ☐ Uses images of text
- ☐ Nondescriptive link text
- ☐ Color used to convey meaning
- ☐ Inadequate color contrast
- ☐ Informative images are missing alternative text
- ☐ Decorative images have alternative text
- ☐ No closed captions
- ☐ No audio transcript
- ☐ Noninclusive language or imagery
- ☐ Flashing imagery
- ☐ Too many emojis
- ☐ Other [*Describe*]

Tool 6-4. Quality Control Checklist Example

Use this list as a starting point for creating a QC test for accessibility.

Alternative (Alt) Text
- ☐ Alt text is present.
- ☐ It's meaningful and appropriate.
- ☐ It's error-free (correct spelling and grammar).
- ☐ Decorative images are tagged appropriately by placing "" in the alt text area or using the authoring tool's function to mark it as decorative.
- ☐ Full image descriptions are also included where appropriate.

Keyboard Navigation
- ☐ You can successfully navigate the course or content using only the keyboard.
- ☐ It follows an accurate progression, meaning items on screen typically progress from left to right and top to bottom (this varies in some regions and languages).
- ☐ Note any keyboard traps where the user gets stuck and can't advance to the next item.

Screen Readers
- ☐ You can successfully use screen reader software to navigate the course or content.
- ☐ Items are read in the correct order.
- ☐ Items are labeled correctly. For example, are buttons designated as buttons?
- ☐ Note any point where you get stuck or advance before you've reviewed all the content.

Color and Contrast

- ☐ The text and background colors pass color contrast testing.
- ☐ Text overlays on images pass color contrast testing.
- ☐ Different states of hyperlinks and buttons pass color contrast testing.
- ☐ Color is not the only indicator used. Additional context (such as text and icons) is added.

Closed Captions

- ☐ All videos include closed captions.
- ☐ Closed captions are accurate.
- ☐ They're synced correctly with the video.
- ☐ They can be turned on and off.
- ☐ Music, background noises, and sounds are described in the captions as appropriate.

Transcript

- ☐ A transcript is available.
- ☐ It's accurate.
- ☐ Music, background noises, and sounds are described in the transcript as appropriate.
- ☐ Visual information is described where appropriate.

Additional Resources

Related Book Recommendations
- *Mismatch: How Inclusion Shapes Design* by Kat Holmes
- *The End of Average: How We Succeed in a World That Values Sameness* by Todd Rose
- *Disability Visibility: First-Person Stories From the 21st Century* edited by Alice Wong
- *Being Seen: One Deafblind Woman's Fight to End Ablesim* by Elsa Sjunneson
- *Design for Belonging: How to Build Inclusion and Collaboration in Your Communities* by Susie Wise
- *Designing Accessible Learning Content: A Practical Guide to Applying Best-Practice Accessibility Standards to L&D Resources* by Susi Miller
- *How to Be an Antiracist* by Ibram X. Kendi
- *White Fragility: Why It's So Hard for White People to Talk About Racism* by Robin DiAngelo
- *The Color of Law: A Forgotten History of How Our Government Segregated America* by Richard Rothstein
- *So You Want to Talk About Race* by Ijeoma Oluo
- *Biased: Uncovering the Hidden Prejudice That Shapes What We See, Think, and Do* by Jennifer L. Eberhardt
- *The Warmth of Other Suns: The Epic Story of America's Great Migration* by Isabel Wilkerson
- *The Hate U Give* by Angie Thomas
- *Why Are All the Black Kids Sitting Together in the Cafeteria?* by Beverly Daniel Tatum
- *Me and White Supremacy* by Layla F. Saad

- *The Fire Next Time* by James Baldwin
- *About Us: Essays from the Disability Series of the New York Times* by Peter Catapano and Rosemarie Garland-Thomson
- *Being Heumann: An Unrepentant Memoir of a Disability Rights Activist* by Judy Heumann

Organizations
- National Organization on Disability
- International Association of Accessibility Professionals
- AbilityPoints
- Accessibility.com
- Disability:IN
- Job Accommodation Network
- Registry of Interpreters for the Deaf

Training and Communities
- Designing Accessible Learning Content Programme is an online course to help you design accessible learning content. To learn more, visit elahub.net/sp/designing-accessible-learning-content-programme.
- Deque University offers online courses to help you prepare for IAAP's web accessibility certifications (free for people with disabilities). To learn more, visit dequeuniversity.com.
- US General Services Administration (GSA) Office of Government-wide Policy (OGP) maintains a wide range of training content and resources. To learn more, visit section508.gov.
- International Association of Accessibility Professionals (IAAP) hosts a wide range of virtual and in-person training opportunities. To learn more, visit accessibilityassociation.org/s/education.
- GSA's "Create Accessible Presentations" has tutorials for creating more accessible PowerPoint presentations. To learn more, visit section508.gov/create/presentations.
- AXSChat is a weekly chat where participants discuss accessibility topics. To learn more, visit axschat.com.

Conferences
- axe-con (hosted by Deque)
- The Accessibility and Inclusive Design Conference (hosted by the Learning and Development Community)

Culture
- Play: How a Blind Warrior Mastered *Street Fighter* Without Sight. Visit youtu.be/UvlhY9eUZQc?si=GuOLhNeLZn_dWe__.
- Microsoft highlights new Xbox accessibility features and the gamers who use them. Visit techcrunch.com/2023/10/18/microsoft-highlights-new-xbox-accessibility-features-and-the-gamers-who-use-them.
- Virtual Reality Accessibility: 11 Things We Learned From Blind Users. Visit equalentry.com/virtual-reality-accessibility-things-learned-from-blind-users.

Book Club Questions

1. In what ways is this book a demonstration of Design for All?
2. Some contributors chose to share a personal experience and others didn't. Do you think it is more important to share lived experiences than example stories?
3. Was there a particular story or example that was surprising or that you hadn't anticipated?
4. This book explains the concept of Design for All from many different perspectives: accessibility (both in terms of general access and accessibility for those with disabilities), inclusion, diversity, equity, and universal design. Was this approach useful to how you think about designing learning experiences? Why or why not?
5. What does Design for All mean to you?
6. Was there something missing from this book that you wish had been included?
7. There was a focus on inclusive mindset across an organization. Do you think that is possible to achieve? Why or why not?
8. Of all the strategies, recommendations, processes, and tools mentioned in this book, what do you think will be the easiest to implement? What will be most difficult? Why?
9. Was there anything in the book that made you feel uneasy or uncomfortable?
10. Do you have a story to share? What did you learn from your own experience and what do you do differently now?

Find more at DesignForAllBook.com.

Endnotes

1. R. Mars, "Invisible Women," *99% Invisible* podcast, September 23, 2019. 99percentinvisible.org/episode/invisible-women.
2. C.C. Perez. *Invisible Women: Data Bias in a World Designed for Men* (New York: Abrams Press, 2019).
3. "Verity Now—A Coalition for Vehicle Equity in Transportation," VERITY (Vehicle Equity Rules in Transportation) NOW, veritynow.org.
4. "Resolution Agreement: South Carolina Technical College System OCR Compliance Review No. 11-11-6002," US Department of Education, February 28, 2013, ed.gov/about/offices/list/ocr/docs/investigations/11116002-b.pdf.
5. "The Universal Design for Learning Guidelines 2.2," CAST, 2018. udlguidelines.cast.org.
6. "DEI," Dictionary.com, 2015, dictionary.com/browse/dei.
7. "Inclusion," *Merriam-Webster*, 2023, merriam-webster.com/dictionary/inclusion.
8. "Microaggressions/Microaffirmations," Justice, Equity, Diversity, and Inclusion (JEDI) Toolkit, Office of Inclusive Excellence and Community Engagement, med.unc.edu/inclusion/justice-equity-diversity-and-inclusion-j-e-d-i-toolkit/microaggressions-microaffirmations.
9. C. Stephanidis, "What Is Design for All?" Interaction Design Foundation, January 1, 2014, interaction-design.org/literature/book/the-encyclopedia-of-human-computer-interaction-2nd-ed/design-4-all.
10. "Disability," WHO (World Health Organization), March 7, 2023, who.int/news-room/fact-sheets/detail/disability-and-health.

11 R. Williams and S. Brownlow, *The Click-Away Pound Report 2019: Revisiting the Online Shopping Experience of Customers With Disabilities, and the Cost to Business of Ignoring Them* (Brighton, UK: Freeney Williams Limited, 2020), clickawaypound.com/downloads/cap19final0502.pdf.

12 "Disability," WHO.

13 E. Meyer and S. Wachter-Boettcher, *Design for Real Life* (New York: A Book Apart, 2016).

14 A. Gibson, "Reframing Accessibility for the Web," *A List Apart*, February 3, 2015, alistapart.com/article/reframing-accessibility-for-the-web.

15 Americans with Disabilities Act of 1990, 42 USC § 12101 (1990).

16 S. Chorn, "I Am Not Broken: The Language of Disability," Bookworm Blues Blog, September 10, 2014, bookwormblues.net/2014/09/10/i-am-not-broken-the-language-of-disability.

17 E. Meyer, "Compassionate Design," An Event Apart video, April 27, 2017, aneventapart.com/news/post/compassionate-design-by-eric-meyeran-event-apart-video.

18 L. Mullican, "From Empathy to Advocacy," *A List Apart*, January 6, 2015, alistapart.com/article/from-empathy-to-advocacy.

19 R. Greene, *Instructional Story Design: Develop Stories That Train* (Alexandria, VA: ATD Press, 2020).

20 "What Is Accessibility?" SeeWriteHear Blog, seewritehear.com/learn/what-is-accessibility.

21 "Web Content Accessibility Guidelines 2.2: Success Criterion 1.3.1. Info and Relationships—Level A," W3C's Web Accessibility Initiative, October 5, 2023, w3.org/TR/WCAG22/#info-and-relationships.

22 "Making Content Usable for People With Cognitive and Learning Disabilities," W3C Working Group Note, April 29, 2021, w3.org/TR/coga-usable.

23 "18F Design Methods: A Collection of Tools to Bring Human-Centered Design Into Your Project," US General Services Administration's Technology Transformation Services Agency 18F, August 10, 2015, methods.18F.gov.
24 "Understanding Disabilities and Impairments: User Profiles," UK Central Digital and Data Office, October 25, 2017, gov.uk/government/publications/understanding-disabilities-and-impairments-user-profiles.
25 EdBuild, *$23 Billion* (Jersey City, NJ: EdBuild, 2019). edbuild.org/content/23-billion/full-report.pdf.
26 L. Landry, "What Is Human-Centered Design?" Havard Business School Business Insights Blog, December 15, 2020, online.hbs.edu/blog/post/what-is-human-centered-design.
27 D. Harwell, "The Accent Gap," *Washington Post*, July 19, 2018, washingtonpost.com/graphics/2018/business/alexa-does-not-understand-your-accent.
28 E. Miller, "Why Innovation Is Critical for Voice Technology's Diverse User Base," *Forbes*, December 17, 2021, forbes.com/sites/forbestechcouncil/2021/12/17/why-innovation-is-critical-for-voice-technologys-diverse-user-base/?sh=76ef648c158c.
29 Americans with Disabilities Act of 1990, 42 USC § 12101 (1990).
30 US DOJ (Department of Justice), *2010 ADA Standards for Accessible Design* (Washington, DC: US DOJ, 2010), ada.gov/assets/pdfs/2010-design-standards.pdf.
31 A.B. Ratto, et al., "What About the Girls? Sex-Based Differences in Autistic Traits and Adaptive Skills," *Journal of Autism and Developmental Disorders* 48, no. 5 (2018): 1698–1711, doi.org/10.1007/s10803-017-3413-9.
32 B.S. Aylward, D.E. Gal-Szabo, and S., Taraman, "Racial, Ethnic, and Sociodemographic Disparities in Diagnosis of Children With Autism Spectrum Disorder," *Journal of Developmental and Behavioral Pediatrics* 42, no. 8 (2021): 682–689. journals.lww.com/jrnldbp/fulltext/2021/11000/racial,_ethnic,_and_sociodemographic_disparities.11.aspx.

33   E. Lobregt-van Buuren, M. Hoekert, and B. Sizoo, "Autism, Adverse Events, and Trauma," chapter 3 in *Autism Spectrum Disorders [Internet]*, ed. A.M. Grabrucker (Brisbane, AU: Exon Publications, 2021), ncbi.nlm.nih.gov/books/NBK573608.

34   S. Saylor, "Steve Saylor's YouTube channel." youtube.com/@SteveSaylor.

35   "Unplayable: Disability and the Gaming Revolution," BBC Radio 4, September 22, 2022, bbc.co.uk/programmes/m000rllh.

36   "M&S Rolls Out Braille Range Including Industry-First Gift," M&S (Marks and Spencer) Press Release, July 19, 2023, corporate.marksandspencer.com/media/press-releases/ms-rolls-out-braille-range-including-industry-first-gift-card.

37   "The Designing Accessible Learning Content Programme," eLaHub, 2023, elahub.net/sp/designing-accessible-learning-content-programme.

38   "Web Content Accessibility Guidelines 2.2: Success Criterion 1.4.1. Use of Color—Level A," W3C's Web Accessibility Initiative, October 5, 2023, w3.org/TR/WCAG22/#use-of-color.

39   CAST, "The Universal Design for Learning Guidelines 2.2," CAST, 2018, udlguidelines.cast.org.

40   "About Universal Design," Centre for Excellence in Universal Design, universaldesign.ie/about-universal-design.

41   CAST, "The Universal Design for Learning Guidelines 2.2."

42   "Summary of Proposed Updates for UDL Guidelines 3.0," CAST, cast.org/impact/summary-of-proposed-updates-for-udl-guidelines-3.0.

43   H. Pashler, M. McDaniel, D. Rohrer, and R. Bjork, "Learning Styles: Concepts and Evidence," *Psychological Science in the Public Interest* 9, no. 3 (2008): 105–119, doi.org/10.1111/j.1539-6053.2009.01038.x.

44   L. Zhang, R.A. Carter, and N.J. Hoekstra, "A Critical Analysis of Universal Design for Learning in the U.S. Federal Education Law," *Policy Futures in Education* 22, no. 4 (2023): 469–474, doi.org/10.1177/14782103231179530.

45 CAST, "Research Evidence," CAST, udlguidelines.cast.org/more/research-evidence#checkpoints.
46 CAST, "The Universal Design for Learning Guidelines 2.2."
47 S. Lambert, "Designing for Accessibility and Inclusion," *Smashing*, April 9, 2018, smashingmagazine.com/2018/04/designing-accessibility-inclusion.
48 D. Na, "Creating an Accessibility Engineering Practice," Daniel Na's blog, September 14, 2017, blog.danielna.com/creating-an-accessibility-engineering-practice.
49 "Photosensitivity and Seizures," Epilepsy Foundation, epilepsy.com/what-is-epilepsy/seizure-triggers/photosensitivity.
50 V. Head, "Designing With Reduced Motion for Motion Sensitivities," *Smashing*, September 8, 2020, smashingmagazine.com/2020/09/design-reduced-motion-sensitivities.
51 D. Gaebel, "A Primer to Vestibular Disorders," The A11Y Project, May 5, 2013, a11yproject.com/posts/understanding-vestibular-disorders.
52 "Color Vision Deficiency," US National Library of Medicine (NLM), medlineplus.gov/genetics/condition/color-vision-deficiency.
53 Lambert, "Designing for Accessibility and Inclusion."
54 Lambert, "Designing for Accessibility and Inclusion."
55 Lambert, "Designing for Accessibility and Inclusion."
56 M. Walker, "Five Golden Rules for Compliant Alt Text," AbilityNet, February 3, 2022, abilitynet.org.uk/news-blogs/five-golden-rules-compliant-alt-text.
57 Lambert, "Designing for Accessibility and Inclusion."
58 "What Is Visual Hierarchy?" Interaction Design Foundation, August 31, 2016, interaction-design.org/literature/topics/visual-hierarchy.
59 M. Sutton, "Links vs. Buttons in Modern Web Applications," MarcySutton.com, July 9, 2016, marcysutton.com/links-vs-buttons-in-modern-web-applications.
60 "How Reading Level Affects Web Accessibility," Bureau of Internet Accessibility, March 15, 2023, boia.org/blog/how-reading-level-affects-web-accessibility.

61 D. Norman, *The Design of Everyday Things* (New York: Basic Books, 2013).
62 J. Cameron, *The Artist's Way: A Spiritual Path to Higher Creativity*, 30th Anniversary Ed. (New York: TarcherPerigee, 2016).
63 "Blindness Statistics," National Federation of the Blind, nfb.org/resources/blindness-statistics.
64 "Web Content Accessibility Guidelines 2.2: Success Criterion 2.4.3. Focus Order—Level AA," W3C's Web Accessibility Initiative, October 5, 2023, w3.org/TR/WCAG22/#focus-order.
65 "Web Content Accessibility Guidelines 2.2: Success Criterion 2.5.8. Target Size (Minimum)—Level AA," W3C's Web Accessibility Initiative, October 5, 2023, w3.org/TR/WCAG22/#target-size-minimum.
66 "Web Content Accessibility Guidelines 2.2: Success Criterion 3.3.4. Error Prevention (Legal, Financial, Data)—Level AA," W3C's Web Accessibility Initiative, October 5, 2023, w3.org/TR/WCAG22/#error-prevention-legal-financial-data.
67 "Unicode Emoji," The Unicode Consortium (Unicode), unicode.org/emoji/techindex.html.
68 "Full Emoji List, v15.1," The Unicode Consortium (Unicode), unicode.org/emoji/charts/full-emoji-list.html.
69 LinkedIn, "Carousels on LinkedIn (No Longer Available)," LinkedIn Help article, December 14, 2023, linkedin.com/help/linkedin/answer/a764804.
70 "Changes of Context," W3C, w3.org/TR/WCAG20/#context-changedef.
71 "Web Content Accessibility Guidelines 2.2: Success Criterion 2.2.2. Pause, Stop, Hide—Level A," W3C's Web Accessibility Initiative, October 5, 2023, w3.org/TR/WCAG22/#pause-stop-hide.
72 "Web Content Accessibility Guidelines 2.2: Success Criterion 3.2.5. Change on Request—Level AAA," W3C's Web Accessibility Initiative, October 5, 2023, w3.org/TR/WCAG22/#change-on-request.

73   "Web Content Accessibility Guidelines 2.2: Success Criterion 2.2.1. Timing Adjustable—Level A," W3C's Web Accessibility Initiative, October 5, 2023, w3.org/TR/WCAG22/#timing-adjustable.
74   *Dyslexia Style Guide* (Nottingham, England: British Dyslexia Association, 2023), cdn.bdadyslexia.org.uk/uploads/documents/Advice/style-guide/BDA-Style-Guide-2023.pdf?v=1680514568.
75   A. Kosari, "Colorblind People Population! Statistics," Colorblind Guide, colorblindguide.com/post/colorblind-people-population-live-counter.
76   "Types of Color Vision Deficiency," NEI (National Eye Institute), August 7, 2023, nei.nih.gov/learn-about-eye-health/eye-conditions-and-diseases/color-blindness/types-color-vision-deficiency.
77   "An Alt Decision Tree," W3C, w3.org/WAI/tutorials/images/decision-tree; "Decorative Images" W3C, w3.org/WAI/tutorials/images/decorative.
78   V. Lewis, "How to Write Alt Text and Image Descriptions for the Visually Impaired," Perkins School for the Blind, July 2023, perkins.org/resource/how-write-alt-text-and-image-descriptions-visually-impaired.
79   "Web Content Accessibility Guidelines 2.2: Success Criterion 1.1.1. Non-text Content—Level A," W3C's Web Accessibility Initiative, October 5, 2023, w3.org/TR/WCAG22/#non-text-content.
80   "Images Must Have Alternate Text," Deque University, dequeuniversity.com/rules/axe/3.5/image-alt.
81   "Web Content Accessibility Guidelines 2.2: Success Criterion 2.3.2. Three Flashes—Level AAA," W3C's Web Accessibility Initiative, October 5, 2023, w3.org/TR/WCAG22/#three-flashes.
82   *The Office*, season 8, episode 2, "The Incentive," directed by Charles McDougall, written by Greg Daniels, Paul Lieberstein, and Ricky Gervais, aired September 29, 2011, on NBC.
83   M. Evans, "Captioned Video Accessibility: 'Stranger Things' Captions, a Fascinating Case Study," Meryl.net Blog, July 26, 2022, meryl.net/stranger-things-captions.

84 DCMP (Described and Captioned Media Program), "Captioning Key—Sound Effects and Music." DCMP Learning Center, dcmp.org/learn/captioningkey/602.

85 K. Linder, *Student Uses and Perceptions of Closed Captions and Transcripts: Results From a National Study* (Corvallis, OR: Oregon State University Ecampus Research Unit, 2016). content-calpoly-edu.s3.amazonaws.com/ctlt/1/images/3PM%20Student%20Survey%20report_final%2010-25-16_Final_Remediated.pdf.

86 "This American Life: A Case Study on How Transcription Boosts Podcast SEO and Engagement," 3PlayMedia, 3playmedia.com/why-3play/case-studies/this-american-life.

87 K. Johnston, "Netflix Reaches Deal to End Lawsuit Over Closed Captioning of Streamed Movies, TV Shows." Boston.com, October 10, 2012, boston.com/uncategorized/noprimarytagmatch/2012/10/10/netflix-reaches-deal-to-end-lawsuit-over-closed-captioning-of-streamed-movies-tv-shows.

88 "Web Content Accessibility Guidelines 2.2: Success Criterion 1.2.5. Audio Description (Prerecorded)—Level AA," W3C's Web Accessibility Initiative, October 5, 2023, w3.org/TR/WCAG22/#audio-description-prerecorded.

89 "Web Content Accessibility Guidelines 2.2: Success Criterion 1.2.7. Extended Audio Description (Prerecorded)—Level AAA," W3C's Web Accessibility Initiative, October 5, 2023, w3.org/TR/WCAG22/#extended-audio-description-prerecorded.

90 "Web Content Accessibility Guidelines 2.2: Success Criterion 1.2.3. Audio Description or Media Alternative (Prerecorded)—Level A," W3C's Web Accessibility Initiative, October 5, 2023, w3.org/TR/WCAG22/#audio-description-or-media-alternative-prerecorded.

91 "Federal Plain Language Guidelines," PlainLanguage.gov, March 2011, Revision 1, May 2011. plainlanguage.gov/media/FederalPLGuidelines.pdf.

92 J. Brooke, "SUS: A 'Quick and Dirty' Usability," *Usability Evaluation in Industry* 189, no. 3 (1996): 189–194.

93 G. Makransky and L. Lilleholt, "A Structural Equation Modeling Investigation of the Emotional Value of Immersive Virtual Reality in Education," *Educational Technology Research and Development* 66, no. 5 (2018): 1141–1164. psycnet.apa.org/record/2018-44416-006.

94 "The Universal Design for Learning Guidelines 2.2." CAST, 2018, udlguidelines.cast.org.

95 "The Universal Design for Learning Guidelines 2.2," CAST, 2018, udlguidelines.cast.org.

96 "Education Brief—Inclusive Education," UCLES (University of Cambridge Local Examinations Syndicate), October 2020, cambridgeinternational-al.org/Images/599369-education-brief-inclusive-education.pdf.

97 "Education Brief—Inclusive Education," UCLES (University of Cambridge Local Examinations Syndicate), October 2020, cambridgeinternational.org/Images/599369-education-brief-inclusive-education.pdf.

98 "Land Acknowledgements: Resources and Recommendations for Creating Land Acknowledgements," ASHE (Association for the Study of Higher Education) LAWG (Land Acknowledgement Working Group), 2020, ashe.ws/landacknowledgements.

99 A. Collins, J.S. Brown, and A. Holum, "Cognitive Apprenticeship: Making Things Visible," *American Educator* (Winter 1991), aft.org/ae/winter1991/collins_brown_holum.

100 J. Stoddard, "Cognitive Apprenticeships: Enhancing Corporate Learning Programs Through Situated Cognition and Problem-Based Learning," Modern Learner Newsletter, June 8, 2023, linkedin.com/pulse/cognitive-apprenticeships-enhancing-corporate-through-stoddard-litd.

101 J.J. Ratey, Spark: *The Revolutionary New Science of Exercise and the Brain* (New York: Little, Brown Spark, 2013).

102 YPulse, "The Majority of Young People Are Using Subtitles When They Watch TV," YPulse, November 22, 2022, ypulse.com/article/2022/11/22/the-majority-of-young-people-are-using-subtitles-when-they-watch-tv.

103 "Deafness and Hearing Loss," WHO (World Health Organization), February 2, 2024, who.int/news-room/fact-sheets/detail/deafness-and-hearing-loss.

104 C. Everett, "Hearing Loss Is More Common Than Diabetes. Why Aren't We Addressing It?" National Council on Aging, August 15, 2023, ncoa.org/adviser/hearing-aids/hearing-loss-america.

105 "Captions/Subtitles," W3C WAI (World Wide Web Consortium's Web Accessibility Initiative), w3.org/WAI/media/av/captions.

106 K. Linder, *Student Uses and Perceptions of Closed Captions and Transcripts: Results From a National Study* (Corvallis, OR: Oregon State University Ecampus Research Unit, 2019), content-calpoly-edu.s3.amazonaws.com/ctlt/1/images/3PM%20Student%20Survey%20report_final%2010-25-16_Final_Remediated.pdf; M.E. Dello Stritto and K. Linder, "A Rising Tide: How Closed Captions Can Benefit All Students," Educause, August 28, 2017, er.educause.edu/articles/2017/8/a-rising-tide-how-closed-captions-can-benefit-all-students.

107 R. Klein, "US Laws for Video Accessibility: ADA, Section 508, CVAA and FCC Mandates," 3Play Media, August 30, 2023, 3playmedia.com/blog/us-laws-video-accessibility.

108 "Web Content Accessibility Guidelines 2.2: Success Criterion 1.2.4. Captions (Live)—Level AA," W3C's Web Accessibility Initiative, October 5, 2023, w3.org/TR/WCAG22/#captions-live.

109 C. Pappas, "6 Tips for Closed Captioning eLearning Courses," *Elearning Industry*, January 6, 2015, elearningindustry.com/6-tips-closed-captioning-elearning-courses.

110 "Use Automatic Captioning," YouTube Help article, 2024, support.google.com/youtube/answer/6373554.

111 "Closed Captioning Services," Rev.com, rev.com/lp/closed-captioning-services-2.

112 "Hiring Qualified Interpreters," NDC (National Deaf Center on Postsecondary Outcomes), Access and Accommodations Resources, nationaldeafcenter.org/resources/access-accommodations/coordinating-services/interpreting/hiring-qualified-interpreters.

113 M. Marzinske, "Speaking Clearly: Help for People With Speech and Language Disorders," Speaking of Health Blog, June 9, 2022, mayoclinichealthsystem.org/hometown-health/speaking-of-health/help-is-available-for-speech-and-language-disorders#.

114 D. Levitt, *Delta CX: The Truth About How Valuing Customer Experience Can Transform Your Business* (Self-published, 2019).

115 M. Papadatou-Pastou, E. Ntolka, J. Schmitz, M. Martin, M.R. Munafò, S. Ocklenburg, and S. Paracchini, "Human Handedness: A Meta-Analysis," *Psychological Bulletin* 146, no. 6 (2020): 481–524, doi.org/10.1037/bul0000229.

116 US Bureau of Labor Statistics. 2024. "Persons With a Disability: Labor Force Characteristics - 2023." News Release, February 22. bls.gov/news.release/pdf/disabl.pdf.

117 K. LaBorie and T. Stone, *Interact and Engage, 2nd Edition! 75+ Activities for Virtual Training, Meetings, and Webinars* (Alexandria, VA: ATD Press, 2022).

118 S. Lambert, "Designing for Accessibility and Inclusion." *Smashing*, April 9, 2018, smashingmagazine.com/2018/04/designing-accessibility-inclusion.

119 "Understanding Conformance," W3C's Web Accessibility Initiative, 2023, w3.org/TR/UNDERSTANDING-WCAG20/conformance.html.

120 "Web Content Accessibility Guidelines 2.2: Success Criterion 2.4.8. Location—Level AAA," W3C's Web Accessibility Initiative, October 5, 2023, w3.org/TR/WCAG22/#location.

121 "Understanding SC 1.2.5: Audio Description (Prerecorded) (Level AA)," W3C's Web Accessibility Initiative, June 20, 2023, w3.org/WAI/WCAG21/Understanding/audio-description-prerecorded.html.

122 "Web Content Accessibility Guidelines 2.2: Success Criterion 2.4.5. Multiple Ways—Level AA," W3C's Web Accessibility Initiative, October 5, 2023, w3.org/TR/WCAG22/#multiple-ways.

123 L. Kalbag, *Accessibility for Everyone* (New York: A Book Apart, 2017).

124 T. Callaghan, D. Greene, R. Shafran, J. Lunn, and S.J. Egan, "The Relationships Between Perfectionism and Symptoms of Depression, Anxiety and Obsessive-Compulsive Disorder in Adults: A Systematic Review and Meta-Analysis," *Cognitive Behaviour Therapy* 53, no. 2 (2023): 121–132. doi.org/10.1080/16506073.2023.2277121.

125 Forbes, "10 Reasons Why DEI Efforts Fail (And How to Ensure They Succeed)," *Forbes*, April 3, 2023, forbes.com/sites/theyec/2023/04/03/10-reasons-why-dei-efforts-fail-and-how-to-ensure-they-succeed.

126 B. Mikkelson, "Etymology of Handicap: Did the Word 'Handicap' Originate With the Disabled's Having to Beg for a Living?" Snopes, January 21, 2021, snopes.com/fact-check/handicaprice.

127 C.S. Dweck, *Mindset: The New Psychology of Success* (New York: Ballantine Books, 2007).

128 "City Council Agenda Memo," Plano City Council, May 22, 2023, plano.novusagenda.com/agendapublic/CoverSheet.aspx?ItemID=8302&MeetingID=3409.

129 B. Little, "When the 'Capitol Crawl' Dramatized the Need for Americans With Disabilities Act," History.com, March 13, 2024, history.com/news/americans-with-disabilities-act-1990-capitol-crawl.

130 M.F. Giangreco, Clearing a Path, 2000, cdi.uvm.edu/islandora/object/uvmcdi-uvmcdi105242.

131 "The Six Nations Confederacy During the American Revolution," National Park Service, Fort Stanwix National Monument, nps.gov/articles/000/the-six-nations-confederacy-during-the-american-revolution.htm.

About the Contributors

Michelle Bartlett, PhD, assistant professor at Old Dominion University, received her PhD in higher education leadership with a cognate in statistics from Clemson University. She currently serves as the professional development trustee for the Association for Career and Technical Education Research, where she leads initiatives to help members learn new research skills. Michelle shares her passion for inclusive training design as the co-founder of the UNITE Design Lab.

Belo Miguel Cipriani, EdD, is a digital inclusion strategist. Through his digital access consulting firm, Oleb Media, he has helped countless organizations build inclusive websites and apps. *HuffPost* referred to him as an "Agent of Change," and *SF Weekly* named him one of the best disability advocates. Tony Coelho, the primary sponsor of the Americans With Disabilities Act, called him an "important voice" in disability writing. Learn more at belocipriani.com.

As a chief operations officer, **Todd Cummings** has successfully worked in ELB Learning's transformation from a startup to a global leader in the L&D industry. His history of working globally and with major organizations contributed to his ability to help this transition. Todd's leadership has fostered a culture of innovation and collaboration, enabling the integration of diverse teams and optimizing processes across multinational structures. He also contributed with others to create Inspire Accessibility with goal of helping everyone participate in learning experiences.

About the Contributors

Betty Dannewitz is a leadership development solutions architect at The Ken Blanchard Companies. With more than 20 years of corporate learning experience, she is an advocate for immersive technology and alternative learning solutions. Betty is recognized industry-wide for her highly creative solutions, including those that use augmented reality, virtual reality, 360-degree video, integrated learning journeys, and digital content creation. She is a sought-after consultant, engaging innovative technology instructor, and regular speaker on the national learning industry conference circuit. Betty is also the founder and CEO of ifyouaskbetty, where she helps learning professionals build new skills, think and design differently, and create immersive and alternative learning experiences.

JD Dillon started his career on the frontline—managing movie theaters and theme parks. After 20 years leading operations and L&D at dynamic organizations like Disney, AMC, and Kaplan, he's become an authority on frontline enablement and a staunch advocate for improving the employee experience. A respected international speaker and author of *The Modern Learning Ecosystem*, JD continues to apply his passion for helping people do their best work every day in his roles as Axonify's chief learning officer and founder of LearnGeek, an insights and advisory practice.

Brian Dusablon, MSW, CPACC, is an accessibility and inclusion advocate who coaches individuals and organizations on improving communication and creating more inclusive experiences. He has a master's in social work and is a Certified Professional in Accessibility Core Competencies. Brian loves traveling, meeting new people, and amplifying diverse voices by listening to and sharing their stories.

Suzanne Ehrlich, EdD, is an associate professor and program director in the Instructional Technology, Training and Development program at the University of North Florida (UNF). She currently serves as a Women in AI Fellow for EdSafeAI. She has presented internationally on implementing the Universal Design for Learning (UDL) framework for improved learner engagement, learning design, and leveraging technology for access. Her research explores topics on the UDL mindset in post-secondary and workplace spaces through a belonging lens. She is a co-founder of UNF's UNITE Design Lab, which is focused on advancing research around UDL to improve training and the workplace through inclusive design.

Diane Elkins is the co-founder of Artisan Learning, a custom learning design firm. She is the co-author of the popular *E-Learning Uncovered* book series and wrote *E-Learning Fundamentals: A Practical Guide* (ATD Press, 2015). She is a founding board member of Inspire Accessibility, a consortium of learning providers looking to champion accessibility in the e-learning industry.

Meryl K. Evans, CPACC, is a TEDx and professional speaker, trainer, and author. Born profoundly deaf, Meryl is a consultant in disability inclusion and accessibility at meryl.net. She's a Certified Professional in Accessibility Core Competencies. The proud native Texan lives in Plano with her family. She spends her free time on crochet projects and trying new things.

Leah Holroyd is the co-director of White Bicycle, a small business based in Essex, UK, which creates bespoke online courses for clients and runs introductory training on digital accessibility. White Bicycle has built online disability inclusion training for the UN World Food Programme, Sony Pictures, and Transport for London. Leah studied modern and medieval languages at the University of Cambridge and went on to work as a learning designer at Epigeum and the University of Canberra. She has a rare form of macular degeneration that affects her central vision. In 2022, she was named one of the UK's Top 10 Female Entrepreneurs to Watch by NatWest and *The Telegraph*. (Photo credit: Sarah Brick.)

Karen Hyder, CTT+, is a trainer of trainers, online-event producer, and speaker coach. She has been using technology to teach about technology since 1991, when she taught software applications courses at Logical Operations in Rochester, New York. In 2017, she was honored with The Learning Guild's Guild Master Award. Currently, Karen supports live, online learning experiences at Hearing First, a not-for-profit that serves professionals earning continuing education units and families supporting children who are deaf or hard of hearing. She is also a certified technical trainer. In addition to her professional work, Karen enjoys rescuing cats and old houses.

Jess Jackson, MEd, MBA, is a seasoned professional with two decades of experience as an intersectional equity speaker, writer, and educational content strategist. She is recognized nationally as an advocate for diversity and inclusion, and has designed award-winning diversity strategies across multiple industries. Jess has authored TorranceLearning's groundbreaking curriculum, Cultivating Racial Equity in the Workplace (CREW), a comprehensive microlearning training program rooted in evidence-informed best practices derived from social psychology research. Jess holds a bachelor's in sociology and Spanish from the University of Michigan and graduated summa cum laude with both her master of education and master of business administration.

Michelle Jackson, CPTD, is the founder and CEO of Tilak Learning Group, where she helps organizations navigate the complexities of creating engaging in-person, virtual, and accessible online learning experiences that deliver tangible results. She has a master's degree in international and intercultural management and is a Certified Professional in Talent Development. Michelle has spoken about accessibility at multiple professional conferences. She lives in Springboro, Ohio, with her husband, Rodney. When she isn't working, she enjoys traveling, horseback riding, home remodeling projects, and playing with her dog, Arthur.

Judy Katz, MBA, MEd, educates and assists organizations that are working to become more neuroaccessible and neuroinclusive. She has a master of business administration, a master of education, and decades of L&D experience, frequently focusing on issues of communication, management, and DEIB (diversity, equity, inclusion, and belonging). She is also AuDHD+ and brings an authentic and research-backed perspective to her work in neurodivergence.

Kassy LaBorie is a virtual training pioneer, professional speaker, author, and the founder of Kassy LaBorie Consulting and Kassy Speaks. She is a facilitator and author of two bestselling books specializing in human connection in a remote world. She has trained thousands of people around the world on topics such as online presenting, virtual learning, remote teams, and using live online technology in engaging and creative ways. Kassy loves helping organizations, teams, and business professionals experience success while working in a digital world, finding ways to take it from "blah" to aha! Connect with her at KassySpeaks.com and KassyConsulting.com.

Mary Henry Lightfoot, MS, NIC Advanced, CI/CT, is the senior digital learning manager at the Laurent Clerc National Deaf Education Center at Gallaudet University and the owner of Interpreting Connections interpreting service. She is a seasoned interpreter and interpreter educator with a wide range of experiences within the field of sign language interpreting. Mary has a rich background in the intersection of community management, online learning, and interpreting. She applies this background to teaching and training online, online project management, and video interpreting services.

David Lindenberg, CPACC, is a senior technical learning and development specialist at SAS Institute. He has more than 15 years of experience as an instructional designer and e-learning developer in corporate, nonprofit, and freelance settings. He has a master of science in instructional design and technology from the University of Memphis. He is also an IAAP Certified Professional in Accessibility Core Competencies.

Jean Marrapodi, PhD, CPTD, has more than 25 years of experience in learning and development across the corporate and higher education sectors. She champions participatory learning, emphasizing the need to accommodate differences. She lives south of Boston, Massachusetts, with two chatty cats vying for the world record in shedding.

Susi Miller is an industry-leading expert on accessible and inclusive learning content. She is the founder and director of eLaHub, which is committed to helping people make all learning content accessible and inclusive—as the default. Author of *Designing Accessible Learning Content*, Susi has more than 30 years of L&D experience in the public, private, and third sectors. Based in Winchester in the UK, she is a

About the Contributors 577

skilled instructional designer and online course developer and a passionate advocate for digital accessibility.

Daron Moore is a seasoned talent and organization development consultant with a passion for fostering inclusive workplaces. With a bachelor of science in management and organizational leadership and extensive experience in L&D operations, he has used his personal experience to help organizations create environments where employees feel seen, heard, and valued. A proud father of three and coach to hundreds, Daron lives in sunny Tampa, Florida.

Alan Natachu is an L&D professional with more than two decades of experience. He pivoted from an artist career, working with the likes of ABC, Disney, and the Smithsonian, to a training career when he was hired as a creative at Apple, where he worked for two years in a technology trainer role. Alan spent a decade in the higher education sector before making the switch to corporate L&D in 2019. He is a presentation geek who loves emerging L&D technologies and films and videos with closed captions, and he's passionate about making all his content accessible.

Cara North, an award-winning learning experience leader, is the founder of and chief learning consultant at The Learning Camel. She's the author of *Learning Experience Design Essentials* and serves as an adjunct in Boise State University's Organizational Performance Workplace Learning (OPWL) program. She lives in Columbus, Ohio, with her partner, Mathew, and their three cats, Bib Fortuna, Pollock Wallace, and Saffron Leiko.

Haley Shust is a passionate Design for All advocate. At Salesforce, she created an accessibility specialist role in hopes of ensuring equitable learning experiences. She is also the co-owner of The Helpful Folks, where she provides strategic, design, and training support for organizations interested in building accessible practices. Haley lives in Chicago, Illinois, with her husband, Dustin, and two Saint Bernards, Eleanor and Herbert. When not at a desk, she spends her time reading, cooking, or training at the gym.

Kristin Torrence is an immersive learning engineer who focuses on applying the learning sciences, instructional design, and data science practices to design, instrument, and validate extended reality (XR) learning solutions. She is the author of the *TD at Work* issue "5 Models for Data-Driven Learning." Kristin has a master's degree in cognitive studies in education with a concentration in intelligent technologies from the Teacher's College of Columbia University. She co-founded XR in LXD, a meetup and community of practice for learning experience designers interested in designing for XR modalities, and is an active member of the Immersive Learning Research Network, XR Women, and the IEEE International Consortium for Innovation and Collaboration in Learning Engineering.

Yvonne Urra-Bazain is an e-learning developer for Briljent whose work is informed by her experience problem solving for state departments, medical companies, sales groups, and a decade of service as a K–6 public educator. Yvonne strives to be a collaborative partner who develops on-brand training and development material to support professionals. She has embraced opportunities to present at virtual and in-person industry conferences to advocate for universal and user-focused accessible design practices.

Index

A

About Us, (Catapano and Garland-Tomson), 407
accessibility
  benefits to everyone of, 17
  compliance feedback, 76–77
  definition of, 8
  designing for, 69, 93
  Gestalt principle and, 259
  growth mindset for, 501
  mobility barriers and, 85–87
  paradox of, 508–509
  pitfalls, examples of, 3–4
  progress in, 499–505, 507–508, 510–513
  starting with, 511–513
  teamwork and, 487–489
  temporary barriers to, 18
  THRIVE (TRV) and, 68
accommodations, 4–6, 445–446, 446–447
alternative (alt) text
  artificial intelligence (AI) and, 189–190
  examples of, 183–188
  image caption versus, 180
  images and, 119–120, 172, 185–187
  keyword stuffing and, 189
  low-bandwidth, use for, 185–187
  WCAG success criteria and, 177
  writing effectively, 119–120, 175, 178–180, 181–183
Artist's Way, The (Cameron)
audio description
  augmented reality (AR) and, 264
  synchronized media and, 237–238
  transcripts, limitations of, 236
  types of, 236
  visual-only information and, 234, 235, 236, 237, 238
  WCAG and, 236

auditory processing challenges, 389–390
augmented reality (AR). *See also* virtual reality (VR)
  accessibility and, 264
  captioning and, 264
  low vision learners and, 264–265
  voice-over narration and, 264
automated speech recognition (ASR), 70, 323

B

Being Heumann (Heumann), 407
braille, 7, 98, 134, 135f

C

closed captioning
  augmented reality (AR) and, 264
  automated captions and, 206–208, 323, 323–324
  benefits to everyone of, 225, 321
  Communications Access Realtime Translation (CART) and, 320
  content consumption alternative, 115
  definition of, 195
  descriptions in, 220–221
  file formats for, types of, 197–199
  key terms related to, 320
  live captioning, definition of, 320
  manual creation of, 208–211
  Microsoft PowerPoint, 328–329
  open captions and, 195, 320
  preferences for, statistics on, 319
  sounds and, nonspeech, 219–220, 273
  standards for, 201–205, 321–322, 323
  subtitles and, comparison, 195–196, 320–321
  tips for, 199–201, 212–218, 325–327

Index

transcript, interactive text and, differences, 196
virtual classroom, in, 382–383
WCAG on flashing elements, 201
web conferencing and, 333
Web Consortium (W3C), 320
color and contrast. *See also* color and contrast checkers
  autism spectrum and, 117
  British Dyslexia Association Dyslexia Style Guide, 164
  color blindness and, 115, 160
  cultural differences and, 115
  dyslexia and, 160
  example of, 25–26
  graphs and, 162, 162f
  macular degeneration and, 159
  noncolor identifiers and, 116
  text on images and, 163, 163f
  virtual reality (VR) and, 272
  WCAG standards for, 160, 162, 168
color and contrast checkers, 160, 161f, 164, 169
color blindness. *See also* color and contrast
  accessibility and, 102–103
  definition of, 166
  secondary cues as aid, 169–170
  statistics, 165
  types of, 166–167
consultants, accessibility
  hiring, factors to consider, 475–476
  interviewing, 477–478
  maintenance and, 476–477
  natural user versus, differences, 474–475
corporate environments, accessibility in. *See also* diversity, equity, inclusion, and belonging (DEIB)
  audits and tools for, 468–469
  blockers, reporting process for, 469–470
  business case for, 460–464
  initiatives, establishing, 452–457
  operationalizing accessibility, 465–467
  training design and, 449–451

D

DEI. *See* diversity, equity, and inclusion (DEI)
Design for Real Life (Meyer and Wachter-Boettcher), 26–27
Designing Accessible Learning Content (Miller), 409
"Designing for Accessibility and Inclusion" (Lambert), 113, 403
"Designing Safer Web Animation for Motion Sensitivity" (Head), 114
digital content, accessibility to. *See also* keyboards, accessibility and
  access needs and, 53–54
  analysis, lenses for, 114–125
  augmented reality (AR) and, 264–265
  benefits to everyone of, 17
  course hierarchy and navigation in, 142
  diverse needs, designing for, 60–62
  drag-and-drop interactions, 29, 53, 127, 264
  evaluating, sources for, 54–55, 55, 58
  interactive elements and, 129–131
  personas, learner-based and, 372–373
  rights, responsibilities, and, 62–63
  strategy for, 127
  time allotted and, flexibility in, 125, 142, 155–156
  virtual reality (VR) and, 267–277
  web accessibility, definition of, 54
disabilities, learning more about, 406–407, 407
disability language and etiquette, 72, 497–499, 500
disability laws and standards. *See also* Web Content Accessibility Guidelines (WCAG)
  Accessibility for Ontarians With Disabilities Act (AODA), 401–402
  Accessible Electronic Documents Community of Practice, The (AED COP), 247
  Americans with Disabilities Act (ADA), 30, 83–84, 400
  European Accessibility Act, 401

European Union Web Accessibility Directive (EN 301 549), 400
International Standards Organization and International Electrotechnical Commission (ISO/TEC 40500:12), 401
Japanese Industrial Standards X 8341 (JIS X 8341), 401
Marrakesh Treaty, 402
Section 508 (US), 239, 400
Web Accessibility Initiative-Accessible Rich Internet Applications Suite (WAI-ARIA), 401
Disability Visibility (Wong, ed.), 407
diversity, equity, and inclusion (DEI), 10
 definition of, 10
 employee resource groups (ERGs), 73
 feedback for, 75–76, 77–78
 graphic examples, 4–5
 progress, barriers to, 10–11
 promoting, 71
 resources for learning about, 72, 73
 training for, 72
diversity, equity, inclusion, and accessibility (DEIA), 458–459
diversity, equity, inclusion, and belonging (DEIB).
 budgeting for, 441
 education for, 439
 inclusive culture, 438, 438–441, 439–440, 442–443
 initiatives, eliciting support for, 440, 441
 initiatives and support, 439
 intercommunication and, 440
 intersectionality and identity and, 440
 progress challenges, 437
drag-and-drop interactions, 29, 53, 127, 264, 373
Dusablon, Brian, 3, 403

E

ELB Learning, 491–496
e-learning. *See* virtual classroom, designing; virtual learning
empathy, cultivating, 71, 72, 87, 87–88, 406

empathy mapping, 32–33, 42, 361
environment, accessibility and
 impact of, 65–66
 redlining, school funding and, 66
epilepsy
 animations and effects and, 114–115
 WCAG and, 201
equality, 4, 4f
equity, 5, 5f
Evans, Meryl, 217
Evanson, Pauli, 450, 451

F

focus order, 138–139
fonts, guidelines for use of, 118–119, 149–150

G

Gestalt principle of similarity, 259

H

human-centered design
 empathy and, 69–70, 72
 inclusion and, 71
 iterative design and feedback and, 70–71

I

images and icons
 alternative (alt) text and, 118–119, 119, 185–187
 cultural differences and, 120
 decorative versus illustrative, 172–173
 screen readers and, 152–153
 value of, determining, 119, 172, 173
 World Wide Web Consortium (W3C) guidance, 172
inclusive design
 collaborative evaluation to measure, 79
 evaluating content through lenses, 113–125
 principles of, 70
 shifting left/left-shift testing, 100
 standardizing and measuring for, 75

Universal Design for Learning, The (UDL), 11–12
inclusive language, 101–102, 103
inclusivity
 activities to advance, 71
 assistive technology (AT) and, 23
 assumptions and, 23
 constructive feedback and, 74
 definition of, 10
 example of, 5, 6f
 Inclusion Solution, the (blog), 4
 language training and, 72
 metrics and comparative analysis to assess, 77
 mindset and, 96–97, 99–100, 100
 promoting diversity and, 71, 74
 teamwork, importance of and, 487–489
 virtual learning environment and, 363
Interact and Engage! 75+ Activities for Virtual Training, Meetings, and Webinars (LaBorie and Stone), 380
Interaction Institute for Social Change, 4–6
International Association of Accessibility Professionals (IAAP), 407
intersectionality
 Crenshaw, Kimberlé, 68
 definition of, 68
 inclusion and, 79–80
 resources and strategies, 72–73
 THRIVE mindset (TRV), 68

K

keyboards, accessibility and
 adaptive keyboards, 136
 assistive devices and, 134
 focus order and, 120–121
 magnifiers and, 136
 mouse navigation and, differences, 133
 tab navigation, 135

L

language, simplifying
 guidelines for developing, 252–260
 headings and sections, 254
 hierarchy principles, 259
 language access, 301
 narrowing content for, 252–253
 organizing content, 253
 paragraphs and topic sentences, 256–257
 Plain Writing Act of 2010, The, 252
 process lists and screen captures for, 258
 term consistency for, 253
 virtual learning environment, in, 363–364
 vocabulary and, 254
 WCAG and, 419
learning design. *See also* Universal Design for Learning, The (UDL); virtual classroom, designing
 accessibility, designing for, 93, 308
 accessibility and, benefits to all, 28–29
 ambiguity in, 94
 assumptions and, 27–28, 93–94
 bias and, overcoming, 28
 controls for learner interaction, 118
 learner-centered approach and, 37
 temporary disabilities and, 28–29
 testing of, 93–95
 undisclosed disabilities and, 29
 varying abilities and, 30, 31
left-handedness
 inclusion and, 354
 statistics on, 354
 universal design principle and, 354
Lewis-Hannah, Karen, 217

M

macular degeneration, 21, 22, 23, 98, 99, 159
microaggressions, definition of, 11
Miller, Susi
 Designing Accessible Learning Content, 409
 eLaHub, 100, 421–422, 428–429
 shifting left/left-shift testing, 100
mobility barriers, 85–87

Index

N
Na, Daniel, 113
navigation of online content. *See also* keyboards and accessibility
 button size, impact of, 145
 interaction cost, 146–147
 "submit" button benefits, 146
neurodivergence. *See also* neurodivergent learners
 definition of, 90
 girls and diagnosis, 89–90
 neurodiversity, definition of, 90
neurodivergent learners. *See also* neurodivergence
 auditory processing challenges, 389–390
 autism spectrum and color/contrast, 117
 e-learning and, 91
 group work, tailoring for, 316
 quality control for accessibility, 485–486
 sensory challenge support, 343–344

P
Patterns Beyond Labels model
 cognitive accessibility and, 300
 cultural accessibility and, 300
 definition of, 299–300
 physical accessibility and, 300
personas, learner-based
 bias and assumptions, avoiding, 50–51
 components of, 40–41
 creation of, 43–47, 59
 diversity, accounting for, 49–50
 empathy map and, 42
 inclusion and, 39
 pitfalls of, 47–48, 49
 purpose of, 39
 stereotyping and, 50
 updating and, need for, 51–52
 validating of, 47
POUR principles of WCAG, 369, 391

Q
quality assurance for accessibility (QA)
 definition of, 481
 differences between QA and QC, 480–481
 recommendations for, 481–482
quality control for accessibility (QC)
 checklist for, 482–483
 definition of, 481
 differences between QA and QC, 480–481
 neurodivergent learners, 485–486

R
readability. *See also* language, simplifying
 elements impacting, 124
 reading levels and, 123

S
screen readers
 audio and video and, 115
 autoplaying and, 115
 case, Pascal and camel, 149–150
 carousels and, 153
 context changes on Web pages and, 154
 emojis and, 150, 151–152, 151f
 focus order and, 138
 hashtags and, 149–150
 headings in content and, 136–137
 images and, 152–153
 JAWS, 2, 29–30, 134
 Microsoft Narrator, 149
 NonVisual Desktop Access (NVDA), 134, 149
 social media and, 149–157
 structure of course and, 121, 124–125
 TalkBack (Google), 134
 technology commonly used, 134
 testing for Web Content Accessibility Guidelines, 429–430
 Unicode Common Locale Repository and, 150
 VoiceOver (Apple), 8, 134, 149
SeeWriteHear, 54
sign language interpreters
 accessibility needs statements and, 335
 budgeting for, 335–336

Registry of Interpreters for the Deaf, 336
services, requesting, 336
working with, 336–337, 340, 341–342
social identity
    conflicts, interpersonal and, 71
    diversity, developing and, 72–73
    empathy, cultivating and, 71–72
    human-centered design and, 69
    imposter syndrome and, 67
    inclusion and, 70
    intersectionality and, 68, 69
    representation gaps and, 67, 68
software, for accessibility. *See also* color and contrast checkers
    Abode Captivate, 1
    Adobe Acrobat, 240, 247
    Articulate Storyline, 120
    JAWS, 2, 29–30, 134
    Lectora, 93
    Microsoft Narrator, 149
    Microsoft PowerPoint, 169, 328–329
    Microsoft's Immersive Reader in Canvas (LMS), 333
    Microsoft Word, 240, 247
    Microsoft Word Dictate and Transcribe, 228
    Microsoft Word Dictate and Transcribe feature, 228
    NonVisual Desktop Access (NVDA), 134, 149
    TalkBack (Google), 134
    VoiceOver (Apple), 8, 134, 149
speech access needs
    aphasia and, 345
    common disabilities and conditions, 391
    inclusion and, 346, 392–393
standards for accessibility. *See also* disability laws and standards; Web Content Accessibility Guidelines (WCAG)
    Accessible Electronic Documents Community of Practice (AED COP), 247
    British Dyslexia Association Dyslexia Style Guide, 164
    definition of, 398–399
    expanding knowledge of disabilities for, 406–407
    identifying and applying, 403, 405–406
    neurodivergence and, 431
    staying current, list for, 404
    transparency and, 423
    types of, 14, 399–400
    US Federal Communications Commission (FCC), 321–322
statistics, disability
    employment and, 367
    hearing loss, 319
    US Bureau of Labor Statistics, 367
    vision loss, 133
    World Health Organization, 17

T

tables in documents
    Accessible Electronic Documents Community of Practice (AED COP), 247
    Adobe Acrobat and, 240, 247
    complex, definition and types of, 241–245
    converting to lists as alternative, 246, 247
    Microsoft Word, ensuring accessibility, 240
    simplicity, value of, 246, 247
    understandability and, 245–246
technology. *See* assistive technology (AT); software, for accessibility
This American Life, 227
THRIVE mindset (TRV)
    definition of, 68
    fostering, steps for, 80–81
transcription. *See also* closed captioning
    accessibility, to increase, 232
    benefits of, 226–228
    Communications Access Realtime Translation (CART), 320
    content consumption alternative, 115
    definition of, 224
    example of, 229–232
    as overlay or stand-alone document, 225–226

Index

U

UDL. *See* Universal Design for Learning, The (UDL)
Unicode Common Locale Repository (CLDR), 150, 151f
Universal Design for Learning, The (UDL)
  accessibility versus, 10
  affective networks/engagement, 106, 287, 290–291t
  Center for Applied Special Technology (CAST), 106
  cognitive accessibility and, 300, 304, 307–308
  community, role of and, 306
  criticism of, 107
  cultural accessibility and, 300, 301, 302, 306–307
  definition of, 9, 10, 106, 287
  engagement in, multiple means of, 106
  example of, HVAC class, 285–294
  framework goals, 287
  guidelines for, 106–107, 308
  mindset and barrier reduction, 299, 302, 303, 305
  Patterns Beyond Labels model and, 299–300
  physical accessibility and, 300, 303, 307
  recognition networks/representation, 106, 288, 290–291t
  strategic networks/action and expression, 106, 288, 290–291t
  using, suggestions for, 108–109

V

virtual classroom, designing. *See also* virtual learning
  accessibility, testing for, 375–376
  alternative response methods, 383–384
  animations and effects in, 114
  augmented reality (AR) and, 263–265
  diverse needs, supporting, 53–54, 374
  headings in content, 136–137
  Image Connect activity, 380, 381–382, 384–386
  interaction and engagement in, 374, 380
  learning management system (LMS) for, 447–448
  lectures, inclusive alternatives to, 379–380
  low bandwidth, alternative (alt) text for, 187–188
  navigation and, 141–142
  personas, learner-based, creating, 372–373
  scripting instructions, 374–375
  structure and, key elements of, 124–125
  template for designing interactive activities, 386–387
  troubleshooting in, preparing for, 375, 378
  tutorials and FAQs in multiple formats, 376
  video use and, 377
virtual instructor-led training (vILT), 315–316, 391–392, 392–393
virtual learning
  accessibility considerations, 359, 362–364
  chat option in, 366
  creation and sharing of materials, 363
  feedback mechanisms in, 264, 360, 363, 364
  inclusivity in, 361
  learner challenges, 367, 370–371
  materials, creation and sharing of, 361–362
  multimodal content, 358–359
  participant preferences, eliciting, 368–369
  personalization and engagement through tools, 359–360
  POUR principles of WCAG, 391
  presentations and pacing, 376–377
  sharing recorded activities, 264
  speech access needs and, 315–316, 391–392, 392–393
  time allotted and flexibility in, 125
  verbal descriptions in, 264
  WCAG, application in, 369
virtual reality (VR)
  accessibility and, 271, 272

Index

controlling, and support, 274–275, 276
iterative testing, 282
physical accessibility and, 274
replicating physical activities, 267–268
user testing and data collection, 278–279, 279–281
visual support and, 271–272, 273
virtual workspaces, barriers in, 357–358
vision and accessibility. *See also* alternative (alt) text; audio description; screen readers
augmented reality (AR) and, 264
color-coding and, 102–103
in-person class, describing visuals for, 317–318
secondary cues for low vision, 169–170
Step-Hear, 332
synchronized media and, 237–238
virtual reality (VR) and, 271–272, 273
visual-only information and, 234, 238, 239
WCAG and, 236
visual hierarchy, principles of, 259

W

W3C. *See* World Wide Web Consortium
WCAG. *See* Web Content Accessibility Guidelines
Web Content Accessibility Guidelines (WCAG)
alternative (alt) text and, 177
audio description and, 236
authoring tool, conformance report or VPAT, 430
case study, practical applications, 420–422
color and contrast and, 102–103, 117–118, 160, 162, 168
complexity of, 57–58, 418–419
exceptions to standards, 416–417
focus order and, 138
Level AAA and, 413–414, 414, 414–415
original intent of, 417–418
POUR principles, 369, 391
screen readers and, 429–430
source classifications, 55
standards for speech access needs lacking, 391
synchronized media, 237–238
testing for, 425–429
understandability principle, 245–246
versions and levels explained, 410–412
virtual learning environment, applying in, 369
World Wide Web Consortium (W3C), 55, 59

About the Editor

Sarah Mercier, MBA, CPACC, specializes in innovative learning technology and strategic implementation of learning solutions. She is an advocate for learner-centered design and is known for her ability to translate highly technical concepts and research into real-world practice.

As the CEO of Build Capable, she leads an organization that prioritizes inclusive design, equity, and accessibility in all aspects of its products and services. Sarah brings together matrix teams of training, design, and technology experts to work with organizations in a wide range of industries, from small, community nonprofits to global corporations.

Sarah is an international facilitator for the Association for Talent Development and a frequent speaker at industry conferences and business events in the areas of instructional and learning technology strategy. Her work has been published in *ATD's 2020 Trends in Learning Technology*, *The Book of Road-Tested Activities*, *TD* magazine, Learning Solutions, and *CLO* magazine, among other training and workforce publications.

Sarah lives in Olympia, Washington, and enjoys searching for local pods of orcas in Puget Sound and rocks to put in her tumbler.